JavaServer Pages™

Xue Bai
Virginia State University

THOMSON

COURSE TECHNOLOGY

Australia • Canada • Mexico • Singapore • Spain • United Kingdom • United States

THOMSON

™

COURSE TECHNOLOGY

JavaServer Pages™

by Xue Bai

Senior Vice President, Publisher:
Kristen Duerr

Managing Editor:
Jennifer Locke

Product Manager:
Barrie Tysko

Developmental Editor:
Lynne Raughley

Production Editor:
Christine Spillett

Associate Product Manager:
Janet Aras

Manuscript Quality Assurance Lead:
Nicole Ashton

Marketing Manager:
Angie Laughlin

Editorial Assistant:
Christy Urban

Cover Designer:
Joseph Lee
Black Fish Design

Compositor:
GEX Publishing Services

Manufacturing Coordinator:
Denise Powers

BRIEF
Contents

TABLE OF
Contents

CHAPTER FOUR
Variables and JSP Control Structures   **93**

CHAPTER FIVE
Scripting with JSP Elements   **129**

Preface

JavaServer Pages™ (JSP™) technology is one of the latest server-based technologies for creating dynamic and interactive HTML pages for your World Wide Web (WWW) site or an organization's intranet/extranet. Using JSP, which is part of the Java™ family, you can develop and easily maintain dynamic, substantive Web pages that are platform independent and that utilize or interact with other resources, such as the Java API and databases. JSP technology allows you to separate the user interface from the business logic by means of XML-like tags and scriptlets, so that you can change the appearance of a Web page, or an entire Web site, without modifying its existing functionality.

This book is designed to prepare you for a career in e-commerce development. This book uses a hands-on approach in which you build JSP Web pages that process form data, generate dynamic content back to client, and interact with databases.

THE INTENDED AUDIENCE

JavaServer Pages is intended for individuals who want to build commercial Web applications, including B2C and B2B Web applications. This book is primarily intended for students who:

- Are considering career opportunities as e-commerce programmers and who want a better understanding of the state-of-the-art Java technology.
- Are interested in gaining hands-on experience with server-based technology.
- Can program in another language but are beginning Web programmers.
- Wish to develop Web-based database driven applications.

This book is designed for e-commerce courses in Management Information Systems or Computer Information Systems. These courses are part of rapidly emerging new programs in schools that aim to prepare students for Web-based application design and implementation, database administration, client/server application development, and Web-based information systems development.

JavaServer Pages aims to teach you everything you need to know about one of the latest server-based technologies. However, students should have some familiarity with general programming concepts and should also be familiar with HTML. You should also be familiar with the Windows operating system and have a basic understanding of how to use the Internet. No prior experience with databases is required. Although not required, knowledge of scripting languages, especially JavaScript, and of an object-oriented programming language, especially the Java programming language, will greatly shorten your learning curve.

THE APPROACH

In *JavaServer Pages*, you learn by doing. To facilitate the learning process, this book explains important concepts about Web/client server architecture, client- and server-side processing, JSP technology and techniques, and using databases with Web pages. Explanations and examples are enhanced with figures and tables. Explanations include integrated exercises that help you conceptualize and build JSP scripts for interactive Web sites. The chapters build on one another, allowing readers to combine concepts to create more sophisticated Web pages. Each chapter also includes Chapter Objectives, a Chapter Summary, Review Questions, Hands-on Projects, and Case Projects that highlight the major concepts that were presented and allow readers to apply their knowledge. The Hands-on Projects are guided activities that let you practice and reinforce the techniques and skills you learn within the chapter and build on the techniques and skills you learned in previous chapters. These Hands-on Projects enhance your learning experience by providing additional ways to apply your knowledge in new situations. Some of the Hands-on Projects are more guided, and others are more challenging, requiring you to write JSP code based on what you have learned in the book thus far. The Case Projects, allow you to use the skills that you have learned in the chapter to create solutions with JavaServer Pages. In particular, a running case project called the Student Record Access System (SRAS) will guide you through chapters to create a whole Web application. The SRAS is for managing a course registration process online. With the SRAS, users can edit their profiles and students can enroll or drop courses, get faculty information, and so on. Faculty members can view the roster for their class. The SRAS project will give you chance to apply the knowledge you gain in each chapter to a real Web application.

OVERVIEW OF THIS BOOK

The examples, steps, projects, and cases in this book will help you achieve the following objectives:

- Learn the JavaServer Pages server-side scripting language
- Learn the architecture of the World Wide Web
- Use both client-side and server-side scripts to create interactive Web pages
- Learn how to design interactive Web pages to allow clients to interact with your Web application
- Create Web pages that interact with relational databases
- Use JavaBeans

- Develop and use custom tags
- Use JSP to develop E-commerce Web applications

Chapter 1 introduces you to the Web client/server architecture, explains the difference between static HTML Web pages and dynamic Web pages, and provides an overview of how to use JSP to create dynamic Web pages. In **Chapter 2**, you learn how to write and use client- and server-side scripts to provide interactive content to clients. In **Chapter 3**, you learn how to use server-side scripts to process client requests. Specifically, you learn how to collect information from Web site visitors, how to send this information to the server, and how to retrieve and process the data on the Web server. In **Chapter 4**, you learn how to use variables in your JSP scripts, and how to use control structures to establish the execution order of JSP script statements. You also learn how to use arrays to store items of similar information, how to manipulate a string object, and how to use the Enumeration object in JSP scripts. In **Chapter 5**, you learn how to use page directives, include directives, include actions, scripting elements, and comments in your JSP pages. In **Chapter 6**, you learn how to use implicit objects in your JSP script. Specifically, you learn how to use implicit objects to obtain header information and client and server related data, to process form input fields, and to control the output stream. In **Chapter 7**, you learn how to use the application object to store information that is accessible to all clients; how to use the session object to maintain state among the requests from a client; and how to use cookies to store information on the client computer. In **Chapter 8**, you learn how to write, compile, and install a bean class; how to use beans to facilitate form processing and to implement business rules for your Web applications; and how to connect a bean with a form. In **Chapter 9**, you learn about variable and bean scopes. Specifically, you learn how to define and use beans in four different scopes, namely, page scope, request scope, session scope, and application scope. In **Chapter 10**, you learn to develop and use a custom tag. In addition, you learn how to involve another page while processing a request, how to define a method in a declaration, and how to handle exceptions. In **Chapter 11**, you learn about databases and database management systems (DBMSs), and you learn how to manipulate a database using the SQL language. Then you learn how to connect to a database from a JSP page, and issue SQL statements and commands from a JSP page. In **Chapter 12**, you learn how to use the IN and BETWEEN operators to add power to your SQL queries, how to get information about a database, and how to use transaction control to preserve data integrity. You also learn how to write JavaBeans to access and process a database. The **Appendix** summarizes the JSP1.2 elements for easy reference.

Each chapter in *JavaServer Pages* includes the following elements to enhance the learning experience:

- **Chapter Objectives:** Each chapter in this book begins with a list of the important concepts to be mastered within the chapter. This list provides you with a quick reference to the contents of the chapter as well as a useful study aid.

- **Step-By-Step Methodology:** As new concepts are presented in each chapter, step-by-step instructions allow you to actively apply the concepts you are learning.

- **Tips:** Chapters contain Tips designed to provide you with practical advice and proven strategies related to the concept being discussed. Tips also provide suggestions for resolving problems you might encounter while proceeding through the chapters.

- **Chapter Summaries:** Each chapter's text is followed by a summary of chapter concepts. These summaries provide a helpful way to recap and revisit the ideas covered in each chapter.

- **Review Questions:** End-of-chapter assessment begins with a set of approximately 20 review questions that reinforce the main ideas introduced in each chapter. These questions ensure that you have mastered the concepts and understand the information you have learned.

 Hands-on Projects: Along with conceptual explanations and step-by-step tutorials, each chapter provides Hands-on Projects, related to each major topic, aimed at providing you with practical experience. Some of the Hands-on Projects provide detailed instructions. As the book progresses, some Projects provide less detailed instructions and require you to apply the material presented in the current chapter. As a result, the Hands-on Projects provide you with practice in implementing JavaServer Pages technology in real-world situations.

 Case Projects: Several cases are presented at the end of each chapter. These cases are designed to help you apply what you have learned in the chapter to real-world situations. They give you the opportunity to independently synthesize and evaluate information, examine potential solutions, and make recommendations, much as you would in an actual business situation. The running Case Project, Student Record Access System, (SRAS), enables to you to follow through on the design and creation of a full-scale Web application.

TEACHING TOOLS

The following supplemental materials are available when this book is used in a classroom setting. All of the teaching tools available with this book are provided to the instructor on a single CD-ROM.

Electronic Instructor's Manual. The Instructor's Manual that accompanies this textbook includes:

- Additional instructional material to assist in class preparation, including suggestions for lecture topics.

- Solutions to all of the in-chapter step-by-step tutorials and end-of-chapter materials, including the Review Questions, Hands-on Projects and possible solutions for the Case Projects.

ExamView®—the ultimate tool for your objective-based testing needs.

ExamView® is a powerful objective-based test generator that enables you to create paper, LAN or Web-based tests from testbanks designed specifically for your Course Technology text. Utilize the ultra-efficient QuickTest Wizard to create tests in less than five minutes by taking advantage of Course Technology's question banks, or customize your own exams from scratch.

PowerPoint Presentations. This book comes with Microsoft PowerPoint slides for each chapter. These are included as a teaching aid for classroom presentation, to make available to students on the network for chapter review, or to be printed for classroom distribution. Instructors can add their own slides for additional topics they introduce to the class.

Data Files. Data Files, containing all of the data necessary for steps within the chapters and the Hands-On Projects, are provided through the Course Technology Web site at **www.course.com**, and are also available on the Teaching Tools CD-ROM, as well as on the CD that accompanies this book.

Solution Files. Solutions to the step-by-step tutorials, end-of-chapter review questions, exercises, Hands-On Projects and Case Projects are provided on the Teaching Tools CD-ROM and may also be found on the Course Technology Web site at **www.course.com**. The solutions are password protected.

ACKNOWLEDGMENTS

This book has been a team effort from the beginning. A big thanks goes to Lynne Raughley, Developmental Editor, who has helped me be a better author. A great thanks goes to Barrie Tysko, Product Manager, for all her support and guidance, and for carrying the team to the finish line. I had a wonderful time with them throughout the writing of this book. Thanks to Dr. Steve Davis, Dr. Fidelis Ikem, Mr. Ji Li, Ms. Lemuria Carter and Mr. Fengguan Bai for providing me guidelines, discussing the structure of the book, and reviewing and editing the early chapters.

I especially want to thank the following reviewers for their invaluable ideas and comments to improve the book: Tsu-Cheng David Chiao, California State University, Fullerton; Guillermo A. Francia, III, Jacksonville State University; Bonnie Ryan-Gauthier, New Brunswick Community College, Moncton Campus; Gene Klawikowski, Nicolet College; Keith Morneau, Northern Virginia Community College, Annandale Campus; Gavin T. Osborne, Saskatchewan Institute of Applied Science and Technology, Palliser Campus; Ryszard F. Paweska, The University College of the Cariboo; Terrance E. Walsh, McDowell Technical Community College.

I want to dedicate this book to my daughter Yuwei, and to my sons, Yuran and Yuzheng, for the sacrifices they had to make during the process of writing, and for their love. A big hug goes to my wonderful wife, Yingjin, for her patience and understanding. The many hours of work would have been impossible and for naught without her daily expressions of love and encouragement.

Read This Before You Begin

To the User

Data Files

To complete the steps and projects in this book, you will need data files that have been created for this book. The data files can be found on the accompanying CD, or your instructor will provide the data files to you. You also can obtain the files electronically from the Course Technology Web site by connecting to **www.course.com**, and then searching for this book title.

Each chapter in this book has its own set of data files that typically are JSP or HTML files. You use files to review the examples and perform the exercises and end-of-chapter projects. Files for each chapter are stored in a separate folder within the folder myjspapp. For example, all data files for Chapter 5 are stored in the folder myjspapp\chapter05. Throughout this book, you will be instructed to open files from these folders.

You can use a computer in your school lab or your own computer to complete the chapters, Hands-on Projects, and Case Projects in this book.

Using Your Own Computer

To use your own computer to complete the chapters, Hands-on Projects, and Case Projects in this book, you will need the following:

- **A 486-level or higher personal computer running Windows 2000 Professional or Windows XP Professional.**

- **Netscape Communicator or Microsoft Internet Explorer browser software.** If you do not have either program, you can download them for free from **www.netscape.com** or **www.microsoft.com**, respectively.

- **A text editor such as Notepad.** You can use any Web page editor such as JBuilder, Homesite, Visual Studio 6.0 and so on.

- **Microsoft Access 2000 or higher.**

- **The Java 2 Software Development Kit (SDK), Standard Edition.** This book uses the version 1.4.0 of the Java 2 SDK, which is supplied by Sun Microsystems, Inc. The software, also referred to as the Java Development Kit (JDK), is included on the book's CD. (It can also be found online at *http://java.sun.com/j2se/1.4.*)

- **Apache Tomcat 4.0.** The examples were tested using Tomcat server 4.0.1, which is contained in the accompanying CD.

- **Data files.** You will not be able to complete the chapters and projects in this book using your own computer unless you have the data files. You can get the data files from the accompanying CD, or you can obtain the data files electronically from the Course Technology Web site by connecting to **www.course.com**, and then searching for this book title. The data files for each chapter should reside in the C:\myjspapp\chapter*n* directory, which is the appropriate directory structure.

  When you download the data files from the Web site and extract them, the default location is C:\myjspapp. The data files for each chapter will then reside in the C:\myjspapp\chapter*n* directory. For example, the data files for Chapter 5 can be found in the folder C:\myjspapp\chapter05.

  To install the data files from the CD, click the **Install** icon for these files, and follow the instructions to install them on your computer. The default location for installing these files is also C:\myjspapp.

- **A Web server and JSP engine allow you to create, save, and execute JSP scripts.** Before you can write and test JSP code, you have to install a Web server and a JSP engine software and configure your system to turn your computer into a Web server. Please note that there is no standard procedure for configuring a Web server; it depends on the Web server software, JSP engine, and operating system. You can use any Web server that supports JSP, or plug in a JSP engine to a Web server. This book uses Apache Tomcat as the JSP container. If you're a beginner, you should use Tomcat, so you can follow the installation and configuration instructions on the following pages to set up a Web server. It is assumed that you are using Windows 2000 Professional, or Windows XP Professional. For other operating systems, see your instructor for details. (You need to install the SDK prior to installing Tomcat Server.)

- **Installing the Java Software Development Kit**

  1. Locate the software j2sdk-1_4_0-win.exe, which is located on the accompanying CD.

  2. Follow the instructions to install Java JDK to your computer. You may change the location of where you install the JDK during installation. The default location is C:\j2sdk1.4.0, and this book assumes that the default location is used.

- **Installing and Configuring Apache Tomcat**

  1. Locate the software jakarta-tomcat-4.0.1.exe, which is located in the software folder on the accompanying CD.

  2. Follow the instructions to install the Tomcat server on your computer. By default, Tomcat will be installed in the directory C:\Program Files\Apache Tomcat 4.0, and this book assumes that the default installation location is used.

  3. Click **Start**, point to **All Programs**, point to **Apache Tomcat 4.0**, point to **Configuration**, and then click **Edit Server Configuration** to open the file server.xml.

4. Insert the shaded code as shown in Figure A:

```
server.xml - Notepad
File  Edit  Format  View  Help

    <!-- Define properties for each web application.  This is onl
         if you want to set non-default properties, or have web a
         document roots in places other than the virtual host's a
         directory.  -->

    <!-- Tomcat Root Context -->
    <!--
      <Context path="" docBase="ROOT" debug="0"/>
    -->

    <Context path="/myapp"
        docBase="c:\myjspapp"
        debug="0"
        reloadable="true" />

    <!-- Tomcat Manager Context -->
    <Context path="/manager" docBase="manager"
     debug="0" privileged="true"/>

    <!-- Tomcat Examples Context -->
    <Context path="/examples" docBase="examples" debug="0"
            reloadable="true">
```

5. Save and close the file.

- **Setting Up System Environment Variables**

    1. On the desktop, right-click the **My Computer** icon, then click **Properties** to open the System Properties dialog box.

    2. Click the **Advanced** tab, then click the **Environment Variables** button to open the Environment Variables dialog box.

    3. On the System variables panel, you should see a list of existing system variables. Use the scroll bar to locate and select the Path variable.

    4. Click the **Edit** button to open the Edit System Variable dialog box.

    5. At the end of the Variable value input field, add the following text:

       `;c:\j2sdk1.4.0\bin;`

    6. Click the **OK** button to close the Edit System Variable dialog box.

    7. Use the scroll bar to navigate all system variables to see whether the variable CLASSPATH has been set. If you can find it, then select the variable and click **Edit**. Add the following text to the end of its current value string in the Edit System Variable window:

       `; c:\j2sdk1.4.0\jre\lib\rt.jar;.;c:\Program Files\`
       `Apache Tomcat 4.0\common\lib\servlet.jar`

       (*Note*: The two lines above should be entered on a single line.)

       Click **OK** to close the Edit System Variable dialog box.

If CLASSPATH does not exist, click the **New** button to open the New System Variable dialog box. In the Variable name input field, type **CLASSPATH**, and in the Variable value input field type the following value:

```
c:\j2sdk1.4.0\jre\lib\rt.jar;.;c:\Program Files\
Apache Tomcat 4.0\common\lib\servlet.jar
```

(*Note*: Enter the two lines above on a single line.)

Click **OK** close the New System Variable dialog box.

8. Click **OK** to close the Environment Variables dialog box.

9. Click **OK** to close the System Properties dialog box.

10. Restart the computer to make the new setting take effect.

■ **Setting Up Your Own Web Application**

1. Create a directory named **myjspapp** under the C: drive

2. Create a directory named **WEB-INF** within the directory C:\myjspapp.

3. Create a directory named **classes** within the directory C:\myjspapp\WEB-INF.

4. Open a new document in your text editor and type in the following code:

```
<?xml version="1.0" encoding="ISO-8859-1"?>
<!DOCTYPE web-app
  PUBLIC "-//Sun Microsystems, Inc.//DTD Web Application
2.3//EN"
  "http://java.sun.com/dtd/web-app_2_3.dtd">
<web-app>
 <session-config>
  <session-timeout>30</session-timeout>
 </session-config>
 <welcome-file-list>
  <welcome-file>index.html</welcome-file>
 </welcome-file-list>
</web-app>
```

5. Save the file as **web.xml** in the folder C:\myjspapp\WEB-INF.

6. Open a new document in your text editor and type in the following code:

```
<HTML>
<HEAD><TITLE>My JSP application</TITLE></HEAD>
<BODY  BGCOLOR="#FFFCCC">
<CENTER><H1>Welcome to my JSP Web site</H1>
<i>Designed by</i><BR><BR>
Your name
</CENTER>
</BODY>
</HTML>
```

7. Save it as **index.html** in the folder C:\myjspapp.

■ **Starting and Stopping Apache Tomcat**

To start Tomcat:

Click **Start**, point to **All Programs**, then point to **Apache Tomcat 4.0**, then click **Start Tomcat**. A Tomcat starting window appears. You can minimize this window, but do not close it.

Note: If you are using Windows XP Professional, Apache Tomcat 4.0 starts automatically when you turn on your computer. To stop Apache Tomcat, you need to open Windows Task Manager, on the Process tab, select the process **tomcat.exe** and click the **End Process** button to stop Apache Tomcat.

To stop Tomcat:

Click **Start**, point to **All Programs**, point to **Apache Tomcat 4.0**, then click **Stop Tomcat**. The Tomcat window closes.

■ **Testing Apache Tomcat Server Installation and Configuration**

Once you have installed and configured the Tomcat server and your Web application, you should check to make sure that it works correctly.

1. Start the Tomcat server if it is not started.

2. Open a browser window and enter the following URL in the address box:

   `http://localhost:8080`

3. You should see the Tomcat default page displayed.

4. Change the URL to:

   `http://localhost:8080/myapp`

5. The default page (index.html) should appear.

   (*Note*: To test any JSP examples, you must keep the Tomcat server running.)

FIGURES

Most of the figures in this book reflect how your screen will look if you are using Windows XP Professional and Internet Explorer version 6.0; your screen will look similar to these figures if you are using Windows 2000 and/or Netscape Navigator, except where noted in the text.

Visit Our World Wide Web Site

Additional materials designed especially for you might be available for your course on the World Wide Web. Go to **www.course.com**. Periodically search this site for more details.

To the Instructor

To complete the chapters in this book, your users must use a set of data files. These files are included in the Instructor's Resource Kit (also note that they are on the student's CD that accompanies the book). They also may be obtained electronically through the Course Technology Web site at **www.course.com**. Follow the instructions in the Help file to copy the data files to your server or standalone computer. You can view the Help file using a text editor such as WordPad or Notepad.

Once the data files are copied, if appropriate, you should instruct your students on how to install the files to their own computers or workstations. This Read This Before You Begin section, on page xviii, includes important details on this.

Please note that to use the SRAS system in Chapters 5–12, students need to sign in on the logon page with a valid user name and password. The database includes three users and three privilege levels, as follows:

Username	Password	Privilege
1	password	administrator
2	password	faculty
3	password	student

The chapters and projects in this book were tested using Windows 2000 and Windows XP Professional with Apache Tomcat 4.0.1, J2SDK 1.4.0, Internet Explorer 6.0, and Netscape 6.2.

If you follow the previous instructions in this section to configure Apache Tomcat 4.0, then the context path is set to http://localhost:8080/myapp, and the all application files are stored in the folder C:\myjspapp. It is worthwhile to mention that you can use any context path name for your Web application and you can also set up a Web application anywhere in the file system by modifying the path and docBase. For example, if you want to use "payroll" as context path and store all Web applications in the folder D:\payrollapplication, then you need modify the shaded code in Figure A on page xix as follows:

```
<Context path="/payroll"
  docBase="d:\payrollapplication"
  crossContent="false"
  debug="0"
  reloadable="true" />
```

And the URL for the Web application is http://localhost:8080/payroll followed by the file name in your application.

Therefore, if you instruct your students to set up the Web application (using the context path name: myapp) in the file system in a location other than C:\myjspapp, then you need to instruct your students to make the corresponding modifications when they follow the instructions to save files in the text.

It is also possible to set up a working folder for each student. If you want each student to create a separate folder to save his/her files, you may do so by creating folders in C:\myjspapp. For example, for John Smith, a folder "john" is created in the folder C:\myjspapp; for Mike Kanet, a folder "mike" is created in the folder C:\myjspapp. Then John Smith will save his files for Chapter01 in the folder C:\myjspapp\john\chapter01, and so on. And the URL should be changed to http://localhost:8080/myapp/john/chapter01/*fileNames*.

COURSE TECHNOLOGY DATA FILES

You are granted a license to copy the data files to any computer or computer network used by individuals who have purchased this book.

1

AN INTRODUCTION TO JSP

In this chapter, you will:

♦ Learn about Web client/server architecture
♦ Learn the difference between static and dynamic Web pages
♦ Learn how dynamic Web pages are generated in JSP
♦ Review various server-side processing technologies
♦ Compare JSP to alternate technologies

JavaServer Pages (JSP) is one of the latest server-based technologies designed for creating dynamic and interactive HTML pages for your World Wide Web (WWW) site or corporate intranet/extranet. As part of the Java™ family, JSP technology enables rapid development of Web-based applications that are platform independent. In this chapter, you will learn about Web client/server architecture, the difference between static HTML Web pages and dynamic Web pages, and how to use JSP to create dynamic Web pages.

Web Client/Server Architecture

To open a Web page on your browser, you usually either type in the URL and then press Enter, or click a hyperlink on a page. Both of these actions send a request for a Web page to a remote computer, which is called a Web server. After receiving the request, the Web server locates the requested page, possibly processes some code in this page, then sends it to the client that requested it, where it is displayed in a Web browser. The process involves at least two components: the Web browser and a Web server. The Web browser resides on the client computer, which sends a request for a Web page; the Web server is a remote computer that accepts and processes the request and sends output to the client. This is known as the client/server model. In this model, the browser simply displays the page sent back from the Web server. For some applications, certain software must be installed on the clients' computer before the client can send requests to the Web server. For example, to use the chatting programs you see on many Web sites, you must first download and install a piece of software onto your computer.

A client/server-based system separates the execution of tasks evenly (hopefully) among processors and makes optimal use of the available resources. A client/server model is made up of a number of components, as shown in Figure 1-1.

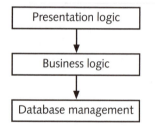

Figure 1-1   Client/server model

A client/server model basically consists of three components: presentation logic, business logic, and database management. Presentation logic typically consists of a graphical user interface of some kind. Business logic governs how data are manipulated. The database management system contains the data that the application requires. The business logic is basically the code that the user calls upon, via the presentation logic, to retrieve the desired data from the database management system. The presentation logic then receives the data and formats it for display.

Based on the distribution of the three components, *N*-tier client/server models have been developed. Figure 1-2 shows a typical model for two-tier client/server architecture.

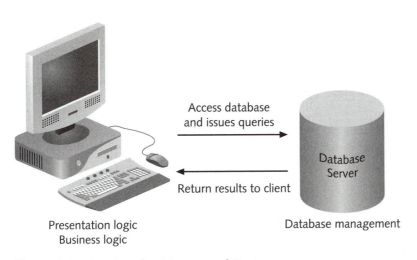

Access database
and issues queries

Database
Server

Return results to client

Presentation logic
Business logic

Database management

Figure 1-2 Two-tier client/server architecture

In the two-tier client/server model, the client typically contains both presentation logic and business logic. The application implementing the business rules is installed in and runs on the client machine, and the application accesses database and issues queries to the database directly. Business logic controls how the data returned from the database is manipulated before it is displayed on the client machine. Since the business logic is implemented on the client side, this relieves the server of heavy computing tasks. However, placing the business logic on the client results in very high maintenance costs, primarily because when business logic changes, the client program must be changed and redistributed. Take, for example, the chat program mentioned above: When the chat program is updated, all clients must download and install the new program. If you separate the business logic from the user interface, you can update the business logic without modifying the client; this separation of business logic from presentation logic is the driving force behind three-tier client/server architecture.

In three-tier client/server architecture, the business logic occupies the middle tier: An application server is used to manage the business logic, a database server handles the data access logic, and the client manages the presentation logic, as shown in Figure 1-3. In the three-tier model, instead of updating the database directly, the client sends a request to the middle tier, which then updates the database. This separation of business logic from the presentation logic adds flexibility to the design of the application. The biggest advantage of the three-tier model is that the business logic can be updated once for all clients; this results in a large savings in deployment costs. On the other hand, multiple user interfaces can be built and deployed without ever changing the business logic.

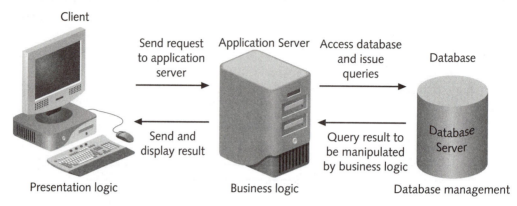

Figure 1-3 Three-tier client-server Architecture

A Web application typically follows a three-tier model, as shown in Figure 1-4. The first tier contains the presentation logic, including the pages that are displayed on the client browser. The second tier is the business logic, which usually consists of scripts or programs governing how data are manipulated. Finally, the third tier provides the second tier with the necessary data. A typical Web application collects data from the user (first tier), sends a request to the Web server, runs the requested server program (second and third tiers), packages the data to be presented in the Web browser, and sends it back to the browser for display (first tier).

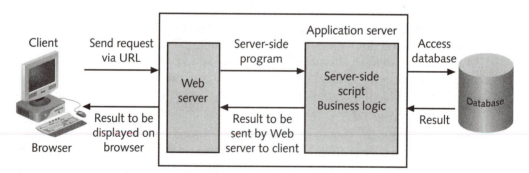

Figure 1-4 Web application architecture

Web applications are server-based. That means there is less maintenance required, because it is not necessary to configure individual client machines. Users can navigate to a Web site without any site-specific setup or configuration. Updates to Web applications are made on the server, and these changes are instantly reflected on client browsers.

In a typical Web client/server model, server-side scripts play a key role in implementing business rules; they also act as a bridge between the presentation and database manipulation functions. JSP, in terms of performance, feasibility for deployment, and scalability, is one of the most effective server-side scripting technologies for implementing presentation and business logic, as well as for interacting with a database system.

STATIC WEB PAGES

If you surf around the Internet today, you have probably noticed that many Web pages are simple compositions of fixed text and images. These Web pages allow you to click text and image links to go to other pages, but their content remains unchanged unless and until they are physically modified. HTML page designers can use tags such as <frame>, <table>, and <font> to improve the appearance of the pages' interface, and they can even incorporate animated images, but they cannot make these pages truly dynamic. These Web pages are called **static Web pages**. The content of a static Web page has been predetermined before it is requested. The content (text, images, hyperlinks, etc.) and appearance of the page is always the same regardless of who visits the page, when they visit it, how they arrive at it, or any other factors. Such a page can be created with any text editor, such as Notepad, and saved as an .htm or .html file.

Static Web pages are often quite easy to spot; sometimes you can pick them out by just looking at the source code of the page. This source code, as shown in the browser, is exactly the same as what the author saved to disk. To make this more understandable, think for a moment about how a static HTML page is displayed on a client browser:

1. A Web page author composes an HTML page and saves it as an .htm or .html file.

2. A user types a page request into the browser, and the request is sent from the browser to the Web server.

3. The Web server receives the page request and locates the .htm/.html page in the local file system.

4. The Web server sends the HTML stream over the Internet to the client browser.

5. The browser interprets the HTML and displays the page.

The following example illustrates the creation and display of a static Web page.

1. Open a new document in your text editor and type in the following code:

```
<HTML>
<HEAD><TITLE>Welcome to JSP</TITLE></HEAD>
<BODY>
<H1>Welcome to JavaServer Pages</H1>
Welcome to the JSP Web site. Here is the class <a
href= "schedule.html">schedule</a> for
Introduction to JSP.
<BR><BR>
If you have any question regarding the schedule, you can
<a href=mailto:instructor@localhost:8080.com>send
e-mail to the instructor.</a>
</BODY>
</HTML>
```

2. Save the file as **example1.html** in C:\myapp\chapter01

3. Load this page using the following URL:
   http://localhost:8080/myapp/chapter01/example1.html

   This page is displayed as shown in Figure 1-5.

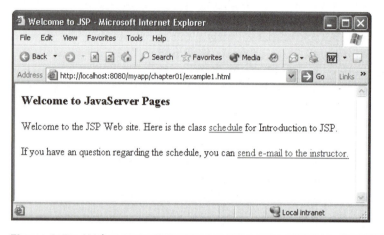

Figure 1-5   Welcome to JSP

Regardless of who you are and when you visit this page, it always looks like the one shown in Figure 1-5. The content of the page is determined when you save the example1.html file to disk.

If you view the source code of this page in a browser, you will see that it is the same as in the file example1.html.

DYNAMIC WEB PAGES

Suppose you are currently designing a Web page for your JSP course. You wish to display a welcome message, "Welcome to Introduction to JSP". This message works for visitors who can read English, but what about those who do not? To make the page accessible to non-English speakers, you could modify the page to display the message in a different language depending upon where a visitor is from. But using HTML alone, it is not possible to obtain information about the visitor. Hence, even though you have designed Web pages using different languages, you would properly not be able to provide them to users who speak different languages. Suppose that you also want to display the current time on the Web server. This can be accomplished easily with JSP or any server-side script, but it is impossible to achieve using HTML alone.

To display the current time to visitors, at least part of the Web page content must be generated when the page is requested. In other words, you need to replace the hard-coded HTML source with code that generates HTML for the page when it is requested.

Specifically, the current time on the Web server must be dynamically generated each time this page is requested. Another example in which the Web page content cannot be predetermined is found in the Student Records Access System (SRAS) Case Project, which is introduced in Chapter 2. To access the system, all users are assigned a unique user ID and a password. After you log on to the system, you are allowed to edit your profile, including changing your address, password, and so on. In fact, all users use the same Web page to edit their profile, but the content displayed on the page can be different. The content is customized to the individual user. When a user requests the Edit Profile page, the user's information is retrieved from a database, and this information, as well as other hard-coded content, is sent back to and displayed on the client browser. You will learn more about dynamic content and how to write JSP to generate it throughout this book.

CREATING DYNAMIC WEB PAGES WITH JSP

JavaServer Pages (JSP) is a server-side scripting language that produces Web pages that can be viewed with any browser. JSP technology allows Web developers and designers to create and maintain information-rich, dynamic Web pages. As part of the Java family, JSP technology enables rapid development of Web-based applications that are platform independent.

To illustrate how JSP can be used to generate dynamic Web pages, you will complete the example discussed above to display the current time on the Web server, as follows.

1. Open a new document in your text editor and type the following code:

```
<HTML>
<HEAD>
<TITLE>Current server time</TITLE>
</HEAD>
<BODY>
<font face="Arial" size=1>
The current date and time on the Web server are:
<%= new java.util.Date() %>
</font>
</BODY>
</HTML>
```

2. Save the file as **example2.jsp** in the folder C:\myapp\chapter01.

3. Open **example2.jsp** in your browser using the following URL:
   http://localhost:8080/myapp/chapter01/example2.jsp

This page is displayed as shown in Figure 1-6.

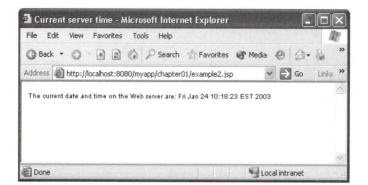

Figure 1-6 Current time on server

The source code of the page as shown in your Web browser is as follows:

```
<HTML>
<HEAD>
<TITLE>Current server time</TITLE>
</HEAD>
<BODY>
<font face="Arial" size=1>
The current date and time on the Web server are:
Mon Jul 16 10:58:09 PDT 2002
</font>
</BODY>
</HTML>
```

This is nothing more than plain HTML code. However, the highlighted part is generated dynamically when this JSP page is requested. The rest of the page is hard-coded in advance. The JSP code <%= new java.util.Date() %> is executed on your Web server and returns the current time on your server; the server sends the newly generated content back to the client browser.

The above example of a dynamic, or built-on-the fly Web page, is a simple one, but there are a couple of situations in which it's essential that Web pages be built in this fashion:

- The Web page is based on the data submitted by the user. For instance, the results pages from search engines and online store order-confirmation pages are specific to particular user requests.

- The Web page uses information from a database. For example, in an online store, all product information, such as item name, price, and inventory level, is stored in a database, and therefore the Web page that displays such information must be dynamically generated.

JSP Versus HTML

A dynamic Web site can be customized to individual visitors. It can reflect the fact that a visitor has visited the site before and can track how much time a visitor spends on each page. It allows visitors to customize the presentation of the Web page they visit. It can obtain data from a database and generate an HTML page on the fly. It can collect information via the browser and access and update a database. It can be customized easily to display the visitor's preferred topics. In general, a dynamic Web site offers the visitor an all-around richer experience.

Here are a few examples of what you can do with JSP that cannot be accomplished with pure HTML:

- Connect to and manipulate a database
- Create pages that can display content of interest to a particular user
- Collect data from users and return information to a visitor based on the data collected
- Modify the content of a Web page by updating a text file or the contents of a database rather than the HTML code itself
- Access file systems via the Internet so that you can read, write, and update files
- Utilize the extensive Java Application Programming Interface

How can JSP generate dynamic pages, while HTML cannot? The key difference between HTML and JSP pages stems from how the Web server deals with them. You will learn more about Web page processing in Chapter 2.

When you type a URL in the address box or location box and press Enter, or when you click a text/image link on a Web page, you are sending a page request to a Web server. A Web server is simply a computer that provides services, such as locating the requested file and sending it back to clients, on the Internet or on a local intranet or extranet. A Web server can accept and process requests for Web pages, images, executable programs, and other files. The Web server responds to each request differently, based on the requested file type. When a Web server receives a request for a Web page, it first checks to see if the page exists in the server system (either on disk or in memory). If the page consists of HTML only, the Web server simply sends the page to the browser, which interprets and displays the page, as shown in Figure 1-7. If it is a JSP page, the JSP code is actually executed on the Web server, and the results are mixed with the existing regular HTML and sent out to a browser, as shown in Figure 1-8.

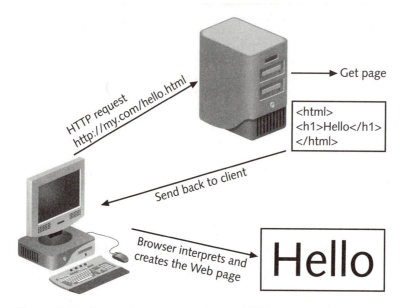

Figure 1-7   Processing a request for an HTML page

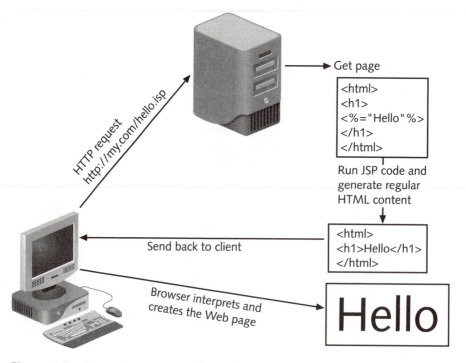

Figure 1-8   Processing a request for a JSP page

CGI, ASP, AND ASP.NET

The earliest server-side processing instructions for managing the interaction between the Web server and client browser were written in Common Gateway Interface, or CGI. The programs that generate dynamic content consequently became known as "CGI programs" or sometimes simply "CGIs." CGI has been around quite a bit longer than JSP and Active Server Pages (ASP), which you will learn about later in this section.

The earliest CGIs were written in a language called C. C programs run fast, because C is compiled into machine language before being executed on a Web server. That is, after it is written, it is converted from a form that humans can understand into machine language, which the computer can understand. There are three disadvantages to this approach. First, it makes it relatively difficult to modify or update applications, because even minor changes require that the whole program be recompiled. Second, C is a relatively "low-level" language. Compared to "high-level" languages, such as Java, more effort may be needed to perform certain computations. Third, it is difficult, if not impossible, to connect to a database using C.

The C language was rapidly replaced as the CGI language of choice by Perl. Perl is good at manipulating text. Perl is an interpreted language, which means it is not compiled in advance. Thus, it is easier to modify a Perl page than a C page. On the other hand, every time a Perl page is requested, the Perl instructions are translated and executed. This translation obviously takes some time, which means that Perl sacrifices speed at runtime in favor of faster development and changes.

Traditional CGI does not directly communicate with the Web server. This adds an extra level to the browser-server model of interaction, which means it requires extra effort to get information on the server side through CGI. For example, with Perl it is not easy to translate relative URLs into physical path names, while with some other server-side scripting languages, such as JSP, you can accomplish this easily, as you will see in future chapters.

ASP is a core feature of Microsoft Internet Information Server (IIS). It provides an extremely versatile development environment. Microsoft ships two languages in the default installation of ASP, Jscript and VBScript. ASP allows programmers to extend the system by using ActiveX objects. Like JSP, ASP overcomes the shortcomings discussed above. Microsoft recently introduced ASP.NET as part of its .NET framework. Unlike classic ASP, ASP.NET is compiled, which greatly improves its performance. Even though ASP.NET is compiled, it does not sacrifice the flexibility of traditional ASP. ASP.NET offers access to any programming languages supported in the .NET framework, including Visual Basic and C# (but not VBScript). ASP and ASP.NET are primarily supported on Windows platforms.

SERVLETS

Servlets are small Java programs that run on a Web server in response to client requests; they generate dynamic content that is sent back to client. Servlets are compiled and represented as .class files. These small Java programs are loaded either on demand or by the server at startup. When a servlet is requested from client, a method or function is called in response to the request. In fact, when a JSP page is requested for the first time, it is compiled into its corresponding servlet. From that point, it is the servlet that handles all requests.

Unlike CGIs, once a servlet has been loaded it remains in memory until the server decides to remove it or the server is shut down. A servlet is loaded either at startup or upon the first client request to it, and after that, every time a client makes a request to the servlet, the server merely runs a method within the servlet. This dramatically reduces the response time from server to client.

Because servlets are written completely in Java, they enjoy the same cross-platform support as any Java program. This "write once, run anywhere" capability allows servlets to be easily distributed throughout an enterprise without rewriting them for each platform. Servlets operate identically without modification whether they are running on UNIX, Windows NT, or any other Java-compliant operating system. Another major advantage of using servlet technology (as JSP does) is that servlets (as well as JSP) can be run on virtually every popular Web server in use today. Many major software vendors currently provide native support for servlets and JSP within their products, including the IBM WebSphere server, BEA WebLogic Application Server, Netscape Enterprise Server, and so on. Servers that do not currently support servlets and JSP require plug-in servlets and a JSP engine from a third party in order to load and run servlets and JSP. For example, JRUN from Live Software, ServletExec from New Atlanta Communications, and Apache Tomcat from the Apache Software Foundation provide servlet and JSP engines to support many popular Web servers, including Microsoft Internet Information Server and Apache Web Server.

WHY USE JSP?

As a server-side scripting language JSP builds pages on top of servlets. So they have all the advantages of servlets.

Unlike CGI, the first time a JSP page is requested, it is compiled into a servlet, and the servlet stays in memory to respond to further requests. This eliminates the need to reload something every time a request for the JSP page is made. Instead, the servlet is loaded once, the first time it is needed; after that it stays active, turning requests into responses as fast as the Web server can send them. This gives JSP pages a speed and scalability advantage over some other server-side scripts. Figure 1-9 illustrates how the Web server processes a JSP page request in more detail.

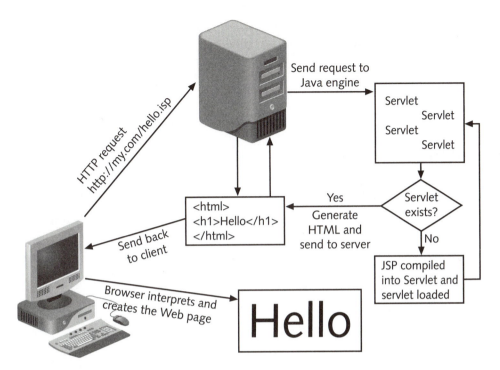

Send request to
Java engine

Servlet
Servlet
Servlet
Servlet

Servlet
exists?

Yes
Generate
HTML and
send to server

No

JSP compiled
into Servlet and
servlet loaded

HTTP request
http://my.com/hello.jsp

```
<html>
<h1>Hello</h1>
</html>
```

Send back
to client

Browser interprets and
creates the Web page

Hello

Figure 1-9   Processing a JSP page request

Because the dynamic part of the JSP page is written in Java, you can exploit the extensive Java API (Application Programming Interface) for networking, database access, distributed objects, and the like. It is powerful, reusable, and portable to other operating systems and Web servers. You are not locked into a single platform.

JSP pages have an advanced feature known as **extensible tags**. This mechanism enables developers to create custom tags, which are introduced in Chapter 10. These extensible tags allow you to extend the JSP page's tag syntax.

CHAPTER SUMMARY

- ❐ A Web server is a computer that provides services via the Internet, intranets, and extranets. To view a Web page, you send the request for that page to a Web server. The Web server accepts your request, locates and processes the page, then sends the results back to your browser.

- ❐ The content of an HTML page is written before the page is requested, while the content of a dynamic page is created when the page is requested. In order to create content dynamically, you must write instructions to tell the Web server what to do. These instructions are executed on the Web server when a Web page is requested.

❏ CGI, Perl, and JSP are means by which you can provide instructions that are run on the Web server. For traditional CGI and Perl, a new process is started for each HTTP request, which produces the overhead of starting the new process. With JSP, the JSP code is compiled into a servlet the first time the page is requested. Thereafter the servlet stays in memory and responds to requests later on. This speeds up the processing time.

REVIEW QUESTIONS

1. With traditional CGI or ASP, a new process is started for each HTTP request. True or False?

2. The JSP code in a JSP page is compiled into a servlet every time it is requested. True or False?

3. In a three-tier client/server architecture, business logic typically resides on the
   _____ .
   a. client machine
   b. client browser
   c. application server
   d. database server

4. In a two-tier client/server model, which of the following components reside(s) on the client side?
   a. presentation logic
   b. business logic
   c. database management system
   d. both a and b
   e. all of the above

5. The first-tier in a Web application contains both presentation and business logic. True or False?

6. A Web application typically follows a three-tier client/server model. True or False?

7. To run JSP code, client browsers must have a JSP engine. True or False?

8. You can use an HTML Web page to get the current time on a Web server and display the time on a client browser. True or False?

9. Because JSP is written in Java, it is cross-platform, which means that JSP is platform independent. True or False?

10. In server-side scripting, content is dynamically generated when the page is requested. True or False?

11. In server-side scripting, the dynamic content is generated on the client browser. True or False?

12. Any browser can properly display a Web page that contains a server-side script, as long as the host Web server has the proper engine to interpret the server-side script. True or False?

13. JSP is browser independent. True or False?

14. JSP is _____ that runs on a Web server.

    a. client-side script

    b. server-side script

    c. HTML

    d. VBScript

15. You cannot use Java API within JSP code. True or False?

16. You cannot mix regular HTML with JSP code in a JSP page. True or False?

17. When a JSP page is compiled, what is it turned into?

    a. an applet

    b. a servlet

    c. an application

    d. a script

HANDS-ON PROJECTS

Project 1-1 Static Versus Dynamic Content

There are many Web sites providing free e-mail account services, such as www.yahoo.com, www.aol.com, www.hotmail.com, and so on. If you do not have an e-mail account accessible from the Internet, you may apply one from the Web sites listed above. In this project, you are required to log on to your e-mail account and open the page where you can edit your personal information. You will see that your information is displayed on that page. Identify which part of the content on the page is prewritten and which is dynamically generated.

Project 1-2 Pure HTML Page Content

In this project, you will create an HTML page, view the page in a browser, and view the page's source code.

1. Open a new document in your text editor and type in the following code:

```
<HTML>
<HEAD><TITLE>Welcome to JSP</TITLE></HEAD>
<BODY>
<H3>Welcome to Introduction to JSP</H3>
In this chapter, you:<br>
<li>learned about Web client/server architecture
```

```
<li>learned the difference between static and dynamic Web
pages
<li>learned how dynamic Web pages are generated in JSP
<li>reviewed various server-side processing technologies
<li>compared JSP to alternate technologies
</BODY>
</HTML>
```

2. Save the file as **project2.html** in the folder C:\myapp\chapter01

3. Load this page using the following URL:
   http://localhost:8080/myapp/chapter01/project2.html

   The page is displayed as shown in Figure 1-10.

4. Click **View** on the menu bar, then click **Source**. You should see the source code of the page, which is the same as in the file project2.html.

5. Close the page and the browser.

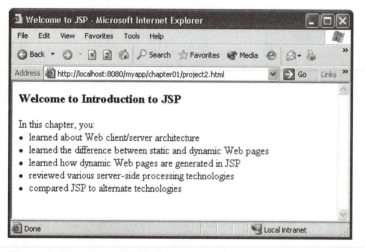

Figure 1-10   Pure HTML demo

Project 1-3 Dynamic Content with JSP

In this project, you will identify which part of the page displayed on browser is generated dynamically.

1. Open the data file **project3.txt** in the folder C:\myapp\chapter01.

2. Save this page as **project3.jsp** in the same folder.

3. Load the page **project3.jsp** using the following URL:
   http://localhost:8080/myapp/chapter01/project3.jsp

4. View the source code of the page in your browser and compare it with the original JSP page code.

5. Identify which part of the page content displayed on your browser is generated dynamically.

6. Close the page and your browser.

Project 1-4 JSP Code in an HTML Page

In this project, you will experience what happens when JSP code is embedded in an HTML page.

1. Open the data file **project3.txt** in the folder C:\myapp\chapter01.

2. Save the file as **project4.html** in the same folder.

3. Load the page project4.html using the following URL:
   http://localhost:8080/myapp/chapter01/project4.html

   If you are using Internet Explorer, this page is displayed as shown in Figure 1-11; if you are using Netscape, it is displayed as shown in Figure 1-12.

4. Write a report explaining why the page is displayed this way, and how dynamic processing would change its appearance.

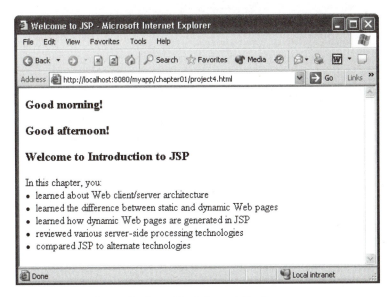

Figure 1-11   Page displayed in Internet Explorer

Figure 1-12   Page displayed in Netscape Navigator

CASE PROJECTS

Web Client/Server Architecture

Write a report that describes how a typical Web application implements the three-tier client/server model. Identify where the three components (presentation logic, business logic, and database management system) are distributed.

Web Server Application

Write a report that describes the function of a Web server application in a typical three-tier Web application architecture.

2

CLIENT-SIDE AND
SERVER-SIDE SCRIPTING

In this chapter, you will:

♦ Use JavaScript to create interactive Web content

♦ Insert client-side script into an HTML page

♦ Insert server-side script into an HTML page

♦ Manipulate a string object using JavaScript

♦ Set up client-side validation

In the previous chapter, you learned that HTML alone cannot provide interactive data on the Internet. To provide dynamic content and to allow clients to interact with Web pages, you need to use client- and server-side scripts as well as HTML. In this chapter, you learn how to write and use client- and server-side scripts to provide interactive content to clients.

SCRIPTING

To extend the capabilities of HTML and add interactive content to your Web pages, you can embed instructions into your Web pages. These instructions are written in one of a number of **scripting languages**, such as JavaScript, VBScript, or JSP, and are executed either on the client or the server. Each scripting language requires its own interpreter. So, VBScript code must be sent to a VBScript interpreter, JavaScript code to a JavaScript interpreter, and JSP code to a JSP interpreter. According to where a script code is interpreted, scripting languages are divided into two categories: client-side and server-side scripts. Client-side scripts are instructions embedded in HTML code; these instructions must be downloaded to the client, where they are executed on the browser. A server-side script, as discussed in Chapter 1, is executed on the Web server before the requested page is sent back to the client.

Client-side Scripts and Browser Dependency

Since client-side scripts are executed by the client browser, the browser must provide the appropriate interpreter to execute the scripting code. All browsers come with built-in engines to support certain client-side scripting languages.

There are two main scripting languages: VBScript and JavaScript. JavaScript was the first client-side scripting language. VBScript is Microsoft's scripting language, and is based on the Visual Basic programming language. Internet Explorer 4 and later versions support both JScript (Microsoft's implementation of JavaScript) and VBScript, while Netscape supports only JavaScript. This means that Netscape does not have a built-in engine to interpret VBScript. In the following exercise you create a client-side script that is browser-dependent.

1. Open a new document in your text editor and type in the following code:

```
<HTML>
<HEAD><TITLE>Client-side Script Example</TITLE></HEAD>
<BODY>
This page was last modified on
<script language="VBScript">
        document.write document.lastModified
</script>
</BODY>
</HTML>
```

2. Save the file as **example1.html** in C:\myjspapp\chapter02.

3. Load this page in Internet Explorer using the following URL:
   http://localhost:8080/myapp/chapter02/example1.html

   This page is displayed as shown in Figure 2-1.

4. Load this page in Netscape. This page is displayed as shown in Figure 2-2.

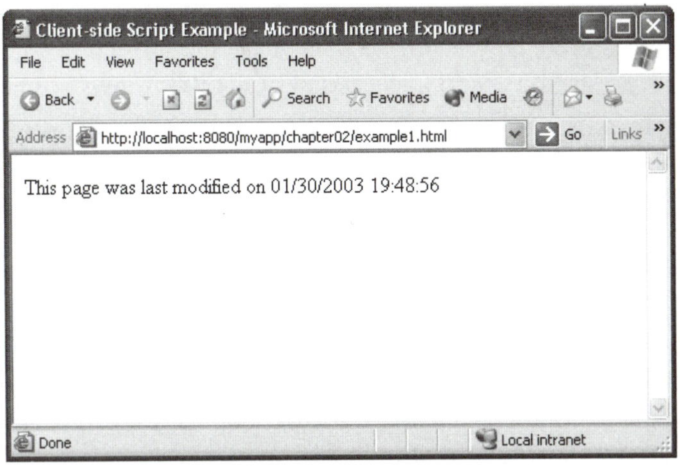

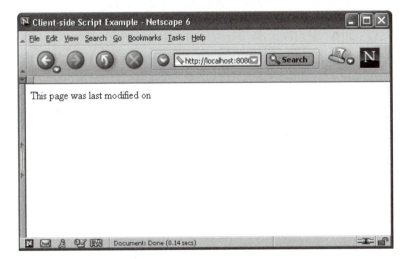

Figure 2-1   VBScript in Internet Explorer

Figure 2-2   VGScript in Netscape

You can see that in Internet Explorer, the last modified time is displayed properly. However, in Netscape, the last modified time is not displayed at all.

The reason is that Netscape does not know how to interpret VBScript. Like all other programming languages, in order for a computer to perform some actions, the instructions must be translated to a language that the computer can understand. Internet Explorer comes with both JavaScript and VBScript engines built-in. These engines intepret

JavaScript and VBScript, ensuring that both scripts can be executed on Internet Explorer. On the other hand, since both browsers have built-in JavaScript engines, a JavaScript script can be executed in both browsers, as illustrated in the following exercise.

1. Open a new document in your text editor and type in the following code:

```
<HTML>
<HEAD><TITLE>Client-side Script Example</TITLE></HEAD>
<BODY>
This page was last modified on
<script language="JavaScript">
    document.write(document.lastModified)
</script>
</BODY>
</HTML>
```

2. Save this page as **example2.html** in C:\myjspapp\chapter02.

3. Load this page in Internet Explorer using the following URL: http://localhost:8080/myapp/chapter02/example2.html

The page is displayed as shown in Figure 2-3.

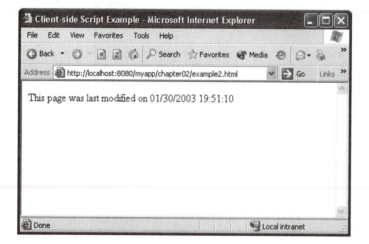

Figure 2-3   JavaScript in Internet Explorer

4. Load the page in Netscape. It is displayed as shown in Figure 2-4.

If you view the page's source code, you will see the same code as the original example2.html file. That means that the Web server sends the original page back to the client's browser. It is the client browser that interprets the scripting instructions and displays the last modified time.

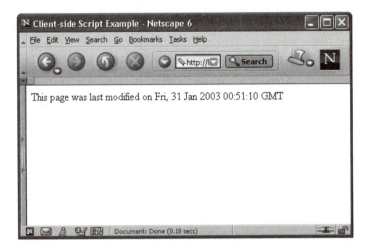

Figure 2-4   JavaScript in Netscape

CLIENT-SIDE SCRIPTING USING JAVASCRIPT

As you learned above, the main disadvantage of client-side scripting is browser dependency. Because VBScript is not supported by Netscape, JavaScript tends to be the language of choice for writing client-side scripts.

You can insert scripts almost anywhere in the body of an HTML page, or between the <HEAD> and </HEAD> tags. Scripts in the <HEAD> of a document load before anything else, which may be important to the functionality of your script. Scripts in the <BODY> are loaded and executed in sequence. In the exercise below, you will write a simple JavaScript program that displays the message "Hello World!"

1. Open a new file in your text editor and type in the following code:

```
<HTML>
<HEAD><TITLE>Hello World</TITLE></HEAD>
<BODY>
<h1>
   <script language="JavaScript">
      document.write("Hello World!")
   </script>
</h1>
</BODY>
</HTML>
```

2. Save this file as **example3.html** in C:\myjspapp\chapter02.

3. Start your browser and load this page using the following URL:
   http://localhost:8080/myapp/chapter02/example3.html

   The page is displayed as shown in Figure 2-5.

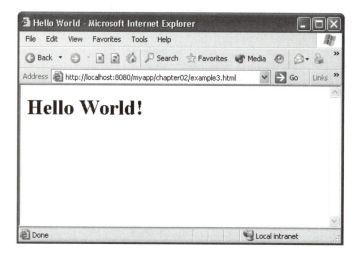

Figure 2-5   Content generated with JavaScript

 To request the page using the URL shown above, you must have Tomcat Server running on your computer; otherwise, this page is not displayed.

Notice that the script tag identifies the scripting language in which the enclosed scripts are written. The code `<script language="JavaScript">` is the opening script tag. This tells the browser to expect JavaScript instead of HTML. The attribute `language="JavaScript"` identifies to the browser which scripting language is being used. The code `document.write("Hello World!")` is the first line of JavaScript. This code writes "Hello World!" into the document window, as seen in Figure 2-5. The code `</script>` identifies the end of script and tells the browser to start expecting HTML again. A `<script>` section can be placed almost anywhere in the page. You will often find scripts at the end of an HTML document, so that the rest of the page can be loaded and rendered by the browser before the interpreter loads and executes the script code. In this way, the whole of the page can be loaded first—rather than alternate chunks of HTML and script. However, if you are using the code to insert something into the page, such as the time and date, you need to place the `<script>` section in the appropriate position within the HTML source.

Inserting Comments into Client-Side Scripts

Some older browsers, such as Netscape 1.x, Microsoft Internet Explorer 3 and earlier, and the America Online (AOL) browser prior to version 4, do not understand JavaScript. In those browsers, the script itself is simply displayed as text on the Web page. To avoid this problem, you can enclose your script within special comment tags <!-- and //-->; any text within these tags is ignored by old browsers. The code above, with these comment tags, is shown below.

```
<HTML>
<HEAD><TITLE>Hello World</TITLE></HEAD>
<BODY>
<h1>
    <script language="JavaScript">
    <!-- Hide script from old browser
        document.write("Hello World!")
    //End hiding script from old browser-->
    </script>
</h1>
</BODY>
</HTML>
```

 If you have a message that you want users of older browsers to see, you can add it into a <NOSCRIPT> tag. This will be processed both by older browsers and by newer browsers when the user has turned off JavaScript (that is, when JavaScript is disabled).

You can also insert comments that are ignored by the scripting engine. You can use comments to describe the purpose of the script, or to explain why you solved a problem in a particular way. These comments can help other programmers to reuse and modify your script. In JavaScript, there are two ways to add comments to your script. One is to use the special tag // to comment out a single line. All text on a line after // is ignored by the scripting engine. To comment out multiple lines use the beginning and ending tags /* and */. All text inserted between /* and */ is ignored by the JavaScript engine. The sample code below shows the Hello World code with comments included.

```
<HTML>
<HEAD><TITLE>Hello World</TITLE></HEAD>
<BODY>
<h1>
    <script language="JavaScript">
    <!-- Hide script from old browser
    /* This script adds the words "Hello World!"
        into the body area of the HTML page
    */
        document.write("Hello World!")
    //End hiding script from old browser-->
    </script>
</h1>
</BODY>
</HTML>
```

Comments can help to make your code accessible to others, but don't overuse them, since too many comments can actually make code difficult to read.

Inserting Client-side Script from an External File

If you expect to use a particular JavaScript program more than once in your Web page, or in more than one Web page, you might wish to create the program in a separate file and then insert it into the HTML code using a URL reference that identifies the location of the file. This way, if you modify the JavaScript program file to add new features or to improve the code's performance, you need only make the changes in one place. When you create a separate file for your JavaScript program, you name it with a .js file extension.

 It is a good practice to use a descriptive name for your file that reminds you what the script does. For example, if you create a JavaScript file to validate an HTML form, you could name the file validation.js.

The <script> tag has an attribute, SRC, that you use when referring to an external script file. The syntax for loading a script file is as follows:

<script language=JavaScript" src="URL_of_javascriptcodefile">

Put your additional JavaScript code here.

</script>

If the JavaScript file is on your local computer system, you use a relative path to point to the JavaScript file. If the JavaScript file is on a server somewhere, you can use the complete URL as the value for the SRC attribute.

In the steps below you rewrite the "Hello World!" example to illustrate how to load JavaScript from a separate file.

1. Open a new document in your text editor and type in the following code:

   ```
   document.write("Hello World!")
   ```

2. Save the file as **helloWorld.js** in the directory C:\myjspapp\chapter02.

3. Open a new document in your text editor and type in the following code:

   ```
   <HTML>
   <HEAD><TITLE>Hello World</TITLE></HEAD>
   <BODY>
   <h1>
       <script language="JavaScript" src="helloWorld.js">
       </script>
   </h1>
   </BODY>
   </HTML>
   ```

2

4. Save this file as **example4.html** in C:\myjspapp\chapter02.

5. Load this page into your browser using the following URL:
   http://localhost:8080/myapp/chapter02/example4.html

   This page is displayed as shown in Figure 2-5.

JavaScript Functions

A **function** is a set of JavaScript instructions or operations that performs a task. Every function has a unique name, and can be invoked, or called, by other parts of the script. By creating a function, you can use a single command to trigger a complex series of actions, repeating the code a number of times within the script. You can also develop generic functions that you can reuse in any script.

 A function can be called as many times as needed during the running of a script.

The syntax for defining a function is as follows:

function functionName(arguments){

      ...

}

The function name is always followed by parentheses, which contain the **arguments**—the information provided to the function for processing. The arguments are followed by an opening brace. The statements that make up the function go on the following lines, and then the function is closed by another brace.

To invoke a function, use the following syntax:

functionName()

A function can return a value. If a value is returned from the function, you must assign it to a variable or use it in an expression. If you do not use the value returned from the function, it is lost.

To create and use a JavaScript function in a Web page:

1. Open a new document in your text editor and type in the following code:

```
<HTML>
<HEAD><TITLE>Display a message window</TITLE>
<script language="JavaScript">
    function alertMessage(message){
        if(message==null)
            alert("Please say something!");
        else
            alert(message);
    }
```

```
   </script>
   </HEAD>
   <BODY>
   <script>
      alertMessage("Hi there")
   </script>
   </BODY>
   </HTML>
```

2. Save the file as **example5.html** in the directory C:\myjspapp\chapter02.

3. Load this file with into browser using the following URL:
   http://localhost:8080/myapp/chapter02/example5.html

   The page is displayed as shown in Figure 2-6.

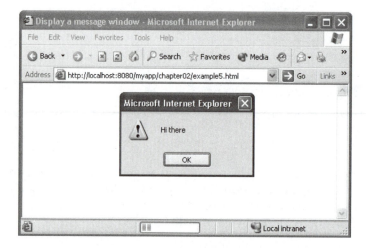

Figure 2-6   JavaScript function

In the example above, there are two script sections. The first one is within the <HEAD> tags, so it is loaded before the HTML interpreter calls the function. In this section, you defined a function that displays in an alert window the message that is given to the function. This function first tests whether information (an argument) is provided when the function is called. If not, the function displays the message "Please say something!"; otherwise, it displays the argument provided when it is called. Unlike C/C++ and Java, in JavaScript, all arguments of a function are optional. That means you can call a function without providing any arguments even though there are several arguments in the function definition.

In the second script section, the function defined in the first section is called to display the message "Hi there."

Since script code is executed in sequence, you must define a function before you can call it. Therefore, it is recommended that you define your functions between the <HEAD> and </HEAD> tags.

In the next exercise, you create a page that prompts a user to input two numbers, and then uses a function to add these two numbers and display the result.

1. Open a new document in your text editor and type in the following code:

```
<HTML>
<HEAD>
<TITLE>add numbers</TITLE>
    <script>
            /*   This function takes two numbers as
arguments and returns the sum of these two numbers
            */
            function add(a,b){
                    var sum
                    sum = a + b
                    return sum
            }
    </script>
</HEAD>
<BODY>
<script>
        var a = prompt("Please input the first number","")
        var b = prompt("Please input the second number","")
        a = parseInt(a)
        b = parseInt(b)
        var sum = add(a,b)
        var s = "The sum of " + a + " and " + b +
                " is <b>" +sum + "</b>"
        document.write(s)
</script>
</BODY>
</HTML>
```

2. Save the file as **example6.html** in the directory C:\myjspapp\chapter02.

3. Load this page into your browser using the following URL:
   http://localhost:8080/myapp/chapter02/example6.html

4. Enter two numbers into the page, and observe that the sum of the two numbers is displayed.

Again, there are two script sections in this example. The first one defines a function that takes two numeric arguments and returns the sum of the two numbers. In the second script section, the first two lines:

```
var a = prompt("Please input the first number","")
var b = prompt("Please input the second number","")
```

prompt the user to input two numbers, and store these numbers in two variables. The prompt method is a built-in JavaScript function. It is passed two parameters: the message to instruct the user to input information, and the default value in the input box.

This function returns the user input as a string. In the following lines two variables are declared to hold the values returned by the prompt function.

```
a = parseInt(a)
b = parseInt(b)
```

These two lines convert strings to integers. The value returned by the prompt function is a string, but the add function expects two numeric parameters. Therefore, the built-in function parseInt is called to do this conversion. The parseInt function has the following form:

parseInt(string, [radix])

The parseInt() function takes an optional integer argument that represents the radix (binary, octal, decimal, and hexadecimal number systems) of the number to be parsed. When the parseInt() function encounters a character that is not a valid numeral for the specified radix, the function returns NaN, which is a reserved value that stands for "Not a Number."

The next line calls the add function, and assigns the value returned by this to a newly declared variable.

```
var sum = add(a,b)
```

The rest of the code forms the message and displays it on the page.

 If you provide a value that is not numeric, the value is displayed on the page as NaN, indicating that the value is not numeric. To reload the file, you can simply click the Reload button on Netscape or the Refresh button on Internet Explorer.

Events and Scripts

An **event** is a user action that triggers activities on the page. For example, loading a Web page when it is requested, clicking a button on a Web page, moving a pointer over an image, and typing into a text input field on a form are all events. You can write scripts that respond to specific actions or events. You can attach a script to some visible element so that the script is executed when the user performs an action on that element (for example, clicking it).

JavaScript deals with events by using commands called event handlers. An action by the user on the page triggers an event handler in your script. Table 2-1 lists a few common event handlers.

Table 2-1   JavaScript Event Handlers

Event Handler	Description
OnLoad	A document or other external element is loaded into the browser.
OnUnload	A document is unloaded from a window or a frame.
onClick	The user clicks an element.
onMouseDown	The user presses a mouse button.
onMouseMove	The user moves the mouse.

Table 2-1 JavaScript Event Handlers (continued)

Event Handler	Description
onMouseOut	The user moves the mouse out of an element.
onMouseOver	The user hovers the mouse over an element.
onMouseUp	The user releases the mouse button.
onSubmit	The user submits a form.
onReset	The user clicks a reset button.
onChange	An element loses focus and the content of the element has changed since it gained focus.

For example, when a user clicks a button, the physical action fires a "click" event. To make your code actually do something in response to the event, you must assign the corresponding event handler to the clicked object. For example, if you want an action to occur when the user clicks a button object, you need to associate an onClick event handler with the button. If you want to perform some tasks after a document loads, you can specify an onLoad event handler that is associated with the BODY element.

The most common way to handle events is to embed the event handler in the HTML tag for the element. All event handlers can be specified as attributes of HTML tags. To associate JavaScript with an event handler, simply assign your JavaScript function to the event handler. Functions assigned to an event handler are called event handler functions and take the following syntax:

Event handler = "functionName()"

For example, the following code opens an alert window that reads "You clicked me!" when a user clicks the button.

```
<input type="button" value="Click Me" onClick="alert('You
clicked me!')">
```

In some cases, you may want to associate more than one function with an event handler. You can do so by assigning multiple functions to an event handler, but these functions must be separated by semicolons, as shown below:

```
<input type="button" value="Click Me" onClick="doFirst();
doSecond()">
```

Event handlers are case insensitive. Therefore, the following two lines are equivalent:

```
<body onLoad="alert('This page has been loaded')">
<body onload="alert('This page has been loaded')">
```

Event handlers as well as attributes of an element are case insensitive. In fact, they are attributes of HTML tags. But JavaScript is case sensitive.

You can pass parameters to an event handler function, just as you would pass them to any function call. A parameter can be a string, a number, or an object. When you use an event handler with an HTML tag element, such as a button, you can use the keyword this to reference the element as an object. Follow the steps below to use the keyword this to pass an object as a parameter to a function.

1. Open a new document in your text editor and type in the following code:

```
<HTML>
<HEAD>
<TITLE>Using this to reference to an element</TITLE>
<script language="JavaScript">
    function convertToUpperCase(anObject){
        anObject.value = anObject.value.toUpperCase()
    }
</script>
</HEAD>
<BODY>
    <form>
            <input type=button value="click me"
onClick="convertToUpperCase(this)">
    </form>
</BODY>
</HTML>
```

2. Save the file as **example7.html** in the directory C:\myjspapp\chapter02.

3. Load this page in your browser using the following URL:
   http://localhost:8080/myapp/chapter02/example7.html

4. Click the button on the page, and note that the label on the button is changed to uppercase.

In this example, the built-in function toUpperCase() is used to convert a string value to uppercase. The function convertToUpperCase() takes an object as parameter and converts its value to uppercase. To call this function, you use the keyword this to reference the button object. So when this button is clicked, the label that is the value of the button is converted to uppercase.

JavaScript and String Objects

Characters are the fundamental building blocks of JavaScript programs. A string object represents any sequence of zero or more characters that are to be treated strictly as text. A string may include characters, digits, and various special characters, such as +, -, *, /, $, and others. A string object provides many methods that facilitate character and substring extraction, case changes, concatenation, and conversion from string lists to JavaScript arrays. Table 2-2 lists the frequently used methods for manipulating string objects.

2

Table 2-2   String Object Methods

Method	Description
charAt(positionIndex)	Returns the character at the location specified by positionIndex. Note the index of the first character is 0. If there is no character at the index location, this function returns an empty string.
indexOf(searchString,index)	Searches for the first occurence of searchString, starting from positionindex. The method returns a starting index of searchString in the source string. If the returned value is –1 then you know the searchString is not in the source string. If the index argument is not provided, the method begins searching from index 0 in the source string.
lastIndexOf(searchString, index)	Returns the position within the current string object where the searchString parameter starts. This method works like the indexOf() method but begins all searches from the end of the string or some index position. Even though searching starts from the end of the string, the index parameter is based on the start of the string, as is the returned value. If there is no match, the returned value is –1.
toLowerCase()	Returns a string with all uppercase characters converted to lowercase.
toUpperCase()	Returns a string with all lowercase characters converted to uppercase.
replace(regexpression, replaceString)	Returns the new string that results when the first occurrence of regexpression is replaced by the replaceString parameter. The original string is unchanged.
split(delimiter)	Splits the source string into an array of strings at each instance of the delimiter string.

The first character in a string is located at index 0. The index of the last character is the length of the string –1.

String objects have a property called length, which contains the number of characters in the string.

In the following exercise, you write JavaScript code to get a character at a specified location from a text field.

1. Open a new document in your text editor and type in the following code:

```
<HTML>
<HEAD>
<TITLE>chatAt method</TITLE>
<script language="JavaScript">
 function getChar(aString, index){
     var c = aString.charAt(index)
     alert("The character at index " + index + " is " + c)
 }
</script>
</HEAD>
<BODY>
<form>
     Message:<input type=text name=txtMsg
         value="Welcome to JSP" size=20>
     Character Index:<input type=text name=txtIndex
         value="0" size=4>
     <input type=button value="Get character"
         onClick="getChar(txtMsg.value,txtIndex.value)">
</form>
</BODY>
</HTML>
```

2. Save the file as **example8.html** in the directory C:\myjspapp\chapter02.

3. Load this page into your browser using the following URL:
   http://localhost:8080/myapp/chapter02/example8.html

4. Click the **Get character** button; a window opens, as shown in Figure 2-7, specifying the first character in the message text field.

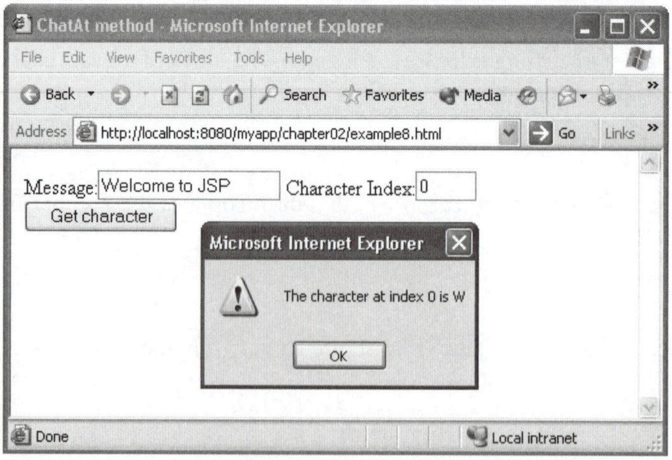

Figure 2-7   Displaying characters at specified locations

In the example above, the function getChar() has two parameters, the source string and the index of a character in the source string. It returns the character located at the specified index location in the source string. The function getChar() is associated with the button's onClick event handler and is therefore triggered when the user clicks the button. You may try to enter several numbers in the Character Index text field, then click Get character button. If the index is less than 0, or greater than the length of the string in the message text field, the function returns an empty string.

If you enter a non-numerical value in the Character index text box, such as a character, a text string, or an empty string (that is, leave it blank), and then click the button, the function returns the first character of the source string. This is because the function charAt()treats non-numerical parameter as zero (Netscape behaves differently).

In order to prevent users from entering these invalid entries, you can modify the code in the previous example, as follows.

1. Open a new document in your text editor and type in the following code:

```
<HTML>
<HEAD>
<TITLE>chatAt method</TITLE>
<script language="JavaScript">
    function getChar(aString, index){
        if(index == "" || isNaN(index)){
            alert("Please enter a number")
        }else if(index < 0 || index >= aString.length){
            alert("Please enter an index between 0 and "
                + aString.length)
        }else{
            var c = aString.charAt(index)
            alert("The character at index " + index +
                +" is " + c)
        }
    }
</script>
</HEAD>
<BODY>
<form>
    Message:<input type=text name=txtMsg
        value="Welcome to JSP" size=20>
    Character Index:<input type=text name=txtIndex
value="0" size=4>
    <input type=button value="Get character"
onClick="getChar(txtMsg.value,txtIndex.value)">
</form>
</BODY>
</HTML>
```

2. Save the file as **example9.html** in C:\myjspapp\chapter02.

3. Load this page in your browser using the following URL:
   http://localhost:8080/myapp/chapter02/example9.html

4. Enter various values in the Character Index text box. Note that if you enter a non-numerical value, an alert window displays the message, "Please enter a number." If you enter a number that is less than zero or greater than or equal to the length of the source string, the message instructs you to enter number between 0 and the length of the source string.

In this above example, you modified the getChar() function to check whether the index parameter is valid using the following code:

```
if(index == "" || isNaN(index)){
        alert("Please enter a number")
}
```

If the index is an empty string or is not a number, a window instructs the user to enter a number. The isNaN() is a JavaScript built-in function. If the parameter is not a numerical value, the function isNaN() returns true; otherwise, it returns false.

```
else if(index < 0 || index >= aString.length){
        alert("Please enter an index between 0 and " +
                aString.length)
}
```

If the index is out of the range, that is, less than zero or greater than or equal to the length of the string, the user is instructed to enter a number between 0 and the length of the string. If the index value passes the validation process, the following statements display the character at the specified index location.

```
else{
        var c = aString.charAt(index)
        alert("This character at index " + index +
                " is " + c)
}
```

String Searches

Often it is useful to search for a character or a sequence of characters in a string. In the following exercise you use the String object methods indexOf and lastIndexOf to search for a substring in a source string.

1. Open a new document in your text editor and type in the following code:

```
<HTML>
<HEAD><TITLE>Search method</TITLE>
<script language="JavaScript">
var source = "In the two-tier client/server model, the ";
source += "application runs on the client machine ";
```

```
source += "and issues queries to the database server."
function search(){
 document.searchForm.first.value =
   source.indexOf(document.searchForm.inputVal.value)
 document.searchForm.last.value =
   source.lastIndexOf(document.searchForm.inputVal.value)
}
</script>
</HEAD>
<BODY>
<form name="searchForm">
   <h1>The string to search is:</h1>
       In the two-tier client/server model, the application
       runs on the client machine and issues queries to the
       database server.<br><br>
   Enter substring to search for:
   <input type=text name=inputVal type=text size=10>
   <input type=button value="Search" onClick="search()">
   <br><br>
   The first occurrence is located at index
   <input type=text name=first size=4><br>
   The last occurrence is located at index
   <input type=text name=last size=4><br>
</form>
</BODY>
</HTML>
```

2. Save the file as **example10.html** in the directory C:\myjspapp\chapter02.

3. Load this page into your browser using the following URL:
   http://localhost:8080/myapp/chapter02/example10.html

4. Enter a substring to search for in the input text field. You should see a page displayed as shown in Figure 2-8.

In the example above, a global variable is declared to store the source string to be searched for:

```
var source = "In the two-tier client/server model, the";
source += "application runs on the client machine and ";
source += "issues queries to the database server."
```

The user types a substring in the HTML form searchForm's inputVal text field and presses the Search button. The function search() is called in response to this onClick() event and performs the search. The results of each search are displayed in the appropriate text fields of the searchForm.

```
document.searchForm.first.value =
       source.indexOf(document.searchForm.inputVal.value)
```

Figure 2-8   Search string demo

You use the string method indexOf() to determine the first occurrence of the source string of the string you typed in the inputVal text field (searchForm.inputVal.value). If the substring is found, the index at which the first occurrence of the substring begins is returned; otherwise, –1 is returned.

```
document.searchForm.last.value =
    source.lastIndexOf(document.searchForm.inputVal.value)
```

You use the string method lastIndexOf() to determine the last occurrence in the source string of the string in the inputVal text field. If the substring is found, the index at which the last occurrence of the substring begins is returned; otherwise, –1 is returned.

 The string methods indexOf() and lastIndexOf() have optional second parameters that you can use to specify the starting index from which the search begins.

String Replacement

In some case, you may need to replace a character sequence with another string. In the steps below, you use the replace() method of a String object to perform replacement in a string.

1. Open a new document in your text editor and type in the following code:

```
<HTML>
<HEAD><TITLE>Replacement method</TITLE>
<script language="JavaScript">
    function replaceString(regexpression, replaceString){
          document.replaceForm.source.value =
            document.replaceForm.source.value.replace
(regexpression, replaceString)
```

```
}
</script>
</HEAD>
<BODY>
<form name=replaceForm>
<TextArea cols=45 rows=5 name=source>
In teh three-tier client/server architecture,
teh business logic is separated into a
middle tier: an application server is used
to manage the business logic, and a database
server handles the data access logic, and
the client manages only the presentation
logic.
</textarea>
   <br><br>
   Replace:<input type=text name=toReplace size=10>
   with:<input type=text name=replaceWith size=10>
   <input type=button value="Replace"
       onClick="replaceString(toReplace.value,
replaceWith.value)">
</form>
</BODY>
</HTML>
```

2. Save the file as **example11.html** in the directory C:\myjspapp\chapter02.

3. Load this page into your browser using the following URL:
   http://localhost:8080/myapp/chapter02/example11.html

4. Notice that there are typos in the text area. The word "the" is purposely typed as "teh". You are going to use the JavaScript program to replace "teh" with "the."

5. Type **teh** in the toReplace text box, and type **the** in the replaceWith text box.

6. Click **Replace**. The first occurrence of the typo "teh" is replaced with "the". Click the button twice to replace all typos.

In the example above, the user specifies the strings used to perform replacements in the source string, then presses the Replace button to replace the first occurrence of the string typed in the toReplace text field with the string typed in the replaceWith input field in the source string (in this case, the source string is the value in the text area). After replacement, the new value is assigned to the text area. If there is more than one occurrence of the string to be replaced, you need to call the function repeatedly until all occurrences have been replaced.

The built-in function replace() returns a new string after replacement, and the original string is unchanged in the process.

SERVER-SIDE SCRIPTING USING JSP

Server-side scripts are executed on the Web server. As with client-side scripts, in order to execute scripts, the server must be equipped with an engine that can interpret the corresponding scripting code. For example, in order to run JSP, the server must be equipped with an engine that can interpret JSP scripts. Since the Web server sends the results (the execution of server-side script) of server-side scripts back to the client browser as regular HTML content, server-side scripts have nothing to do with the client browser. That means that the server-side scripts will work with any browser.

In Chapter 1 you learned that JSP is server-side script, and that JSP files, which must have the extension .jsp, contain a mixture of HTML code and JSP script. This JSP script is read by the server, which interprets the JSP instructions and translates them into appropriate HTML code. The server then returns the whole file as pure HTML, which is interpreted by the client browser.

There are two ways to identify server-side scripts within your HTML code, so that the Web server can interpret them correctly:

- <% ... %> server script delimiters
- XML (Extensible Markup Language) based syntax

The second method is introduced in Chapter 5. The syntax for using the server script delimiters is:

```
<%
     ...JSP script code goes here
%>
```

When the Web server encounters the special tags <% and %>, it recognizes the statements within the tags as server-side script, and executes instructions on the server side.

In order for a Web server to recognize the tags <% and %> and treat them as server-side script, the file must be saved with .jsp extension. Otherwise, the server will send the script code to the client without executing it on the server.

In the following exercise, you create a simple server-side script.

1. Open a new document in your text editor and type in the following code:

```
<HTML>
<HEAD><TITLE>server-side scripts</TITLE>
<META HTTP-EQUIV = "REFRESH" CONTENT = "10,
URL=example12.jsp">
</HEAD>
<BODY>
The time on the server is:
<%= new java.util.Date() %>
```

```
</BODY>
</HTML>
```

2. Save this file as **example12.jsp** in the directory C:\myjspapp\chapter02.

3. Load this page in your Web browser using the following URL:
   http://localhost:8080/myapp/chapter02/example12.jsp

   This page is displayed as shown in Figure 2-9.

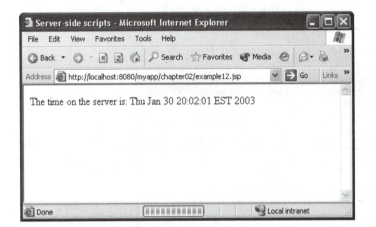

Figure 2-9   Current time on the Web server

Notice also that the time is updated every 10 seconds. The META tag is used to set the refresh interval for the page:

```
<META HTTP-EQUIV = "REFRESH" CONTENT = "10,
URL=example12.jsp">
```

The CONTENT attribute specifies the number of seconds (10) until the URL attribute's value (server-client.jsp) is requested.

To illustrate where a client-side and a server-side script are executed, look at the following example. This example uses both client-side and server-side script in a JSP file. The client-side script displays the current time on the client computer, and the server-side script displays the current time on the Web server.

1. Open a new document in your text editor and type in the following code:

```
<HTML>
<HEAD><TITLE>server-side vs. client-side scripts</TITLE>
<META HTTP-EQUIV = "REFRESH" CONTENT = "10,
URL=example13.jsp">
</HEAD>
<BODY>
The time on the client is:
<script>
```

```
document.write(new Date())
</script>
<br><br>
The time on the server is:
<%= new java.util.Date() %>
</BODY>
</HTML>
```

2. Save this the file as **example13.jsp** in the directory C:\myjspapp\chapter02.

3. Load this page in your Web browser using the following URL:
http://localhost:8080/myapp/chapter02/example13.jsp

This page is displayed as shown in Figure 2-10.

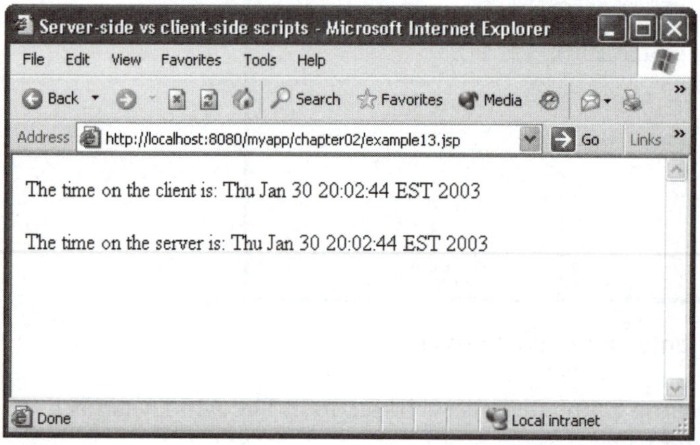

Figure 2-10 Server-side script versus client-side script

If you view the page on the same computer on which the Tomcat Server is running, you will notice that the current time on the client is exactly the same as on the server. If you are running Windows NT Server or Windows 2000 Server, and accessing this page from another computer, the client time and server time may be different.

In the example above, when the page is requested, the server interprets the server-side script embedded in this page and executes the instruction, which is a simple JSP expression:

```
<%= new java.util.Date() %>
```

This statement returns the current time on the server, and the newly generated content, together with the rest of the HTML, is sent back to the client. A JSP expression is a very nice tool for embedding values within your HTML code. Anything between <%= and %> will be evaluated, converted to a string on the Web server, and then sent to the client browser. The server does not interpret the client-side script.

```
<script language="JavaScript">
        document.write(new Date())
</script>
```

This code is treated as HTML on the server and is sent to the client unchanged. The client browser interprets this client-side script, which gets the current time on the client, and displays it on the page. You may verify this by looking at the source code of the page displayed.

CLIENT-SIDE VALIDATION

There are some tasks that can be performed on either the client or the server. For example, you might design a Web site that requires clients to log on using their user ID and password before they are allowed to access the rest of the site. Validation of the logon page can be performed on the client or on the server. In practice, a client-side script is often used for validation, in order to reserve server resources for other tasks. Client-side validation reduces the number of requests the server receives and therefore reduces the amount of work the server must perform.

In the following exercise, you design a guest book for clients. The guest book requests the user's name, e-mail address, and comments. The name and e-mail address are required, so you use client-side script to validate the form information before it is sent to the server for processing. (Note that since you have not yet learned how to retrieve information on the server, you simply validate the information on the client-side when a user clicks a button.)

1. Open a new document in your text editor and type in the following code:

```
<HTML>
<HEAD><TITLE>Validation</TITLE>
<script language="JavaScript">
function validatingForm(){
if(document.guestForm.guestName.value.length == 0){
   alert("Please enter your name.")
   document.guestForm.guestName.focus()
   return
}
if(document.guestForm.email.value.length == 0){
   alert("Please enter e-mail address.")
   document.guestForm.email.focus()
   return
}
alert("The following information entered\nName:"+
   document.guestForm.guestName.value  +
   "\nEmail address:" +
   document.guestForm.email.value +
   "\nComments:"+
   document.guestForm.comments.value)
}
</script>
</HEAD>
```

```
<BODY>
<h1>Please sign our Guest Book ...</h1>
<form name=guestForm>
    <table border=0>
        <tr><td align=right>Your name:</td>
            <td><input type=text name=guestName
size=25></td>
        </tr>
        <tr><td align=right>Email address:</td>
            <td><input type=text name=email
size=25></td>
        </tr>
        <tr>
        <td valign=middle align=right>Comments:</td>
        <td><TextArea rows=5 cols=35 name=comments>No
comment.</TextArea>
        </td>
        </tr>
    </table>
    <br>
    <input type=button value="Validate form"
onClick="validatingForm()">
    <input type=reset value="Clear form">
</form>
</BODY>
</HTML>
```

2. Save the file as **example14.html** in the directory C:\myjspapp\chapter02.

3. Load this page into your browser using the following URL:
   http://localhost:8080/myapp/chapter02/example14.html

4. Click the **Validate form** button without entering a username; an alert dialog box opens, indicating that you need provide user name, as shown in Figure 2-11.

In the code above, the function validatingForm() is called to respond to the onClick() event of the Validate form button. If either the guestName or e-mail text field is empty, an alert dialog box notifies the user that the text field needs to be filled. Otherwise, a window opens listing the information the user entered.

```
if(document.guestForm.guestName.value.length == 0){
        alert("Please enter your name.")
        document.guestForm.guestName.focus()
        return
}
```

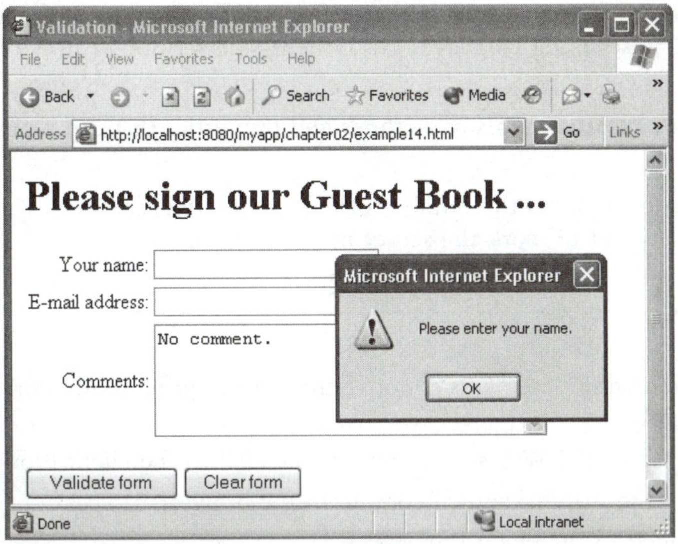

Figure 2-11   Client-side validation

The code above tests whether the guestName text field is empty. If it is empty, an alert window instructs the user to enter a name, and the guestName text field gets the focus.

```
if(document.guestForm.email.value.length == 0){
        alert("Please enter email address.")
        document.guestForm.email.focus()
        return
}
```

The code above tests whether the e-mail text field is empty. If it is empty, an alert window instructs the user to enter an e-mail address, and the focus moves to the e-mail text field.

This validation could be performed on the server, but it is more efficient to validate the form before sending it to the server, which performs the processing to add the username and e-mail address to the guest book.

CHAPTER SUMMARY

- ❑ A script or scripting refers to lines of instructions that tell the computer to accomplish a specific task. A client-side script is downloaded and executed on the client browser, while a server-side script is executed on the Web server. The results are sent to the client browser as regular HTML content.

- ❑ Both client-side script and server-side script can be embedded in an HTML page to provide interactive content.

- ❑ In order to run scripts, appropriate engines must be installed on the computer.

❑ Client-side scripting has some limitations, such as browser dependency, since not all browsers support all scripting languages. Also, client-side scripting can be viewed on the client.

❑ The string object encapsulates many methods and properties that can be used with JavaScript.

❑ Client-side validation reduces the number of requests the server receives and therefore reduces the amount of work the server must perform.

REVIEW QUESTIONS

1. Which of the following statements about client-side scripting is(are) correct? Select all that apply.

   a. It is interpreted on the Web server and downloaded to the client browser.

   b. You can view the original source code from the browser.

   c. It is downloaded to the client browser.

   d. It is interpreted on the client browser.

2. Which of the following statement(s) about server-side scripting is(are) correct? Select all that apply.

   a. You can view the original scripting source code from the browser.

   b. It is downloaded to the client browser.

   c. It is interpreted on the client browser.

   d. It is interpreted on the Web server.

3. To run VBScript in a browser, an engine that can interpret VBScript code must be provided to the browser. True or False?

4. Internet Explorer 6.0 supports both JavaScript and VBScript. True or False?

5. Netscape 6.0 supports both JavaScript and VBScript. True or False?

6. The first character of a string object has an index of _____.

   a. 0

   b. 1

   c. 5

   d. 10

7. Regarding the function replace(), which of the following statements is(are) correct. Select all that apply.

   a. It returns a string.

   b. The original string will be modified.

   c. The original string remains unchanged.

   d. The string returned by this function is the same as the original string.

8. Client-side script is browser dependent. True or False?

9. Server-side script is browser dependent. True or False?

10. To interpret server-side script, the browser must support the scripting language. True or False?

11. Which of the following is more appropriate for validating a form? Select all that apply.

    a. client-side script

    b. server-side script

    c. JavaScript

    d. VBScript

12. In JavaScript, the function call: `"Hello World".indexOf("l")` returns:

    a. 2

    b. 3

    c. 4

    d. 10

13. In JavaScript, the function call: `"Hello World".lastIindexOf("l")` returns:

    a. 2

    b. 3

    c. 9

    d. 10

14. In JavaScript, the function call: `"Hello World".indexOf("L")` returns:

    a. 2

    b. 3

    c. 10

    d. –1

15. In JavaScript, if a function is defined to take three arguments, then you must provide three parameters when this function is called. True or False?

16. In JavaScript, the function call: `"Hello World".charAt(11)` returns:

    a. "H"

    b. "d"

    c. an empty string

    d. "Hello World"

17. In JavaScript, the function call: `"Hello".charAt("A")` returns:

    a. "H"

    b. "e"

    c. an empty string

    d. "A"

18. Client-side script is viewable on the client browser. True or False?

19. Server-side script is viewable by the client. True or False?

20. In JavaScript, the function call: `"Hello".charAt("Hello".length)` returns:

 a. "o"

 b. "H"

 c. an empty string

 d. 5

21. In JavaScript, the function isNaN("123") returns:

 a. True

 b. False

 c. 1

 d. 2

HANDS-ON PROJECTS

Project 2-1 Client-side Validation

In this project, you create a logon page to validate user IDs and passwords. The user ID must be a numerical value. The password field must contain no fewer than 4 and no more than 15 characters.

1. Open a new document in your text editor and type in the following code:

```
<HTML>
<HEAD><TITLE>Hands-on project1</TITLE>
<script language="JavaScript">
        /* The function validate() is to validate the userID
        and password fields. The userID must be a numeral
        value; the length of password should be less than
        15. If any of them does not meet the requirement,
        the user is notified to correct it.
     */
    function validate(){
            if(document.logonForm.userID.value == ""){
                    alert("Please enter user ID.")
                    document.logonForm.userID.focus()
                    return
            }
            if(isNaN(document.logonForm.userID.value)){
                    alert("The user ID should be a number.")
                    document.logonForm.userID.value = ""
                    document.logonForm.userID.focus();
                    return
```

2

```
              }
              if(document.logonForm.password.value == ""){
                    alert("Please enter a password.")
                    document.logonForm.password.focus()
                    return
              }
              if(document.logonForm.password.value.length <4 ||
                document.logonForm.password.value. length>15){
                    alert("The length of the password "+
                        +"must be between 4 and 15.")
                    document.logonForm.password.value = ""
                    document.logonForm.password.focus()
                    return
              }
              // Perform other actions here
        }
    </script>
    </HEAD>
    <BODY>
    <form name=logonForm>
        <table border=0>
        <tr><td align=right>User ID:</td>
              <td><input type=text name=userID size=10></td>
        </tr>
        <tr><td align=right>Password:</td>
              <td><input type=password name=password size=10>
    </td>
        </tr>
        <tr><td> </td>
              <td><input type=button value=logon
    onClick="validate()">
                        <input type=reset>
              </td>
        </tr>
        </table>
    </form>
    </BODY>
    </HTML>
```

2. Save the file as **project1.html** in C:\myjspapp\chapter02.

3. Load this page into your browser using the following URL:
   http://localhost:8080/myapp/chapter02/project1.html

   The page is displayed as shown in Figure 2-12.

4. Enter some invalid values in the User ID and Password fields, and you should get a message notifying you that the values are invalid.

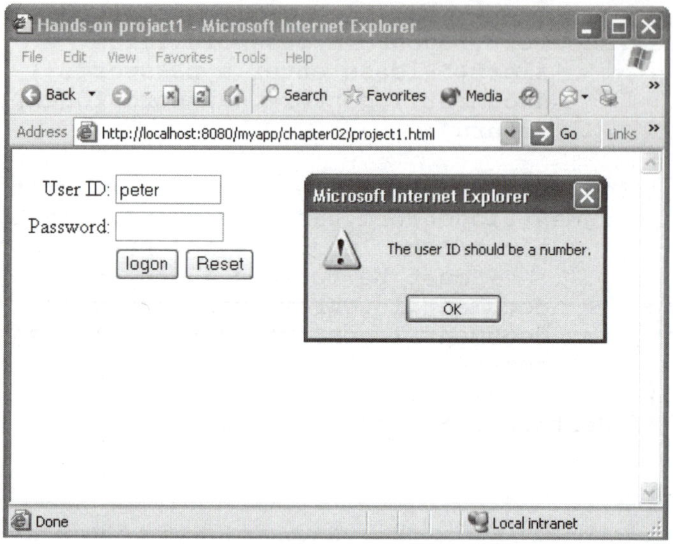

Figure 2-12 Validating a logon page

Project 2-2 Replacement Operation on a String

In this project, you will modify the script in project2.txt data file to improve its functionality.

1. Open the file **project2.txt** page in C:\myjspapp\chapter02.

2. Save the file as **project2.html** in the same directory.

3. Modify the function replaceString() so that all occurrences of a string are replaced by a new string. (*Hint*: Use a loop structure to check whether the original string still contains the old String; if it does, replace it with the new string and go to the next iteration.)

4. Save the file.

5. Load this page into your Web browser using the following URL:
   http://localhost:8080/myapp/chapter02/project2.html

6. Try to replace "teh" with "the". This time, when you click the **Replace** button once, all instances of "teh" should be replaced with "the".

Project 2-3 Split String

In this project, you write JavaScript code to split a sentence into its component words.

1. Create a Web page, and save it as **project3.html** in the directory
   C:\myjspapp\chapter02

2. Add the basic HTML tags.

3. Insert the following JavaScript between <HEAD> and </HEAD> tags:

```
<script language="JavaScript">
    function splitString(aString){
            var anArray = aString.split(" ");
            var words=""
            for(var i=0; i<anArray.length; i++){
                    words = words + anArray[i] + "\n"
            }
            document.splitForm.output.value = words
    }
</script>
```

4. Add the following code in the body of the Web page:

```
<form name=splitForm>
    Enter a sentence to split into words.<br>
    <input type=text name=inputVal size=25>
    <input type=button value="Split"
        onClick="splitString(inputVal.value)"><br>
    <br>
    The sentence split into words is<br>
    <TextArea name=output rows=8 cols=25></TextArea>
</form>
```

5. Save the file as **project3.html** in C:\myjspapp\chapter02.

6. Load this page into your browser using the following URL:
   http://localhost:8080/myapp/chapter02/project3.html

7. Type a sentence in the text box, and then click the **Split** button. You should see a page similar to the one shown in Figure 2-13.

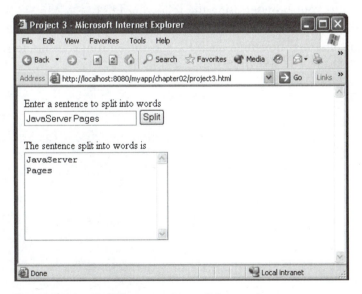

Figure 2-13 Splitting a sentence into words

Project 2-4 Occurrence of a String

In this project, you write JavaScript code to count the number of occurrences of a string in a sentence.

1. Create a Web page and save it as **project4.html** in the folder: C:\myjspapp\chapter02.

2. Add the basic HTML tags.

3. Write a function in JavaScript that takes two parameters, the source string and the search string, and returns the number of occurrences of search string in the source string. (*Hint*: Use a loop structure.)

4. Add the following code in the body of the page:

```
<form name=countForm>
<TextArea cols=45 rows=8 name=source>
In the three-tier client/server architecture,
the business logic is separated into a
middle tier: an application server is used
to manage the business logic, and a database
server handles the data access logic, and
the client manages only the presentation
logic.
</textarea><br>
Substring to count:
<input type=text name=inputVal size=10>
<input type=button value="Count"
onClick="count(source.value,inputVal.value)"><br>
</form>
```

5. Save this file as **project4.html** in C:\myjspapp\chapter02.

6. Load this page into your browser using the following URL:
   http://localhost:8080/myapp/chapter02/project4.html

7. Type a word into the text box, then click the **Count** button; you should see a window similar to the one shown in Figure 2-14.

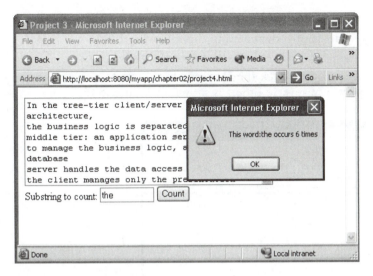

Figure 2-14 Word count

Project 2-5 Reversing Sentence

In this project, you will create a Web page to display the character sequence in a string in reverse order.

1. Open a new document in your text editor and type in the following code:

```
<HTML>
<HEAD><TITLE>Project 5</TITLE>
<script language="JavaScript">
        function reverse(aString){
                var s = ""
                for(var i=0; i<aString.length; i++){
                s =  aString.charAt(i) + s
        }
        return s
        }
</script>
</HEAD>
<BODY>
<form name=reverseForm>
        Enter a sentence<br>
        <input type=text name=inputVal size=30><br>
        <input type=button value="Reverse"
onClick="output.value=reverse(inputVal.value)"><br>
        The characters in reverse sequence<br>
        <input type=text name=output size=30>
</form>
</BODY>
</HTML>
```

2. Save the file as **project5.html** in C:\myjspapp\chapter02.

3. Load this page into your browser using the following URL:
http://localhost:8080/myapp/chapter02/project5.html

4. Type in a string and then click the **Reverse** button; the characters in the string should be displayed in reverse order, as shown in Figure 2-15.

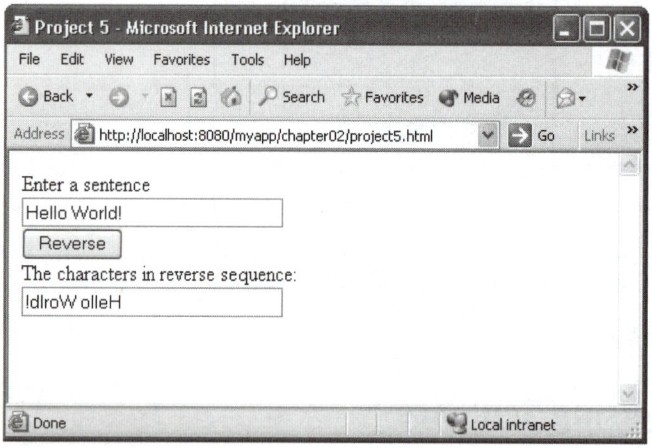

Figure 2-15   Reverse character sequence

CASE PROJECTS

Student Record Access System: logon page

You have been hired to develop a system, called the Student Record Access System (SRAS), to facilitate students' access to their academic records via the Internet. With the SRAS, students will be able to view courses taken and grades received. To access the system, each student must have a user ID and password, so the system must provide a logon page. In this project, you design the logon page for the system. The logon page contains two input fields, one for user ID, the other for password, as well as a Logon (submit) button, and a Reset button. Your job is to create the logon page and write JavaScript to validate the values entered in the input fields when a user clicks the Logon button. The validation rules are as follows:

1. Both the user ID and password fields must be filled in when the user clicks the Logon button.

2. If the user ID field is empty when the user clicks the Logon button, a message window instructs the user to enter a user ID, and then the user ID field gets the focus to facilitate user input.

3. If the password field is empty when the user clicks the Logon button, a message window instructs the user to enter a password, and then the password field gets the focus to facilitate user input.

4. The length of the password must be between 5 and 15 characters; otherwise, a message window should instruct the user to enter a valid password.

Temperature Conversion

Create a Web page to help people with temperature conversion. This page converts a Fahrenheit temperature to a Celsius temperature, and vice versa. Therefore, there are two text input fields: one for Fahrenheit, and the other for Celsius. It also includes two buttons that call JavaScript functions that perform the conversions.

Note: Use the following formula to perform the appropriate conversion:

Celsius = (Fahrenheit - 32)*5/9

Validating Guest Book Input Fields

You are asked to design a guest book page for a Web application. The guest book page has the following elements: input fields for name, e-mail address, phone number, and comments; a Register button, and a Reset button. The name, e-mail address, and phone number are required. The phone number must be a numerical value. Your job is to design this page and write JavaScript code to validate the information when the user tries to register.

3

BASIC FORM-PROCESSING TECHNIQUES

In this chapter, you will:

♦ Design a form to collect information from users
♦ Use the GET method to send form information to the server
♦ Use the POST method to send form information to the server
♦ Retrieve information from a form
♦ Output information to users
♦ Use variables to store information obtained from a form

In Chapter 2, you learned the difference between client-side scripting and server-side scripting. In this chapter, you will learn how to use server-side scripts to process client requests. Specifically, you will learn how to collect information from Web site visitors, how to send this information to the server, and how to retrieve and process the data on the Web server.

COLLECTING AND SUBMITTING FORM INFORMATION

Forms play a key role in communications between Web page visitors and servers. A form serves as a container that holds controls such as text fields, labels, buttons, and images. Some of these controls may be invisible. Most, but not all, form controls are created in a document as input elements.

The first set of tags you use to set up the structure of a form are the form tags, <FORM> and </FORM>. For example:

```
<FORM NAME="formName" ACTION="getUserName.jsp"
METHOD="POST">
<!--form elements go inside of form tags -->
</FORM>
```

A form has several attributes, and each attribute has a name and a value. A value can be assigned to an attribute with an assignment operator, that is, the equal sign. For example, in the above code the equal sign is used to assign the value: "getuserName.jsp" to the ACTION attribute. The form above has three attributes. The first, NAME, contains the name of the form. Note that the NAME attribute is required if you want form controls processed on the client side; otherwise, it is optional. For example, you can dynamically set the ACTION attribute of the form using JavaScript on the client-side. In this case, you have to use the form's name to access the ACTION attribute. The second attribute, ACTION, specifies the name of the JSP file that should be opened when the form is submitted. This file is used to retrieve and process form data. The third attribute, METHOD, determines which of two ways (POST or GET) the browser will use to send information to the server. The differences between these two methods are discussed in the next section.

The ACTION attribute of the form tells the browser what page is going to be opened when the form is submitted. After the user submits data, the browser automatically requests the file specified in the ACTION attribute. It is good practice to put the value of an attribute in double quotes, although it is not required.

The input fields on a form are called **controls** and are usually (but not always) created with the <INPUT> tag. One such control is a text box. You create a text input field using the following code:

```
<FORM NAME="frmName" ACTION="getUserName.jsp"
METHOD="POST">
<INPUT TYPE = "TEXT" NAME="lastName">
</FORM>
```

The input field has two attributes, TYPE and NAME. The TYPE attribute specifies the input type, in this case, a text field into which the user inputs a last name. The second attribute, NAME, is the more important one: each control in a form must have a NAME. The data entered by the user is retrieved by referencing the name of its control field.

Without a name, the data stored in the control field cannot be retrieved. As in any programming language, you use a variable name to reference the value stored in that variable; you use the value assigned to the NAME attribute to reference that control.

The code below illustrates how to add a label to the text input field:

```
<FORM NAME="frmName" ACTION="getUserName.jsp"
METHOD="POST">
Your Last Name:<INPUT TYPE = "TEXT" NAME="lastName">
</FORM>
```

In the exercise below you create a form that contains three input fields.

1. Open a new document in your text editor and type in the following code

```
<HTML>
<HEAD><TITLE>Form example</TITLE></HEAD>
<BODY>
<FORM NAME="frmName" ACTION="getUserName.jsp"
METHOD="POST">
Your First Name:<INPUT TYPE = "TEXT" NAME="firstName">
<br>
Your Middle Name:<INPUT TYPE = "TEXT" NAME="middleName">
<br>
Your Last Name:<INPUT TYPE = "TEXT" NAME="lastName">
</FORM>
</BODY>
</HTML>
```

2. Save the file as **example1.html** in C:\myjspapp\chapter03.

3. Load this page into your browser using the following URL:
   http://localhost:8080/myapp/chapter03/example1.html

   The page is displayed as shown in Figure 3-1.

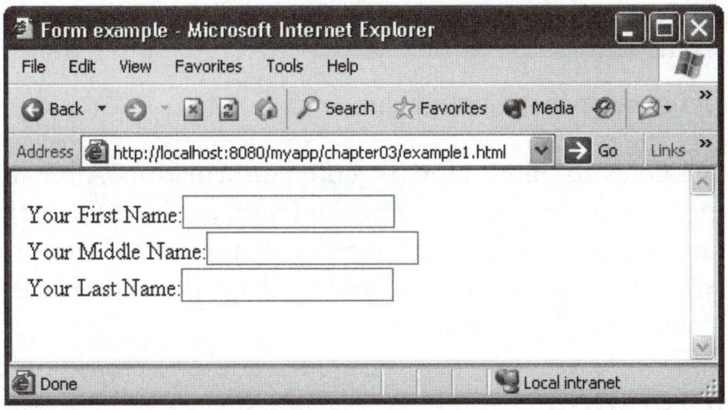

Figure 3-1   Example1.html shown in a browser

You can also specify a default value for an input control. All input controls have an attribute called VALUE. The default value of an input control is assigned to its VALUE attribute.

1. Open a new document in your text editor and type in the following code:

```
<HTML>
<HEAD><TITLE>Form example</TITLE></HEAD>
<BODY>
<FORM >
<INPUT TYPE = "TEXT" NAME="txtField" VALUE="This is the
default text.">
</FORM>
</BODY>
</HTML>
```

2. Save the file as **example2.html** in C:\myjspapp\chapter03.

3. Load this page into your browser using the following URL:
   http://localhost:8080/myapp/chapter03/example2.html

   The resulting page is shown in Figure 3-2.

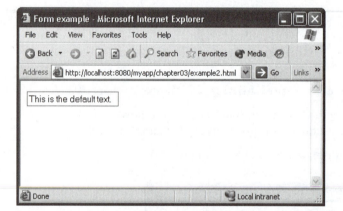

Figure 3-2   Assign a default value to an input field

Here you used text input fields to allow users to enter information. After information has been collected from a form, you can retrieve and process it. Information can be retrieved and prosessed on the client side, but normally it is retrieved and processed on the server side. Before the information can be processed on the server side, the form from which data is collected must be submitted.

Submitting Form Information

In order to process form data, you need to submit the form to the server, and then retrieve and process data on the server side. To submit a form, the submit() method of the form must be called. You can explicitly call the submit method or you can include a Submit button on the form. The Submit button is a built-in button control. When the user clicks this button, the form's submit method is called. In the steps below you use the submit input control button to submit a form.

1. Open a new document in your text editor and type the following code:

```
<HTML>
<HEAD><TITLE>Submit a form</TITLE></HEAD>
<BODY>
<FORM NAME="frmName" ACTION="getUserName.jsp"
METHOD="POST">
Your First Name:<INPUT TYPE = "TEXT" NAME="firstName">
<br>
Your Middle Name:<INPUT TYPE = "TEXT" NAME="middleName">
<br>
Your Last Name:<INPUT TYPE = "TEXT" NAME="lastName"><br>
<INPUT TYPE=SUBMIT VALUE="Submit">
<INPUT TYPE=RESET VALUE="Reset">
</FORM>
</BODY>
</HTML>
```

2. Save the file as **example3.html** in C:\myjspapp\chapter03.

3. Load this page in your browser using the following URL:
   http://localhost:8080/myapp/chapter03/example3.html

   Enter the values in the text fields. The page should look similar to the one shown in Figure 3-3.

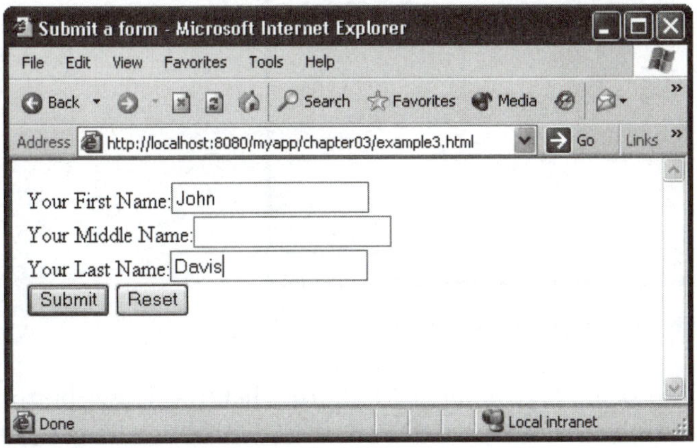

Figure 3-3 Submit a form

The Submit and Reset button tags generally have two attributes. The first declares the type of button, and the second specifies the value (that is, the text displayed on the button). The Submit button is used to submit the form to the server, and the Reset button is used to clear the form and reset all input values to their default values, if any. The type must be "SUBMIT" for a submit button and "RESET" for a reset button. The VALUE will appear to the user and thus can be anything you like, as long as you type it in quotes.

1. Open a new file in your text editor and type in the following :

```
<HTML>
<HEAD><TITLE>Reset button in a form</TITLE></HEAD>
<BODY>
<FORM NAME="frmName" ACTION="getValue.jsp" METHOD="POST">
<INPUT TYPE="TEXT" NAME="txtField" VALUE="This is the
default value"><br>
<INPUT TYPE=SUBMIT VALUE="Submit"><br>
<INPUT TYPE=RESET VALUE="Reset">
</FORM>
</BODY>
</HTML>
```

2. Save the file as **example4.html** in C:\myjspapp\chapter03.

3. Load this page into your browsing using the following URL:
   http://localhost:8080/myapp/chapter03/example4.html

   The page is displayed as shown in Figure 3-4.

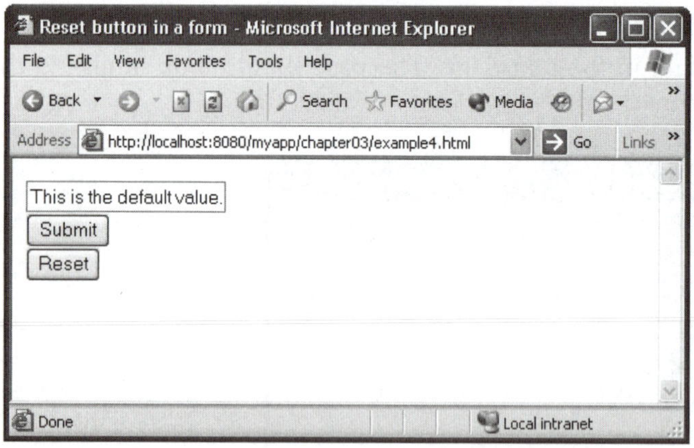

Figure 3-4 Example4.html shown in the browser

Try to enter new text into the text input field. If you click the Reset button, the text in the text input field changes back to its default value: "This is the default value." When the Submit button is clicked, the page specified as the ACTION value in the form will be opened and displayed. Since you have not created the file getValue.jsp yet, the browser displays a message saying that the page cannot be found. In the steps below you create the file named getValue.jsp in the same folder as example4.html.

1. Open a new document in your text editor and type in the following code:

```
<HTML>
<HEAD><TITLE>Get the value in a text field</TITLE></HEAD>
<BODY BGCOLOR="#FFFCCC">
Your value in the text field:
</BODY>
</HTML>
```

2. Save the file as getValue.jsp in C:\myjspapp\chapter03.

3. Reload the page example4.html in your Web browser, type a sentence into the text input field, and then click the **Submit** button. This opens the page getValue.jsp, as shown in Figure 3-5.

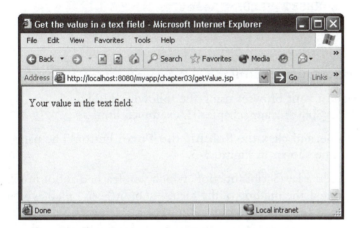

Figure 3-5 getValue.jsp shown in the browser

Whoops! Where is the value you entered? You did enter a sentence in the text input field but it is not displayed here! This problem occurs because you have not yet written code in getValue.jsp to process the data. After you enter information into the text input fields and click the Submit button, all the information is sent to the server. On the server side, you can retrieve and process data collected from the form and output this information to the user by writing code within the getValue.jsp file. You learn how to do this later in the chapter.

The second way to submit a form is to call the submit method of the form explicitly, as illustrated in the steps below.

1. Open a new document in your text editor and type in the following code:

```
<HTML>
<HEAD><TITLE>Submit a form by calling the submit method
</TITLE>
<SCRIPT LANGUAGE="javascript">
    function submitForm(){
            document.frmName.submit()
    }
```

```
</SCRIPT>
</HEAD>
<BODY>
<FORM NAME="frmName" ACTION="getUserName.jsp"
METHOD="POST">
Your First Name:<INPUT TYPE = "TEXT" NAME="firstName">
<BR>
Your Middle Name:<INPUT TYPE = "TEXT" NAME="middleName">
<BR>
Your Last Name:<INPUT TYPE = "TEXT" NAME="lastName"><BR>
<INPUT TYPE=BUTTON VALUE="Submit the Form" onclick=
" submitForm()">
<INPUT TYPE=RESET VALUE="Reset">
</FORM>
</BODY>
</HTML>
```

2. Save the file as **example5.html** in C:\myjspapp\chapter03.

3. Load this page in your browser using the following URL:
   http://localhost:8080/myapp/chapter03/example5.html

4. Enter your name, and click the **Submit the Form** button. The page appears
   similar to the one shown in Figure 3-3.

In the steps above, you add a JavaScript function, which you learned about in Chapter 2.
When this function is called, the method of the form—submit()—is called, which in turn
submits the form to the server. The function submitForm() is associated with the event
handler of the submit button, so when the user clicks the button, the function
submitForm() is executed.

 It is always convenient to use a Submit button to submit a form. However, in
many cases, when you need to validate a form before sending it to a Web
server, you need to use a regular button and associate your JavaScript validation code with the onClick event handler of the button.

There are two HTTP methods that you can use to send a form to a server: POST and
GET. You can change the method by setting the value of the form's METHOD attribute.
These methods determine whether the form element data is sent to the server appended
to the ACTION attribute of the URL or as a transaction message body.

The GET Method

When you use the GET method, the data is appended to the end of the designated URL
after a question mark. The URL is the one specified as the ACTION value in a form. If you
do not explicitly set the METHOD attribute for a form, by default the form is sent using
the GET method. The following example demonstrates how you use the GET method.

1. Open a new document in your text editor and type in the following code:

```
<HTML>
<HEAD><TITLE>Submit a form with the get method</TITLE>
</HEAD>
<BODY>
<FORM NAME="frmName" ACTION="getUserName.jsp"
METHOD="GET">
Your First Name:<INPUT TYPE = "TEXT" NAME="firstName">
<br>
Your Middle Name:<INPUT TYPE = "TEXT" NAME="middleName">
<br>
Your Last Name:<INPUT TYPE = "TEXT" NAME="lastName"><br>
<INPUT TYPE=SUBMIT VALUE="Submit">
<INPUT TYPE=RESET VALUE="Reset">
</FORM>
</BODY>
</HTML>
```

2. Save the file as **example6.html** in C:\myjspapp\chapter03.

3. Open a new document in your text editor, and type in the following code:

```
<HTML>
<HEAD><TITLE>Get user information</TITLE></HEAD>
<BODY>
Your name is:
</BODY>
</HTML>
```

4. Save the file as **getUserName.jsp** in the folder C:\myjspapp\chapter03.

5. Load example6.html in your browser using the following URL:
   http://localhost:8080/myapp/chapter03/example6.html

6. Enter your name in the appropriate text input fields as shown in Figure 3-6, and then click **Submit**. A new page is displayed, as shown in Figure 3-7.

In the URL shown in Figure 3-7, note that the data has been appended to the end of the designated URL, as follows:

http://localhost:8080/myapp/chapter03/getUserName.jsp?firstName=
Mike&middleName=R&lastName=Davis

The value appended to the URL after the question mark is called a **query string**. The question mark here is used to separate the URL and the query string. In this case, the query string is generated in the following way: Each text input field and its value create a pair of name/value strings, wherein the name and value are separated by an equal sign. Each pair of name/value strings is separated by ampersands.

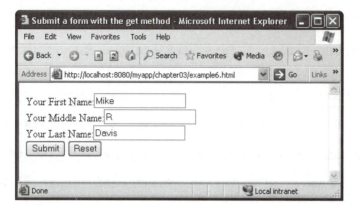

Figure 3-6   Get method

Figure 3-7   Query string

The POST Method

When you use the POST method, the form element data is sent to the server as a transaction message body. Unlike the GET method, the POST method does not append form element data to the URL. Note that when the POST method is used, you can generate a query string by attaching a queryString to the URL directly. In the following example, you use the POST method to send form data to the server.

1. Open a new document in your text editor and type in the following code:

```
<HTML>
<HEAD><TITLE>POST method</TITLE></HEAD>
<BODY>
<FORM NAME="frmName" ACTION="getText.jsp?action=update"
METHOD="POST">
```

```
<INPUT TYPE="TEXT" NAME="txtField" VALUE=""><br>
<INPUT TYPE=SUBMIT VALUE="submit"> <br>
<INPUT TYPE=RESET VALUE="clear form">
</FORM>
</BODY>
</HTML>
```

2. Save this file as **example7.html** in C:\myjspapp\chapter03.

3. Open a new document in your text editor and type in the following code:

```
<HTML>
<HEAD><TITLE>Get data entered from JSP file</TITLE>
</HEAD>
<BODY BGCOLOR="#FFFCCC">
The data you entered:
</BODY>
</HTML>
```

4. Save this page as **getText.jsp** in C:\myjspapp\chapter03.

5. Load the page example7.html in your Web browser using the following URL:
http://localhost:8080/myapp/chapter03/example7.html

6. Enter some data into the text input field as shown in Figure 3-8, and then submit the form. A new page is displayed as shown in Figure 3-9.

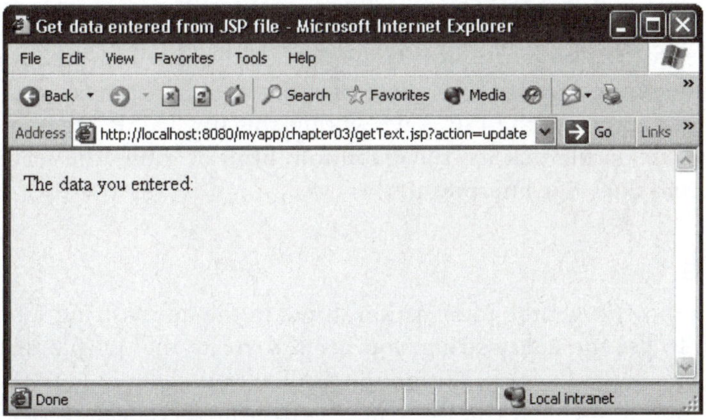

Figure 3-8 POST method

You see that the query string is appended to the URL, but the text input field and its value are not included in the query string. Again, the text you entered is not displayed here because you have not written JSP code to encapsulate the information in the form yet. In the following section, you learn how to retrieve and process data collected from a form.

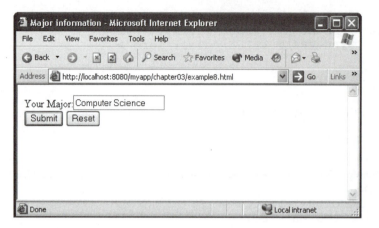

Figure 3-9   JSP with POST method

RETRIEVING FORM INFORMATION USING THE REQUEST OBJECT

After you collect form information, it must be sent to the server for processing. When a user submits a form, all information encapsulated within the form is sent to and processed on the server side by the file specified as the value of the ACTION attribute of the form. You must write the JSP code in this file to retrieve and process form information, and then to provide output to users.

Recall that in order for the server to process the data encapsulated in the form, the file specified as the value of the ACTION attribute of the form must have the extension .jsp so that the server can interpret the JSP codes within this file. If JSP codes are inserted into a plain HTML file (a file that has the extension .html or .htm), the server treats it as regular HTML and does not interpret it.

The Query String

First, you will learn how to get the information stored in the query string submitted via the GET method. To get the query string, you need to create the .jsp file that is specified as the ACTION value of a form. Within the .jsp file, you can mix HTML tags with JSP code, but you must follow standard JSP syntax so that the server can recognize which parts are JSP code. In the example below, you create a form and a .jsp file to retrieve the form information stored in a query string.

1. Open a new document in your text editor and type in the following code:

```
<HTML>
<HEAD><TITLE>Major information</TITLE></HEAD>
<BODY>
<FORM NAME="frmName" ACTION="getMajor.jsp" METHOD="GET">
```

```
Your Major:<INPUT TYPE = "TEXT" NAME="major"><BR>
<INPUT TYPE=SUBMIT VALUE="Submit">
<INPUT TYPE=RESET VALUE="Reset">
</FORM>
</BODY>
</HTML>
```

2. Save the file as **example8.html** in the folder C:\myjspapp\chapter03.

3. Open a new document in your text editor and type in the following code:

```
<HTML>
<HEAD><TITLE>Get and display your major</TITLE></HEAD>
<BODY>
Your major is: <%= request.getQueryString() %>
</BODY>
</HTML>
```

4. Save this page as **getMajor.jsp** in the folder C:\myjspapp\chapter03.

5. Open your browser and load the page using the following URL: http://localhost:8080/myapp/chapter03/example8.html

6. Enter your major information as shown in Figure 3-10, and then click the **Submit** button. The query string is retrieved and displayed on the page getMajor.jsp, as shown in Figure 3-11.

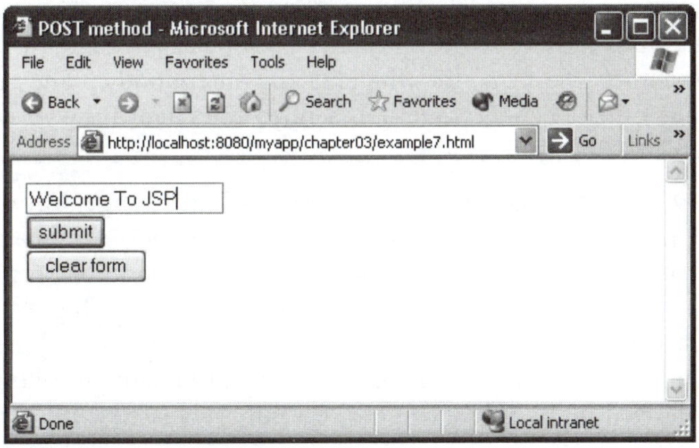

Figure 3-10   Major form collection

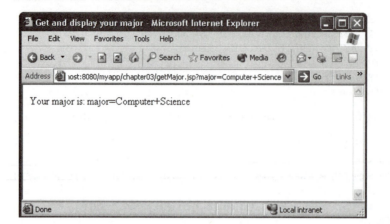

Figure 3-11   Get major information

The JSP code `<%= request.getQueryString() %>` in the getMajor.jsp file success-fully retrieves the query string and displays it in your browser. Recall that all code inside the special tags starting with <% and ending with %> is interpreted on the server. The request object is one of the implicit objects predefined in JSP; you will learn more about the JSP request object in Chapter 6. You use the code `request.getQueryString()` to get whatever is appended to the URL as a query string. In the code above, an equal sign follows <%. There must be no spaces between the tag <% and the equal sign. If there is, you will get a syntax error message. The syntax <%= an expression %> is a shortcut used to generate output. Thus the code `<%= request.getQueryString() %>` means "get the query string and insert the string into the HTML content body." The newly gen-erated content, as well as other HTML content, is sent to the client browser, where the contents are interpreted and displayed.

You may have already noticed that the query string looks strange. Your major is "Computer+Science" instead of "Computer Science." You learn more about this prob-lem in Chapter 6. For now you can solve this problem by using another technique to get the value stored in the pair of name/value format in the query string. As discussed in the previous section, a query string takes the name/value format, and all name/value pairs are separated by ampersands. For each name/value pair, the name is followed by an equal sign, which is followed by its value. To get the value associated with a name, you write JSP code to perform this task.

To do so, you would modify the code in getMajor.jsp as follows:

```
<HTML>
<HEAD><TITLE>Get and display your major</TITLE></HEAD>
<BODY>
Your major is: <%= request.getParameter("major") %>
</BODY>
</HTML>
```

The code `request.getParameter("major")` retrieves the value associated with the name "major" and displays this value in the browser.

Form Processing Techniques

After data has been collected and sent to the Web server, you need to write JSP code to retrieve and process these data. In the following example, you build your first dynamic Web page, which can be customized according to user preferences. You design a form that allows users to specify their preferences for page background color, font color, and font size. You also provide space to allow users to type in a message. The message is displayed on another page, according to the user's preferences.

1. Open a new document in your text editor and type in the following code:

```
<HTML>
<HEAD><TITLE>My page preference</TITLE></HEAD>
<BODY>
<FORM METHOD=post ACTION="example9.jsp"  name=form1>
<TABLE BORDER="0" align="center">
    <TR><TH colspan=2>Create My Page Preference Creator
</TH></TR>
    <TR><TD ALIGN=right>Your Name: </TD>
        <TD ALIGN=left><INPUT NAME="myName" size=24></TD>
    </TR>
    <TR><TD ALIGN=right VALIGN=top>Your Message: </TD>
        <TD ALIGN=left VALIGN=top><TEXTAREA name=message
rows=3></TEXTAREA></TD>
    </TR>
    <TR><TH colspan=2 align=middle>Please Indicate Your
Preference</TH></TR>
    <TR><TD ALIGN=right >Background Color:</TD>
        <TD ALIGN=left><INPUT name=bgColor></TD>
    </TR>
    <TR><TD ALIGN=right VALIGN=center>Your message Color:
</TD>
        <TD ALIGN=left><INPUT name=fontColor></TD>
    </TR>
    <TR><TD ALIGN=right>Font Size:</TD>
        <TD><INPUT name=fontSize></TD>
    </TR>
    <TR><TD colspan=2 ALIGN=middle VALIGN=center><INPUT
type=submit value=Submit>
    <INPUT type=reset value=Reset>
    <P></P>
    <P></P></TR>
</TABLE>
</FORM>
</BODY>
</HTML>
```

3

2. Save the page as **example9.html** in the C:\myjspapp\chapter03. This is the page on which the user specifies preferences.

3. Open a new document in your text editor and type in the following code:

```
<HTML>
<HEAD><TITLE>Get your preference</TITLE></HEAD>
<BODY BGCOLOR="<%= request.getParameter("bgColor")%>">
Hello, <%= request.getParameter("myName") %>,
here is your message displayed using your preferences:
<br>
<br>
<font color="<%= request.getParameter("fontColor")%>"
   size="<%= request.getParameter("fontSize") %>">
   <%= request.getParameter("message")%>
</font>
</BODY>
</HTML>
```

4. Save this file as **example9.jsp** in the folder C:\myjspapp\chapter03. This is the page with which you retrieve and process the user's preferences.

5. Load the page example9.html in your browser using the URL: http://localhost:8080/myapp/chapter03/ example9.html

6. Enter your preferences, and then click the **Submit** button to send the information to the server. The example9.jsp page is then activated on the server and displays results in the browser. Notice that this page is customized to your preferences.

7. Click the **Back** button on your browser, enter different preferences, and then click the **Submit** button. Notice that example9.jsp is displayed differently each time you change your preferences.

In the file example9.html, you begin the form with <FORM>. The <FORM> tag must contain an ACTION attribute to tell the browser which page to use on the server-side to process information when the user clicks the Submit button. In the example above you use `ACTION="example9.jsp"`. You also use the POST method to send the form. Then, you provide four text input fields to type in name, preferred page background color, font color, and font size. You also provide one textarea control so that the user can include a message. You display all fields within a table to achieve alignment. Each input field and the textarea control is assigned a name. Without a name, you can still display an input field in your browser, but the server cannot retrieve information from the fields. In the above example, you did not specify the input type for the four text input fields. For the input field, the default type is TEXT. For example, the following two lines of code are the same:

```
<INPUT TYPE=TEXT NAME=text1>
<INPUT NAME=text1>
```

The code `<TEXTAREA name=message rows=3></TEXTAREA>` creates an input space that allows users to enter a multiple-line message. The Submit button is used to send information collected on the form to the server, and the Reset button is used to clear the form.

After a user enters information into the form and clicks the Submit button, the information is sent to the server. Next, all information from the form is retrieved on the server side. The code `request.getParameter("a field name")` retrieves the data stored in each field, and then you use the values retrieved here to set up the page.

The first line of the body of the HTML code is:

```
<BODY BGCOLOR="<%= request.getParameter("bgColor")%>">
```

The code `request.getParameter("bgColor")` retrieves the value the user entered in the form in example9.html. Then, the value is assigned to the attribute BGCOLOR that determines the background color of the page. For example, assume that a user enters "yellow" into the text field named "bgColor." In example9.jsp, "yellow" is assigned to BGCOLOR. Since the code `<%= request.getParameter("bgColor")%>">` is processed on the server side before this page is sent back to the browser, the browser is going to receive `<BODY BGCOLOR="yellow">`. You can verify this by using the View Source command on your browser. The following code is used to get the username entered by the user:

```
Hello, <%= request.getParameter("myName") %>: here is your
message displayed using your preferences:
<%= request.getParameter("myName") %>
```

If you entered Steve in the myName field on the form, then the text displayed on the browser is: Hello, Steve, here is your message displayed using your preferences:

The following code is used to set the font color and size for the message that will be displayed:

```
<font color="<%= request.getParameter("fontColor")%>"
size="<%=
request.getParameter("fontSize") %>">
<%= request.getParameter("message")%>
</font>
```

Here, you use `request.getParameter("fontColor")` to get the font color and assign it to the color attribute of the font. You use `request.getParameter("fontSize")` to obtain the font size and set the size attribute of the font. Then, you use `request.getParameter("message")` to retrieve the message the user entered followed by the font closing tag. Assume that a user typed "blue" in the fontColor field, 7 in the fontSize field, and "This is a message." in the message field. If you use the View Source command on your browser, the source code is displayed as follows:

```
<HTML>
<HEAD><TITLE> Get your preference</TITLE></HEAD>
```

```
<BODY BGCOLOR="yellow">
Hello, Steve, here is your message displayed using your
preferences:<br>
<br>
<font color="blue" size="7">
This is a message.
</font>
</BODY>
</HTML>
```

In the next section, you learn in detail how to output a message to the browser with JSP code.

SENDING OUTPUT TO THE USER

If you want an HTML page to display the message "Hello World!", you type it into the page. You do not even need a tag. However, if you want to display the same message in a JSP page, you must write JSP code that generates the message in HTML.

There are several ways to write output to users with JSP code. One of them you should already be familiar with:

```
<%= "Your message goes here." %>
```

The equal sign tells the server to insert into the file as HTML content whatever follows (and then the content along with other HTML content is sent to client browser). So in order to display "Hello World!" on the browser, the JSP code should look like this:

```
<%= "Hello World!" %>
```

There is no space between <% and =. If there is, the server sends an error message to the requesting user. You will learn more about JSP syntax in Chapter 5.

When the server interprets this code, it inserts the string "Hello World!" into the page as if you had inserted the following simple HTML text:

```
Hello World!
```

You can also use this method to write HTML tags into the page. For example, to add a horizontal line to the page using JSP code, you can put the <HR> tag into the page as follows:

```
<%= "<HR>" %>
```

In the following exercise, you use this technique to send output to the user.

1. Open a new document in your text editor and type the following code:

```
<HTML>
<HEAD><TITLE>JSP output example 1</TITLE></HEAD>
```

```
<BODY>
<%= "<hr size=2 color=red>" %>
<%= "<font size=4 face=Arial color=green>" %>
<%= "Welcome to JavaServer Pages" %>
<%= "</font>" %>
<%= "<hr size=2 color=red>" %>
</BODY>
</HTML>
```

2. Save this file as **example10.jsp** in the folder C:\myjspapp\chapter03.

3. Start your browser and run the page, which looks like the one shown in Figure 3–12.

Welcome to JavaServer Pages

Figure 3-12 Output HTML tags

 To optimize performance, you should always use the .html extension when saving pages that contain no server-side scripts.

In the page example10.jsp, the first line after the <BODY> tag is:

```
<%= "<hr size=2 color=red>" %>
```

Before sending anything to the requesting user, the Web server interprets the code and generates the text: <hr size=2 color=red>, which displays a horizontal line on the screen. The next line is:

```
<%= "<font size=4 face=Arial color=green>" %>
```

This code outputs the text:<font size=4 face=Arial color=green> that starts the font format tag specifying the font size, font name, and font color. The line:

```
<%= "Welcome to Beginning JSP" %>
```

outputs the text message: Welcome to JavaServer Pages. The line:

```
<%= "</font>" %>
```

outputs the closing tag </font> for the font. Finally, the line:

```
<%= "<hr size=2 color=red>" %>
```

outputs <hr size=2 color=red>, which creates another horizontal line in your browser.

Another way to generate output is to use one of the implicit objects defined in JSP, the out object. You will learn more about the out object in Chapter 6. For now you can use the out object to display text on the Web page. To use the out object to do this, you use out.print("your message goes here") within the tags <% and %>. The syntax is simple:

```
<%
    out.print("Hello World!");
%>
```

This is equivalent to <%= "Hello World!" %>, but there is no "=" sign when out is used. The code out.print("Hello World!") is a statement in JSP, and it ends with a semicolon. (In JSP, all statements must end with a semicolon. You can put many statements in the same line as long as they are separated with semicolons. You will learn more about JSP syntax in Chapter 5.) Unlike the first output method, <%= %>, with the out.print method, you can put many statements within a single pair of <% %> tags. You can modify the page example10.jsp as follows:

1. Open a new document in your text editor and type in the following code:

```
<HTML>
<HEAD><TITLE>JSP output example 1</TITLE></HEAD>
<BODY>
<%
    out.print("<hr size=2 color=red>");
    out.print("<font size=4 face=Arial color=green>" );
    out.print("Welcome to JavaServer Pages" );
    out.print("</font>" );
    out.print("<hr size=2 color=red>");
%>
</BODY>
</HTML>
```

2. Save the file as **example11.jsp** in the folder C:\myjspapp\chapter03.

3. Load this page using the following URL:
http://localhost:8080/myapp/chapter03/example11.jsp

   This page is displayed the same as the one in Figure 3-12.

However, if you view the source code, you see that all the output goes to the same line, as follows:

```
<HTML>
<HEAD><TITLE>JSP output example 1</TITLE></HEAD>
<BODY>
<hr size=2 color=red><font size=4 face=Arial color=green>
Welcome to JavaServer Pages</font><hr size=2 color=red>
</BODY>
</HTML>
```

3

In order to overcome this problem and make your page source more readable, you may use out.println("your message") instead of out.print("your message"). The out.println feeds the message to the next line.

In the following example, you use this output technique to create a page that allows users to specify a preferred font color and size, and displays messages in a specified font format.

1. Open a new document in your text editor and type in the following code:

```
<HTML>
<HEAD><TITLE>My page preferences</TITLE></HEAD>
<BODY>
<FORM METHOD=post ACTION="example12.jsp" name=form1>
<TABLE BORDER="0" align="center">
    <TR><TH colspan=2>My Font Preference Creator</TH></TR>
    <TR><TD ALIGN=right VALIGN=top>Your Message: </TD>
        <TD ALIGN=left VALIGN=top>
            <TEXTAREA name=message rows=3>
            </TEXTAREA>
        </TD>
    </TR>
    <TR><TH colspan=2 align=middle>Please Indicate Your
Preferences</TH></TR>
    <TR><TD ALIGN=right VALIGN=center>Your Preferred Font
Color:</TD>
        <TD ALIGN=left>
            <select name=fontColor>
                <option value="Yellow">Yellow
</option>
                <option value="Green">Green</option>
                <option value="Red">Red</option>
                <option value="Blue" selected>Blue
</option>
                <option value="Black">Black</option>
            </select>
        </TD>
    </TR>
    <TR><TD ALIGN=right>Your Preferred Font Size:</TD>
        <TD>
            <select name=fontSize>
                <option value="1">1</option>
                <option value="2">2</option>
                <option value="3" selected>3</option>
```

```
                        <option value="4">4</option>
                        <option value="5">5</option>
                        <option value="6">6</option>
                </select>
            </TD>
        </TR>
        <TR><TD colspan=2 ALIGN=middle VALIGN=center>
            <INPUT type=submit value=Submit>
            <INPUT type=reset value=Reset>
        <P></P>
        <P></P></TR>
    </TABLE>
    </FORM>
    </BODY>
    </HTML>
```

2. Save the file as **example12.html** in the folder C:\myjspapp\chapter03.

3. Open a new document and type in the following code:

```
<HTML>
<HEAD><TITLE>JSP output example 2</TITLE></HEAD>
<BODY>
Your message is displayed using your preferred font
format as follows:<br><br>
<%
out.println("<hr size=2 color=red>");
out.print("<font size= ");
out.print(request.getParameter("fontSize"));
out.print(" color= ");
out.print(request.getParameter("fontColor"));
out.println(">");
out.println(request.getParameter("message"));
out.println("</font>" );
out.println("<hr size=2 color=red>");
%>
</BODY>
</HTML>
```

4. Save this page as **example12.jsp** in the folder C:\myjspapp\chapter03.

5. Start your browser and view the page example12.html.

6. Type a message that you want displayed on the next page and specify your favorite font color and size from the font color and font size drop-down lists (see Figure 3-13), then click the **Submit** button. The example12.jsp page appears, as shown in Figure 3-14.

In this example, you use many out.print and out.println statements, which is rather tedious. But you do not have to use JSP output techniques for every output message. Since you can mix HTML tags with JSP code, you can simply write HTML code when you don't need to use JSP code. For example, if you want your JSP page to display the text "Hello World!" on a browser, you can write JSP code to do so, but it's easier to simply type Hello World into your JSP page.

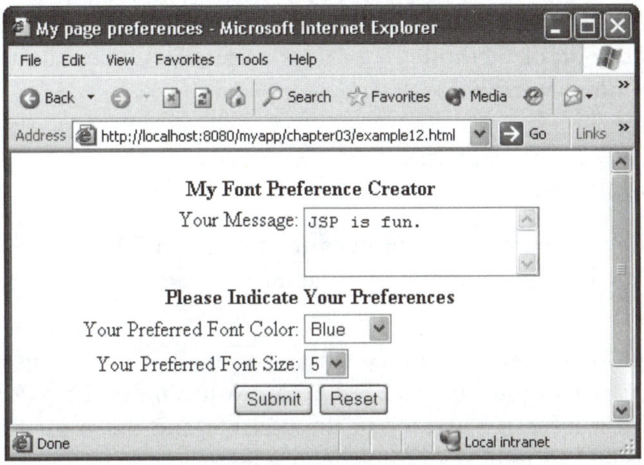

Figure 3-13   Font preference

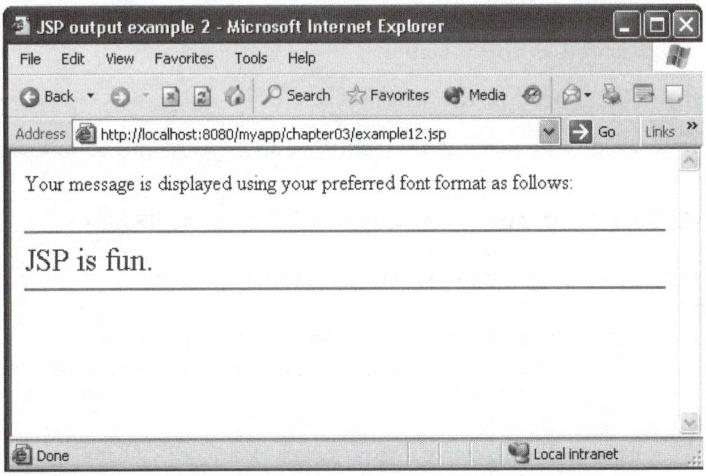

Figure 3-14   Processed font preference

You can get the same result by using the first output method: <%= %>. For example, the JSP code in example12.jsp can be replaced with the following code:

```
<hr size=2 color=red>
<font size=<%=request.getParameter("fontSize")%>
color=<%= request.getParameter("fontColor")%> >
<%= request.getParameter("message") %>
```

```
</font>
<hr size=2 color=red>
```

This code looks more concise. You mix JSP code within HTML tags by using the first output method. So when do you use the output shortcut <%= %>, and when do you use the out.println method? When you want to output text or user output mixed with HTML tags, the shortcut output method <%= %> is preferred. Under all other conditions, out.print may be more suitable.

STORING FORM INFORMATION

There are many situations in which you will need to store form information and use it later in your JSP scripts. Like all programming languages, JSP uses variables to temporarily store information.

A **variable** is a location in computer memory where a value is stored for use by a program. In JSP script, all variables must be declared before you can use them. After a variable has been declared, a value can be stored in the variable, and this value can be used throughout your JSP page. In the next example, you will:

- Declare a variable.

- Store a value in the variable.

- Use the value stored in the variable.

- Change the value stored in the variable.

1. Open a new document in your text editor and type in the following code:

```
<HTML>
<HEAD><TITLE>Instance Variable</TITLE></HEAD>
<BODY>
<form method=post action="example13.jsp">
    <table border=0>
            <tr><td align=right>Your Name:</td>
                    <td align=left><input name="name" size=25>
</td>
            </tr>
            <tr><td align=right>Your Major:</td>
                    <td align=left><input name="major" size=25
> </td>
            </tr>
            <tr><td colspan=2 align=center>
                <input type=submit value="Submit">
                <input type=reset>
                </td>
            </tr>
    </table>
```

```
</form>
</BODY>
</HTML>
```

2. Save this page as **example13.html** in the folder C:\myjspapp\chapter03.

3. Open a new document and type in the following code:

```
<HTML>
<HEAD><TITLE>Instance Variable</TITLE></HEAD>
<BODY>
<%
 String yourName;
 String yourMajor;
 yourName = request.getParameter("name");
 yourMajor = request.getParameter("major");
%>
Hello, <%= yourName %>:<br>
Your major is: <%= yourMajor %>
</BODY>
</HTML>
```

4. Save this file as **example13.jsp** in the folder C:\myjspapp\chapter03.

5. Start your browser and run example13.html using the following URL:
   http://localhost:8080/myapp/chapter03/example13.html

6. Type in your name and major on the page, then click the **Submit** button. You will see that the name and major you entered are displayed on the new page.

The form within the example13.html is used to collect the user's name and major. After the user enters a name and major and clicks the Submit button, the form is sent to the server along with the new page request for example13.jsp. Before the new page is sent back to the browser, the server processes the JSP code within this page. Let's examine the JSP code within the new requested JSP page.

The first JSP code segment, the code inside <% and %> is:

```
<%
 String yourName;
 String yourMajor;
 yourName = request.getParameter("name");
 yourMajor = request.getParameter("major");
%>
```

The first line of the segment tells the server to begin a section of JSP code. The second line declares a variable called yourName having the data type String. A variable in JSP is declared in this way:

```
Data_Type  variable_Name;
```

Data_Type specifies the type of a value that can be stored in the variable; for example, int, float, char, and String are data types defined in JSP. Data types are discussed Chapter 4. The text following data type is the variable name. A variable name is any valid identifier. An **identifier** is a series of characters consisting of letters, digits, and underscores that do not begin with a digit. Here are examples of how to declare variables:

```
String aString;
int anIntegerVariable;
char a_char_variable;
```

In the example13.jsp, you declare two variables:

```
String yourName;
String yourMajor;
```

These two variables have the data type String. After a variable has been declared, a value of the proper data type can be stored in that variable by assignment. For example, you declare a String variable and store a String value in it as follows:

```
String s;
s = "This is a string.";
```

After a value has been stored in a variable, you can use that value by using the variable name in you JSP code.

In example13.jsp, you get the data from the form and assign the value to the corresponding variables.

```
yourName = request.getParameter("name");
```

This statement performs the following tasks: the request object gets the data stored in the "name" input field in the form in the example13.html page. The code request.getParameter("name") gets the data and returns the value having the data type of String. Then, the returned value is assigned to the variable yourName. After this statement, the name you entered into the name input field is retrieved and assigned to the variable yourName. The following code gets and assigns your major to the variable yourMajor.

```
yourMajor = request.getParameter("major");
```

Once values are stored in the variables, you can use them by referencing the variable name, as follows:

```
Hello, <%= yourName %>:<br>
Your major is: <%= yourMajor %>
```

The code <%= yourName %>, uses the value stored in the variable: yourName, and outputs the value to the user. Similarly, the code <%= yourMajor %> uses the value stored in yourMajor and outputs the value to the user.

USING BASIC JSP TECHNIQUES

In the example below, you use basic JSP techniques to create a Web site that uses a form to collect data, and a response page that processes this data.

As part of a plan to provide a seminar on Basic JSP Techniques, you plan to set up a Web site that asks visitors to sign in if they want to attend your seminar. In the sign-in form, you plan to ask visitors to provide the following information:

- Name
- Major
- The date of the seminar the visitor wants to attend

Then, you have your Web server create a sign-in sheet on the browser with the visitor's name, major, and the date information written in.

1. Open a new document in your text editor, and type in the following code:

```html
<HTML>
<HEAD><TITLE>Sign-in sheet</TITLE></HEAD>
<BODY>
<form method=post action="example14.jsp">
   <table border=0>
           <tr><td colspan=2 align=center>
                  <font color=blue size=6>
              Sign-in Sheet Template for my Basic JSP
Techniques Seminar
              </font><br><br><br>
              </td>
       </tr>
       <tr><td align=right>Your Name:</td>
           <td align=left><input name="name" size=25>
</td>
       </tr>
       <tr><td align=right>Your Major:</td>
           <td align=left><input name="major" size=25>
</td>
       </tr>
       <tr><td align=right>Preferred Seminar Date:</td>
           <td align=left><input name="date" size=25>
</td>
       </tr>
       <tr><td colspan=2 align=center>
              <input type=submit value="Submit">  
<input type=reset>
          </td>
       </tr>
   </table>
</form>
</BODY>
</HTML>
```

2. Save this page as **example14.html** in the folder C:\myjspapp\chapter03.

3. Open a new document and type in the following code:

```
<HTML>
<HEAD><TITLE>Sign-in sheet</TITLE></HEAD>
<BODY>
<%
 String yourName;
 String yourMajor;
 String date;
 yourName = request.getParameter("name");
 yourMajor = request.getParameter("major");
 date = request.getParameter("date");
%>
Name: <%= yourName %><br>
Major: <%= yourMajor %><br>
Preferred Seminar Date: <%= date %> <br><br>
Hello, <%= yourName %>: <br><br>
<font color=blue size = 5>Welcome to <font color=red>
'JSP Basic'</font> Seminar</font> <br><br>
Please sign this sheet and bring it with you when you
attend the seminar on <%= date %><br><br>
Your Signature: _____
</BODY>
</HTML>
```

4. Save this page as **example14.jsp** in the folder C:\myjspapp\chapter03.

5. Open example14.html page in your browser. A sign-in sheet template is displayed. See Figure 3-15. Type in your name, your major, and the date, and then click the Submit button. The example14.jsp page renders a sign-in sheet for you.

The solution is contained in two pages. The first page contains a form with input fields for the user to enter data. The form in the first page contains the ACTION attribute, with the value "example14.jsp" indicating that example14.jsp will be opened when the form is submitted.

In order to create a sign-in sheet in the page example14.jsp, you need to get the information the user entered, then use this information to generate sheet. See Figure 3-16.

```
<%
 String yourName;
 String yourMajor;
 String date;
 yourName = request.getParameter("name");
 yourMajor = request.getParameter("major");
 date = request.getParameter("date");
%>
```

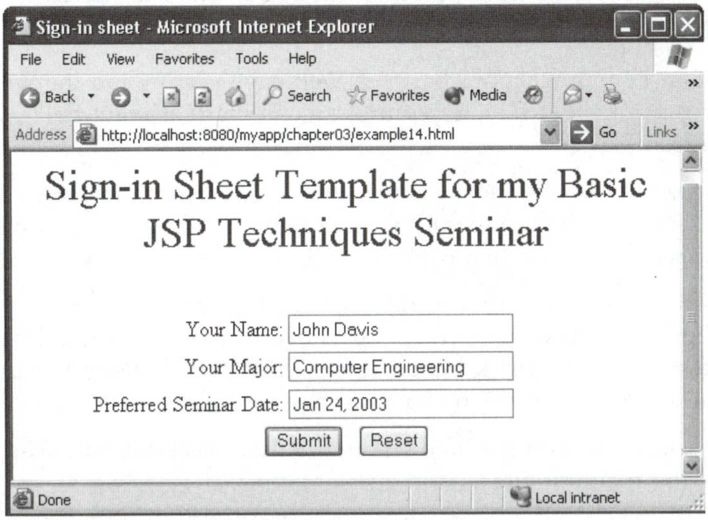

Sign-in Sheet Template for my Basic JSP Techniques Seminar

Your Name: John Davis
Your Major: Computer Engineering
Preferred Seminar Date: Jan 24, 2003
Submit   Reset

Figure 3-15   Sign-in sheet template

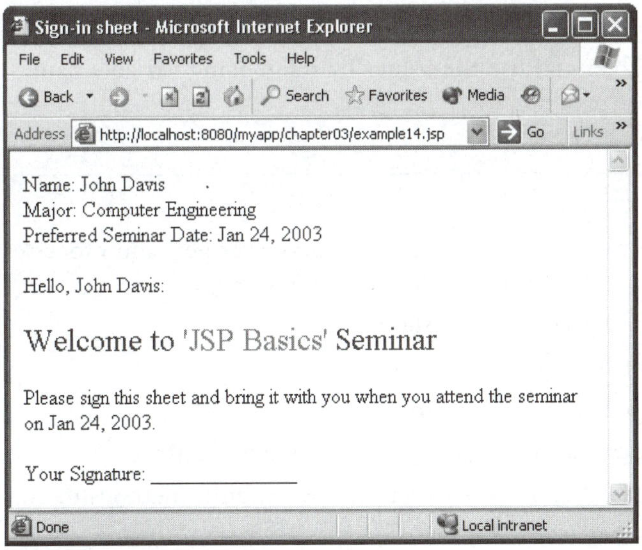

Name: John Davis
Major: Computer Engineering
Preferred Seminar Date: Jan 24, 2003

Hello, John Davis:

Welcome to 'JSP Basics' Seminar

Please sign this sheet and bring it with you when you attend the seminar on Jan 24, 2003.

Your Signature: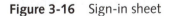

Figure 3-16   Sign-in sheet

In the code above, you first declare three variables: yourName, yourMajor, and date. Then you use the request object to get the user's name and major, and the date of the seminar, assigning each value to its corresponding variable. Then you can use the values anywhere in the program by referencing the variable names.

In the remaining the code, you mix JSP code with HTML to generate the sign-in sheet. You use the values stored in yourName and date twice. As a matter of fact, you can use the value stored in a variable as many times as you need.

CHAPTER SUMMARY

❏ Forms are used in communications between Web page visitors and the Web server. A form serves as a container for user controls, including text input fields, select control, and buttons.

❏ There are two ways to submit a form to the Web server. You can include a Submit button on the form, which the user clicks when finished filling in the form. Or, you can write a JavaScript function that explicitly calls the submit method of the form.

❏ There are two ways to send a form to the server: GET and POST. When you use the GET method, the data in the form is appended to the end of the designated page's URL after a question mark. When you use the POST method, the form data is sent to the server as part of the transaction message body.

❏ After a form has been sent to the Web server, the data encapsulated in the form is retrieved using the request object.

❏ To send output to the user, you can use the shortcut syntax: <%= expression %>. There is no space between <% and the "=" sign. You can also use the out object to send output to a user.

❏ You can declare and use variables within JSP code. You can store the data retrieved from a form in variables and use the values by referencing variable names in your JSP code.

REVIEW QUESTIONS

1. To send a form to the Web server such that the server gets and processes the data encapsulated in the form, you must (choose all that apply):

   a. assign the ACTION attribute of the form

   b. include a submit button on the form

   c. include a reset button on the form

   d. make sure the destination page has the file extension .jsp

2. Briefly describe the differences between the two submit methods discussed in this chapter.

3. The ACTION attribute value can be assigned with a JavaScript function call. True or False?

4. In order for the Web server to process data stored in an input field in a form, the name attribute of the input field must be set. True or False?

5. The name attribute of a form must be set in order for the Web server to be able to process the data in the form. True or False?

6. In order to use a function to call the submit method of a form, the name attribute of the form must be set. True or False?

3

7. You cannot mix HTML tags with jsp code in a jsp page file. True or False?

8. A queryString is appended to the URL when a form is submitted via the _____ method.

9. If you put JSP code in an HTML file that has the file extension .html, then after the page is displayed on your browser, you will see the original JSP code when you view the page's source. True or False?

10. A variable can be used without declaration in JSP. True or False?

11. After a value has been assigned to a variable, the value stored in the variable cannot be changed. True or False?

12. Briefly describe how to use values stored in variables.

13. The value stored in a variable can be used only once. True or False?

14. A query string can be generated by appending a query string to the URL specified as ACTION value in a form when the GET method is used. True or False?

15. Briefly describe the differences between out.print("message") and out.println("message").

16. What can happen if you forget to set the ACTION attribute of a form?

17. If you put the code `<%= "Hello World!" %>` in an HTML file, what is displayed when you view this file in your browser?

18. In JSP, all statements end with a semicolon. True or False?

19. If you write the JSP code `<%= "Hello World!"; %>` in a .jsp file, what would be sent to the client browser when this page is requested?

20. When you declare a variable, you must precede the variable name with _____ .

HANDS-ON PROJECTS

Project 3-1 Registration Form

You plan to provide several seminars on the following topics: An Overview of E-Commerce, Introduction to JSP, HTML Design, and Topics on Client/Server Architecture. You will provide a registration form that:

❑ Allows visitors to select the topic of interest from a drop-down list

❑ Provides a text input field for the visitor's name

❑ Allows visitors to specify their college major from a drop-down list naming the departments in your school, for example, MIS, Computer Science, Computer Engineering, E-Commerce, and Accounting

❑ Allows a visitor to select a preferred seminar date from a drop-down list

In this project, you provide a registration form, and you will design another page to process the data when a user submits the registration form.

1. Open a new document in your text editor and type in the following code:

```
<HTML>
<HEAD>
<TITLE>Sign-in sheet template</TITLE>
</HEAD>
<BODY bgcolor="#fffccc">
<form method=post action="project2.jsp">
<table border=0>
 <tr>
  <td colspan=2 align=center>
  <font color=blue size = 6>
  Seminar Series Sign-in Sheet Template
  </font><br><br><br>
  </td>
 </tr>
 <tr><td align=right>Your Name:</td>
  <td align=left><input name="name" size=25></td>
 </tr>
 <tr><td align=right>Seminar Series:</td>
  <td align=left>
  <select name="seminar" >
  <option value="Overview on E-Commerce" selected>Overview
on E-Commerce
  <option value="Introduction to JSP">Introduction to JSP
  <option value="HTML Design">HTML Design
  <option value="Topics on Client/Server Architecture">
Topics on Client/Server Architecture
  </select>
  </td>
 </tr>
 <tr><td align=right>Department:</td>
  <td align=left>
  <select name="department" >
  <option value="MIS" selected>MIS
  <option value="Computer Science">Computer Science
  <option value="Computer Engineering">Computer
Engineering
  <option value="E-Commerce">E-Commerce
  <option value="Accounting">Accounting
  </select>
  </td>
 </tr>
 <tr><td align=right>Seminar Date:</td>
  <td align=left>
  <select name="date">
   <option value="Tuesday, Jan 21, 2003">Tuesday, Jan 21,
2003
```

```
       <option value="Friday, March 21, 2003">Friday,
March 21, 2003
       <option value="Tuesday, June 17, 2003">Tuesday,
June 17, 2003
       <option value="Monday, July 21, 2003">Monday, July 21,
2003
    </select>
    </td>
  </tr>
  <tr><td colspan=2 align=center>
    <input type=submit value="Submit">
    <input type=reset>
    </td>
  </tr>
</table>
</form>
</BODY>
</HTML>
```

2. Save this page as **project1.html** in the folder C:\myjspapp\chapter03.

In the following project, you will design the page project2.jsp specified as the ACTION value on this page.

Project 3-2 Processing Registration Form

In this project, you will process the data on the registration form and generate registration form for users. You must complete Project 3-1 before completing this project.

1. Open a new file in your text editor and type in the following code:

```
<HTML>
<HEAD><TITLE>Sign-in sheet</TITLE></HEAD>
<BODY>
<%
 String yourName;
 String seminar;
 String department;
 String date;
 yourName = request.getParameter("name");
 seminar = request.getParameter("seminar");
 department = request.getParameter("department");
 date = request.getParameter("date");
%>
Name: <%= yourName %><br>
Department: <%= department %><br>
Seminar Date: <%= date %> <br><br>
Hello, <%= yourName %>: <br><br>
<font color=blue size = 5>Welcome to <font color=red>
<%= seminar %></font> Seminar</font> <br><br>
```

```
Please sign this form and send it to the seminar holder
before you attend the seminar on <%= date %><br><br>
Your Signature: _____
</BODY>
</HTML>
```

3. Save this page as **project2.jsp** in the folder C:\myjspapp\chapter03.

4. Load the page project1.html, which you created in project 1, in your browser using the following URL:
   http://localhost:8080/myapp/chapter03/project1.html

5. Fill in the fields on the form and click the **Submit** button. A registration form should be displayed.

Project 3-3 Process Guestbook

In the guest book example you worked on in Chapter 2, you wrote code to validate the required fields on a form. Here you will create a destination page to retrieve and display the data collected from the guest book sign-in form.

1. Open the file project3.txt in the folder: C:\myjspapp\chapter03 and save it as **project3.html**.

2. Open a new file in your text editor and type in the following code:

```
<HTML>
<HEAD><TITLE>Guest book</TITLE></HEAD>
<BODY>
<h2>Thanks for registering in the guest book.<br>
    Here is the information you provided:<br>
    Your Name: <%= request.getParameter("guestName") %><br>
    E-mail Address: <%= request.getParameter("email") %>
<br>
    Your Comments: <%= request.getParameter("comments")
%><br>
</h2>
</BODY>
</HTML>
```

3. Save the file as **project3.jsp** in C:\myjspapp\chapter03.

4. Load project3.html in your browser using the following URL:
   http://localhost:8080/myapp/chapter03/project3.html

5. Enter your information in the sign-in form, and then click the **Validate form** button. The function validate() is called to validate the information first and then the function submit() is called if all required information has been entered. Finally the data is processed in the file project3.jsp.

Project 3-4 Get User Authorization Data

In this project, you will design a page to retrieve on the server the user ID and password entered on a logon page.

1. Open the file project4.txt in the folder C:\myjspapp\chapter03 and rename it project4.html in the same folder. This file includes a logon form that is used to accept a user ID and password.

2. Open a new document in your text editor and type in the following code:

```
<HTML>
<HEAD><TITLE>Logon information</TITLE></HEAD>
<BODY>
Logon Information<br><br>
User ID: <%= request.getParameter("userID") %><br>
Password: <%= request.getParameter("password") %><br>
</BODY>
</HTML>
```

3. Save the file as project4.jsp in C:\myjspapp\chapter03.

4. Open project4.html using the following URL:
   http://localhost:8080/myapp/chapter03/project4.html

5. Enter a user ID and password, and then click the logon button. The user ID and password is displayed on the page.

Project 3-5 Sending Data with GET Method

In this project, you use the GET method to send form data so you can compare the difference between using the GET and POST methods to send form data.

1. Open the file project5.txt in the folder C:\myjspapp\chapter03 and save it as **project5.html** in the same folder. Examine the file to determine what data is being collected on the form.

2. Open a new document in your text editor and write JSP code to retrieve the data collected on the form in the page project5.html.

3. Save the file as **project5.jsp** in the folder C:\myjspapp\chapter03.

4. Load the page project5.html using the following URL:
   http://localhost:8080/myapp/chapter03/project5.html.

5. Fill in the guest book, and then click the **Sign-in** button. The data should be retrieved and displayed. Note that the data collected on the form are attached to the designated destination page's URL.

Project 3-6 Online Book Store

In this project, you will design a Web page that allows customer to ask questions via the Internet.

1. Open the file project6.txt in C:\myjspapp\chapter03 and save it as **project6.html** in the same folder. This file includes a form to collect user computer information.

2. Open a new document in your text editor and type in the following code:

```html
<html>
<head><title>Help desk</title>
</head>
<body>
You submitted the following data:<br><br>
CPU: <%= request.getParameter("cpu")%><br>
Memory: <%= request.getParameter("memory")%>M<br>
Question: <%= request.getParameter("question")%><br><br>
Your question will be processed soon.
</body>
</html>
```

3. Save the file as **project6.jsp** in the folder C:\myjspapp\chapter03.

4. Load the page project6.html using the following URL:
   http://localhost:8080/myapp/chapter03/project6.html

5. Provide data on the displayed form and submit the form. The page processes and displays the data.

CASE PROJECTS

SRAS System: Retrieving and Storing Data

In the previous chapter, you designed the logon page for the SRAS system and wrote JavaScript code to validate the form. In this project, you send this page to the Web server, create a JSP file to retrieve the user data from the logon form, and store it in variables for later use.

Information Collection

To enhance your Web application, you decide to design a Web page to collect suggestions from clients. You plan to request names, e-mail addresses, and comments. The information will be sent to and processed on the server. After retrieving the data, you will display the collected information on a page.

Customize Pages

The project manager of an online store has asked you whether it is possible to allow clients to customize the pages they visit, for example, by specifying the background and font colors. Create a page that requests users' preferences, which are then sent to the Web server. Use variables to store user preferences. After you retrieve and store the data in variables, display a page that reflects the user preferences.

4

VARIABLES AND JSP CONTROL STRUCTURES

In this chapter, you will:

♦ Declare and use variables in JSP scripts
♦ Learn about the JSP data types
♦ Learn control structures in JSP scripts
♦ Use logical operators in JSP scripts
♦ Manipulate strings in JSP scripts
♦ Declare and use arrays in JSP scripts
♦ Create and use Enumeration objects

Variables and control structures are a fundamental part of any programming language. You use variables to store information so that you can retrieve it anywhere in your program. You use control structures to determine the order in which statements are executed. In this chapter, you will learn how to use variables in your JSP scripts and how to use control structures to establish the execution order of JSP script statements. You will also learn how to use arrays to store items of similar information, how to manipulate a string object, and how to use the enumeration object in a JSP script.

VARIABLES IN JSP

A **variable** is a location in the computer's memory where a data value is stored, or a location that references another location where an actual object resides. There are two types of data types in JSP: primitive data types and classes. For primitive data types, the data value is stored in the location specified by the variable name; for classes, the actual data value is stored somewhere in memory, and the data value is referenced by using the variable name. In the string manipulation example in Chapter 2, you declared several variables with the data type String, which is a class. The value of a String object is retrieved by referencing these variable names.

Variable Declaration

To use a variable in a JSP script, you need to declare it first. Several variables of the same data type may be declared in one declaration or in multiple declarations. A declaration includes a data type and a list of variable names:

dataType vName1, vName2;

The following are examples of variable declarations:

```
int x,y;
char a;
String s1,s2;
```

The examples use data types int, char, and String. You will be introduced to additional data types such as long, Boolean, float, and short in this chapter.

Assignment

After a variable is declared, you can assign a value to that variable by using an assignment statement. The syntax for the assignment is one of the following formulations:

variable = value;
variable = expression;

For example, consider the following code:

```
x = 1;
a = 'A';
```

An **expression** represents a computation involving values, variables, and operators, as shown, for example, in the following code:

```
area = radius * radius*3.14;
```

The variable on the left can also be used in the expression on the right, as follows:

```
x = x + 2;
```

In an assignment statement, the data type of the variable on the left must be compatible with the data type of the value on the right. For example, after you declare a variable x as int data type, the assignment x="hello" is illegal. You cannot assign a string to an int variable.

Often, variables have initial values. You can declare a variable and initialize it in one step. For example, consider the following code:

```
String message = "Hi, there.";
```

This is equivalent to the following two statements:

```
String message;
message = "Hi, there.";
```

Naming Variables

A variable's name can be any valid identifier. An identifier is a series of characters, consisting of letters, digits, and underscores, that does not begin with a digit. JSP script is case sensitive—uppercase and lowercase letters are different, so varname and VARNAME are different identifiers. A variable name can be any length; all of the following are valid identifiers:

```
String s;
String aLongVariableNameButStillValid;
int an_integer_variable_name;
```

Variable names cannot contain spaces or dashes.

Choosing meaningful variable names helps make your programs more readable, without the excessive use of comments.

JSP Primitive Data Types

A **data type** describes the information that a variable stores. For example, int variables store integers, or whole numbers. A variable's data type also determines how many bytes of memory are required to store that variable.

Each data type has a range of values. Memory space is allocated to store each variable according to its data type. JSP provides eight primitive data types. Six of them are numeric; one is character, used for characters in Unicode encoding; and one is Boolean, used for true/false values.

Numerical Data Types

JSP, like Java, has six numeric data types, four for integers and two for floating-point numbers. Table 4-1 lists the six numeric data types, along with their value ranges and storage sizes.

Table 4-1   Numeric data types

Name	Range	Storage Requirement
byte	-2^7 to $2^7 - 1$	1 byte
short	-2^{15} to $2^{15} - 1$	2 bytes
int	-2^{31} to $2^{31} - 1$	4 bytes
long	-2^{63} to $2^{63} - 1$	8 bytes
float	$-3.4E38$ to $3.4E38$	4 bytes
double	$-1.7E308$ to $1.7E308$	8 bytes

The Character Data Type

The character data type is used to represent a single character. Unlike the String data type, a character value is enclosed within single quotation marks. For example, consider the following code:

```
char letter = 'A';
char numChar = '6';
```

The first statement assigns character A to the char variable letter. The second statement assigns the numerical character 6 to the char variable numChar. Consider the following statement:

```
char numChar = 6;
```

In this statement, 6, an int value, is assigned to a character variable. In fact, in JSP, an int value and a char value are interchangeable. So, the following statement is legal in JSP:

```
int anInteger = 'A';
```

In the above statement, the character value 'A' is assigned to an int variable: anInteger. The value assigned to the int variable is the ASCII/ANSI code for the character 'A', which is 65.

 A **casting operator** is used to convert variables of one type to another. You can assign a char variable to an int variable without an explicit cast, but you must provide an explicit cast to convert an int to a char value. You can, however, assign a literal of an int value to a char variable without explicit cast. A **literal** is a primitive data type value that appears directly in a program. For example, in the code **char aChar = 56;** 56 is a literal.

The char type denotes characters in the Unicode encoding scheme. Because Unicode is designed to handle essentially all characters in all written languages in the world, it is a

2-byte code. This allows 65,635 characters, unlike ASCII/ANSI, which is a 1-byte code, allowing only 255 characters. The familiar ASCII/ANSI code that you use in Windows programming is a subset of Unicode. More precisely, it is the first 255 characters in the Unicode character set.

 Unicode characters are more often expressed in terms of a hexadecimal encoding scheme that runs from '\u0000' to '\uFFFF', which is beyond the scope of this text.

The following example illustrates the conversion of characters into their corresponding ASCII/ANSI codes.

1. Open the data file example1.jsp, which is located in the folder C:\myjspapp\chapter04.

2. Add the shaded code shown in Figure 4-1.

```html
<HTML>
<HEAD><TITLE>Char to ANSI conversion</TITLE></HEAD>
<BODY>
<table align=center border=0>
        <tr><td align=center>Character</td>
                <td align=center>ANSI Code</td>
        </tr>
        <tr><td align=center colspan=2><hr width=150></td>
        </tr>
        <tr><td align=center> A </td>
                <td align=center> <%= (int)'A'%> </td>
        </tr>
        <tr><td align=center> B </td>
                <td align=center> <%= (int)'B'%> </td>
        </tr>
        <tr><td align=center> C </td>
                <td align=center> <%= (int)'C'%> </td>
        </tr>
        <tr><td align=center> D </td>
                <td align=center> <%= (int)'D'%> </td>
        </tr>
        <tr><td align=center> E </td>
                <td align=center> <%= (int)'E'%> </td>
        </tr>
        <tr><td align=center> F </td>
                <td align=center> <%= (int)'F'%> </td>
        </tr>
        <tr><td colspan=2 align=center> <hr width=150> </td>
        </tr>
</table>
</BODY>
</HTML>
```

Figure 4-1 Example1.jsp

3. Save the file.

4. Load this page in your browser using the following URL:
   http://localhost:8080/myapp/chapter04/example1.jsp

   The page is displayed as shown in Figure 4-2.

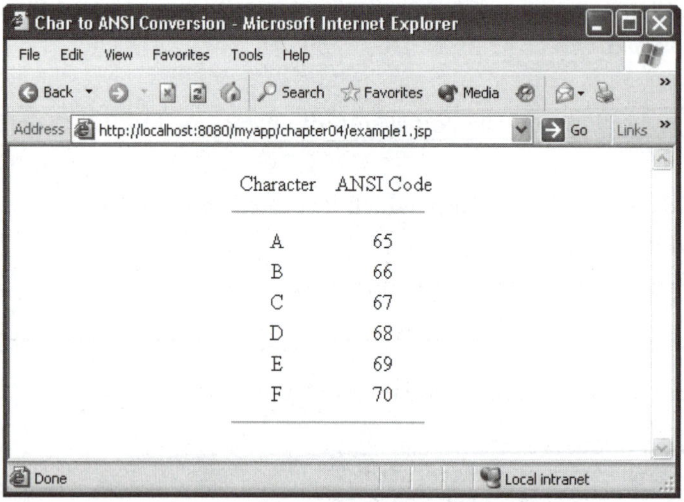

Figure 4-2   Convert characters to ANSI code

Boolean Data Type

The Boolean data type has two values, true and false. It is used for logical testing with the relational operators. Boolean values are an integral part of control structures such as if…then statements, while loops, and for loops. You will learn about control structures later in this chapter.

ARITHMETIC OPERATIONS

Most programs perform arithmetic calculations. The usual arithmetic operators (+ − * / %) are used for addition, subtraction, multiplication, division, and modulus (integer remainder) operations. These operators are summarized in Table 4-2. The / operator denotes integer division if both operands are integers, and floating-point division otherwise. For example, in integer division 15/9 is 1, and 14/4 is 3. Note that any fractional part in integer division is simply discarded. However, 14/4.0 is 3.5.

Note the use of various special symbols that are not used in algebra. The asterisk (*) indicates multiplication, and the percent sign (%) is the modulus operator that gives an integer remainder (i.e., the mod function). The modulus operator is an integer operator that can be used only with integer operands. The expression $x \% y$ yields the remainder after x is divided by y. Thus, 6 % 4 yields 2, and 23 % 5 yields 3.

Table 4-2   Arithmetic operators

Operation	Arithmetic Operator	Algebraic Expression	JSP Expression
Addition	+	x + y	x + y
Subtraction	–	x – y	x – y
Multiplication	*	x * y	x * y
Division	/	x / y	x / y
Modulus	%	x mod y	x % y

Shortcut Operators

It is common to use the current value of a variable, modify it, and then reassign the modified value back to the same variable. For example, consider the following code:

```
x = x +2;
```

There is another way to perform the same operation more concisely. The statement can be expressed as:

```
x += 2;
```

The += is called a **shortcut operator**. The common shortcut operators are shown in Table 4-3.

Table 4-3   Shortcut operators

Operators	Example	Equivalent
+=	x += 5	x = x + 5
–=	x –= 5	x = x – 5
*=	x *= 5	x = x * 5
/=	x /= 5	x = x / 5
%=	x %= 5	x = x % 5

Increment/Decrement Operators

The most common operations performed with a numeric variable are adding or subtracting one. JSP scripting uses both increment and decrement operators: ++ for increment and -- for decrement. These operators can be used in prefix or suffix notation. x++ or ++x adds one to the current value of the variable x, and x-- or --x subtracts one from it. For example:

- x++ is equivalent to $x = x + 1$;
- ++x is equivalent to $x = x + 1$;

- $x--$ is equivalent to $x = x - 1$;
- $--x$ is equivalent to $x = x - 1$;

If an increment or decrement operator is a prefix to the variable, it is referred to as the preincrement or predecrement operator, respectively. If an increment or decrement operator is a suffix to the variable, it is referred to as the postincrement or postdecrement operator, respectively. Preincrementing or predecrementing a variable causes the variable to increment or decrement by 1 before it is used in the expression. Postincrementing or postdecrementing a variable causes the current value of the variable to be used in the expression in which it appears, then the variable value is incremented or decremented by 1.

 With the preincrement or predecrement operator, the new value is used in the expression; with the postincrement or postdecrement operator, the old value is used in the expression.

Increment and decrement operators can be applied to any numeric variable. These operators are often used in loop statements. Loop statements are the structures that control how many times an operation or a sequence of operations is performed in succession. You will learn about loop statements and other control structures later in this chapter.

The following example illustrates how increment and decrement operators work in an expression.

1. Open a new document in your text editor and type in the following code:

```
<HTML>
<HEAD><TITLE>Increment and decrement</TITLE></HEAD>
<BODY>
The following code illustrates how increment and
decrement operators work.<br><br>
<% int x = 10; %>
The initial value of x is <%=x %>.<br><br>
The result of the expression &lt;%= x++ %&gt; is
<%= x++ %>.<br>
The current value of x is <%=x %>.<br>
The result of the expression &lt;%= ++x %&gt; is
<%= ++x %>.<br>
The current value of x is <%=x %>.<br>
The result of the expression &lt;%= x-- %&gt; is
<%= x-- %>.<br>
The current value of x is <%=x %>.<br>
The result of the expression &lt;%= --x %&gt; is
<%= --x %>.<br>
The current value of x is <%=x %>.<br>
</BODY>
</HTML>
```

2. Save the file as **example2.jsp** in the directory C:\myjspapp\chapter04.

3. Load this page in the browser using the following URL:
   http://localhost:8080/myapp/chapter04/example2.jsp

This page is displayed as shown in Figure 4–3.

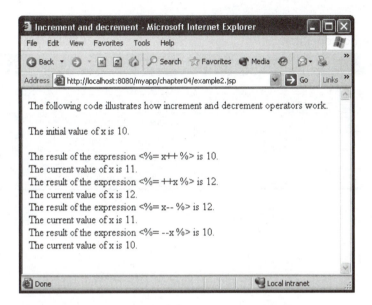

Figure 4-3   Increment and decrement operators

CLASSES

Classes are data types other than primitive data types. You define class type variables in the same way you define primitive data type variables. Look at the following examples:

```
String message = "Hi, there.";
java.util.Date today = new java.util.Date();
```

The variables declared above have class data types. These kinds of variables are usually called objects. The main difference between primitive data type variables and objects is that an object encapsulates both data members and methods, which is one of the key features of object-oriented programming languages. This encapsulation enables you to use the object's methods to perform computations. A String object, for example, provides many methods, such as, length() and indexOf(), that you can use to manipulate the string. You will learn more about classes and objects in Chapter 8.

COMPARISON OPERATORS

There are two kinds of operators associated with values: comparison operators and logical operators. Logical operators are introduced later in this chapter. Comparison operators can be used in expressions that result in a Boolean value. Table 4-4 lists the comparison operators.

Table 4-4   Comparison operators

Operator	Example	Meaning
==	x == y	x is equal to y.
!=	x != y	x is not equal to y.
>	x > y	x is greater than y.
>=	x >= y	x is greater than or equal to y.
<	x < y	x is less than y.
<=	x <= y	x is less than or equal to y.

For example, consider the following code:

```
int x = 2;
int y = 3;
```

Then the expression x>y results in a Boolean value of false.

CONTROL STRUCTURES

Control structures allow you to specify the order in which statements in a program are executed. Any computing problem can be solved by executing a series of actions in a specific order. Controlling the order in which statements are executed is as integral to the programming process as writing the action statements themselves. Consider the following situation: You are developing a Web application for a banking system. The system allows customers to view their accounts and perform transactions; it also allows managers to view all customer accounts. Both managers and users access the banking system from the same logon page. However, after verifying the user ID and password, the system should direct different types of users to different pages. If the user is a bank manager, all user information should be available; if the user is a bank customer, only account information pertaining to that customer should be available. To create such a system, you need to write action statements that are or are not executed, depending upon whether certain conditions are met.

Conditional Statements

There are two types of conditional statements: the simple if statement; and the if...else statement. The simple if statement is used to perform some actions if and only if the condition is true; no alternate actions are executed if the condition is false. In an if...else statement, the set of actions that are executed differ according to whether the condition is true or false.

The Simple if Statement

The simple conditional statement is called single-selection structure because it simply selects or ignores actions. It has the following syntax:

if (condition) statement;

Or:

if (condition) {
      statement(s);
}

If the condition is true, the statement(s) is(are) executed. The difference between the two forms above is that the first form executes a single statement if the condition is true, and the second form executes all statements included within the curly braces. For example:

```
<% if (yourGrade >= 60) {
        out.println("passed");
}
%>
```

In the code above, the condition tests whether the value stored in the variable yourGrade is greater than or equal to 60. If the condition is true, the content containing the message "passed" is generated. Otherwise, no action is taken. Because the code contains only one statement, you can use the first form of the simple if statement, without enclosing it in braces.

 It is always good practice to include opening and closing braces in all control structures, including the simple if statement discussed above. Braces make your program more readable.

Since you can mix HTML code with JSP code, you may modify the above code as follows:

```
<% if (yourGrade >= 60) { %>
        passed
<% } %>
```

It is recommended that you always use the second form of the simple if statement and enclose your actions statements in curly braces. This is especially important when you mix HTML code with JSP code, since the first form (without braces) treats all HTML code following the conditional statement as single statement until the next JSP script code. The following example illustrates this problem:

1. Open a new document in your text editor and type in the following code:

```
<HTML>
<HEAD><TITLE>if statement example</TITLE></HEAD>
<BODY>
This example demonstrates the potential problem that a<br>
<b>if</b> statement without braces may cause.<br><br>
<% int x = 3; %>
<% if(x >3) %>
 The value of x is greater than 3.
 This is the end of the example.
</BODY>
</HTML>
```

2. Save the file as **example3.jsp** in the directory C:\myjspapp\chapter04.

3. Load this page in the browser using the following URL:
   http://localhost:8080/myapp/chapter04/example3.jsp

4. Note that only the messages before the JSP script are displayed on the page. If you view the source code of the page in the browser, you will notice that none of the HTML tags after the if statement are even sent to the browser!

The if...else Statement

In the simple if statement, some actions are performed when the specified condition is true. If the condition is false, nothing is done and the actions are ignored. In many cases, you may want to perform different actions, depending on whether a condition is true or false. You can use if...else to perform this task. The syntax is as follows:

```
If (condition) {
        Statement(s);
}else{
        statement(s);
}
```

Although the braces are not required when there is only a single action statement in the block, you should always use them, especially if you are mixing HTML code with JSP code.

If the condition is true, the statements for the true case block are executed; otherwise, the statements for the else case (false case) block are executed. Consider the following example:

```
<% int yourGrade = 89; %>
<% if (yourGrade >=60 ) { %>
        passed
```

```
<% } else { %>
      failed
<% } %>
```

The above code generates the content with the message "passed" or "failed," depending on the value stored in the variable yourGrade.

The statement inside the if or the if...else statements can be any legal JSP statement, including another if or if...else statement. The inner if statement is called a nested if statement. This nested if statement can contain another if statement. In fact, there is no limit to the depth of the nesting. The following example uses nested if statements to output the letter grade according to the numerical grade.

1. Open a new document in your text editor and type in the following code:

```
<HTML>
<HEAD><TITLE>Another if statement example</TITLE>
</HEAD>
<BODY>
Enter your score and click the "Get letter grade" button.
<form name=gradeForm action=example4.jsp method=post>
    Your score:<input type=text name=score size=4>
    <input type=submit value="Get letter grade">
</form>
</BODY>
</HTML>
```

2. Save the file as **example4.html** in the directory C:\myjspapp\chapter04.

3. Open a new document and type in the following code:

```
<HTML>
<HEAD><TITLE>Another if statement example</TITLE></HEAD>
<BODY>
<% String strScore = request.getParameter("score") ;
 int score = Integer.parseInt(strScore);
%>
Your letter grade:
<% if(score >= 90 ){ %>
    A
<%}else{
    if(score >= 80){%>
          B
<%}else{
          if(score >= 65){%>
                C
<%          }else{%>
                  F
<%                }
    }
```

```
    } %>
    </BODY>
    </HTML>
```

4. Save the file as **example4.jsp** in the directory C:\myjspapp\chapter04.

5. Load the page example4.html using the following URL:
   http://localhost:8080/myapp/chapter04/example4.html

6. Type a score on the page form, and then click the **Get Letter Grade** button; your letter grade is displayed on another page.

In some cases, you may want to assign a value to a variable that is subject to a certain condition. For example, the following statement assigns a string "passed" to the variable grade if the score is greater than or equal to 60, and "failed" if the score is less than 60.

```
<% if (score >=60){
        grade = "passed";
}else{
        grade = "failed";
}%>
```

Alternately, you can use a shortcut if statement to achieve the same result:

```
<% grade = (score >=60)?"passed":"failed"; %>
```

You can use the shortcut if statement for simple assignment only; you cannot mix HTML code within the shortcut if statement structure.

Loops

Loops are structures that control the repeated execution of a block of statements. A loop structure contains two parts: the statements to be executed, and the condition that determines whether the execution of the statements continues. The first part is called the loop body, and the second part is called the continue-condition. A single execution of the loop body is referred to as an iteration of the loop. After each iteration, the condition is reevaluated. If the condition is true, the statements in the loop body are executed again. If the condition is false, the loop terminates and your program continues executing after the loop structure.

There are three types of loop structures: the for loop, the while loop, and the do loop.

The for Loop

The syntax of the for loop is as follows:

for (initialize-control-variable; condition-testing; modifying-condition){
    statements;
}

The for loop structure starts with the keyword for, followed by the three control elements, which are enclosed within parentheses, followed by statements, or the loop body. The three control elements, which are separated by a semicolon, control how many times the loop body is executed and when the loop terminates. For example, the following code outputs "Welcome to JSP" 10 times:

```
<% for(int i = 0; i<10; i++){ %>
     Welcome to JSP<br>
<% } %>
```

The first control element, int i=0, declares and initializes the control variable *i*. The control variable tracks how many times the loop body has been executed.

The next element, i< 10, which is the condition-testing statement, is a Boolean expression. This expression is evaluated at the beginning of each iteration. If the condition is true, the loop body is executed. If it is false, the loop terminates and the program control moves to the line following the loop structure.

The modifying-condition statement, i++, modifies the control variable. This statement is executed after each iteration. Usually, a modifying control variable statement either increments or decrements the control variable. Eventually, the value of the control variable forces the condition to become false.

The first control element can be placed outside of the for loop structure. In the following example, the control variable *x* is declared and initialized before the for loop, so it is not contained in the for loop. But you still need a semicolon before the second control element.

```
<%     int x =0;
       for( ; x< 10; x++) { %>
       Welcome to JSP<br>
<% } %>
```

You can place the remaining two control elements anywhere in the loop body. The following for loop produces the same result.

```
<%     int x = 0;
       for(; x < 10; ){%>
       Welcome to JSP<br>
<%     x++; } %>
```

In the following example you create a loop in a JSP script. In this example, you use both a nested for loop and if statement to display a multiplication table.

1. Open a new document in your text editor and type in the following code:

```
<HTML>
<HEAD><TITLE>Multiplication table</TITLE></HEAD>
<BODY>
<h2>Multiplication Table</h2>
<table border=1>
<tr><td width=20> </td>
```

```
<% for(int i=1; i<=9; i++){%>
  <th align=center width=20><%=i%></th>
<%}%>
</tr>
<% for(int r=1; r<=9; r++){%>
  <tr><th><%=r%></th>
        <%for(int c=1; c<=9; c++){%>
             <td align=center><%= c*r%></td>
        <%}%>
  </tr>
<%}%>
</table>
</BODY>
</HTML>
```

2. Save the file as **example5.jsp** in the directory C:\myjspapp\chapter04.

3. Load this page using the following URL:
   http://localhost:8080/myapp/chapter04/example5.jsp

   In this example, a nested loop is used to create a multiplication table.

The while Loop

The syntax of the while loop is as follows:

while (condition-testing){
       statements;
}

The loop body is executed repeatedly as long as the condition remains true. For example, consider the following code:

```
int i = 0;
While(i < 10){
       Out.println("Welcome to JSP<br>");
       i--;
    }
```

This code generates the text "Welcome to JSP" 10 times.

In most cases the for loop can be represented with an equivalent while loop, as follows:

initialize-control-variable;
while (condition-testing){
       statements;
       modifying-condition;
}

In the following example, you use a while loop to calculate the squares of 1 to 25 and display the results in a nice format.

1. Open a new document in your text editor and type in the following code:

```
<HTML>
<HEAD><TITLE>Squares</TITLE></HEAD>
<BODY>
<table border=0 align=center>
<tr><th align=center>Number</th>
    <th align=center>Square</th>
</tr>
<% int i=1; %>
<% while (i<=25) {%>
<tr><td align=center><%= i %> </td>
    <td align=center><%= i*i %></td>
</tr>
<% i++;%>
<%}%>
</table>
</BODY>
</HTML>
```

2. Save the file as **example6.jsp** in the directory C:\myjspapp\chapter04.

3. Load this page using the following URL:
   http://localhost:8080/myapp/chapter04/example6.jsp

   You should see the page displaying the numbers from 1 to 25 and the corresponding squares.

The do Loop

The do loop is similar to the while loop. In the while loop, the condition is tested at the beginning of the loop before the body of the loop is executed. The do loop tests the condition after the body of the loop is executed; therefore, the loop body is always executed at least once. The syntax of the do loop is as follows:

```
do{
     statements;
} while(condition-testing);
```

For example, the following code outputs numbers from 1 to 10:

```
<%      int counter = 1;
        do { %>
<%= counter %> <br>
<%      }while (++counter <=10); %>
```

Switch Structure

The if conditional structure can be cumbersome when you are handling multiple selections with many alternatives. In these cases, it is more convenient to use the switch structure rather than nested if statements.

The **switch structure** consists of a series of case labels and an optional default case. The syntax of the switch structure is as follows:

```
switch (switch-expression){
case value1:     statements1;
                 break;
case value2:     statements2;
                 break;
...
case valueN:     statementsN;
                 break;
default: statements-for-default-case;
}
```

The switch expression must result in an integral value, such as char, byte, short, or int, and must always be enclosed in parentheses. When a switch structure is executed, your program looks for the first case value that matches the switch-expression value, and the statements in that case are executed. If no match is found, the default statements are executed if the default case is provided in the switch structure.

The **break statement** causes the program to proceed with the first statement after the switch structure. The break statement is used because the cases in a switch structure would otherwise run together. If break is not used anywhere in a switch structure, then each time a match occurs in the structure, the statements for all remaining cases will also be executed.

In the following example, you design a Web page to allow customers to check the CD interest rate for a 1-, 3-, and 5-year CD.

1. Open the data file example7.jsp, which is located in the folder C:\myjspapp\chapter04.

2. Add the shaded code shown in Figure 4-4.

3. Save the file.

4. Load this page in the browser using the following URL: http://localhost:8080/myapp/chapter04/example7.jsp

5. Select a year from the selection list, and then click the **Submit** button to display the corresponding interest rate.

Break statements are essential in switch structures. If you delete the break statements in the above example, then run the page and select 1 year from the list, all of the interest rates for 1, 3, and 5 years, as well as the default message are displayed.

```
<HTML>
<HEAD><TITLE>Switch example</TITLE></HEAD>
<BODY>
<form action="example7.jsp" method="post">
        <select name=year>
        <option value="0">
        <option value="1"> 1 year
        <option value="3"> 3 year
        <option value="5"> 5 year
        </select>
        <input type=submit value="Submit">
</form>
<% String s = request.getParameter("year"); %>
<% float rate = 0.0f;%>
<% if( s != null) { %>
<% int year = Integer.parseInt(s);
        switch(year){
        case 1: out.println("The interest rate for a 1 year CD is <B>4.5%</B>");
                    break;
        case 3: out.println("The interest rate for a 3 year CD is <B>5.8%</B>");
                    break;
        case 5: out.println("The interest rate for a 5 year CD is <B>7.9%</B>");
                    break;
        default:
                    out.println("Please select a year from the list.");
        }
%>
<% } %>
</BODY>
</HTML>
```

Figure 4-4   Example7.jsp

Break and Continue Statements

The break and continue statements alter the flow of control. The **break statement**, when executed in a for loop, while loop, do loop, or switch structure, causes the program to immediately exit from that structure. Program execution continues with the first statement after the structure. The break statement is usually used in a loop structure to stop iteration, or to skip the remaining cases in a switch structure. For example, the following code outputs 1 through 5 and then stops:

```
<% for(int i=1; i<=10; i++) { %>
     <% if (i == 6) break; %>
     <%= i %><br>
<% } %>
```

The **continue statement**, when executed in a for, while, or do loop, ends the current iteration, and proceeds with the next iteration of the loop. For example, the following code outputs the numbers from 1 to 10, except 6:

```
<% for(int i=1; i<=10; i++) { %>
     <% if (i == 6) continue; %>
     <%= i %><br>
<% } %>
```

LOGICAL OPERATORS

Comparison operators are usually used to test a single condition. In many cases, it is more convenient to use multiple-condition testing in a single statement. The logical operators are used to perform more complex condition testing by combining simple conditions.

Logical operators operate on Boolean values to generate new Boolean values. Table 4-5 lists the logical operators used in JSP.

Table 4-5   Logical operators

Operator	Meaning
!	Logical NOT
&&	Logical AND
||	Logical OR
^	Logical exclusive

The logical NOT (!) operator returns true if the Boolean value of the expression is false, and false if the Boolean value of the expression is true. The logical AND returns a true value if and only if the Boolean value of both operands is true. The logical OR returns true if the Boolean value of at least one of the operands is true. The logical exclusive operator returns true if and only if the two operands have different Boolean values. Tables 4-6 through Table 4-9 are the truth tables for the various operators.

Table 4-6   Truth table for the logical NOT (!) operator

Operand	!operand
true	false
false	true

Table 4-7   Truth table for the logical AND (&&) operator

operand1	operand2	operand1 && operand2
false	false	false
false	true	false
true	false	false
true	true	true

Table 4-8   Truth table for the logical OR (||) operator

operand1	operand2	operand1 || operand2
false	false	false
false	true	true
true	false	true
true	true	true

Table 4-9   Truth table for the logical exclusive (^) operator

operand1	operand2	operand1 ^ operand2
false	false	false
false	true	true
true	false	true
true	true	false

For example, given two integer variables x=2 and y=5, the following expressions evaluate to true:

- x >1 && y<8
- x >10 || y <8
- !(x>10)
- (x>10)^(y>2)

The following expressions evaluate to false:

- x > 1 && y >5
- x <1 || y>10
- !(x>2)
- (x>1)^(y<10)
- (x>10)^(y<4)

STRING MANIPULATION

A **string** is a series of characters that is treated as a single unit. You have already used string variables in your JSP script; the value returned by the code `request.getParameter("paraName")` is a string. In a JSP script, a string is an object that encapsulates many methods that you can use to manipulate it, such as substring extraction, case change, and concatenation. In the following sections, you will learn the most frequently used methods of the string object.

Retrieving String Length and Characters

You can get the length of a string by invoking the length() method. For example, the following code displays the length of the string "Welcome to JSP", which is 14:

```
<%= "Welcome to JSP".length() %>
```

You can use the method charAt(index) to retrieve a specified character in a string, where the index value is between 0 and the string's length − 1. For example, the following code displays the character W:

```
<%= "Welcome to JSP".charAt(0) %>
```

If the index is out of range (less than 0 or greater than or equal to the length of the string), the code returns an error message indicating that an exception has occurred. You will learn about exceptions in Chapter 10.

String Concatenation

You can concatenate two or more strings using the plus sign (+). For example, the following code combines the three strings: "Welcome", " to ", and "JSP" into one string, and assigns the string to a newly declared variable called aCombinedString:

```
<% String aCombinedString = "Welcome" + " to " + "JSP"; %>
```

You can also concatenate strings and numbers. When you do this, the number is converted to a string and then concatenated. The following code outputs the text "Hello 123":

```
<% String s = "Hello " + 1 + 2 + 3; %>
<%= s %>
```

Locating Characters and Substrings

You can use the methods indexOf() and lastIndexOf() to search for a specified character or substring in a string. The code `"Hello World!".indexOf('W')` returns the index of the first occurrence of the character W in the string, which is 6. If the specified character is not found in the string, it returns −1. The code `"Hello World!".indexOf("ll")` returns the starting index of the first occurrence of the substring ll, which is 2.

The indexOf() method can take another parameter that specifies the starting index from which the search of the string begins. The lastIndexOf() method is similar to the indexOf() method, but it begins searching from the end of the string and proceeds to the beginning of the string.

Extracting Substrings from a String

You can use the substring() method to extract a substring from a string. For example, the code `"Hello World!".substring(6)` returns the substring "World!". This method takes one integer parameter, which specifies the starting index from which characters are copied in the original string. The substring returned contains a copy of the characters from the starting index to the end of the string. The code `"Hello World!".substring(6, 8)` returns the substring "Wo". This method takes two parameters. This first specifies the starting index from which characters are copied in the original string. The second specifies the index one beyond the last character to be copied. If the parameters are out of the range of the string, the code returns an error message indicating that an exception has occurred.

4

ARRAYS

Variables are fine for storing individual items of data. However, if you want to store a group of similar items, for example, employee IDs in an organization, then an array is a better choice. An **array** is a group of contiguous memory locations that all have the same name and same type. To refer to a particular element in the array, you specify the name of the array and the index of the particular element in the array.

You must declare an array before you can use it. The syntax for declaring an array is as follows:

DateType[] arrayName;

Or:

DataType arrayName[];

Like variables, arrays occupy space in memory. When you declare a variable, a memory space is reserved for that variable. The declaration of an array, however, does not allocate any memory, so you cannot assign elements to the array until you allocate space in memory by using the new operator. Consider the following example:

```
int c[] = new int[10];
```

This declares and allocates 10 elements for integer array c. The preceding statement can also be performed in two steps, as follows:

```
int c[];
c = new int[10];
```

After an array is allocated, you can treat the elements in the array as regular variables for assignment and retrieval. For example, consider the following code:

```
<%      int c[] = new int[10];
        for(int i=0; i<c.length; i++)
            c[i] = i*i;
%>
<% for(int i=0; i<c.length; i++){ %>
<%= c[i] %> <br>
<% } %>
```

Note the expression `c.length` in the for loop condition; it is used to determine the length of the array. An array index is always an integer that starts with 0. The index of the last element in an array is the length of the array − 1.

 If the index is out of the range of an array, the code returns an error message indicating that an exception has occurred.

You can allocate and initialize the elements of an array in the array declaration. For instance:

```
int c[] ={1,2,3,4,5,6,7,8,9,10};
```

The code creates a 10-element integer array c, and the first element is initialized to 1, the second to 2, and so on. This method automatically allocates space in memory for the array, and thus does not use the operator new.

 When an array is allocated, the size of the array is fixed and cannot be altered without modifying the code.

ENUMERATION

JSP is built on the top of Servlet, which is based on the Java programming language; therefore JSP can use almost all of the Java APIs. One of these APIs is **Enumeration**. The Java utility library provides the Enumeration interface, which is very useful in JSP script-ing. The Enumeration interface has two methods, hasMoreElements() and nextElement(). You will use these two methods frequently in your JSP scripts, because many of the objects in JSP scripts have methods that return references to an Enumeration object.

The method hasMoreElements() tests if an Enumeration object contains more elements. It returns true as long as the enumeration object contains at least one more element to provide when the nextElement() method is called; otherwise, it returns false. The nextElement() method returns the next element of an Enumeration object if the Enumeration object has at least one more element to provide.

The following example illustrates how to get a reference to an Enumeration object and how to use these methods in a JSP script.

1. Open the data file example8.txt, which is located in the folder C:\ myjspapp\chapter04, and save it as **example8.html**.

2. Add the code shaded in Figure 4-5.

```
<HTML><HEAD><TITLE>Enumeration</TITLE></HEAD>
<BODY bgcolor="#ffffff">
<form method=post action="example8.jsp" name=theForm>   
<center>
<b>Registration Form</b>
<table width=400 cellpadding=2 cellspacing=0 border=0>
<tr><td colspan=2><hr size=0></td></tr>
<tr><td align=right>First Name:</td>
  <td ><input name="firstName" size=10 maxlength=50 ></td>
</tr>
<tr><td align=right>Last Name:</td>
    <td><input name="lastName" size=10 maxlength=50 ></td>
</tr>
<tr><td align=right >Language &amp; Content:</td>
      <td><select name="language">
            <option selected value="English">English
            <option value="Chinese">Chinese
            <option value="French">French
            <option value="German">German
            <option value="Korean">Korean
            <option value="Spanish">Spanish
            <option value="other">[other]</option>
          </select></td>
</tr><tr><td align=right>Zip/Postal Code:</td>
<td ><input name="zipCode" size=8 maxlength=15 >   
      Gender:
      <select name="gender">
      <option value="" selected>---
      <option value="male">male
      <option value="female">female</option>
      </select>
</td>
</tr><tr><td align=right>Occupation:</td>
      <td><select name="occupation"><option value="" selected >[select
      occupation]
            <option value="executive">executive/managerial
            <option value="professional">professional (doctor, lawyer, etc.)
            <option value="academic">academic/educator
            <option value="computer">computer technical/engineering
            <option value="others">others
            </select></td>
```

Figure 4-5   Example8.jsp

```
</tr><tr><td colspan="2"><hr></td></tr>
<tr><td align=center colspan="2">
      <input type=submit value="Submit This Form">
</td></tr></table></form>
</BODY></HTML>
```

Figure 4-5   Example8.jsp (continued)

3. Save the file as **example8.html** in the directory C:\myjspapp\chapter04.

4. Open a new document and type in the following code:

```
<HTML>
<HEAD><TITLE>Enumeration</TITLE></HEAD>
<BODY>
<table>
<tr><th width=100 align=left>Data Item</th>
   <th>Information</th>
</tr>
<tr><td colspan=2><hr></td></tr>
<%
   java.util.Enumeration enu =
request.getParameterNames();
   while(enu.hasMoreElements()){
           String s = (String)enu.nextElement();
%>
   <tr><td><%= s %> </td>
           <td><%= request.getParameter(s) %>
   </tr>
<%}%>
</table>
</BODY>
</HTML>
```

5. Save the file as **example8.jsp** in the directory C:\myjspapp\chapter04.

6. Load the page example8.html using the following URL:
http://localhost:8080/myapp/chapter04/example8.html

7. A registration form is displayed. Fill in the form as shown in Figure 4-6 and then click **Submit This Form**. The information you entered is displayed on another page, similar to the one shown in Figure 4-7.

There are six control elements on the registration form, and the information collected from the form is sent to the server. On the server side, you use another technique to retrieve and process the information.

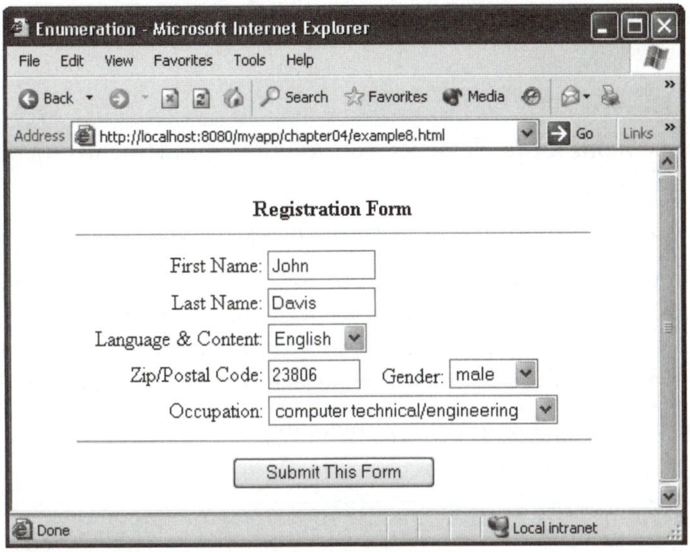

Figure 4-6   Registration form

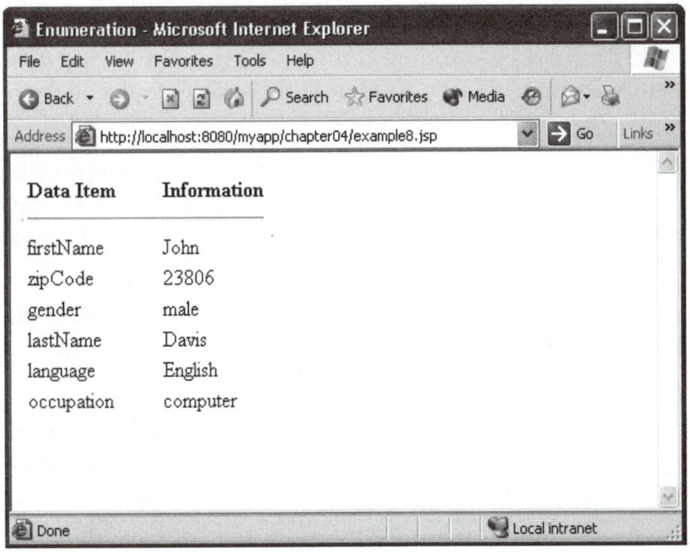

Figure 4-7   Registration information

The following code returns an enumeration reference and assigns the enumeration to an Enumeration variable (or an Enumeration object reference). The Enumeration contains references to these strings that are the control names on the requesting form.

```
java.util.Enumeration enu = request.getParameterNames();
```

This following statement tests if this Enumeration contains more elements that reference the control names:

```
enu.hasMoreElements();
```

If this Enumeration contains more elements, you use the nextElement() method to get the next element, as follows:

```
String s = (String)enu.nextElement();
```

Since this method returns an object, you need to explicitly cast the object to a string. The string is then assigned to a string variable *s*. The string variable *s* contains a control name on the form, the method `request.getParameter(s)` returns the value entered to that control. Both the control name and its value are displayed on the page.

You will learn more about the Enumeration object in Chapter 6.

CHAPTER SUMMARY

❑ A variable is a location in the computer's memory where a data value is stored. When code references a variable name, the value stored in that location is retrieved.

❑ All variables must be declared before they can be used in a JSP script. A variable name must be a valid identifier that consists of letters, digits, and underscores and that does not begin with a digit.

❑ There are two types of control structures that alter the the execution order of your program: the conditional selection structure and the loop structure. In the conditional selection structure, the execution of actions depends on certain conditions. The loop structure controls the repeated execution of actions.

❑ Logical operators facilitate multiple-condition testing in a single statement. There are four logical operators: logical NOT (!), logical AND (&&), logical OR (||), and logical exclusive (^).

❑ A string object provides many methods that you can use to perform manipulations on it, such as substring extraction, case change, location of a specified character or substring, and concatenation.

❑ An array is a group of continuous memory locations that all have the same name and type. To refer to a particular element in the array, you specify the name of the array and the index of the particular element in the array.

❑ The Enumeration interface has two methods, hasMoreElements() and nextElement(). The hasMoreElements() method tests if the enumeration contains more elements. It returns true as long as the Enumeration object contains at least one more element; it returns false otherwise. The nextElement() method returns the next element of the Enumeration if the Enumeration object has at least one more element to provide.

REVIEW QUESTIONS

1. In JSP, a variable must be declared before it can be used. True or False?

2. A character can be assigned to an int variable. True or False?

3. A string can be assigned to an int variable. True or False?

4. The expression `9 % 4` yields:

   a. 1

   b. 2

   c. 3

   d. 5

5. The expression `10/4` yields:

   a. 2

   b. 4

   c. 2.5

   d. 3

6. The expression `10/4.0` yields:

   a. 2

   b. 4

   c. 2.5

   d. 3

7. Assume that an int variable x has been declared and initialized to 5. The JSP code `<%= (x>5?x--:x++) %>` then returns:

   a. 5

   b. 4

   c. 3

   d. 2

8. Assume that an int variable x has been declared and initialized to 5. The JSP code `<%= (x>5?--x:++x) %>` then returns:

   a. 3

   b. 4

   c. 5

   d. 6

9. The difference between a while loop and do loop is that the loop body in the do loop is executed at least once. True or False?

10. The case value in a switch structure can be a string. True or False?

11. Assume that the case values are 1, 2, 3, and 4 in a switch structure, and the switch-expression yields 1. If there is no break statement in the switch structure, then all statements in the switch structure are executed. True or False?

12. The expression `(1>9)^(3<4)`, yields a Boolean value of true. True or False?

13. The expression `(0>4) || (3<5)` yields a Boolean value of false. True or False?

14. The statement `"Welcome to JSP".substring(0)` returns which of the following substrings?

    a. "W"

    b. "Welcome to JSP"

    c. "elcome to JSP"

    d. "Welcome"

15. The statement `"Welcome to JSP".indexOf("come",4)` returns:

    a. 3

    b. 4

    c. 7

    d. –1

16. The statement `"Welcome to JSP".indexOf("come")` returns:

    a. 3

    b. 4

    c. 7

    d. –1

17. The statement `"Welcome to JSP".charAt(4)` returns:

    a. l

    b. c

    c. o

    d. m

18. Assume that a string variable s is declared and initialized to "Welcome to JSP". In this case, the expression `s.indexOf(s.length())` causes an exception. True or False?

19. The expression `"Welcome " + 12 + 3` yields which of the following strings:

    a. "Welcome 123"

    b. "Welcome 15"

    c. "Welcome 312"

    d. none of the above

20. The expression `"Welcome 123".lastIndexOf("123", 9)` returns which of the following:

    a. 8

    b. 9

    c. 10

    d. −1

21. You can store both integer and string values in the same array. True or False?

22. The index of the last element in the array c is:

    a. c.length

    b. 0

    c. c.length + 1

    d. c.length − 1

23. The hasMoreElements() method returns a Boolean value. True or False?

HANDS-ON PROJECTS

Project 4-1 Sales Commission I

In this project, you create an if statement in a Web page to help salespeople calculate their commissions based on the following rules:

Sales Amount (Inclusive)	Commission Rate
$1 – $2000	3 percent
$2001 – $5000	4 percent
$5001 – $10000	7 percent
$7001 and above	10 percent

1. Open the data file project1.txt and save it as **project1.jsp** in the directory C:\myjspapp\chapter04.

2. Add an if statement to implement the rules specified in the above table to calculate sales commissions, and save the file.

3. Load this page using the following URL:
   http://localhost:8080/myapp/chapter04/project1.jsp

4. Enter sales amount and click the button to display the commission on the page.

Project 4-2 Enumeration

In this project, you will improve example8.jsp, which you created in this chapter, so that only those data items with values are displayed.

1. Open the data file project2.txt and save it as **project2.html** in the folder C:\myjspapp\chapter04. This file contains a form similar to the one in example8.html.

2. Open a new document in your text editor and type in the following code:

```
<HTML>
<HEAD><TITLE>Project 4-2</TITLE></HEAD>
<BODY>
<table>
<tr><th width=100 align=left>Data Item</th>
    <th>Information</th>
</tr>
<tr><td colspan=2><hr></td></tr>
<%
    java.util.Enumeration enu =
request.getParameterNames();
    while(enu.hasMoreElements()){
            String s = (String)enu.nextElement();
            String v = request.getParameter(s);
            if(v.equals(""))
                    continue;
%>
    <tr><td><%= s %></td>
            <td><%= v%>
    </tr>
<%}%>
</table>
</BODY>
</HTML>
```

3. Save the file as **project2.jsp** in the directory C:\myjspapp\chapter04.

4. Load the page project2.html using the following URL: http://localhost:8080/myapp/chapter04/project2.html

5. Leave some fields on the form blank and click the **Submit This Form** button. Those items with no information are not displayed.

Project 4-3 Using the Switch Structure

In this project, you will use a switch structure to generate a truth table for each of the logical operators:

1. Open the data file project3.txt and save it as **project3.jsp** in C:\myjspapp\chapter04.

2. Look at the code and make sure you understand the logic used to generate the truth table for logical NOT, AND, and OR operators.

3. Add code inside the switch structure to implement the truth table for the logical exclusive operator.

4. Save this file.

5. Load this page using the following URL:
   http://localhost:8080/myapp/chapter04/project3.jsp

6. Select a logical operator to display its associated truth table, which should appear similar to the one shown in Figure 4–8.

4

Project 4-3 - Microsoft Internet Explorer

File   Edit   View   Favorites   Tools   Help

Back   ·   ·   Search   Favorites   Media

Address   http://localhost:8080/myapp/chapter04/project3.jsp?index=2   Go   Links

Truth table for:

Logical AND (&&)

operand1	operand2	operand1 && operand2
false	false	false
false	true	false
true	false	false
true	true	true

Done   Local intranet

Figure 4-8   Truth table

Project 4-4 Searching for Strings

In this project, you will use loop structures to access individual elements in an array that stores all usernames. You can specify certain criteria and list those names that meet the criteria.

1. Open the data file project4.txt and save it as **project4.jsp** in the directory C:\myjspapp\chapter04.

2. Add code to perform the search operation. List all names that satisfy the search criteria.

3. Save this file.

4. Load this page using the following URL:
http://localhost:8080/myapp/chapter04/project4.jsp

5. Enter the search criteria and click the button. The names that meet the specified criteria are displayed on the page, which should appear similar to the one shown in Figure 4-9.

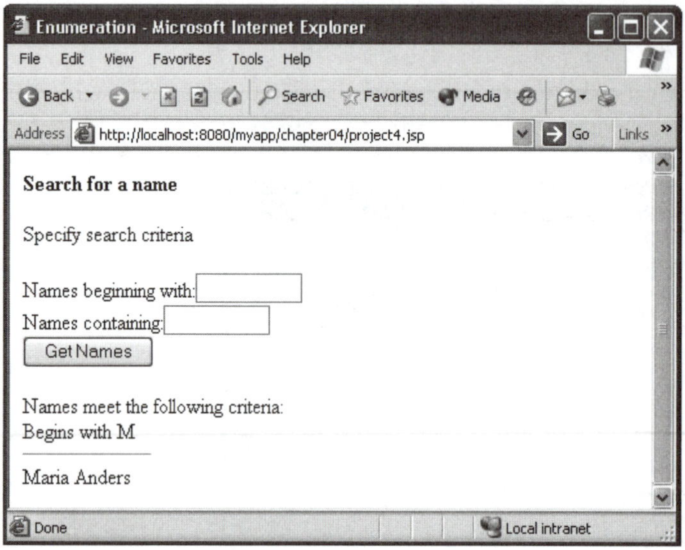

Figure 4-9   Search for names

Project 4-5 Sales Commissions II

In Project 4-1, you designed a Web page to help salespeople calculate their commissions. It works fine as long as you provide a numerical value in the amount of sales input box. If you forget to provide a number, an error occurs. In this project, you are required to fix this problem, so that if no sales amount is entered, a message is displayed on the page to notify users that the amount of sales is required.

1. Open and save the data file project5.txt as **project5.jsp** in the folder C:\myjspapp\chapter04.

2. Modify the code so that if no sales amount is entered, a message is displayed indicating that a sales amount is required.

3. Load this page and test it to see whether it works properly.

Project 4-6 Transactions

In this project, you will design Web pages to allow customers to transfer money from their checking accounts to their saving accounts, and vice versa. To transfer money, the account must contain at least the amount of money to be transferred. Otherwise, the transaction should not be processed. Assume that the amount in the checking account is $2000 and the amount in the savings account is $500.

1. Open and save the data file project6.txt as **project6.html** in the folder C:\myjspapp\chapter04. It contains the form for transferring money between checking and savings accounts.

2. Open a new document in your text editor and save the file as **project6.jsp** in the folder C:\myjspapp\chapter04.

3. Add JSP code to transfer money between the two accounts.

4. Save this file and load project6.html using the following URL: http://localhost:8080/myapp/chapter04/project6.html

5. Test the code you wrote in Step 3 to see whether a transaction is implemented properly.

CASE PROJECTS

SRAS: Improving the Logon Page

In a previous chapter you created a logon page for the SRAS. Basically, there are three groups of users in the system: administrators, faculty, and students. Each group has different privileges when accessing the system. In this project, you modify the logon.jsp page so that it displays a welcome message that is specific to the group of which the user is a member.

Online Produce

You are hired by a small fruit store. To expand sales, the manager asks you to develop a Web application so customers can order four types of fruit online: apples, oranges, bananas, and grapes. On the Web site, you should include four input text fields in which a customer can enter the amount of each fruit they want to buy, a Submit button, and a Reset button. You should also display the unit price for each type of fruit. After a customer places an order, display a page containing the order information, including the fruit type, the amount purchased, a subtotal for each type of fruit, and the total charge.

Client Calendar

The manager of your consulting firm asks you to develop a page that displays a calendar for the current month when a client visits the Website. Today's date should be highlighted on the calendar.

5

SCRIPTING WITH JSP ELEMENTS

In this chapter, you will:

♦ Use JSP page directives to determine some characteristics of JSP pages

♦ Use JSP include directives and actions to incorporate content from other files

♦ Use simple JSP scripting elements

♦ Use JSP comments to make your code more readable

As you learned in previous chapters, a JSP page consists of template data and JSP elements. Template data is plain HTML, which the JSP processor passes on to the browser untouched. JSP elements are executed on the server. JSP elements fall into four groups: directives, scripting elements, comments, and actions. Directives are messages to the JSP engine that apply to the entire page, and they are organized into three categories that configure JSP parameters or extend the page's code: the page directive, the include directive, and the taglib directive (which you will learn about in Chapter 10). Scripting elements are subdivided into declarations, expressions, and code fragments (or scriptlets). Comments are used to document the code; JSP has two types of comments, content comments and JSP comments. In this chapter, you will learn how to use page directives and include directives, and how to incorporate action, scripting elements and comments in your JSP pages.

PAGE DIRECTIVES

Among the three JSP directives, the **page directive** is the most complicated. It supports a wide range of attributes and functionalities. Page directive attributes apply to the entire JSP page; you use them to set the script language, import Java classes, configure the output buffer, control the session, and so forth. You can use the page directive anywhere in the JSP file, but it's good coding style to place it at the top of the file.

The basic syntax of the page directive is as follows:

<%@ page attribute1="value1" attribute2="value2" attribute3=... %>

Alternately, you can write the page directive in an XML-based syntax, as follows:

<jsp:directive.page attribute1="value1" attribute2="value2" attribute3=... />

Because the first style appears more frequently in JSP pages, you will use it in the examples that follow. Table 5-1 lists the page directive's attributes.

Table 5-1   The page directive's attributes

Attribute and Example Values	Default	Description
language="java"	"java"	Specifies the language used by the page. Currently only Java is supported.
extends="javax.servlet.http.HttpServlet"	None	Defines the parent class of the generated servlet. Rarely used in practice.
import="java.util.*,java util.Vector"	None	Specifies a comma-separated list of packages or classes. If used, it must be placed at the top of the file.
session="true|false"	"true"	Specifies if the page participates in an HTTP session. True means session data is available to the page.
buffer="none|8kb|sizekb"	"8kb"	Specifies the buffering model for the output stream to the client. If the value is "none," then all the output is written directly to the ServletResponse.
autoFlush="true|false"	"true"	If true, the script flushes the output buffer when it's full.
isThreadSafe="true|false"	"true"	Indicates whether or not multiple requests can be handled simultaneously.
info="text"	None	Specifies page information that can be accessed via the Servlet.getServletInfo() method.
errorPage="record/pagenotfound.jsp"	None	Indicates the relative path to JSP pagehandling exceptions. This page will be designated isErrorPage="true".
isErrorPage="true|false"	"false"	Specifies whether the page is an error handler.
contentType="text/html; charset=ISO-8859-1"	"text/html" ISO-8859-1	Specifies the mime type and character set of the JSP and final pages.

Import Attribute

The import attribute describes the types (usually a Java class) that are available to the scripting environment. Java **class** is a data type containing data members and methods. There are many prewritten classes, and you can also write your own classes. Classes enable the programmer to model objects that have **attributes** (represented as data members) and **behaviors** (represented as methods). You can use these data members and/or methods in your JSP code. For example, the class Date contains useful methods that deal with dates and times; you can declare an object of type Date from this class and use this object reference to handle dates and times. (You will learn more about classes in Chapter 8.) Once a class has been defined, the class name can be used to declare objects of the class. However, before you can use these prewritten classes or your own classes in your JSP code, you need to specify where these classes can be found. Java classes are grouped in a collection called a package. The **packages** are referred to collectively as the Java class library or the **Java Applications Programming Interface (Java API)**.

Java contains hundreds of classes you can use in your JSP code. These classes are grouped into a number of packages. Packages are organized in a hierarchical structure, just like the nested subdirectories on your hard drive. You can use the public classes in a package in two ways. The first is simply to give the full name of the package. Recall the example in Chapter 2, in which, you used `<%= new java.util.Date() %>` to get the time on your Web server. In that example, to use the class Date, you included the entire path with the class name. That is obviously tedious. The simpler, and more common, approach is to use the **import** attribute of the page directive. When a Java class is imported into a JSP page, you can reference this class without explicitly specifying the class package names. Consider the following scenario: In your JSP code, you may want to use the larger of two integer variables, say var1 and var2. If you don't use classes, you have to write code to compare the values of the two variables, and then decide which of them is greater, as follows:

```
<%  int theLargerOne = var1;
    if(var1 < var2){
            theLargerOne = var2;
    }
%>
```

There is a class Math, which has a method called max that helps to decide which of the two numbers is greater. You can use this method to perform the same operation in the code above, as follows:

```
<% int theLargerOne = Math.max(var1, var2); %>
```

Notice that the code above does not specify where the Math class can be found. In fact, the following packages are imported into JSP pages automatically: java.lang.*, javax.servlet.*, javax.servlet.jsp.*, javax.servlet.http.*, and possibly some server-specific classes. A package name followed by the ".*" string means that all the public classes in this package are available to this JSP page. Since the class Math is in the package: java.lang.Math, you do not need to import the Math class in order to use it in your JSP code.

There are two types of methods defined in a class: the static method and the instance method. You can use the static method without declaring an object, but you must declare an object in order to use an instance method.

In some cases, you may want to use classes from different packages. All classes imported are separated with commas. For example, if you want to use classes from both the java.util package and the java.sql package, you can import these packages using the following code:

```
<%@ page import="java.util.*,java.sql.*" %>
```

It is possible that some classes in different packages have the same class name. For example, both the java.util and java.sql packages contain a class called Date. If you import the Date class from both packages, you must explicitly declare the Date class using full class path. The following code generates error messages:

```
<%@ page import="java.util.*, java.sql. *" %>
<%= new Date() %>
```

Given this code, the JSP container displays an error message regarding the ambiguous class for java.util.Date and java.sql.Date because they have the same class name. To resolve this, you should use the fully qualified class name as follows:

```
<%@ page import="java.util.*, java.sql.*" %>
<%
  java.util.Date date = new java.util.Date();
%>
The current time on the Web server is: <%= date %>
```

Session Attribute

The HTTP protocol is a stateless protocol; that is, the maintenance of a state across multiple requests is not supported within the protocol itself. What if you want to hold client information across multiple requests? For example, in an online shopping system, each item ordered must be added to a client's ongoing order. The order must maintain its state, and each order must be associated with a customer. JSP solves this problem by providing support for session management, a mechanism used to turn the HTTP stateless protocol into a stateful protocol. A **session** begins when any user requests a JSP page for the first time. The session attribute specifies how the page uses the predefined session object in JSP. If the attribute value is "true," then the predefined (implicit object) session is bound to the existing session if one exists; otherwise, a new session is created and bound to the implicit session object. If the session attribute is not specified, the default setting is true. If the attribute value is false, then no session is created, and attempts to access the session object result in errors at the time the JSP is translated into a servlet. The following example illustrates how the session attribute works.

1. Open a new document in your text editor and type in the following code:

```
<%@ page import="java.util.*" session="true" %>
<HTML>
<HEAD><TITLE>Session attribute</TITLE></HEAD>
<BODY>
Is this a new session? <%= session.isNew() %><br>
Current time: <%= new Date() %> <br>
<% Date date = new Date(session.getCreationTime()); %>
The session was created on :<%= date %><br>
</BODY>
</HTML>
```

2. Save the file as **example1.jsp** in the folder C:\myjspapp\chapter05.

3. Open your browser and load the page using the following URL:
   http://localhost:8080/myapp/chapter05/example1.jsp

   This page is displayed as shown in Figure 5-1.

 Before loading this page, quit all browser windows and then open your browser and load this page. A session begins when a user requests a JSP file for the first time. If you loaded a JSP page, then a session exists already (assuming that it has not expired yet, which is discussed in Chapter 7), and your page indicates that the session is not new, and when this session was created.

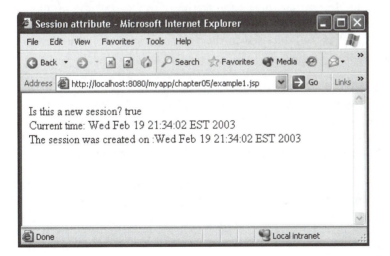

Figure 5-1   Session attribute example

In example1.jsp, the session attribute is set to true. So the implicit session object is created when a user requests any JSP file for the first time. If you request this page again (by clicking the Refresh button on the browser), a session already exists, so the page displays a message indicating that the session is not new. That is, the implicit session object is bound to the existing session. If the session attribute is set to false, you cannot use the implicit session variable in your JSP. Try to set the session attribute in example1.jsp to false, and reload this page. You will get error messages indicating that the session is not defined. If you set the session attribute to false, you need to declare a session variable; the newly declared session variable is bound to the session if a session exists; otherwise, a new session is created.

1. Open a new document in Notepad and type in the following code:

```
<%@ page import="java.util.*" session="false" %>
<HTML>
<HEAD><TITLE>Session attribute</TITLE></HEAD>
<BODY>
<% HttpSession mySession = request.getSession(true); %>
Is this a new session? <%= mySession.isNew() %><br>
Current time: <%= new Date() %> <br>
<% Date date = new Date(mySession.getCreationTime()); %>
The session created on :<%= date %><br>
</BODY>
</HTML>
```

2. Save this file as **example2.jsp** in the folder C:\myjspapp\chapter05

3. Open your browser and load this page using the following URL:
http://localhost:8080/myapp/chapter05/exmple2.jsp

In this example, you set the session attribute to false. So the implicit session object reference is not available in this page. The session variable: mySession (of type HttpSession) declared in the page performs the same way as the implicit session variable.

Turning off session tracking (by setting the session attribute to false) may save significant amounts of server memory on high-traffic sites. However, because the sessions are associated with a user, and not with individual pages, it does not help to turn off session tracking for one page unless you also turn it off for related pages that are likely to be visited in the same client session.

A session begins when a user requests any JSP page for the first time. Requesting an HTML page will not start a session.

Buffer Attribute

The buffer attribute indicates that you will manually control when the HTML output stream is sent back to the client browser. The buffer attribute specifies the size of the buffer used by the implicit out variable. Use of this attribute takes one of two forms:

```
<%@ page buffer="sizekb" %>
<%@ page buffer="none" %>
```

If the value is none, then there is no buffering and all output is written directly to the clients. If a buffer is specified, then output is buffered, with a buffer size not less than the specified size. For example, `<%@ page buffer="16kb" %>` means that the document content should be buffered and not sent to the client until at least 16 KB have been accumulated or the page is completed. The default buffer size is server specific, but must be at least 8 KB.

The size of the buffer can only be specified in kilobytes, and the suffix "kb" is mandatory. The following example illustrates how to set the buffer attribute and how the buffer attribute affects the output stream that is sent back to client.

1. Open a new file in your text editor and type in the following code:

```
<HTML>
<HEAD><TITLE>Buffer attribute</TITLE></HEAD>
<BODY>
<%@ page  buffer="16kb" %>
The buffer attribute is set to "16kb"<br>
<hr align=left width=250 color=red>
Let's send some text to the HTML output stream<br>
The content is buffered.
<% out.clear(); %>
The buffered content is cleared from the buffer.<br>
</BODY>
</HTML>
```

2. Save this page as **example3.jsp** in the folder C:\myjspapp\chapter05.

3. Open your browser and load this page using the following URL: http://localhost:8080/myapp/chapter05/example3.jsp

   This page is displayed as shown in Figure 5-2.

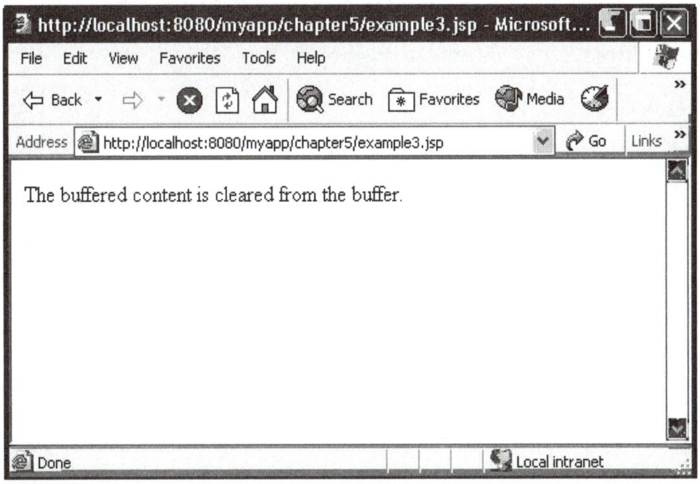

Figure 5-2 Output stream and buffer attribute

In this example, the buffer size is set to 16 KB. This means that the output stream is not sent to the client until the buffered content reaches the buffer size or this page is complete. Since the content in this page is far less than the buffer size, in order to test whether the content is buffered before it is sent to the client, you use the implicit variable out and call the clear method to clear the buffered content from the output stream. The method out.clear() clears whatever is buffered in the output stream. Therefore, the previous buffered content is not sent to the client. The following example illustrates how the output stream is sent to the client when the buffer attribute is set to "none."

1. Open a new document in your text editor and type in the following code:

```
<HTML>
<HEAD><TITLE>Buffer attribute</TITLE></HEAD>
<BODY>
<%@ page  buffer="none" %>
The buffer attribute is set to "none".<br>
<hr align=left width=250 color=red>
Let's send some text to the HTML output stream.<br>
The content is not buffered.
<% try{
     out.clear();
  }catch(Exception e){}
%>
The buffered content is not cleared.<br>
</BODY>
</HTML>
```

2. Save this page as **example4.jsp** in the folder C:\myjspapp\chapter05.

3. Open your browser and load this page using the following URL:
http://localhost:8080/myapp/chapter05/example4.jsp

This page is displayed as shown in Figure 5-3.

Notice the code segment:

```
<% try{
     out.clear();
  }catch(Exception e){}
%>
```

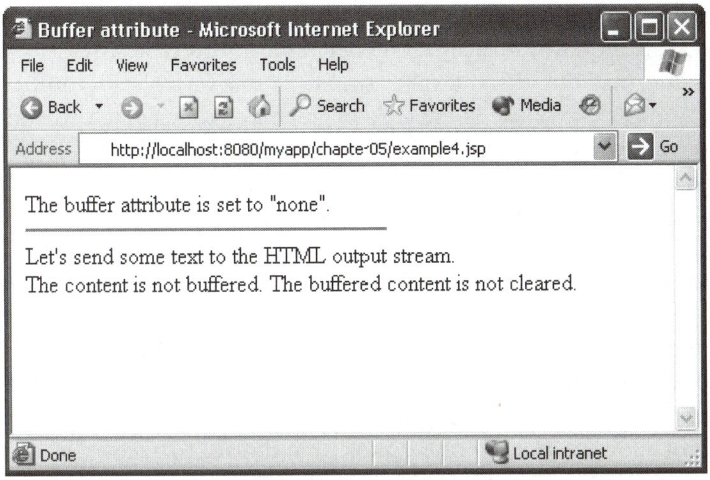

Figure 5-3   Output stream without buffering

Since the out.clear() method is illegal when the buffer size is set to "none," when this page is translated, the illegal statement is thrown as an exception. An **exception** is an indication that a problem occurred during the program's execution. You will learn more about exceptions in Chapter 10. When an exception occurs in your program, you must handle it; otherwise, your program terminates. For now, you just need to know to use the try/catch block to try to clear the buffer if there is buffering. Without the try/catch statement, you will get error messages and the page cannot be loaded.

> Even if you set the buffer attribute to false, the JSP container, for example the Tomcat server you use in this text, may still do some buffering, so there is no guarantee that the content will be sent immediately. You can always force the buffered content to be sent immediately by calling the flush method of the implicit out variable.

IsThreadSafe Attribute

Before discussing the isThreadSafe attribute, consider the following scenario: You are designing a Web page that will assign each visitor a user ID when the user visits your Web site for the first time. The following code segment assigns an ID to visitors:

```
<%! int idNumber = 0; %>
<%
    String userID = "Your user id is: " + idNumber;
    out.println(userID);
    inNumber++;
%>
```

The code <%! int idNumber = 0; %> declares a variable: idNumber with the initial value 0. The first visitor is assigned 0 and the value increments by 1, so the second visitor is assigned 1, then the value increments by 1, and so on. Each request for a JSP page is processed via a thread. A **thread** is a process that handles client requests by executing code sequentially. Each client request for this page generates a thread that requests access to this code segment. Assume that the current value stored in the variable idNumber is 10. Joe requests this page, and a thread called "Thread A" is generated to execute this code segment. Shortly after this, Lynne visits this page and another thread, called "Thread B," is generated. Thus, there are two threads executing the code segment simultaneously. Within "Thread A," after Joe is assigned the ID number 10, the code out.println(userID) is executed. Before executing the next statement to increment the value stored in the idNumber variable, "Thread B" executes the code and assigns Lynne the value stored in the variable, which is still 10. "Thread A" updates the value of the variable, so the value of the variable is 11. Then, "Thread B" also updates the value, so that after the two requests have been processed, the value stored in the variable idNumber is 12. Therefore, the ID 11 is never assigned to a visitor. In such a scenario, two visitors are assigned the same user ID! To prevent this from happening, you must not allow more than one visitor (one thread) to access this code segment at the same time. Once a thread enters the block of code, no other thread can enter the same block until the first one exits (finishes the execution of the code block). Another term for exclusively accessing the code block is **synchronization**. JSP handles this by using the isThreadSafe attribute.

As you know already, your JSP page is ultimately compiled into a Java servlet class. The isThreadSafe attribute indicates whether the generated servlet is capable of responding to multiple simultaneous requests safely. Use of the isThreadSafe attribute takes one of the following forms:

```
<%@ page isThreadSafe="true" %>
<%@ page isThreadSafe="false" %>
```

If the isThreadSafe attribute is set to true, you assume that concurrently executing users' requests does not result in inconsistent results from an unexpected ordering of thread executions. If this attribute value is set to false, no more than one thread can execute the JSP code at one time. In this case, if a thread executes the code segment, the next thread must wait until the first one finishes execution. This means that the system queues up all requests and processes a single request at a time.

In some cases (such as when tracking page access counts), you may not care if two visitors occasionally get the same ID value, but in other cases (such as when assigning user IDs), identical values can spell disaster. If you do not specify this attribute, the default value is set to true.

The autoFlush, errorPage, and isErrorPage Attributes

The autoFlush attribute is used to specify whether the buffered output should be sent (flushed) automatically when the buffer is filled. The syntax of the autoFlush attribute is as follows:

```
<%@ page autoFlush="true" %>
<%@ page autoFlush="false" %>
```

The default value is "true" and indicates that the buffer should be flushed when it is full. A value of false, which is rarely used, indicates that the JSP container should throw an exception when the buffer overflows. This stops the processing of the JSP page. For example, if you have no control over the size of the dynamic content you generate, and you want to ensure that the processing is aborted if the content reaches a certain limit on buffering, you can set the autoFlush attribute to false. A value of false is illegal when you are using buffer="none", which means that when there is no output buffer for your JSP page, you cannot set the JSP container to throw an exception on the assumption that the output buffer will become full.

In some cases, an error may occur when JSP code is executed on the server. If this happens, the program execution stops at the point where the error occurs and the server generates messages telling you that a problem (an exception) occurred during the program's execution that is not handled in your JSP code. (These messages are written to the Tomcat server log file.) For example, consider the following example, in which you try to divide a number by zero.

1. Open a new file in your text editor and type in the following code:

```
<HTML>
<HEAD><TITLE>Error occurs</TITLE></HEAD>
<BODY>
<%@ page buffer="none" %>
Try to divide a number by zero.<br>
<% int numerator = 19, denominator=0; %>
The numerator is <%= numerator %><br>
The denominator is <%= denominator %><br>
<%= numerator/denominator %>
This message will not be displayed because an error
occurs and it is not handled.
</BODY>
</HTML>
```

2. Save this file as **example5.jsp** in the folder C:\myjspapp\chapter05.

3. Load this page using the following URL:
   http://localhost:8080/myapp/chapter05/example5.jsp

   This page is displayed as shown in Figure 5-4.

5

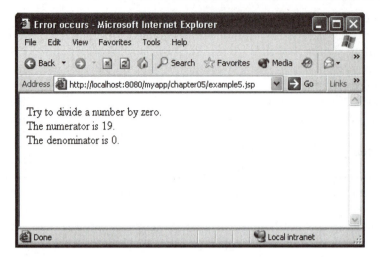

Figure 5-4   Divide by zero exception

You can handle JSP exceptions within the same JSP page or in another JSP page. You can use the errorPage attribute to specify a JSP page that processes any exceptions that are not handled in the current page. This attribute uses the following syntax:

<%@ page errorPage="relative URL" %>

The exceptions are automatically made available to the designated error page by means of the implicit exception variable.

The isErrorPage attribute indicates whether or not the current page can act as the error page for other JSP pages. Use of isErrorPage takes one of the following forms:

```
<%@ page isErrorPage="true" %>
<%@ page isErrorPage="false" %>
```

When the attribute is set to true, the implicit exception variable can be accessed via this page. The default value is false since most JSP pages do not serve as error pages. The following example illustrates how to use the errorPage and isErrorPage attributes.

1. Open a new file in your text editor and type in the following code:

```
<HTML>
<HEAD><TITLE>Handling exceptions</TITLE></HEAD>
<BODY>
<%@ page isErrorPage="true" %>
This page handles exceptions that occur in other JSP
pages.<br><br>
The following exception occurred:<br><br>
<font size=-1 face="Arial">
<%= exception.toString() %>
</font>
</BODY>
</HTML>
```

2. Save this page as **errorPage1.jsp** in the folder C:\myjspapp\chapter05.

3. Open a new document in your text editor and type in the following code:

```
<HTML>
<HEAD><TITLE>Error handled in errorPage</TITLE></HEAD>
<BODY>
<%@ page errorPage="errorPage1.jsp" %>
Enter the amount of money you want to deposit:<br>
<form action="example6.jsp" method="POST">
 <input type=text name=depositAmount>
 <input type=submit value="Submit">
 <input type=reset>
</form>
<%
 String depAmt = request.getParameter("depositAmount");
 if(depAmt != null){
   double depositAmount = Double.valueOf(depAmt)
   .doubleValue();
   out.println("The amount you want to deposit:" +
   depositAmount);
 }
%>
</BODY>
</HTML>
```

4. Save this as **example6.jsp** in the folder C:\myjspapp\chapter05.

5. Open your browser and load example6.jsp using the following URL:
   http://localhost:8080/myapp/chapter05/example6.jsp

6. Enter a numerical value in the deposit amount input field, then click the **Submit** button. The amount you entered is displayed on the page.

7. Enter some non-numerical value this time. When you submit the form, an exception occurs when the code tries to parse a non-numerical value as a double value. The execution of the program is directed to the errorPage1.jsp, which is specified in the errorPage attribute, and the exception is processed in that page.

INCLUDE FILES

When you design a Web application, you may want to provide the same navigation links and footer on each of the pages. To do so, you could write the code for these elements into each page. This is tedious, however, because you must remember to put these elements into each page, and make sure they are correct and identical across the pages. Worst of all, sooner or later will come the day when you want to modify the footers or add more navigation links, and you will have to go back and edit them on each page.

In JSP, you can avoid this scenario by placing the code containing the navigation links and footer in separate files. You can include other HTML or JSP files within a JSP file so that when you need to modify the navigation links or footer, you just need to modify two files: the navigation links file and the footer file.

You can apply this technique when all pages in a Web application share common elements, such as headers, footers, and navigation bars. There are two ways to include files in a JSP page: static includes, via the JSP include directive, and dynamic includes, via the JSP include action.

Including Files at Page Translation Time

The JSP include directive is used to include within the current page another page's content. It has the following syntax:

<%@ include file=" relative URL %>

Or, in tag format:

<jsp:directive.include file=" relative URL" />

When you use this method to include a file, the content of the specified page is read at translation time (when it is converted into its corresponding servlet) and is merged with the original page when the page is requested for the first time.

The included file can contain static content, such as HTML and plain text, or it can be a JSP file. Its contents are merged with the page that includes it, and the resulting page is converted into a servlet at translation time. The following example illustrates how the include directive works.

1. Open a new document in your text editor and type in the following code:

```
<HTML>
<HEAD><TITLE>Course Technology</TITLE></HEAD>
<BODY>
<table border=1 cellspacing=0 cellpadding=2>
<tr><td bgcolor="#fffccc"><a href="#">Series</a></td>
  <td bgcolor="#fffccc">
<a href="#">Student Download</a></td>
  <td bgcolor="#fffccc">
<a href="#">Instructor Resources</a></td>
</tr><tr>
  <td bgcolor="#dddccc"><a href="#">Home</a></td>
  <td bgcolor="#dddccc"><a href="#">About Us</a></td>
  <td bgcolor="#dddccc"><a href="#">Contact</a></td>
  <td bgcolor="#dddccc">
<a href="#">Find Your Rep</a></td>
<tr>
</table>
```

2. Save this page as **navigation.html** in the folder C:\myjspapp\chapter05.

3. Open a new document in your text editor and type in the following code:

```
<%@ include file="navigation.html" %>
<hr color=red>
The navigation bar is merged from the included file "<b>
navigation.html.</b>"
</BODY>
</HTML>
```

4. Save this file as **example7.jsp** in the folder C:\myjspapp\chapter05.

5. Open your browser and load example7.jsp using the following URL:
   http://localhost:8080/myapp/chapter05/example7.jsp

As shown in Figure 5-5, the navigation links are merged into the original page.

If you modified the file navigation.html by adding more links and then reloaded example7.jsp, the newly added links would not be displayed on the page. The content in the included file is merged into the page that includes it when the page is requested for the first time, that is, when the page is translated into its corresponding servlet. The servlet converted from the JSP stays in memory until the JSP container removes it from memory, or until the server is down. Therefore, even if you modify the included content, when the original file (the file that contains the included page) is requested again, the servlet remains the same, so the content merged from the included file is not changed. That is why the include directive is called a static include.

Figure 5-5   Include directive

 You can convince the JSP container that the JSP page was modified by adding a space anywhere in the JSP code. Then the JSP page is translated when it is next requested.

Including Files at Request Time

You can include files at request time by using the <jsp: include> action. It uses the following syntax:

<jsp:include page="Relative URL" flush="true" />

The included file can be a plain HTML page, a CGI script, a servlet, or another JSP page. The action does not merge the actual contents of the specified page at translation time. The page is included each time the JSP page is requested. This means that whenever you modify the included file, the changes are reflected the next time the page is requested. You use the flush property to flush the output buffer of the current page before the new file is included. Currently, this property must be set to true.

In contrast to the JSP include directive, the processing of the included file happens at page request time. The output of the inserted file is placed into the current page when the action tag is processed at request time.

1. Open a new file in your text editor, and type in the following code:

```
<HR>
Copyright © 2003 CT.
</BODY>
</HTML>
```

2. Save this page as footer.html in the folder C:\myjspapp\chapter05.

3. Open a new document in your text editor and type in the following code:

```
<HTML>
<HEAD><TITLE>Include action</TITLE></HEAD>
<BODY>
The footer is merged from the included file
"<b>footer.html</b>"
<jsp:include page="footer.html" flush="true"/>
```

4. Save the file as **example8.jsp** in the folder C:\myjspapp\chapter05.

5. Open your browser and load example8.jsp using the following URL:
http://localhost:8080/myapp/chapter05/example8.jsp

6. You see the footer is displayed on this page. Now modify the file footer.html as follows:

```
<hr>
Copyright © 2002 CT. All rights reserved.
</BODY>
</HTML>
```

After saving this page and reloading example8.jsp, the newly added content is displayed.

Additional information may be passed to the included page by using <jsp:param> tag, as shown below. These parameters can be read by the included page.

```
<jsp:include page="footer.jsp" flush="true">
        <jsp:param name="year" value="2002" />
        <jsp:param name="pageOwner" value=
"Course Technology" />
</jsp:include>
```

The following example illustrates how to use the <jsp:param> tag and how to read these parameters in the included page.

1. Open a new document in your text editor and type in the following code:

```
<hr>
Copyright © <%= request.getParameter("year") %>
<%= request.getParameter("pageOwner") %>.
All rights reserved.
</BODY>
</HTML>
```

2. Save it as **footer.jsp** in the folder C:\myjspapp\chapter05.

3. Open a new document in your text editor and type in the following code:

```
<HTML>
<HEAD><TITLE>Include action</TITLE></HEAD>
<BODY>
The footer is merged from the included file
"<b>footer.jsp.</b>"
<jsp:include page="footer.jsp" flush="true" >
<jsp:param name="year" value ="2003" />
<jsp:param name="pageOwner"
value ="Course Technology" />
</jsp:include>
```

4. Save it as **example9.jsp** in the folder C:\myjspapp\chapter05.

5. Load this page using the following URL:
   http://localhost:8080/myapp/chapter05/example9.jsp

   This page is displayed as shown in Figure 5-6.

5

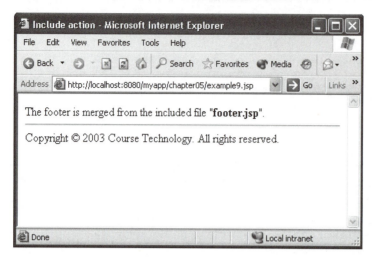

Figure 5-6   Read parameters in included page

In the page example9.jsp, two parameters are provided in the include action; these parameters are read in the included page, footer.jsp.

 There are no spaces in the following include action tags: <jsp:include ...>, <jsp:param ...>, </jsp:include>. Otherwise, an exception occurs.

JSP SCRIPTING ELEMENTS

A JSP page needs scripting code—normally Java code—to make it live. You need to use scripting elements to insert the Java code. There are three forms of scripting elements: declarations, expressions, and scriptlets.

Declarations

A **declaration** is used to declare variables and methods in the scripting language used in a JSP page. The variables and methods declared are inserted into the servlet class generated when the JSP container translates the JSP page. A declaration has the following syntax:

<%! Variable and method %>

Take, for example, the following page hit count code:

```
<%! private int count = 0;
    public int getCount(){
        return ++count;
    }
%>
```

The variable count in the above example is initialized when the JSP page is initialized and is available to the getCount() method, which is declared after it. Declarations do not produce any output to the output stream. If you try to output to the output stream, an exception occurs.

JSP Expressions

A JSP expression inserts the value of the expression directly into the output stream. It has the following syntax:

<%= Expression(s) %>

Below is the page hit count code, modified so that the counter number is displayed:

```
<%! private int count = 0;
    public int getCount(){
        return ++count;
    }
%>
Welcome! This is the <%= getCount() %> time this page has
been visited!
```

When this page is accessed, the expression getCount() is evaluated, the value returned by the expression is an int value (1, 2,...,), which is converted into a string and inserted into the output stream.

JSP Scriptlets

A scriptlet is a code fragment that is executed at request-processing time. Basically, you can embed any valid Java language code inline between the <% and %> tags. The basic syntax is:

<% scriptlets %>

Below is the page hit counter code, with the addition of a JSP scriptlet:

```
<%@ page import="java.util.Calendar" %>
<%! private int count = 0;
    public int getCount(){
        return ++count;
    }
%>
<% Calendar calendar = Calendar.getInstance();
   int hourOfDay = calendar.get(Calendar.HOUR_OF_DAY);
   if(hourOfDay <= 12){
%>
 Good morning!
<%}
   else if(hourOfDay <= 18){
```

```
%>
 Good Afternoon!
<% }
  else{
%>
 Good Evening!
<% } %>
This is the <%= getCount() %> time this page has been
visited!
```

Note how the if...else structures are created by the multiple scriptlets.

Unlike JSP declarations, in which you can declare only variables and methods, you can include any JSP scripts in JSP scriptlets. You can declare variables, define methods, and send output to the output stream. But the variables defined in JSP declarations and JSP scriptlets have different durations. The **duration** of a variable (also called its lifetime) is the period during which that variable exists in memory. Some variables exist briefly, some are repeatedly created and destroyed, and others exist for the entire execution of your Web application.

JSP has variables of **instance duration**. Variables of instance duration exist from the point at which the corresponding servlet that defines them is loaded into memory, usually when a JSP page is requested for the first time (when the JSP is converted to a servlet). JSP has other variables of **local duration**. Local variables are created when program control reaches their declaration; they exist while the block in which they are declared is active, and they are destroyed when the block in which they are declared is exited. All variables declared in the JSP declaration have instance duration; all variables declared in scriptlets have local duration. The following example illustrates the difference between the variables declared in a JSP declaration and those in scriptlets.

1. Open a new document in your text editor and type in the following code:

```
<HTML>
<HEAD><TITLE>Variable duration</TITLE></HEAD>
<BODY>
<%! int count1 = 0; %>
<% int count2 = 0; %>
<% count1++; count2++; %>
Use the counter variable declared in JSP declaration.<br>
<b>This page has been accessed
 <font size=6 color=red><%= count1 %> </font>
 <% if(count1 == 1) { %>
  time.
 <% }else{ %>
  times.
 <% } %>
 </b><br><br>
Use the counter variable declared in JSP sriptlet.<br>
<b>This page has been accessed
```

```
<font size=6 color=red><%= count2 %> </font>
<% if(count2 == 1) { %>
 time.
<% }else{ %>
 times.
<% } %>
</b><br><br>
<a href="example10.jsp">Reload this page</a>
</BODY>
</HTML>
```

2. Save the file as **example10.jsp** in the folder C:\myjspapp\chapter05.

3. Load this page using the following URL:
   http://localhost:8080/myapp/chapter05/example10.jsp

When this page is displayed for the first time, you see that both counter variables give the right information. Click the Reload this page link to reload the page several times. Each time the page is reloaded, the page counter variable declared in the JSP declaration increments by one, while the counter variable declared in JSP scriptlet does not increment, as shown in Figure 5-7. Because the variable count1 declared in the JSP declaration has instance duration, this variable is loaded when you request this JSP page for the first time, and the variable stays in the memory. Subsequent requests for this page all use the same variable: count1, which exists in memory already. However, the variable count2 declared in the JSP scriptlet is created, and initialized to 0, each time the page is requested.

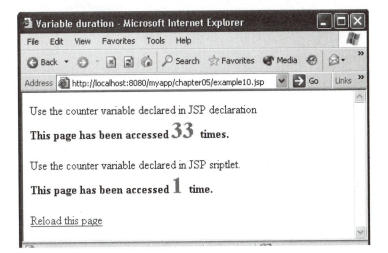

Figure 5-7   Variable duration

COMMENTS

Comments improve your program's readability and are ignored when the program is translated. JSP has two types of comments: content comments and JSP comments. Content comments use the same syntax as comments in HTML:

```
<!-- content comments  -->
```

Content comments are sent back to the client via the response output stream in the generated document. Since they are comments, they are not displayed on the browser, but can be viewed via the browser's View Source command. Content comments can include dynamic data if a JSP expression is included inside the tag. For example:

```
<!-- JSP Page = <%= javax.servlet.http.HttpUtils.getRequest
URL(request)%> -->
```

If you include this comment in your JSP page, the real page URL will replace the JSP expression when the page is requested, and you can view it in the source code.

JSP comments usually document what the JSP page is doing or comment out portions of the code that are not needed. Those comments, also called server-side comments, are not sent back to the client and can only be viewed in the original JSP page. When the JSP container processes the page, the JSP comments are totally ignored. Use of JSP comments takes one of the following three forms:

```
<%--
multiple-line comments
-- %>
<%
    /* Multiple-line
        comments */
%>
<% //single-line comment %>
```

Now you will insert both content comments and JSP comments into the code to complete the page hit counter example.

1. Open the data file example11.jsp, which is located in the folder C:\mjspapp\chapter05.

2. Add the shaded code in Figure 5-8 to insert various types of comments.

3. Save the file as **example11.jsp** in the folder C:\myjspapp\chapter05.

4. Load this page using the following URL:
   http://locahost:8080/myapp/chapter05/example11.jsp

```
<%@ page import="java.util.Calendar" %>
<!-- This is a content comment. The URL of this JSP page is
<%= javax.servlet.http.HttpUtils.getRequestURL(request)%>
-->
<HTML>
<HEAD><TITLE>JSP comments </TITLE></HEAD>
<BODY>
<%-- declare a counter variable
    and a method to increment count by 1
    at every request for the page
--%>
<%! private int count = 0;
    public int getCount(){
        return ++count; // increment count by 1 and returns
    }
%>
<%-- get the time of the day for greetings --%>
<%
 /* get an instance of calendar object by using
    a static method defined in the class
    Calendar
  */
  Calendar calendar = Calendar.getInstance();
  int hourOfDay = calendar.get(Calendar.HOUR_OF_DAY);
  if(hourOfDay <= 12){
%>
 Good morning!
<% }else if(hourOfDay <= 18){ %>
 Good Afternoon!
<% } else { %>
 Good Evening!
<%  } %>
This page has been visited <%= getCount() %> times!
</BODY>
</HTML>
```

5

Figure 5-8   Comments added to example11.jsp

After this page is displayed, use the View Source command to view the source code.
Note that the content comments are sent to clients, while the JSP comments are not.

Every JSP page should begin with a comment describing the purpose of
the page.

CHAPTER SUMMARY

❑ A JSP directive affects the overall structure of the servlet that is generated from the JSP page. There are three types of directives: page directives, include directives, and taglib directives.

❑ The page directive supports a wide range of attributes and functionalities. The attributes apply to the entire JSP page, and you use them to set the script language, import Java classes, configure the output buffer, and control the session.

❑ The include directive allows you to insert a file into the servlet class at the time the JSP file is translated into a servlet. The include action allows you to add the included file in the response when the original JSP page is requested.

❑ A declaration is used to declare variables and methods in the scripting language used in a JSP page. The variables and methods declared are inserted into the servlet class generated when the JSP container translates the JSP page. Variables declared in JSP declarations have instance duration.

❑ A JSP expression is used to insert the value of the expression directly into the output stream.

❑ A scriptlet is a code fragment that is executed at request-processing time. Basically, you can embed any valid Java language code within a scriptlet. Variables declared in scriptlets have local duration.

❑ There are two types of comments you can use in a JSP file: content comments, and JSP comments. Content comments are sent back to the client, while JSP comments are not.

REVIEW QUESTIONS

1. Which of the following packages is/are imported into a JSP page automatically?

   a. java.util.*

   b. java.lang.*

   c. javax.servlet.*

   d. javax.servlet.jsp.*

   e. javax.servlet.http.*

2. All classes imported are separated with:

   a. ,

   b. .

   c. ?

   d. &

3. Which of the following can be used to hold client information across multiple requests?

a. a variable declared in a JSP declaration

b. a variable declared in a scriptlet

c. the implicit session variable

d. the implicit out variable

4. A session begins when any user requests a JSP page for the first time. True or False?

5. Each client can have only one session. True or False?

6. Which of the following statements sets the buffer size of the page directive to 16 KB?

a. `<%@ page buffer="16" %>`

b. `<%@ page buffer="16 kilobytes" %>`

c. `<%@ page buffer="16kb" %>`

d. `<%@ page buffer="16000" %>`

7. Suppose the size of the content to be sent to the client is 20 KB. If the buffer size is set to 8 KB, then how many times is the buffer flushed? (Assume that the Web server sends the content only when the buffered content reaches the buffer size or the page is complete).

a. 1

b. 2

c. 3

d. 4

8. If the isThreadSafe attribute is set to "false," no more than one thread can execute the JSP code at one time. True or False?

9. Assume that you set the page directive attributes as `<%@ page buffer="8kb" autoFlush="false" %>` and that the page sends 10 KB of content to a client. When a client requests this JSP page, which of the following occurs?

a. The content is sent to the client.

b. An exception occurs and the content is not sent to the client.

c. No exception occurs but the content is not sent to the client.

d. Only the first 8 KB of content is sent to the client.

10. The JSP include _____ inserts the contents of the included file when the primary page is converted into a servlet.

11. The JSP include _____ inserts the contents of the included file each time the primary page is requested.

12. If you want a page that uses an include file to reflect the updated content of its included file, you should:

    a. use an include directive

    b. use an include action

    c. reload the page using the refresh button on browser

    d. open the page in another browser window

13. If you include a file using the include action and want to read parameters added in the include action tags (<jsp:param>) in the included file, then the included file must have the extension:

    a. .jsp

    b. .html

    c. .htm

    d. .pl

14. You insert the following JSP code segment in a JSP page: `<%! int aNum = 0; %> <% aNum++; %>`. Assume that this page has been requested 10 times by client A and 5 times by client B. The value stored in the variable aNum is:

    a. 10

    b. 15

    c. 5

    d. 0

15. You insert the following JSP code segment in a JSP page: `<% int aNum = 0; aNum++; %>`. Assume that this page has been requested 10 times by client A and 5 times by client B. The value stored in the variable aNum is:

    a. 10

    b. 15

    c. 5

    d. 0

16. Which of the following statements is correct?

    a. Variables declared in scriptlets are created every time the JSP page is requested.

    b. Variables declared in scriptlets are created only the first time the JSP page is requested.

17. Which of the following statements is correct?

    a. Variables declared in a JSP declaration are created every time the JSP page is requested.

    b. Variables declared in a JSP declaration are created the first time the JSP page is requested.

18. Which of the following comments in a JSP page is sent to the client when the page is requested?

   a. `<!--some comments -->`

   b. `<%-- some comments --%>`

   c. `<% /* some comments */ %>`

   d. `<% //some comments %>`

19. Which of the following forms of comments support(s) multiple-line comments in a JSP page? (Select all that apply.)

   a. `<!--some comments -->`

   b. `<%-- some comments --%>`

   c. `<% /* some comments */ %>`

   d. `<% //some comments %>`

20. _____ are used for documentation purposes.

HANDS-ON PROJECTS

Project 5-1 Handling Exceptions

In this project, you use the isErrorPage attribute to specify a JSP page that serves as the error-handling page.

1. Open and save the data file errorPage2.txt as **errorPage2.jsp** in the folder C:\myjspapp\chapter05.

2. Create a new document in your text editor and save it as **project1.jsp** in the folder C:\myjspapp\chapter05.

3. Add page directive and specify that exceptions will be processed in errorPage2.jsp.

4. Add the following code:

```
<HTML>
  <HEAD><TITLE>Handling Exceptions</TITLE></HEAD>
<BODY>
<%
 String sx = request.getParameter("x");
 String sy = request.getParameter("y");
 if(sx == null){
%>
This page performs the modulus operation.<br>
The expression x%y yields the remainder <br>
after x is divided by y.<br><br>
<% }
```

```
      else {
        int x = Integer.parseInt(sx);
        int y = Integer.parseInt(sy);
        int remainder = x % y;
  %>
   The <%= x %>%<%= y%> yields <%= remainder %><br><br>
  <% } %>
  Please enter two numbers in the following fields:<br>
  <form action="project1.jsp" method="POST">
   x:<input type=text name=x size=10><br>
   y:<input type=text name=y size=10><br>
   <input type=submit value=submit>
   <input type=reset>
  </form>
  </BODY>
  </HTML>
```

5. Save this file as **project1.jsp** in the folder C:\myjspapp\chapter05.

6. Load project1.jsp using the following URL:
   http://localhost:8080/myjspapp/chapter05/project1.jsp

7. Enter two numbers in the x and y input field, and then click the **Submit** button.
   The result of x%y is displayed.

8. Enter a non-numeric value in the x input field, and then click the **Submit** button.
   This time an error message is displayed, indicating that the value you entered is
   non-numeric (you may use the Back button on the tool bar of your browser and
   enter other values).

Project 5-2 The Include Directive

In this project, you use the include directive to include a file in a JSP page.

1. Open the data file newyorktemperature.txt and save it as
   newyorktemperature.jsp in the folder C:\myjspapp\chapter05.

2. Open the data file project2.txt and save it as **project2.jsp** in the folder
   C:\myjspapp\chapter05.

3. Follow the instructions within the code to add an include directive right below
   the instruction <%-- insert include directive below --%>.

4. Save the file.

5. Load project2.jsp using the following URL:
   http://localhost:8080/myjspapp/chapter05/project2.jsp

6. This page displays the temperature in New York as 89. Now change the temperature
   to 95 in the file "newyorktemperature.jsp," and reload this page by pressing **F5**, or by
   clicking the **Refresh** button on your browser. The temperate displayed is still 89. This
   occurs because you used the include directive to include a file. The included file is
   merged into the original JSP page when the original page is converted into a
   servlet, so the changed temperature is not updated in the servlet.

Project 5-3 The Include Action

In this project, you use the include action to include a file in another JSP page.

1. Open the data file project3.txt and save it as **project3.jsp** in the folder C:\myjspapp\chapter05.

2. Follow the instruction within the code to add an include action right below the instruction: `<%-- insert include action below --%>`.

3. Save the file

4. Load this page using the following URL:
   http://localhost:8080/myjspapp/chapter05/project3.jsp

5. Change the temperature in New York to 95, and refresh this page by pressing **F5**. The new temperature is displayed.

Project 5-4 Design a Guest Book Using a JSP Declaration

In this project, you design a guest book to allow users to sign in. Users can view the list of users in the guest book.

1. Open the data file project4.txt and save it as **project4.jsp** in the folder C:\myjspapp\chapter05.

2. Follow the instructions within the code to display the user list.

3. Save the file.

4. Load this page using the following URL:
   http://localhost:8080/myapp/chapter05/project4.jsp

5. You can sign the guest book or view the users in the guest book.

Project 5-5 Create News Headlines

In this project, you create news headlines using the include action. The news items are updated on the main news page automatically.

1. Create three news item files: **item1.html**, **item2.html**, and **item3.html** in the folder C:\myjspapp\chapter05, and then add some content in each of these files.

2. Create a new document in your text editor and save the file as **project5.jsp** in the folder C:\myjspapp\chapter05.

3. Add code to include the three pages, item1.html, item2.html, and item3.html, that you created in Step 1.

4. Save the file.

5. Load this page using the following URL:
   http://localhost:8080/myapp/chapter05/project5.jsp

   This page displayed should be similar to the one shown in Figure 5-9.

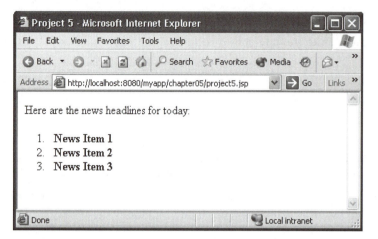

Figure 5-9   News headlines

Project 5-6 Read a File from the Local File System

In this project, you use the java.io.* package to read content from a file in the local file system and display the content on your browser.

1. Open the data file project6.txt and save as it **project6.jsp** in the folder C:\myjspapp\chapter05.

2. Follow the instructions within the code to add code to display the content read from the file.

3. Save the file.

4. Load the page project6.jsp using the following URL: http://localhost:8080/myapp/chapter05/project6.jsp

    This page is displayed as shown in Figure 5-10.

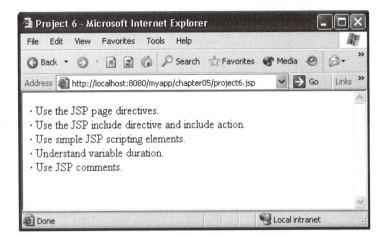

Figure 5-10   Read data from a file

Project 5-7 Write Data to a File

Sometimes you must save data collected from clients to a file on the local file system. In this project, you use the java.io.* package to interact with the file system. You use a TextArea field as an editorial tool to allow clients save data to file on the local file system.

1. Open the data file **project7.txt** and save it as **project7.jsp** in the folder C:\myjspapp\chapter05.

2. Read the code and try to understand how to read data from a file and process data by using the API from the package java.io.*

3. Load this page using the following URL: http://localhost:8080/myapp/chapter05/project7.jsp

4. Enter some text, and then click the **Submit** button. The data you entered in the TextArea is saved in the file C:\myjspapp\chapter05\project7Data.txt.

5. Open the file C:\myjspapp\chapter05\project7Data.txt to confirm that the data was stored in this file.

CASE PROJECTS

SRAS: Limiting the Number of Tries to Log on to SRAS

In the previous chapter you created a logon page for the SRAS. Now, the manager feels that this page needs to be improved so that if a user fails three times to log on to the system, instead of directing the user to try to log on again, another page is displayed that instructs the user to contact the system administrator. In this way, you can reduce the amount of unnecessary requests that are sent to the Web server. Before you can work on this project, you need to register the database used for this case as an ODBC data source.

Please note that from this chapter forward, to use the SRAS system you need to sign in on the logon page with a valid user name and password. The database includes three users and three privilege levels, as follows:

Username	Password	Privilege
1	password	administrator
2	password	faculty
3	password	student

You will learn about ODBC data sources as well as databases in Chapters 11 and 12.

1. Open the Control Panel, and from the folder list, open the folder Administrative Tools. You should see Data Sources (ODBC) in the list. Double-click Data Source (ODBC) to display the ODBC Data Source Administrator window, as shown in Figure 5-11. Select the User DSN tab if it is not selected.

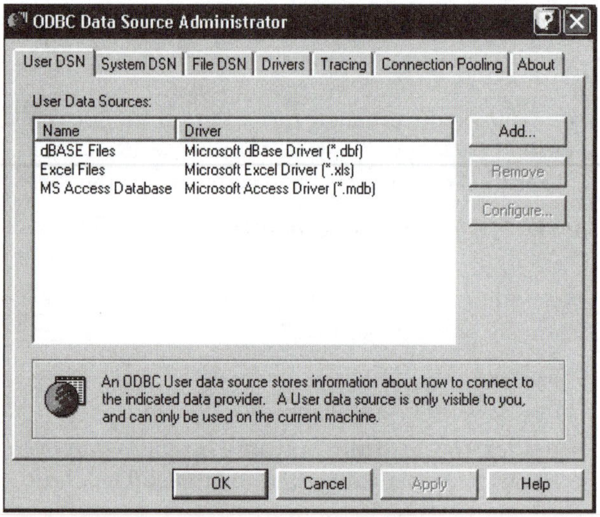

Figure 5-11   ODBC Data Source Administrator dialog box

2. Click the Add button on this window. The Create New Data Source dialog window is displayed, as shown in Figure 5-12. From the driver name list, select Driver do Microsoft Access Driver (*.mdb), then click the Finish button.

3. The Microsoft Access Setup dialog box is displayed, as shown in Figure 5-13. In the Data Source Name field, enter SRASDSN, then click the Select button to select the database you have created in the above section. Locate SRAS.mdb in the folder C:\myjspapp\chapter05\sras\, select this database, and then click OK twice to go the back to ODBC Data Source Administrator dialog box. Click OK to close the window.

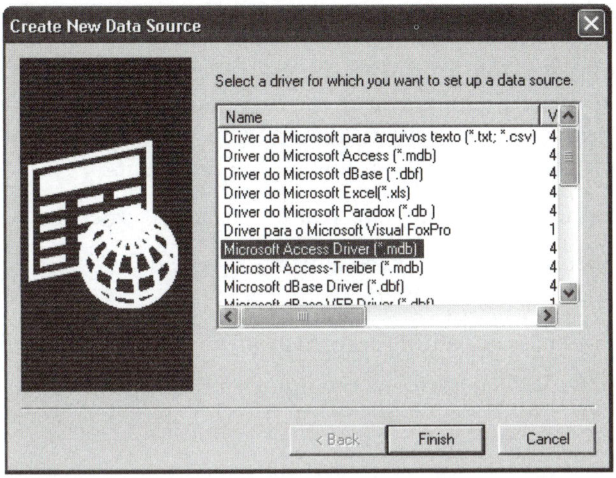

Figure 5-12   Create New Data Source dialog box

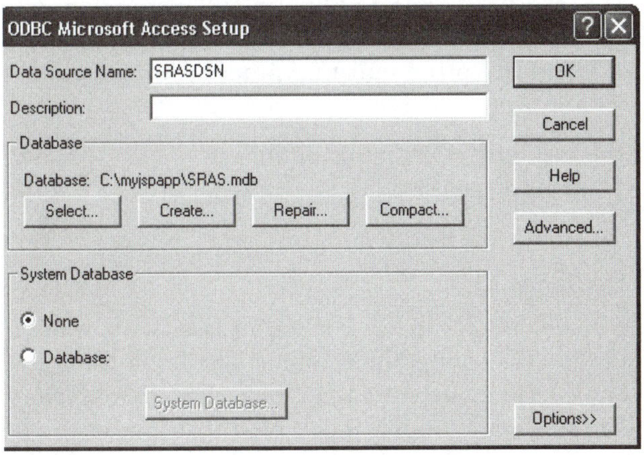

Figure 5-13   ODBC Microsoft Access Setup dialog box

Now, you have set the ODBC data source. Open the data file main.txt and save it as main.jsp in the same folder. Follow the instruction within the code to accomplish the task as specified.

Creating a Guest Book

You are asked to create a guest book for a Web site. All the guest books you have done before have a drawback: the guest data is lost if the server goes down. Therefore, your manager asks you to save the registered guests' information permanently on your local file system. The guest book should meet the following requirements:

❑ When a user signs your guest book, the data will be written to the file.

❑ A user will be able to view guests who have already signed in. The data is obtained from the file where the guest data is stored.

❑ Prevent more than one user from writing information to the guest book file.

(*Hint*: you need to import java.io.* to perform any input/output operation on your local file system.)

Online News Editing Tools

You are hired by a local news broadcast station. The manager asks you to develop a Web page to display headline news every day. The headline news is stored in four different files: item1.html, item2.html, item3.html, and item4.html. The main news page should display the four news items. To speed up the updating process, you are asked to provide the following functions:

❑ Allow reporters to edit the headline news items online

❑ Always display the updated headlines on the main news page

CT-Online

CT-Online is a startup company made up of JSP enthusiasts who want to create a compelling, up-to-the-minute site for selling books online. The book list is always subject to change. Assume that all books' names are stored in a file called "bookName.txt" in the local file system. You are asked to design a book index page that lists all the book names in that file. When the file bookName.txt is updated, the index page should always reflect the updated data.

6

PROCESSING THE CLIENT REQUEST

In this chapter, you will:

♦ Learn how to use JSP implicit objects

♦ Use the request object to obtain header, client, and server information

♦ Process form input fields using the request object

♦ Get and use arrays using the request object

♦ Control the output stream using the out object

In the previous chapter, you learned how to use page directives and simple JSP scripting elements. However, in order to make your JSP scripts function and interact with clients more effectively, you usually need to use the methods provided by objects. JSP has several implicit objects that you can use in your JSP scripts. In this chapter, you will learn how to use these objects to obtain header information and client- and server-related data, to process form input fields, and to control the output stream.

THE IMPLICIT OBJECTS

To process a client request, the Web server must execute the following steps:

1. Retrieve the data related to the request

2. Process the data

3. Send output to the client

When you use scripting elements in a JSP page, the JSP container makes a number of objects available. These objects are called **implicit objects**, because you can use them without explicitly declaring them in your page. These objects are instances of classes defined by the servlet and JSP specifications. Among these objects are:

- request
- response
- out
- session
- application
- exception

Implicit objects cannot be accessed from the JSP declaration. Using implicit variables in a JSP declaration results in compilation errors when the JSP is converted into a servlet. In this chapter, you will learn about the request, response, and out objects. The application and session objects are discussed in more detail in Chapter 7. The exception object is discussed in Chapter 10.

REQUEST OBJECT

Each time you request a JSP page, the JSP container creates a new instance of the request object. This object contains information about the request and the invoked page, including headers, client and server information, request URL, cookies, and session and input data. You have learned how to get the input data encapsulated in a form in Chapter 3. You will learn how to get other types of information from the request object in detail in the following sections.

 You can use the implicit objects in JSP expressions or scriptlets, but not in declarations.

Getting Header Information

HTTP requests can have a number of associated HTTP headers. These headers provide some extra information about the request. You can use the header information to customize the content you send to the client. There are dozens of possible headers; Table 6-1 lists several commonly used request headers.

Table 6-1 Common HTTP request headers

Header Name	Description
accept	Specifies the media type, Multipurpose Internet Multimedia Extensions (MIME), that the client prefers to accept. All media types are separated by commas.
user-agent	Gives information about the client software, including the browser name and version as well as information about the client computer. For example, Mozilla/4.0 (compatible; MSIE 6.0b; Windows NT 5.1) indicates that it is Microsoft Internet Explorer running on Windows XP.
referer	Gives the URL of the document that refers to the requested URL (that is, the document that contains the link the client followed to access this document).
accept-language	Indicates the default language setting on the client machine.

To get the value of a header, use the following syntax:

```
request.getHeader("header name");
```

This method returns a string containing information about the header passed as a parameter. For example, the code `request.getHeader("Referer")` returns the value of the header "Referer". Header names are not case sensitive, so, for example, `request.getHeader("Referer")` and `request.getHeader("referer")` are interchangeable. If a header name is not supported on a request, the getHeader method returns a null value.

The request object provides the method getHeaderNames, which returns an enumeration object containing all headers in the request. The following example illustrates how to use this method to get all header names and then use these header names to get corresponding header values.

1. In your text editor, open the data file example1.jsp, which is located in the folder C:\myjspapp\chapter06.

2. Add the code shaded in Figure 6-1.

```
<%@ page import="java.util.*" %>
<HTML>
<HEAD><TITLE>Header information</TITLE></HEAD>
<BODY>
<%
  String action = request.getParameter("action");
  if(action !=null && action.equals("getHeader")){
%>
<%
  Enumeration enu = request.getHeaderNames();
%>
<table border=1>
<tr>
  <th align=center colspan=2>Get header information using request object</th>
</tr>
<tr>
  <th align=center>Header Name</th>
  <th align=center>Header Value</td>
</tr>

<% while(enu.hasMoreElements()){
    String headerName = (String)enu.nextElement();
%>
    <tr>
      <td align=center> <%= headerName %> </td>
      <td align=center> <%= request.getHeader(headerName) %> </td>
    </tr>
<% } %>
</table>
<% } else{ %>
<a href="example1.jsp?action=getHeader">Request a page and display headers</a>
<% } %>
</BODY>
</HTML>
```

Figure 6-1 Additional code entered in example1.jsp

3. Save the file.

4. Load the page using the following URL:
   http://localhost:8080/myapp/chapter06/example1.jsp

5. Click the link on the page. The page is similar to the one shown in Figure 6-2.

In this example, `request.getHeaderNames()` returns an enumeration of all header names on the current request. Two methods associated with an enumeration object obtain all header names, and then the request object method getHeader obtains the header values.

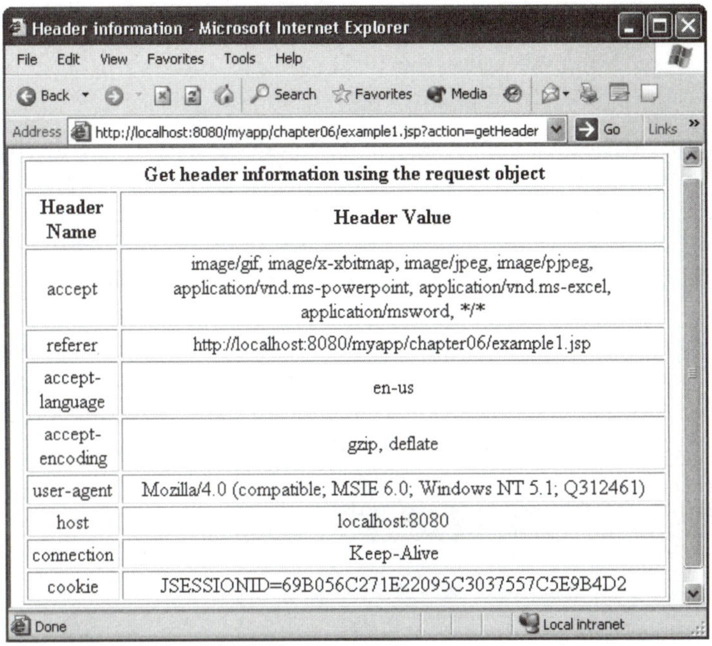

Get header information using the request object	
Header Name	Header Value
accept	image/gif, image/x-xbitmap, image/jpeg, image/pjpeg, application/vnd.ms-powerpoint, application/vnd.ms-excel, application/msword, */*
referer	http://localhost:8080/myapp/chapter06/example1.jsp
accept-language	en-us
accept-encoding	gzip, deflate
user-agent	Mozilla/4.0 (compatible; MSIE 6.0; Windows NT 5.1; Q312461)
host	localhost:8080
connection	Keep-Alive
cookie	JSESSIONID=69B056C271E22095C3037557C5E9B4D2

Figure 6-2 Header information

In some situations, you may want to send different content, depending on which browser a client uses. In this case, you must first determine the browser type. The following example illustrates how to identify the browser and send a different message based on the browser type.

1. Open a new document in your text editor, and type the following code:

```
<HTML>
<HEAD><TITLE> Detect browser</TITLE></HEAD>
<BODY>
<%  String userAgent = request.getHeader("User-Agent"); %>
<% if(userAgent.indexOf("MSIE") != -1){ %>
    You are using Internet Explorer
<% }else if(userAgent.indexOf("Netscape") != -1){ %>
    You are using Netscape Navigator
<% }else{ %>
    You are using a browser other than Netscape Navigator
or Internet Explorer
<% } %>
</BODY>
</HTML>
```

2. Save the file as **example2.jsp** in the folder C:\myjspapp\chapter06.

3. Load this page using the following URL:
   http://localhost:8080/myapp/chapter06/example2.jsp

Try to load this page in various browsers. This JSP code should detect the browser and display the appropriate message. In this example, the method of the request object getHeader("user-agent") returns a string that contains the client's browser and operating system information. If the client uses Microsoft Internet Explorer, the string should contain a substring "MSIE", so the method indexOf("MSIE") returns the index of the substring. If it returns −1, it means that the string does not contain "MSIE", and the code continues testing for other browsers. If the client browser is Netscape Navigator, the string should contain a substring "Netscape". If the client is using Netscape Navigator, the method indexOf("Netscape") should return an index of the substring other than −1. Figure 6-3 and Figure 6-4 show this page properly detecting the browsers.

Figure 6-3 Example2.jsp displayed in Internet Explorer

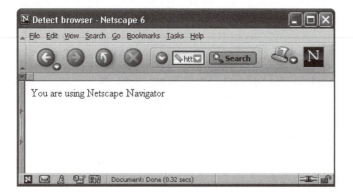

Figure 6-4 Example2.jsp displayed in Netscape Navigator

Getting Client and Server Information

Companies like to know where the visitors to their Web sites come from. With this information, a company can develop strategies to target various market segments. You can easily collect visitor information using the request object. The request object provides various methods you can use to get the client and server information, including the client computer name, client computer IP, Web server name, and Web server port. Every computer that is connected to the Internet has an IP address. The **Internet Protocol (IP)** is an identifier for a computer or device on a TCP/IP network. Networks using the TCP/IP protocol route messages according to the IP address of the destination. Computers can be given a randomly assigned IP address, or they can have a static IP address. Regardless of how it is assigned, the IP address must be unique. A computer may also have a name associated with its IP. You can get this sort of client and server information as follows: `request.getRemoteAddr()` returns the IP address of the client; `request.getRemoteHost()` returns the name of the client computer (if the computer does not have a name, the IP address is returned); `request.getServerName()` returns the Web server name; `request.getServerPort` returns the number of the port on which the Web server is running. The following example shows how to use these methods to get the client and server information.

1. In your text editor, open the data file example3.jsp, which is located in the myjspapps\chapter06 folder.

2. Add the four shaded lines of code in Figure 6-5 to get both client and server information.

```
<HTML>
<HEAD>
<TITLE>Client/server information</TITLE>
</HEAD>
<BODY>
Client Information:<br>
<font face="Arial" size=1>
Your computer name: <%= request.getRemoteHost() %> <br>
Your computer IP address: <%= request.getRemoteAddr() %>
</font>
<br><br>
The Web server information:<br>
<font face="Arial" size=1>
The Web server name: <%= request.getServerName() %><br>
The running port number of Web server: <%= request.getServerPort() %>
</font>
</BODY>
</HTML>
```

Figure 6-5 Additional code entered in the example3.jsp document

3. Save the file.

4. Load the page, using the following URL:
   http://localhost:8080/myapp/chapter06/example3.jsp

   This page displays client and Web server information, like the page shown in Figure 6-6.

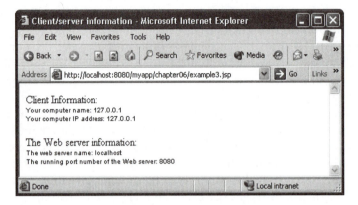

Figure 6-6   Client and Web server information

Form Collections

In previous chapters, you learned how to collect and retrieve information using forms. Now you will learn more about the elements used to build a form. These input elements include text, password, TextArea, hidden, select, checkbox, and radio inputs.

Text, Password, TextArea, and Hidden Fields

The input elements in a form can hold data that are sent to the Web server for processing. For example, when you fill in the text boxes on a form and press the Submit button, all of the values you entered are sent to the Web server.

Text fields are used to accept single-line information, such as names, addresses, job titles, telephone numbers, and so on. A text field is one of the most versatile input elements. There are three additional attributes that can be used with a text field:

- maxlength. Sets the maximum allowable length of the field, in characters

- size. Sets the width, in characters, of the input box that appears on the page

- value. Sets initial value for the text field

The following sample code creates a field that handles state abbreviations, and that includes a default value.

```
<input type="text" name="state" size="4" maxlength="2"
value="VA">
```

Notice the difference in the values for the maxlength and size attributes. The size attribute is larger, allowing for a little more display room, although the input is still limited to two characters by maxlength. This method is used to compensate for the way some browsers handle the text. If size were only two characters, certain two-letter pairs wouldn't fit in the box for display.

Password fields are similar to text fields, except that the characters typed into the text box by the user are converted to asterisk or bullet symbols for privacy. Use of password fields takes the following form:

           `<input type="password" name="fieldname">`

All the attributes associated with text fields can be applied to password fields.

Hidden fields are another type of text field, but they are not displayed. A hidden field provides a way to send information to the server that cannot be changed by the user. Hidden fields are often used to pass information from one page to another. For example, if a user types a name or address on one form, the JSP script processes it and includes it on a second follow-up form that retains the information in a hidden field. This makes it easier for the user because the user doesn't have to supply the information again. Use of hidden fields takes the following form:

           `<input type="hidden" name="fieldName" value="hidden data">`

 Even though the field is hidden from view on the browser, the user can still see it by viewing the HTML source code. Therefore, the hidden input field is not a good place to store private data.

The **TextArea** input type uses its own tag. It accepts multiple lines. A TextArea allows the user to enter larger amounts of information. The syntax for a TextArea is as follows:

           `<TextArea name="fieldname" rows="numberOfRows" cols="number`
              `OfColumns">`

           `</TextArea>`

The rows and cols attributes are used to control the number of rows and columns displayed, respectively.

In the following example, you will use all of these input fields in a Web page that posts course materials. In order to access these materials, the client must set up an account first. The example uses three pages: the first page asks a client to set up a user ID and a password, the second page collects the client's information, and the third one displays all information collected from the first two pages.

1. In your text editor, open the data file example4–1.jsp, which is located in the folder C:\myjspapp\chapter06.

2. Add the code shaded in Figure 6-7 to specify the destination file to process the data collected on the form in example4–1.jsp.

```
<HTML>
<HEAD>
<TITLE>Form collecting</TITLE>
</HEAD>
<BODY>
<form action="example4-2.jsp" method="POST">
<table align=center boder=1>
<tr><td colspan=2>Get a CT ID and password for access to course materials
online!</td>
</tr>
<tr><td colspan=2><hr width=400></td>
</tr>
<tr><td align=right>User ID:</td>
    <td align=left><input type=text name="userID" size=15></td>
</tr>
<tr><td align=right>Password:</td>
    <td align=left><input type=password name="password" size=15></td>
</tr>
<tr><td colspan=2 align=center><input type=submit value="Submit"></td>
</tr>
<tr><td colspan=2><hr width=400></td>
</tr>
</form>
</BODY>
</HTML>
```

Figure 6-7   Additional code entered in example4-1.jsp

3. Save the file.

4. In your text editor, open the data file example4-2.jsp, which is located in the folder C:\myjspapp\chapter06.

5. Enter the code shaded in Figure 6-8. The code you are required to enter retrieves the user ID and password collected on the form in example4-1.jsp and stores them as hidden fields.

```
<HTML>
<HEAD>
<TITLE>Form processing</TITLE>
</HEAD>
<BODY>
<form action="example4-3.jsp" method="POST">
<table align=center boder=1>
<tr><td colspan=2>Please provide the following information:</td>
</tr>
<tr><td colspan=2><hr width=400></td>
</tr>
```

Figure 6-8   Additional code entered in example4-2.jsp

```
<tr><td align=right>Name:</td>
    <td align=left><input type=text name="userName" size=25></td>
</tr>
<tr><td align=right>Address:</td>
    <td align=left><input type=text name=address size=25></td>
</tr>
<tr><td align=right>City:</td>
    <td align=left><input type=text name=city size=25></td>
</tr>
<tr><td align=right>State:</td>
    <td align=left>
      <input type=text name=state size=4 maxlength=2>
      Zip:<input type=text name=zip size=10 maxlength=5>
    </td>
</tr>
<tr><td colspan=2 align=center><input type=submit value="Submit"></td>
</tr>
<tr><td colspan=2><hr width=400></td>
</tr>
<!-- use hidden fields to hold the information collected from previous form-->
<input type=hidden name=userID
        value="<%= request.getParameter("userID") %>">
<input type=hidden name=password
        value="<%= request.getParameter("password") %>">
</form>
</BODY>
</HTML>
```

Figure 6-8 Additional code entered in example4-2.jsp (continued)

6. Save the file.

7. Now, you will create a file to process data collected on the form in example4-2.jsp, including hidden fields. Open the data file example4-3.jsp, which is located in the folder C:\myjspapp\chapter06. Enter the code shaded in Figure 6-9.

8. Save the file.

9. Load the page example4-1.jsp, using the following URL: http://localhost:8080/myapp/chapter06/example4-1.jsp

The page is displayed as shown in Figure 6-10.

```
<HTML>
<HEAD>
<TITLE>Form processing</TITLE>
</HEAD>
<BODY>
Here is the information collected from two previous forms:
<hr width=350 align=left>
User ID:<%= request.getParameter("userID") %><br>
Password:<%= request.getParameter("password") %><br><br>
<%= request.getParameter("userName") %><br>
<%= request.getParameter("address") %><br>
<%= request.getParameter("city") %>
, <%= request.getParameter("state") %>
 <%= request.getParameter("zip") %>
<hr width=350 align=left>
</BODY>
</HTML>
```

Figure 6-9   Additional code entered in example4-3.jsp

10. Enter a user ID and password and click the **Submit** button. The example4-2.jsp file is requested and displayed, as shown in Figure 6-11, for example. The user ID and password information is retrieved and stored in hidden fields on the form in example4-2.jsp.

11. Enter a name and address and click the **Submit** button to send the data collected on the form, as well as the hidden data, to example4-3.jsp. Example4-3.jsp retrieves and displays data, as shown, for example, in Figure 6-12. That is, the third page retrieves all information collected on the first two forms and displays the information.

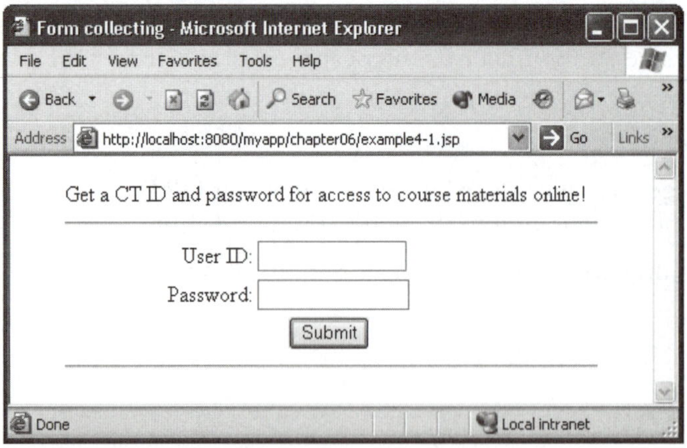

Figure 6-10   Example4-1.jsp

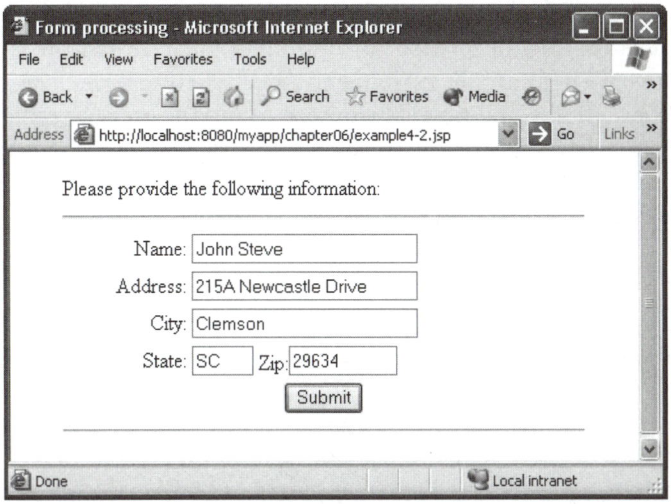

Figure 6-11   Example4-2.jsp

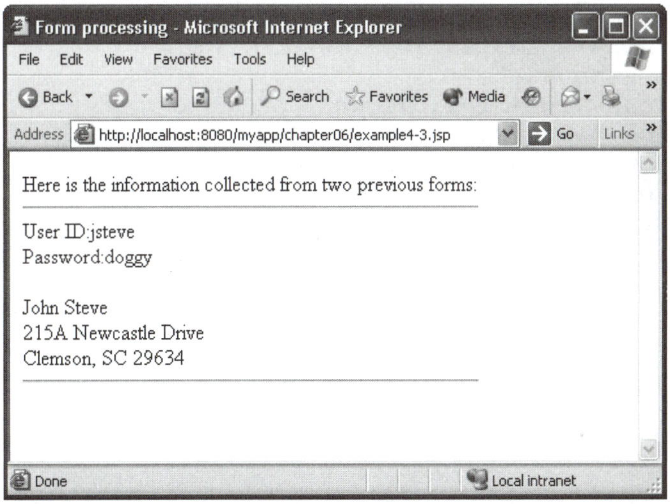

Figure 6-12   Example4-3.jsp

Select Fields

The **select** input field uses the <select> and </select> tags to provide a list of options from which the user may select. Your browser displays a <select> field as a drop-down list box. The use of select input fields takes the following syntax:

```
<select name="fieldname" size=n multiple>
<option value="value" selected>Option1 text
...additional options
</select>
```

The size attribute controls how many lines are visible at one time. If you don't specify a value, the size defaults to 1. If the number of options is greater than the size, a drop-down list box is displayed. The multiple attribute controls whether users may select multiple items from the list. If the multiple attribute is omitted, only one item may be selected.

 To select multiple items from a scrolling list, hold down the Ctrl key and click the items you want to select.

The option tag is used to add items. It can contain two optional attributes: selected and value. The value attribute of the selected item is submitted as the value of the select field. The option text is the text that follows each option tag. The option text is displayed on the list. If the value attribute is not specified, the value of that option defaults to its option text.

1. Open a new document in your text editor, and type in the following code:

```
<HTML>
<HEAD><TITLE>Select input field</TITLE></HEAD>
<BODY>
<form action="example5.jsp" method=POST>
  <select name=state>
    <option value=MI>Michigan
    <option value=NC>North Carolina
    <option >South Carolina
    <option value=VA selected>Virginia
  </select>
  <input type=submit value="submit this form">
</form>
</BODY>
</HTML>
```

2. Save the file as **example5.html** in the folder C:\myjspapp\chapter06.

3. Open a new document in your text editor and type in the following code:

```
<HTML>
<HEAD><TITLE>Processing select field</TITLE></HEAD>
<BODY>
The state value you selected is:
<%= request.getParameter("state") %>
<br><br>
<a href="example5.html">Go back and try again</a>
</BODY>
</HTML>
```

4. Save the file as **example5.jsp** in the folder C:\myjspapp\chapter06.

5. Load example5.html, using the following URL:
   http://localhost:8080/myapp/chapter06/example5.html

In this example, the selected option defaults to "Virginia". You may select another item and submit the form. The selected option value is displayed. Because the value attribute for "South Carolina" is not set, if you select "South Carolina" from the list, the option text is displayed.

Checkboxes and Radio Buttons

The **checkbox** input element is a small box that the user clicks to place or remove a check mark. The use of checkboxes takes the following syntax:

<input type=checkbox name="fieldname" value="a value"
CHECKED>Descriptive text

The value is what is sent to the Web server if a checkbox is checked. The CHECKED attribute controls the initial status of the checkbox. Following a checkbox, descriptive text indicates what the user is selecting (or not).

 The descriptive text for a checkbox usually comes after the checkbox, but it doesn't matter whether you put it before or after its corresponding checkbox.

Radio buttons are similar to checkboxes, but they present a range of choices. Only one radio button in a group is selected at one time. The use of radio buttons takes the following syntax:

<input type=radio name="fieldname" value="field value"
checked>Descriptive text

The following example illustrates how to use checkboxes and radio buttons.

1. In your text editor, open the data file example6.jsp, which is located in the folder C:\myjspapp\chapter06.

2. Enter the shaded code shown in Figure 6-13, which adds two radio buttons and four checkboxes.

```
<HTML>
<HEAD>
<TITLE>Checkbox and radio button</TITLE>
</HEAD>
<BODY>
<% String gender = request.getParameter("gender");
   String music = request.getParameter("music");
   if( gender !=null){
%>
    Gender: <%= gender %><br>
<% }
   if(music != null) {
%>
   Music types you listen to:<%= music %>
<% } %>
<hr width=250 align=left>
<form action="example6.jsp" method="POST">
  Gender:
    <input type=radio name=gender value="Female">Female
    <input type=radio name=gender value="Male">Male
  <br><br>
  What types of music do you listen to?<br>
  <input type=checkbox name=music value=Rock>Rock
  <input type=checkbox name=music value=Jazz>Jazz
  <input type=checkbox name=music value=Classical>Classical
  <input type=checkbox name=music value=Pop>Pop
  <br><br>
  <input type=submit value="Submit">
</form>
<hr width=250 align=left>
</BODY>
</HTML>
```

Figure 6-13   Additional code entered in the example6.jsp document

3. Save the file.

4. Load the page, using the following URL:
   http://localhost:8080/myapp/chapter06/example6.jsp

5. Select a gender, click to check the music type(s) you listen to, and click the
   Submit button. The information should be displayed on the top of the page,
   as on the page shown in Figure 6-14.

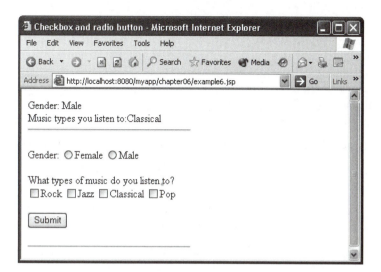

Figure 6-14 Working with checkboxes and radio buttons

In the example above, if you check more than one music type, only the first checked music type is displayed. For example, if you check all music types and submit the form, then you see that only the first music type is displayed. In the following section, you will learn how to handle multiple checkbox selections.

Working with Arrays

The JSP script you wrote in the previous example can't retrieve more than one selected music type. To fix this problem, you could assign each checkbox a different name, but this is not the most efficient method.

In fact, a similar problem arises whenever multiple values are associated with a single object. Fortunately, the request object provides another method that you can use to get all the values associated with a single form element. The syntax is as follows:

```
request.getParameterValues("elementName");
```

This method returns a String array containing all values associated with the element. If the element name does not exist in the requesting form—that is, no checkbox or radio button has been selected—it returns null. To access these values, you must use an array. For example, to get all checked music types in the previous example, you can use the following code:

```
<% String music[] = request.getParameterValues("music");
    if(music != null && music.length != 0){
        out.println("Music types you listen to: <br>");
        for(int i=0; i<music.length; i++){
```

```
                                   out.println(music[i] + "<br>");
                    }
              }
        %>
```

Before you go on to process the array, you must check whether the array is null or not. If you try to manipulate a null array, an exception occurs. Typically, you use a repetition structure to go through the array and extract each value.

The following example illustrates how to get all values associated with a select field.

1. In your text editor, open the file example7.jsp, which is located in the folder C:\myjspapp\chapter06.

2. Add the shaded code shown in Figure 6-15, which retrieves all values associated with an input field as an array and processes the array.

```
<HTML>
<HEAD><TITLE>Multiple values of a select field</TITLE></HEAD>
<BODY>
What are your favorite fruits?<br>
<form action="example7.jsp" method="POST">
   <select name="fruits" size=4 MULTIPLE>
     <option value="Apple">Apple
     <option value="Grape">Grape
     <option value="Banana">Banana
     <option value="Orange">Orange
     <option value="Peach">Peach
   </select>
   <br>
   <input type=submit value="Submit">
</form>
<hr width=200 align=left>
Your favorite fruits list:<br>
<%
   String fruit[] = request.getParameterValues("fruits");
   if(fruit != null && fruit.length != 0){
     for(int i=0; i<fruit.length; i++){
       out.println(fruit[i] + "<br>");
     }
   }
%>
</BODY>
</HTML>
```

Figure 6-15 Additional code added in the file example7.jsp

3. Save the file.

4. Load the page, using the following URL:
   http://localhost:8080/myapp/chapter06/example7.jsp

5. Select more than one fruit type and submit the form; all selected fruit types are displayed on your favorite fruit list. (Use the Shift or Ctrl keys to select multiple items from the list.)

The code `String fruit[] = request.getParameterValues("fruits")` gets all selected values and assigns the returned values to an array. Then an if statement is used to test whether the value returned is null. If the returned value is not null, a for loop navigates all elements of the array, and then displays your favorite fruit types list.

As for the select field, if the size is set to 1, or the size attribute is omitted (the default value is 1), the first item on the list is selected by default; if the size is set to a value other than 1, no item is selected by default.

You can use the getParameterValues() method on all form elements. It returns an array containing values associated with the elements that have the same name attribute.

Before you process an array returned by the getParameterValues() method, you must check whether the array is null. If you try to access an array that is null, an exception occurs.

The names of request object input fields are case sensitive. For example, "UserID" and "userID" are treated as two different parameters when used in the method getParameter.

The request object also has a getParamterNames() method. This method returns an enumeration object containing all the names of request parameters (the name attributes of all fields on a form). The returned value is an enumeration object. This function is useful if the form is generated dynamically and the JSP page does not know in advance all the names of the fields in the form. The following example illustrates how to use the getParameterNames() method to retrieve all field names on a form.

1. In your text editor, open the file example8.jsp, which is located in the folder C:\myjspapp\chapter06.

2. Add the shaded code shown in Figure 6-16, which retrieves all field names encapsulated in the request.

```
<%@ page import="java.util.*"%>
<HTML>
<HEAD>
<TITLE>Using getParameterNames() method</TITLE>
</HEAD>
<BODY>
<%
<%
  Enumeration names = request.getParameterNames();
    while(names.hasMoreElements()){
      String name = (String)names.nextElement();
      out.println(name+"<br>");
    }
%>
<hr width=250 align=left>
<form action="example8.jsp" method="POST">
  Gender: <input type=radio name=gender value="Female">Female
          <input type=radio name=gender value="Male">Male
  <br><br>
  What types of music do you listen to?<br>
  <input type=checkbox name=music value=Rock>Rock
  <input type=checkbox name=music value=Jazz>Jazz
  <input type=checkbox name=music value=Classical>Classical
  <input type=checkbox name=music value=Pop>Pop
  <br><br>
  <input type=submit value="Submit">
</form>
</BODY>
</HTML>
```

Figure 6-16   Additional code added to the file example8.jsp

3. Save the file.

4. Load the page, using the following URL:
   http://localhost:8080/myapp/chapter06/example8.jsp

5. Check gender and music types and submit the form. Your page should look like the one shown in Figure 6-17. The field names on the form are displayed on the top of this page.

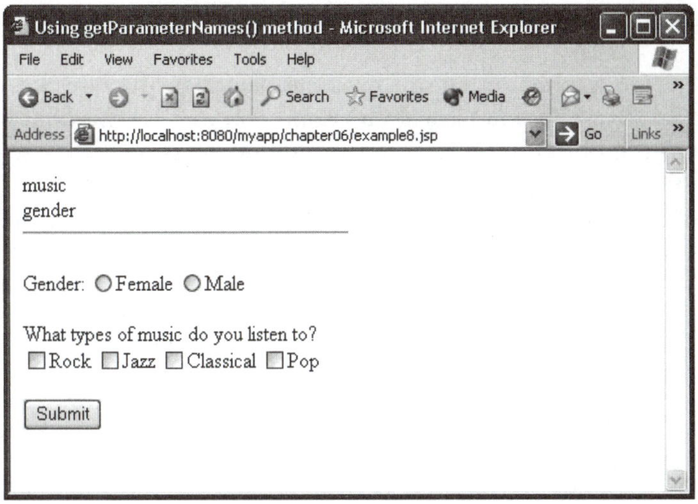

Figure 6-17 Using the getParameterNames() method

RESPONSE OBJECT

The response object controls output that the server sends to the client. It is an instance of the javax.servlet.http.ServletResponse class, which is imported automatically when your JSP page is converted into a servlet. The response object provides methods that you can use in your JSP script to set headers, add cookies, and control how information is returned to clients.

Cookies

Many commercial Web sites store information on client computers. For example, if you have a Yahoo e-mail account, you might notice a checkbox on the logon page asking whether you want to remember your ID on this computer. If you select this checkbox, you are not required to enter your user ID when you log on again. This kind of information stored on the client machine is called a cookie. A **cookie** is a small piece of textual information that a Web site sends to a browser, and that the browser returns to the same Web server during a later visit. It can contain an encoded username and password, shopping-cart contents, user identification, and so on. A cookie is a name and value pair and has several attributes, such as maximum age, which indicates how long the cookie should remain on the client's computer; domain, which specifies what Web server can access the cookie; and path, which specifies the URL of the resource on the server that can see the cookie. The response object provides a method to add a cookie to the response header. You will learn how to create and use cookies in Chapter 7.

THE OUT OBJECT

You use the out object to send an output stream to the client. The out object is an instance of javax.servlet.jsp.JspWriter. As you have always done, you can use the print and println methods provided by this object to add text to the response message body. The out object is usually used within scriptlets (within the symbols <% and %>), when it is convenient. You may use a JSP expression to output text to the output stream. For example, when you embed a message generated from JSP code into HTML content (for example, to output the value of a variable), it might be more appropriate to use a JSP expression. But there are many circumstances where the print/println methods may be more convenient. For example, look at the following JSP script:

```
<%
  int sum = 0;
  for(int i =0; i<=9; i++)
         {
           sum = sum +i;
           out.println("sum is:"+sum);
         }
%>
```

This scriptlet uses the out object to print the running total of integer values from zero to nine. If you want to use a JSP expression to do this, then you must break down the scriptlet to insert the JSP expression, as follows:

```
<%
          for (int i=0 ; i<=9; i++){
                sum += i;
%>
                sum is <%= sum %>
<% } %>
```

So it is more appropriate to use the println() method in this case.

Flushing Buffered Content

In Chapter 5, you learned how to set the buffer size in a page directive. The size you specify is the minimum buffer size. The JSP container may use a larger buffer than the one you specify. So the content is accumulated in the buffer to at least the specified buffer size, or until the page is complete, before it is sent to the client, or flushed. However, you can at any point in your code use the flush method to force buffered content to be flushed, regardless of the specified buffer size. To force buffered content to be flushed, use the following syntax:

out.flush()

It is not necessary to use the flush method when the buffer attribute is set to none. However, the JSP container may still do some buffering even if you disable the buffering, and you can still use the flush method to force the buffered content to be sent immediately.

 When buffered content exceeds specified buffer size, the container may indirectly invoke the flush method to flush the buffer.

Clearing the Buffer

You can write JSP script to erase the buffered content. The out object provides two methods to clear the buffered content. They take the following syntax:

```
out.clear()
and:
out.clearBuffer()
```

Both methods can be used to clear the contents of the buffer.

The following example illustrates how to control the output stream by using the flush and clear methods.

1. Open a new document in your text editor, and type in the following code:

```
<%@ page buffer="8kb" %>
<HTML><HEAD><TITLE>Control output stream</TITLE></HEAD>
<BODY>
This message is buffered.<br>
Flush buffered content now.<br>
<%
  out.flush();
%>
Previously buffered content has been sent.<br>
New content is buffered.<br>
Erase buffered content now.
<%
  out.clearBuffer();
%>
<br><br>
The second buffered content is erased and this message is
 buffered.<br>
After this page is complete, buffered content is flushed.
</BODY>
</HTML>
```

2. Save the file as **example9.jsp** in the folder C:\myjspapp\chapter06.

3. Load the page, using the following URL:
   http://localhost:8080/myapp/chapter06/example9.jsp

   The page is displayed as shown in Figure 6-18.

Figure 6-18   Clearing the buffer

The buffer size is set to 8 KB (the default buffer size), so the response content must be buffered to at least the specified buffer size before it is flushed. The message is far smaller than the buffer size, so it is stored in the buffer until the flush method is called. Calling the flush method forces the buffered content to be sent immediately, so the content is displayed on your browser. Then the content accumulates in the buffer again. But calling clearFlush erases the buffered content; then the last message is buffered. When the page is complete, the buffered content is sent to the output stream and is displayed on your browser. That is why only the first and last paragraphs are displayed.

Closing the Output Stream

The out object provides a method that allows you to explicitly stop output that is being sent to the client. This method has the following syntax:

    out.close()

When this method is called, the buffered content is flushed before the output stream is closed. In fact, the JSP container automatically includes a call to close the output stream when a page is complete.

Once the output stream has been closed, calling the close method has no effect, but calling the flush method generates an exception. The following example illustrates how to use the close method to close an output stream.

1. Open a new document in your text editor, and type in the following code:

```
<%@ page buffer="8kb" %>
<HTML><HEAD><TITLE>Explicitly close the output stream
</TITLE></HEAD>
<BODY>
Messages that appear before closing the output stream<br>
```

```
Close the output stream now.<br>
<%
  out.close();
%>
The output stream has been closed. So this content will
not be sent to client.
</BODY>
</HTML>
```

2. Save the file as **example10.jsp** in the folder C:\myapp\chapter06\ example10.jsp

3. Load the page, using the following URL:
   http://localhost:8080/myapp/chapter6/example10.jsp

   The page is displayed as shown in Figure 6-19.

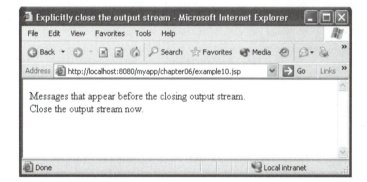

Figure 6-19   Closing the output stream

So, the out object enables the buffering of output content for the JSP page. Buffering gives the JSP programmer control when handling the output data. It allows the entire page to be processed before it is sent out to the browser, so when something goes wrong, you can abort the current page. Or you can send whatever is ready to the browser as soon as possible.

CHAPTER SUMMARY

- ❐ The request object provides methods that allow you to retrieve header information as well as information about the client and server.

- ❐ There are many input fields you can use to collect information from clients. The information is sent to and processed on the Web server. The request object provides methods to retrieve input field information.

❐ The request object provides a method that allows you to access all values associated with the same field name on the form. The method returns all values as an array.

❐ The response object provides a method that you can use to create cookies.

❐ The out object provides a variety of methods that allow you to control how response data are sent back to clients.

REVIEW QUESTIONS

1. The JSP container makes available several objects you can use to facilitate the processing of client requests. These objects are called (choose all that apply):

   a. implicit objects

   b. implicit variables

   c. predefined objects

   d. predefined classes

2. Which of the following objects can provide information about a client browser?

   a. response

   b. out

   c. request

   d. cookie

3. The method request.getHeaderNames() returns _____.

   a. an enumeration object

   b. a string

   c. an array

   d. null

4. The parameter passed to the method `request.getHeader("headerName")` is case sensitive. True or False?

5. Which of the following headers contains the user's browser information?

   a. user-agent

   b. accept

   c. referer

   d. accept-language

6. Which of the following input fields is not displayed on your browser?

   a. text

   b. password

   c. TextArea

   d. hidden

7. If the size and maxlength attributes are set to 10 and 6, respectively, the maximum number of characters you can enter in this text field is:

   a. 10

   b. 6

   c. 4

   d. 16

8. Calling the method `request.getParameterValues("products")` returns (choose all that apply):

   a. a String array

   b. an enumeration object

   c. a string

   d. null

9. If the size attribute of a select field is not specified, then the first item on the option list is selected by default. True or False?

10. If the size attribute of a select field is set to 4, which of the following statements is correct?

    a. The first item is selected by default.

    b. The last item is selected by default.

    c. The first four items are selected by default.

    d. No default item is selected.

11. Which of the following input fields is often used to pass information from one form to another form on a different page?

    a. text

    b. TextArea

    c. hidden

    d. password

12. There are five checkboxes on a form and all of them have the same name, music. Assume all of them are checked. The code `request.getParameter("music")` on the Web server returns _____.

    a. a string containing all values of the five checkboxes

    b. a string containing the value of the first checkbox

    c. null

    d. a String array containing all values of the five checkboxes

6

13. A cookie takes which of the following formats?

    a. text

    b. image

    c. executable

    d. none of the above

14. Which of the following output methods is more convenient if you want to simply insert the value of a variable into plain HTML code?

    a. a JSP expression

    b. the println method of the out object

15. The message "Hello World!" is buffered but has not been sent out yet. Calling the method out.close() results in the following (choose all that apply):

    a. The message is sent to the client and displayed on the browser.

    b. The buffered content is discarded.

    c. No further content is buffered.

    d. No further content is written to the output stream.

16. Calling the clearBuffer() method of the out object will cause all buffered contents to be sent to the client. True or False?

17. The flush method of the out object causes all buffered content to be flushed immediately. True or False?

18. Which of the following statements is true?

    a. The name attribute of a field must be set in order for the Web server to be able to retrieve the value associated with that field.

    b. The value attribute of a password field must be set.

    c. You cannot assign a default value to a TextArea field.

    d. All radio buttons with the same name belong to the same group.

19. Which of the following is used to set the default selected item for a select field?

    a. selected

    b. checked

    c. multiple

    d. size=1

20. Which of the following packages is/are imported automatically when a JSP page is converted into a servlet?

    a. java.util.*

    b. java.lang.*

    c. javax.servlet.*

    d. javax.servlet.jsp.*

    e. javax.servlet.http.*

HANDS-ON PROJECTS

Project 6-1 Working with Select Input Field Elements

In this project, you will design a form and add two select fields with different attributes, to provide a list of options. (*Hint:* You may use Figure 6-13 to design this page.)

1. Open a new document in your text editor and save it as **project1.jsp** in the folder C:\myjspapp\chapter06.

2. Add the basic HTML tags as indicated below:

```
<HTML>
<HEAD>
<TITLE>Select Input Field</TITLE>
</HEAD>
<BODY>
```

3. Add an HTML form. The action is set to the same page because this page will collect and process the form information.

4. Add two select elements with different names. Specify the size attribute of the first select element to 1, the second one to 4. Then add the following option list for both of the select elements as follows:

```
<option value="Apple">Apple
<option value="Grape">Grape
<option value="Banana">Banana
<option value="Orange">Orange
<option value="Peach">Peach
```

5. Add JSP code to retrieve the selected item from the select elements and store the retrieved data in two variables.

6. Output the data collected on the form.

7. Add the following HTML tags to complete this file:

```
</BODY>
</HTML>
```

8. Save the file.

9. Load the page using the following URL:
   http://localhost:8080/myapp/chapter06/project1.jsp

10. Without selecting any item from either select field, click the **Submit** button. The default item values are displayed, as shown in Figure 6-20.

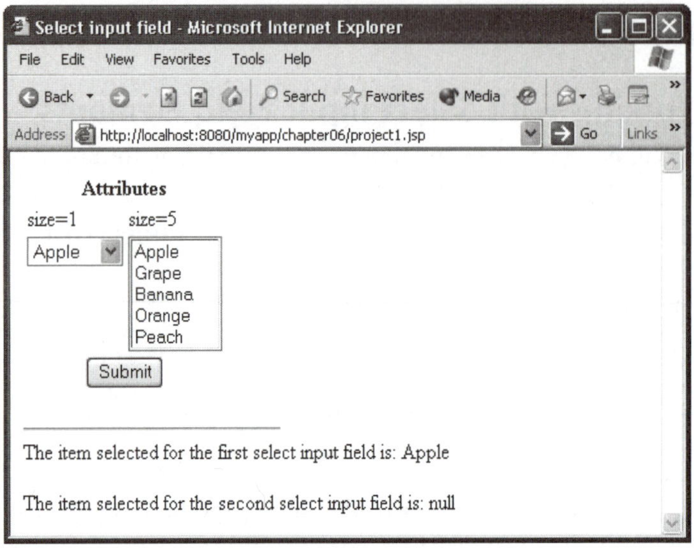

Figure 6-20 Select elements

Notice that if the size attribute is not set, the first item is selected by default. Otherwise, no default item is selected.

Project 6-2 Checkbox and Select Fields

In this project, you will design a virtual library search criteria Web page. This project contains two pages. The first page is used to collect search criteria; the second page is for retrieving information collected from the first page. There are two kinds of form elements, checkbox and select. The group of checkbox fields, named "categories", allow a user to specify which categories to browse. The select field lets the user choose multiple options from different topics.

1. Design an HTML page, as shown in Figure 6–21, and save this file as **project2.html** in the folder C:\myjspapp\chapter06.

2. Create another file to process data collected on the form in project6.html and display these data on the page you created in Step 1. If a user did not select any topics from the topic list, display a message to indicate this.

3. Load project2.html, using the following URL:
   http://localhost:8080/myapp/chapter06/project2.html

   This page should look like the one shown in Figure 6–21.

4. Specify the categories and topics and submit the form. The specified search criteria are then displayed, as shown in Figure 6-22.

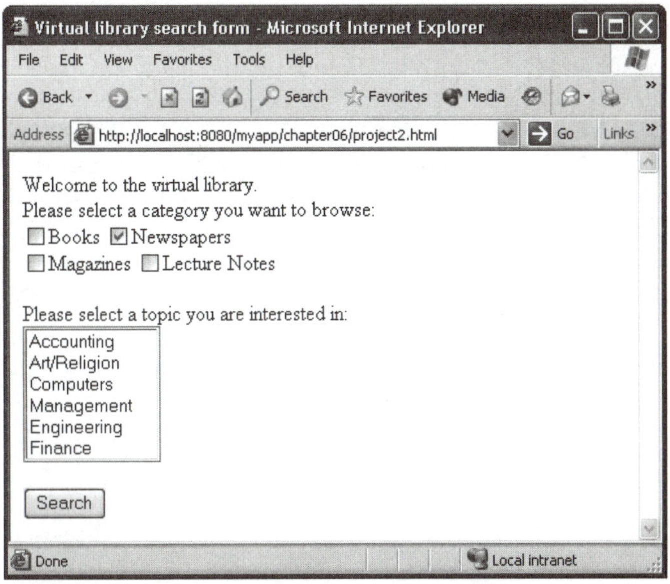

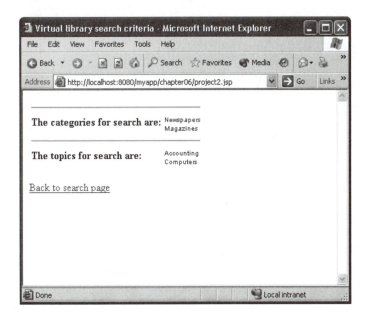

Figure 6-21   Specifying search criteria form

Figure 6-22   Processing search form data

6

Project 6-3 Working with an Array

In order to retrieve values associated with an input field, the name attribute must be set. You can use the method request.getParameter("fieldname") to retrieve whatever is collected from that field. However, when there is more than one value attached to that field, this method returns only the first available value. In fact, different input fields can have the same name attribute. In such a case, the method will return the value of the first element of the name. To get all values, you can use request.getParameterValues("fieldname"). This method returns all values associated with the fields that have the same name attribute. In this project, all input fields have the same name attribute, so you must use the second method to get all values.

1. Open the data file project3.jsp, which is located in the folder C:\myjspapp\ chapter06.

2. Add JSP code to collect data, and display the data right after the horizontal line on this page.

3. Save the file.

4. Load the page, using the following URL:
   http://localhost:8080/myapp/chapter06/project3.jsp

5. Fill in data for all input fields and submit the form. A page like the one shown in Figure 6-23 is displayed.

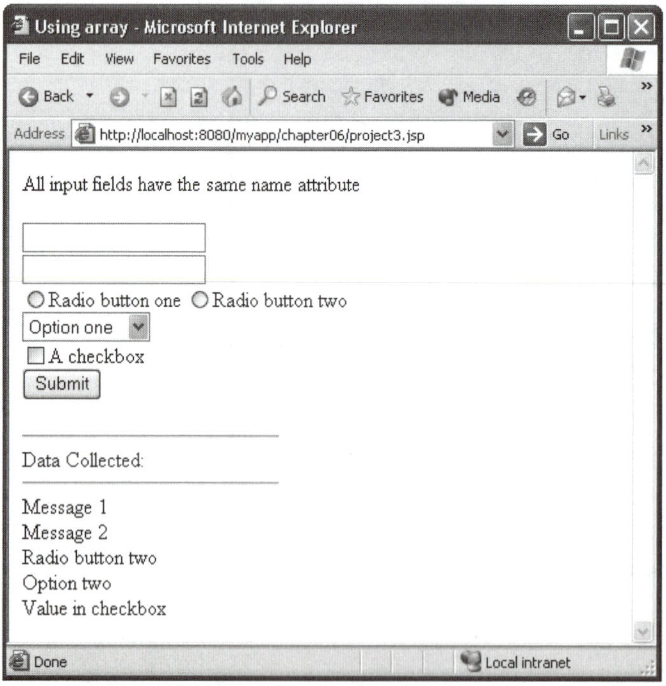

![Using array - Microsoft Internet Explorer window. Address: http://localhost:8080/myapp/chapter06/project3.jsp. Text reads "All input fields have the same name attribute" with two text input boxes, two radio buttons "Radio button one" and "Radio button two", a dropdown "Option one", a checkbox "A checkbox", and a Submit button. Below a horizontal line: "Data Collected:" followed by "Message 1", "Message 2", "Radio button two", "Option two", "Value in checkbox".]

Figure 6-23   Working with an array

Project 6-4 Get All Field Names and Their Values

In this project, you use getParameterNames() to retrieve all field names, and then use these names to get their corresponding values.

1. Open the data file project4.txt and save it as **project4.html** in the folder C:\myjspapp\chapter06. This page contains a form with several input fields. The data collected on the form will be sent to project4.jsp.

2. Create a new document in your text editor, and save it as **project4.jsp**.

3. Add code to retrieve the input field names, as specified in the file project4.html, by using the method getParameterNames(), and use the names with the method getParameter() to get the values corresponding to these names. Then display these input field names and their values in an HTML table.

4. Save the file.

5. Load the page project4.html, using the following URL:
   http://localhost:8080/myapp/chapter06/project4.html

6. Fill in the form and submit the form. If you entered text in both of the text input fields, only the data entered in the first text input field are displayed.

Project 6-5 Get All Values Associated with an Input Field

In Project 6-4, you miss some values if there is more than one value associated with an input field. For example, the two text input fields have the same name, so only the data in the first text input field are retrieved. In this project, you will modify Project 6-4 so all values will be retrieved.

1. Open the data file project4.txt and save it as **project5.html** in the folder C:\myjspapp\chapter06.

2. Change the action in the form to project5.jsp.

3. Open project5.jsp, which is located in the folder C:\myjspapp\chapter06.

4. Add the following code right below the horizontal line tag on the page, to get all input field names and retrieve all values associated with each input name, then display these names and values in an HTML table:

```
<table>
  <tr><th>Field Name</th><th>Input Field Value</th>
  </tr>
<%
    // get all field names.
    Enumeration allNames = request.getParameterNames();
    while(allNames.hasMoreElements()){
      String name=(String)allNames.nextElement();
      out.println("<tr><td>" + name +"</td><td>");
```

6

```
String[] values = request.getParameterValues(name);
if(values == null)
  out.println(" </td></tr>");
else{
  for(int i=0; i<values.length; i++){
    out.println(values[i] + "<br>");
  }
  out.println("</td></tr>");
}
}
%>
</table>
```

5. Save the page.

6. Load project5.html, using the following URL:
   http://localhost:8080/myapp/chapter06/project6.html

Project 6-6 Invoice Generator

In this project, you will provide a form that allows a client to enter items purchased and amounts; an invoice is then generated based on the data entered. Use Figure 6-24 and Figure 6-25 as guidelines to complete this project. Figure 6-24 lists three items and three input fields corresponding to these items. After a user enters a quantity of each item to buy and clicks the Submit button, an invoice is generated, as shown in Figure 6-25.

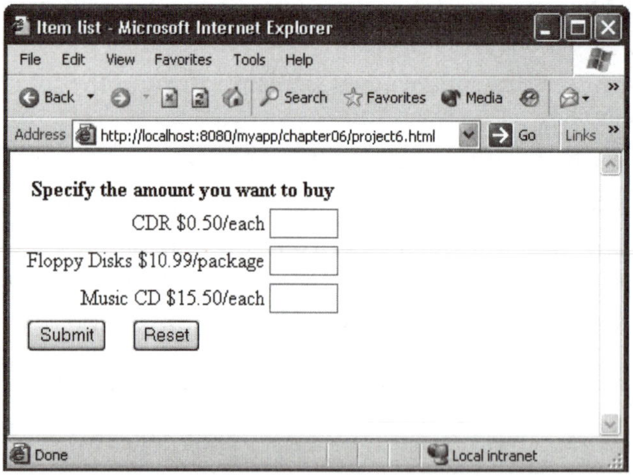

Figure 6-24   Item list

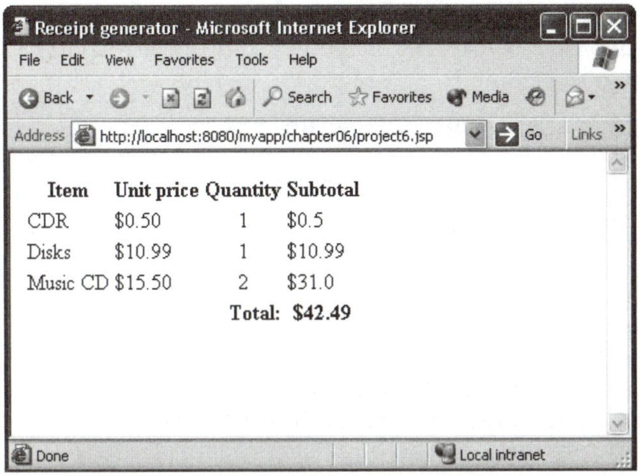

Figure 6-25   Invoice

1. In the folder C:\myjspapp\chapter06, create an HTML form called **project6.html** that lists all items (list at least three items). Each item is followed by a text input field to allow customers to enter the quantity.

2. Provide the unit price for each item.

3. In the same folder, create another file called **project6.jsp** that is used to process data collected from the form in project6.html. This page is used to retrieve data collected from the form and generate an invoice for the client.

4. The invoice should include the item name, quantity, unit price, subtotal for each item, and total price. Then calculate the tax based on a tax rate of 5%, and show the total charge for the purchase.

Project 6-7 Tracking Visitors

In this project, you will track whether a visitor is accessing your page for the first time. If it is the first visit, display a message saying so; otherwise, welcome the visitor back.

1. Create a new document in your text editor, and save the file as **project7.jsp** in the folder C:\myjspapp\chapter06.

2. Add the following code to import the java.io.* package and basic HTML tags:

```
<%@ page import="java.io.*" %>
<HTML>
<HEAD><TITLE>Tracking visitors</TITLE></HEAD>
<BODY>
```

3. Write JSP code to get remote IP address:

```
<%
    String userIP = request.getRemoteAddr();
%>
```

4. Add the following code to check whether a user is visiting this page for the first time or has visited this page before. If it is the first time, display a message saying so; otherwise, display a "welcome back" message.

```
String vPath = "chapter06/tracking.txt";
    String rPath=
getServletConfig().getServletContext().getRealPath(vPath);
    FileInputStream fis =
     new FileInputStream(rPath);
    InputStreamReader in = new InputStreamReader(fis);
    BufferedReader br = new BufferedReader(in);
    String tempIP=null;
    boolean found = false;
    while( (tempIP=br.readLine())!=null){
       if(tempIP.equalsIgnoreCase(userIP)){
           found=true;
           break;
       }
    }
    br.close();;
    if(found){
       out.println("You have visited this Web site"+
               "before.<br>");
       out.println("<h2>Welcome back!</h2>");
    }else{
       out.println("This is your first visit"+
               "to this site.<br>");
       out.println("<h2>Welcome!</h2>");
       // if this is the first visit to this page,
       // write user's IP to the files
       FileOutputStream fos =
          new FileOutputStream(rPath, true);
       PrintStream ps = new PrintStream(fos);
       ps.println(userIP);
       ps.close();
    }
%>
</BODY>
</HTML>
```

5. Save the file.

6. Load the page, using the following URL:
   http://localhost:8080/myapp/chapter06/project7.jsp

7. Because this is your first visit to the page, the system displays a greeting message.

8. Reload the page; the system welcomes you back.

Project 6-8 Design an HTML Page

In this project, you will use JSP script to design an HTML page that contains a form.

1. Open the data file project8.jsp, which is located in the folder C:\myjspapp\ chapter06. Go through the code to understand how to design HTML pages using JSP code.

2. Add code to the first while loop by following the instructions provided.

3. Save the file.

4. Load the page, using the following URL: http://localhost:8080/myapp/chapter06/project8.jsp

   The page is displayed as shown in Figure 6-26.

5. Select a field type and provide a name and default value for that field, then click the **Add Field** button to add fields to the form to be created.

6. Click the **Complete** button to create a form.

7. Click the link to the newly created form.

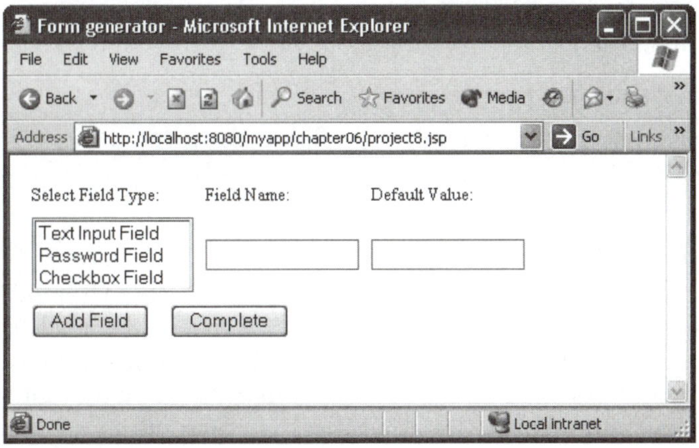

6

Figure 6-26   Designing a HTML page online

Validation in this project is minimal. Otherwise, the code would be much longer. You may add or modify the code to make this project more robust.

CASE PROJECTS

SRAS: Edit Profile

In a previous chapter, you added functionality to the SRAS project by providing a link to allow users to edit their profiles. In this project, you will complete the profile-editing page. You will also design a header file that is included on all pages except the main.jsp page. The header file will contain links to all pages that the user is allowed to view (remember that different user types have different access privileges to the SRAS). However, the header should not include a link to the page on which it is included. For example, when a user views the profile.jsp page, the header should not include a link to the profile.jsp page. Modify the data file profile.jsp, which is located in the folder C:\myjspapp\chapter06\sras. Add code to validate the password, which must contain at least five and no more than 15 characters. Create a header.jsp, file that meets the requirements specified above, and then include header.jsp in the file profile.jsp so the links are displayed on the top of the profile.jsp page.

Joe's Pizzeria

A small pizza place, Joe's Pizzeria, is interested in reaching customers via the Internet. You are hired to develop a Web page that allows customers to place orders online. On this Web page, the customer is asked to specify the following information:

❑ the pizza size (small, medium, or large)

❑ the number of pizzas

❑ the preferred toppings

❑ the delivery method (pickup, deliver)

After the client provides all the information and submits the form, the information collected from the form is displayed.

Music Library Search

The XYZ entertainment company hires you to develop a Web site to extend their business over the Internet. This company carries music CDs. First, you need to provide a page that allows clients to view all the music that is currently available, or to search for special music. All data are stored in a text file containing the composer and the music title. Each record takes one line in the file, and the composer and music title are separated by a tab. Clients can also search for music written by a particular composer.

Survey Form Generator

This is a relatively complex Case Project. You plan to provide a service to those who want to conduct surveys on the Internet. Clients who want to conduct a survey can design their survey and post it on your Web site. The survey results are usually stored in a database. You can use all your JSP skills to allow clients to design a survey form on your Web site. You are responsible for designing the Web site, which provides the following functions:

1. The first page includes a form that collects the surveyor's information, including contact name, company name, contact phone number, and address. This information is used as the survey form's footer.

2. After the client fills in and submits the form to your Web server, you provide a page that includes another form to allow the client to design survey questions. Information collected from the previous form is retrieved and stored in hidden fields on the second form. The client can design one survey question at a time. Before more questions can be added, the previous question must be submitted to the server, and again, the survey questions are stored in hidden fields.

3. The second form also includes a Complete button. When this button is clicked, you generate a survey form and save this survey form as survey.html. This survey form can be used to collect information from users, and it is then processed on the Web server.

4. Create another JSP page that is used to process the information collected from the survey form.

6

7

APPLICATIONS, SESSIONS, AND COOKIES

In this chapter, you will:

♦ Learn what a Web application is

♦ Use the application object to store information that is accessible to all clients

♦ Use the session object to maintain information across successive requests

♦ Create cookies

♦ Send cookies to the client browser, using the response object

♦ Read cookies using the request object

Because the HTTP protocol is connectionless, you cannot retain information between successive requests. But frequently you need to track information that was sent in a previous request. For example, a shopping cart must maintain its state so it knows what's already been added to it. In this chapter, you will learn how to use the application object to store information that is accessible to all clients, how to use the session object to maintain state among the requests from a client, and how to use cookies to store information on the client computer.

WEB APPLICATIONS

Web sites are also called Web applications. A **Web application** is a group of files, for example HTML/XML documents, Web components (servlets and JSP pages), and other resources that reside in either a directory structure or an archived format known as a Web Archive (WAR) file. A Web application resides on a central server and provides services to a variety of clients. It typically consists of the following components:

- Web server. The platform on which the application runs. The Web server provides services on the Internet, or on a local intranet, or on an extranet.

- Documents. A mixture of static documents and active documents. When a client requests a static file, the Web server simply locates the file and sends it back to the client without processing it. The static document is interpreted on the client browser. When a client requests an active document, the Web server processes the document before sending it back to the client. Typically, the Web server executes the server-side scripts and generates new content. What the server sends back to the client is usually plain HTML content.

- Document Processing Engine. Software installed on the Web server that processes the active documents. This is often part of the server, for example, the JSP engine.

A Web application can reside anywhere in the file system. In fact, Tomcat comes with several Web applications. You can find these applications in tomcat_root/webapps/. For example, if you installed Tomcat in the folder C:\Program Files\Apache Tomcat 4.0, which is the default directory when you install Tomcat4.0, then you see several Web applications in the folder C:\Program Files\Apache Tomcat 4.0\webapps\, called ROOT, manager, and examples.

THE APPLICATION OBJECT

One of the main characteristics of a Web application in the JSP container is its relationship to the implicit **application object**. Each Web application has one and only one application object, and this object can be shared by all application users. By extension, you can use this object to hold references to other objects that can be accessed by all users.

Application Variables

The application object provides a variety of methods that allow you to store information that is accessible to all clients. Since these variables can be accessed throughout the Web application, they are called **application variables**. Application variables can be initialized when you configure the Web server and/or the Web application, or can be created by using the application object in a JSP file. In the following section, you will learn how to set the application variables as initial parameters when you configure a Web application. You will also learn how to create application scope variables in a JSP file.

Application variables are useful for storing information that's used on all JSP pages in your Web application. For example, you may want to make the webmaster's e-mail address available throughout the Web application. Then, if the e-mail address changes, instead of editing all JSP pages, you simply change the application variable in one place.

Initialization Parameters

If you have followed the instructions in this book to set up your own Web application, you know that every Web application has a subdirectory called WEB-INF, and in this directory resides a file called web.xml. The file web.xml describes the application layout to the Tomcat Web server. The Tomcat server allows you to set initialization parameters in this file. These parameters are set as name/value pairs, and they are accessible throughout the Web application.

To set initialization parameters, you need to modify the web.xml file associated with that Web application, as illustrated in the steps below.

1. Open the file web.xml in your text editor; this file is located in C:\myjspapp\WEB_INF.

2. Add the code shaded in Figure 7-1.

```
<?xml version="1.0" encoding="ISO-8859-1"?>

<!DOCTYPE web-app
    PUBLIC "-//Sun Microsystems, Inc.//DTD Web Application 2.3//EN"
    "http://java.sun.com/dtd/web-app_2_3.dtd">
<web-app>
 <context-param>
   <param-name>webmaster</param-name>
   <param-value>webmaster@myeducationonline.com</param-value>
 </context-param>
 <context-param>
   <param-name>jdbcDriver</param-name>
   <param-value>sun.jdbc.odbc.JdbcOdbcDriver</param-value>
 </context-param>
 <context-param>
   <param-name>dbURL</param-name>
   <param-value>jdbc.odbc.clientDB</param-value>
 </context-param>
  <session-config>
    <session-timeout>30</session-timeout>
  </session-config>
  <welcome-file-list>
    <welcome-file>index.html</welcome-file>
  </welcome-file-list>
</web-app>
```

Figure 7-1   Additional code added to web.xml

3. Save and close the file.

4. Shut down the Tomcat server, then restart it to make the new configuration take effect.

The syntax for using XML element tags to set up initialization parameters takes the following form:

```
<context-param>
  <param-name>variable name</param-name>
  <param-value>value</param-value>
</context-param>
```

All initialization parameters consist of two child elements, between the tags <context-param> and </context-param>. The tags <param-name> </param-name> specify the parameter name or variable name; the tags <param-value> </param-value> set the initialization value for the parameter.

Now that you have set initialization parameters for your Web application, the JSP pages in your Web application can access them. You use the application object to access these variables. The syntax to get an initialization parameter is as follows:

application.getInitialParameter("parameterName")

This method returns a string containing the value of the named parameter. If the parameter does not exist, it returns a null value. The application object also provides another method that allows you to get all initialization parameter names. The syntax is as follows:

application.getInitialParameterNames()

This method returns the names of the initialization parameters as an enumeration of string objects. If there is no initialization parameter, it returns an empty enumeration. This is useful when you do not know the initialization parameter name, or when you want to list all the parameters. The following example illustrates how to get the initialization parameters.

1. Open a new document in your text editor and type in the following code:

```
<%@ page import="java.util.*" %>
<HTML>
<HEAD><TITLE>Initialization parameters</TITLE></HEAD>
<BODY>
<table align=center order=1>
 <tr><th align=center colspan=2>Initialization
Parameters</th></tr>
 <tr><th align=center>Parameter Name</th>
   <th align=center>Parameter Value</th>
 </tr>
<%
  Enumeration enu= application.getInitParameterNames();
  while(enu.hasMoreElements()){
    String paramName= (String)enu.nextElement();
%>
```

```
      <tr><td align=center><%= paramName %> </td>
        <td align=center><%=
  application.getInitParameter(paramName) %></td>
        </tr>
  <% } %>
  </table>
  </BODY>
  </HTML>
```

2. Save the page as **example1.jsp** in the folder C:\myjspapp\chapter07.

3. Load the page, using the following URL:
   http://localhost:8080/myapp/chapter07/example1.jsp

   The page is displayed as shown in Figure 7-2.

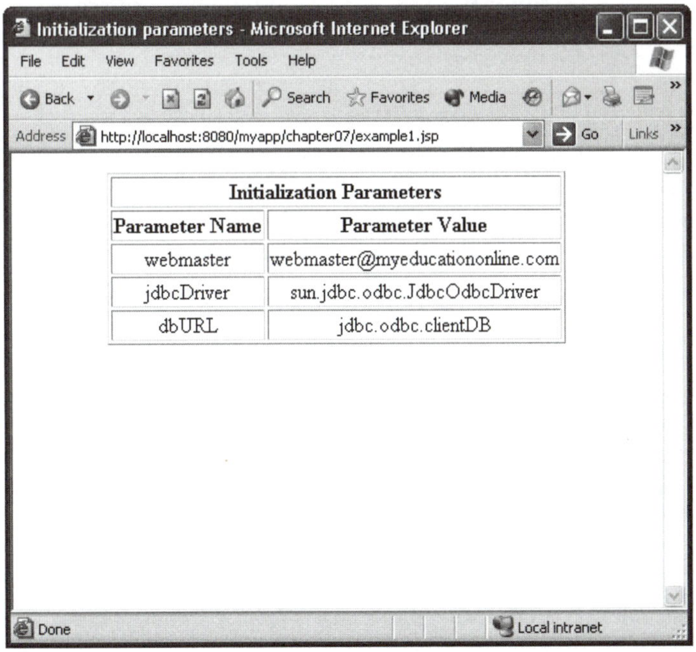

Figure 7-2   Initialization parameters

Setting Application Variables in JSP Pages

In addition to the initialization parameters you learned in the previous section, you can create application variables in your JSP code. To do this, you set new attributes to the application object and associate the new attributes with objects. These objects have **application scope**, since they are available to all JSP pages in the Web application. However, they cannot be referenced directly in JSP pages. In order to refer to these objects, you have to use the attribute that an object is bound to. The syntax to set a new attribute is as follows:

application.setAttribute("attribute name", an_object)

This method binds an object to a given attribute name. After an object is bound to an attribute, you can refer to the object via its attribute. The object is an instance of Java classes. For example, a date object, an array, or a string object can be bound to attributes. The syntax for referring to an object associated with an attribute is as follows:

application.getAttribute("attribute_name")

This method returns an object bound to the attribute with the given name; if there is no attribute by that name, it returns a null value. The following example illustrates how to set and get these attributes in JSP pages.

1. Open the data file example2-1.jsp, which is located in the folder C:\myjspapp\chapter07.

2. Add the code shaded in Figure 7-3, which sets a new attribute binding a string object.

```
<HTML>
<HEAD><TITLE>Set attributes</TITLE></HEAD>
<BODY>
<% /*set a date attribute */
 if(application.getAttribute("date") == null){
    application.setAttribute("date", new java.util.Date());
 }
%>
This page was first visited on <%= application.getAttribute("date") %>
<br><br>
Please use the following form to set attributes<br>
that are accessible from all JSP pages in this Web<br>
application.<br><br>
<form action=example2-1.jsp method=post>
 Attribute name:<input type=text name=attributeName><br>
 A string bound to the attribute: <input type=text name=attribute><br><br>
 <input type=submit value="submit this form">
</form>
<%
 String attrName = request.getParameter("attributeName");
 String attr = request.getParameter("attribute");
 if(attrName != null && attrName.length() != 0){
    application.setAttribute(attrName, attr);
 }else{
%>
<hr>
 Please enter attribute name and a string and then submit the form.
<% } %>
<hr>
<a href="example2-2.jsp">Get Attribute</a>
</BODY>
</HTML>
```

Figure 7-3   Additional code added to the example2-1.jsp file

3. Save the file.

4. Open the data file example2-2.jsp, which is located in the folder C:\myjspapp\chapter07.

5. Add the code shaded in Figure 7-4, which retrieves the attribute and the object bound to the attribute.

```
<%@ page import="java.util.*" %>
<HTML>
<HEAD><TITLE>Get attributes</TITLE></HEAD>
<BODY>
To get an attribute, please enter an attribute name<br>
and then submit the form. Then the attribute should be<br>
displayed, if it exists.<br><br>
<form action=example2-2.jsp method=post>
 Attribute name:<input type=text name=attributeName><br>
 <input type=submit value="submit this form">
</form>
<%
 String attrName = request.getParameter("attributeName");
 if(attrName != null){ %>
   <br>
   The attribute name: <b><%= attrName %> </b><br>
   The string bound to the attribute: <b><%= application.getAttribute(attrName)
 %></b>
<% } %>
<hr>
<a href="example2-1.jsp">Set Attribute</a>
</BODY>
</HTML>
```

Figure 7-4   Additional code added to the example2-2.jsp file

6. Save the page.

7. Open the page example2-1.jsp, using the following URL: http://localhost:8080/myapp/chapter07/example2-1.jsp

   The page is displayed as shown in Figure 7-5.

8. Enter some attribute names and values, and then submit the form.

9. Click the link **Get Attribute**. The page example2-2.jsp is requested and displayed as shown in Figure 7-6.

10. Enter an attribute name you created on the previous page, and submit the form. If the attribute does exist, the object bound to the attribute is displayed as a string; if it does not exist, a null value is displayed instead.

11. Enter **date** in the attribute name input field and submit the form. What is displayed?

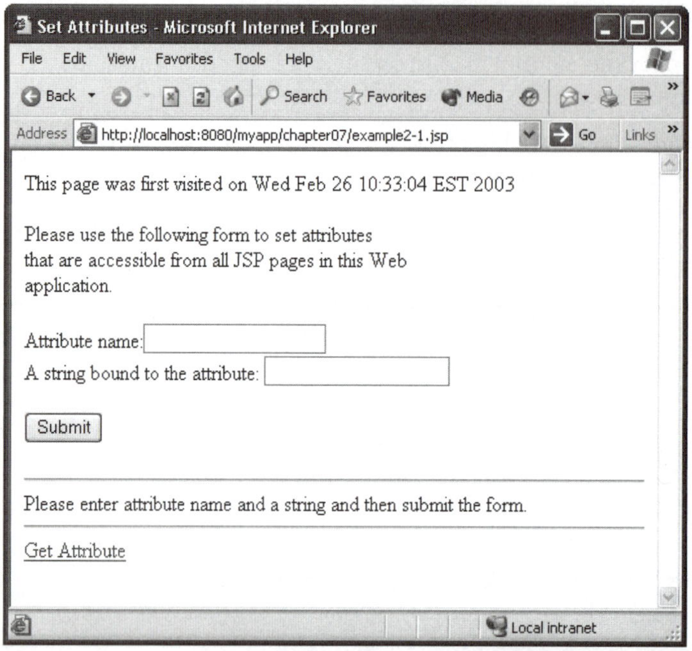

Figure 7-5   Setting the application object attribute

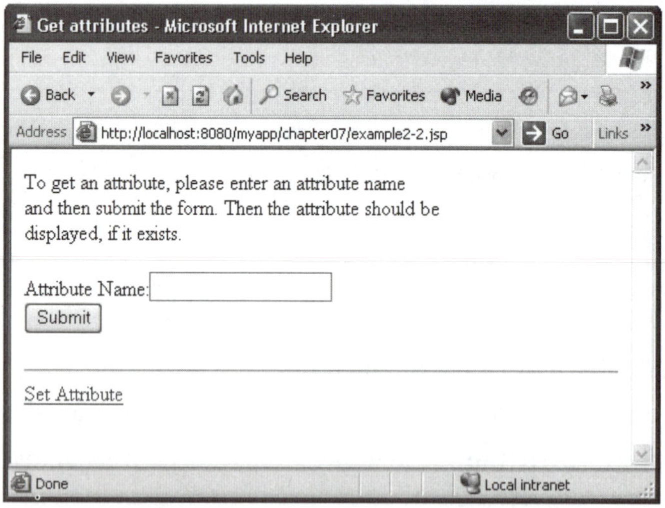

Figure 7-6   Getting the application object attribute

As you see in Figure 7-5, the first line displays the date when this page was first visited. The time remains the same regardless of who visits this page and when they visit, because the date attribute is set only once, when this page is requested for the first time (assuming the date attribute has not already been set by another JSP page).

The application object also provides methods that allow you to list all attribute names, and even delete an attribute. The syntax for listing all attribute names takes the following form:

application.getAttributeNames()

This method returns an enumeration object containing the attribute names available for all JSP pages in the Web application.

To delete an attribute, use the following syntax:

application.removeAttribute("attributeName")

This method removes the attribute with the given name. After removal, subsequent calls to getAttribute("attributeName") to retrieve the attribute's value will return null.

When you use the setAttribute() method to set an attribute, if the name specified is already being used for an attribute, this method removes the old bound object and binds the name to the new object.

THE SESSION OBJECT

The HTTP protocol is stateless, meaning that each time a client requests a Web page, it opens a separate connection to the Web server. There is no connection or information sharing between successive requests. What if you want to hold information that is particular to a client across multiple requests? For example, when a client is using a shopping system, each separate request might add an item to the client's ongoing order. This order must maintain its state across requests in order to maintain the entire ongoing transaction. Also, when the client wants to check out, how does the server determine which previously created order is the correct one? The process of trying to maintain state across multiple requests is referred to as session management, the idea being that all of a user's requests for pages from a Web server during a given period of time are actually part of the same interactive session.

There are several solutions to the session management problem. You can use hidden fields to hold information from successive requests, as discussed in Chapter 5. However, there are some disadvantages to this approach: first, every page must be dynamically generated to include new hidden fields; second, the page request carrying hidden fields cannot be interrupted. If the user exits the browser, or visits a page that does not contain the hidden fields, all hidden fields may be lost.

You can also use cookies to store and retrieve information in successive requests. But using cookies for this purpose can be tedious: you must use a unique identifier to associate a cookie with the right client; you must set an appropriate expiration period; and you must retrieve cookies from the client computer for each request.

The other solution is to use URL rewriting. With this technique, the client appends some extra data on the end of each URL. URL rewriting is not discussed in this text.

JSP provides an excellent solution to the session management problem: the session object. The session object is one of the implicit objects, so you do not need to declare it in order to use it. The session object enables JSP applications to maintain state information. Typically, a session object is used by applications consisting of several pages. For example, a shopping cart application might have a page that places user selections into the session object, enabling subsequent pages to access the information. In Chapter 5, you learned how to set a session attribute in the page directive. You also learned that a session begins when a client requests a JSP page for the first time. In the following sections, you will learn how to use the session object to store information across multiple requests.

Creating the Session Object

A session object is created when a client browser first requests a JSP page. A session is then associated with all requests from within the same browser window. The following example illustrates when a session object is created.

1. Open the HTML file example3.html, which is provided in the folder C:\myjspapp\chapter07.

2. Open a new document in your text editor, and type in the following code:

```
<%@ page import="java.util.*" %>
<HTML>
<HEAD><TITLE>Create a session</TITLE></HEAD>
<BODY>
<%
  if(session.isNew()){
%>
  A new session has begun.<br>
<% } else { %>
  The session already exists.<br>
<% } %>
  This session was created at:
  <b><%= new Date(session.getCreationTime()) %></b><br>
  This session was last accessed on:
  <b><%= new Date(session.getLastAccessedTime()) %></b>
  <br><br>
  <a href="example3.html">back to example3.html</a>
</BODY>
</HTML>
```

3. Save the file as **example3.jsp** in the folder C:\myjspapp\chapter07.

4. Open a new browser window and load example3.html, using the following URL: http://localhost:8080/myapp/example3.html

The page is displayed as shown in Figure 7-7.

5. Read the message displayed on the page, then click the link on this page to request the example3.jsp page. A new page is displayed, as shown in Figure 7-8, indicating that a new session has begun, along with the information about when the session was created and the time at which it was last accessed.

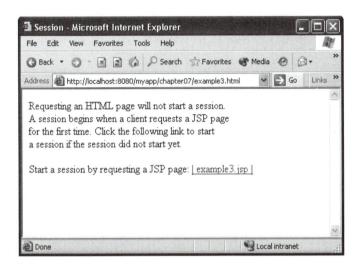

Figure 7-7   Requesting an HTML page

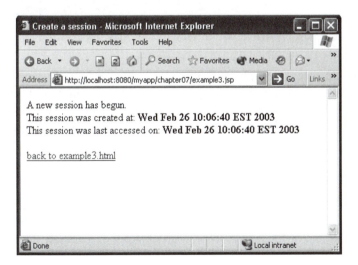

Figure 7-8   Requesting a JSP page

Make sure you open a new browser window when you load this page. If you load the page in an existing browser window, a session may exist already.

Internet Explorer maintains a different session in each browser window, while Netscape Navigator maintains the same session across all browser windows. Therefore, if you are using Netscape, you need to close all browser windows to test this example.

When you request the example3.html page, a session does not begin, because the requested file is an HTML page. A session begins only when you request a JSP page for the first time.

The session object provides methods that you can use to get information about the session object itself. The most frequently used methods include:

- isNew()

- getCreationTime()

- getLastAccessedTime()

The method session.isNew() returns a Boolean value indicating whether the session is newly created. The method session.getCreationTime() returns the time in milliseconds (a long data type) at which this session was created. The method session.getLastAccessedTime() returns the last access date and time of the session, in milliseconds. In the example above, you construct dates using the returned milliseconds to display both the session creation date and time and the last access date and time of the session object.

If you use the links on the pages to move between these two pages, you should see that the creation time of the session remains the same, while the last access time changes each time you request the example3.jsp page.

The session object in the above example is associated with the browser window in which the pages are displayed. Therefore, the session is actually associated with a browser window, and not with the user. To verify this, open another browser window and load the page example3.html, then click the link on the page to load example3.jsp. You see that a new session is created.

Storing Information in a Session Object

After a session is created, you can store information in the session object. To store information, you must set attributes of the session object, and associate the new attributes with objects. You use the following syntax to bind an object to a given attribute name:

session.setAttribute("attributeName", anObjectReference)

The following code segment sets three attributes that bind username, user ID, and password string objects with these attribute names.

```
session.setAttribute("username", "Joe Davis");
session.setAttribute("userID", "jdavis");
session.setAttribute("password", "jdsecret");
```

If an object has been bound to an attribute name, then the object is replaced with the newly bound object. For example, the code `session.setAttribute("username", "Joe Davis")` binds the string "Joe Davis" with the attribute "username". If you set the attribute later on, like this: `session.setAttribute("username", "John Smith")`, the old string object "Joe Davis" is replaced with the new one. So "John Smith" is now bound to the attribute.

After objects have been bound to attributes of the session object, you can use them via the session object. Since the session is associated with the client, not the request, these objects are available to all requests made by the same client, and therefore can be accessed by all JSP pages that are requested by the client.

 The method for storing objects in a session is setAttribute(String s, Object o).

7

Using Information Stored in the Session Object

After you have associated objects with attribute names in a session object, you can use the session method to get references to these objects. The syntax for getting a reference to a bound object takes the following form:

session.getAttribute("attributeName")

This method returns an object reference to the object bound to an attribute in this session. If no object is bound under the specified attribute name, it returns a null value. The following example illustrates how to bind objects with attributes in a session object, and how to use these bound objects within the same session.

1. Open the data file example4-1.jsp, which is located in the folder C:\myjspapp\chapter07.

2. Add the code shaded in Figure 7-9.

```
<%@ page import="java.util.*" %>
<HTML>
<HEAD><TITLE>Session attributes</TITLE></HEAD>
<BODY>
<% /*bind the date when this client accesses this page
  for the first time within the current active session */
 if(session.getAttribute("date") == null){
   session.setAttribute("date",new Date());
 }
```

Figure 7-9   Additional code added to example4-1.jsp

```
%>
You visited this page on <%= session.getAttribute("date") %>.
<br><br>
Please use the following form to bind a string object<br>
with an attribute in the session object. The bound object<br>
is accessible from all JSP pages within your session.<br><br>
<form action=example4-1.jsp method=post>
 Attribute name:<input type=text name=attributeName><br>
 String value to be bound: <input type=text name=attribute><br><br>
 <input type=submit value="Submit">
</form>
<%
 String attrName = request.getParameter("attributeName");
 String attr = request.getParameter("attribute");
 if(attrName != null && attrName.length() != 0){
   session.setAttribute(attrName, attr);
 }else{
%>
 <hr>
 Please enter an attribute name and a string value and then submit the form.
<% } %>
<hr>
<a href="example4-2.jsp">Get These Bound String Objects</a>
</BODY>
</HTML>
```

Figure 7-9 Additional code added to example4-1.jsp (continued)

3. Save the file.

4. Open the data file example4–2.jsp.

5. Add the code shaded in Figure 7-10.

```
<%@ page import="java.util.*" %>
<HTML>
<HEAD><TITLE>Session attributes</TITLE></HEAD>
<BODY>
To get a bound object, please enter an attribute name<br>
and then submit the form. Then the bound object should be<br>
displayed as a string, if it exists.<br><br>
<form action=example4-2.jsp method=post>
 Attribute Name:<input type=text name=attributeName><br>
 <input type=submit value="Submit">
</form>
<%
```

Figure 7-10 Additional code added to example4-2.jsp

```
String attrName = request.getParameter("attributeName");
if(attrName != null){ %>
  <br>
  The attribute name: <b><%= attrName %> </b><br>
  The bound object displayed as a string:
  <b><%= session.getAttribute(attrName) %></b>
<% } %>
<hr>
<a href="example4-1.jsp">Bind Objects</a>
</BODY>
</HTML>
```

Figure 7-10   Additional code added to example4-2.jsp (continued)

6. Save the file.

7. Load page example4-1.jsp, using the following URL:
http://localhost:8080/myapp/chapter07/example4-1.jsp

The page is displayed as shown in Figure 7-11.

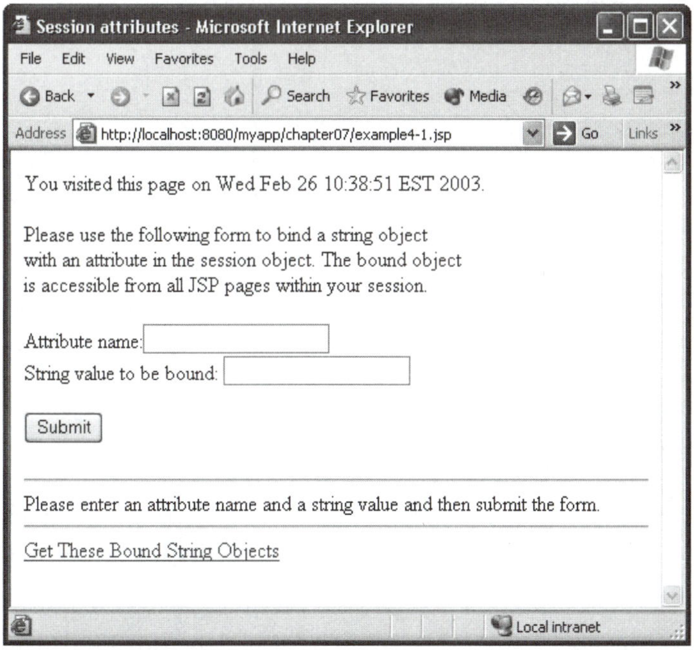

Figure 7-11   Binding objects with attributes in a session object

8. On this page, you can enter an attribute name and a string value to be bound to that attribute, and then submit the form.

9. Click the link on the page to display example4-2.jsp, as shown in Figure 7-12.

10. On this page, enter the attribute name you entered in the previous page; the attribute name and the string value bound with that attribute are displayed. If you enter an attribute name that has not been set, a "null" value is displayed. Again, these attributes are associated with the current session. If you try to access these attributes from another browser window (another session, assuming you are using Internet Explorer), you will get null values (assuming that no attributes have been set with the same names in the current session). To verify this, keep the current browser window, open, open another browser window and load page example4-2.jsp, using the URL http://localhost:8080/myapp/chapter07/example4-2.jsp. Then enter the attribute name you set in the previous session. You see that a "null" value is displayed.

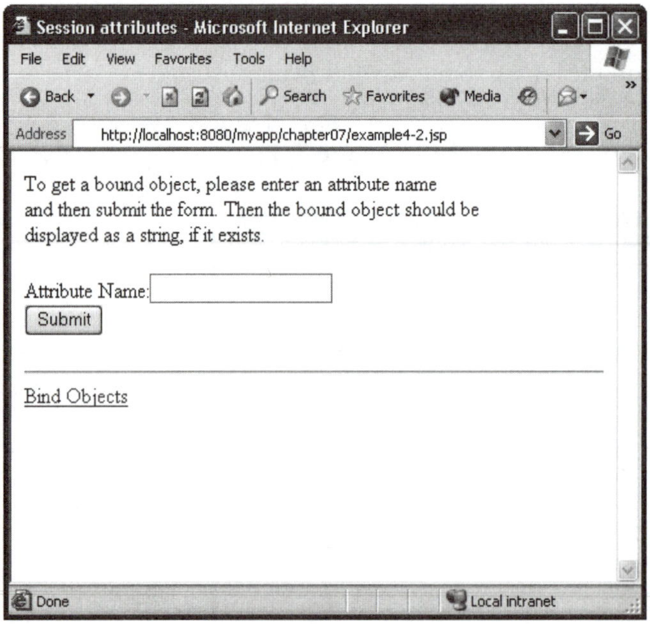

Figure 7-12   Retrieving a bound object

The session object also provides a method that allows you to list all attribute names in a session object. The syntax to list all attribute names takes the following form:

session.getAttributeNames()

This method returns an enumeration object containing the attribute names in the session object.

The return type of the method getAttribute is Object, so you have to do a type-cast to determine what specific type of data was associated with that attribute name in the session.

The method for retrieving stored objects in a session is the getAttribute("attributeName") method.

Remove Attribute

An attribute can be removed from a session. The syntax to remove an attribute takes the following form:

session.removeAttribute("attributeNameToRemove")

This method removes the object bound with the specified attribute name from this session. If the session does not have an object bound with the specified name, this method does nothing.

Expire Session Object

A session automatically becomes inactive, or expires, when the amount of time between client requests exceeds a certain interval, known as the **timeout** period. When a session expires, all objects bound to the session object are eventually reclaimed by the JSP container. Given that HTTP is a stateless protocol, there is no way for the JSP container to know that a user has left the Web site and is no longer using the session. Indeed, the user may even have exited the Web browser altogether, but the server is not aware of that. How does the server decide, then, that a client is no longer using a session? Each session object keeps track of the last time it was requested by a JSP page or servlet. After a predetermined period of time has elapsed without a request—for example, a user leaves the browser window idle— the user's session simply expires, and is no longer valid. At this point, all system memory associated with the session object, including all objects bound to the session object, is ready to be released. The next time the user returns to the site, an empty session object is created; no information is carried over from previous sessions that have expired.

You can explicitly expire a session by using one of the session methods. The syntax for expiring a session takes the following form:

session.invalidate();

This method expires the session and unbinds any objects bound to it.

A session may not be available even though it is not expired. As discussed earlier, a session is actually associated with a browser window. If a user closes the browser window, the session associated with the browser window is not available anymore, but it is not expired, assuming that the session is active when the browser window is closed.

The JSP server comes with a default session duration that specifies how long a session object is kept alive between client requests. The default session timeout is 30 minutes in Tomcat4.0, unless you change the session timeout time. You can set this time period in your JSP page. The syntax to set session duration takes the following form:

session.setMaxInactiveInterval(durationInSeconds)

The parameter in this method specifies the time, in seconds, between client requests before the JSP container will invalidate the session. A negative time duration indicates that the session should never expire.

The method session.getMaxInactiveInterval() returns the maximum time interval, in seconds, that the JSP container keeps this session open between client requests. After this interval, the JSP container expires the session.

The following examples illustrate how to use the methods discussed above.

1. Open the data file example5.jsp, which is located in the folder C:\myjspapp\chapter07.

2. Add the code shaded in Figure 7-13.

```jsp
<%@ page import="java.util.*" %>
<HTML>
<HEAD><TITLE>Session methods</TITLE></HEAD>
<BODY>
<% //test whether the session is new. The session is new when
 //this page is the first page the client requested or the
 //current session expired
 if(session.isNew()){
   out.println("A new session has begun.<br>");
 }
%>
 This session was created on
  <b><%= new Date(session.getCreationTime()) %></b><br>
 This session was last accessed on
  <b><%= new Date(session.getLastAccessedTime()) %></b><br>
 <hr width=250 align=left>
<%
 String interval = request.getParameter("seconds");
 if(interval != null){
   int seconds = Integer.parseInt(interval);
   session.setMaxInactiveInterval(seconds);
 }
%>
 The default max inactive interval for this session:
  <%= session.getMaxInactiveInterval() %> seconds
<br><br>
<form action=example5.jsp method=post>
 Set a new max inactive interval in seconds:
 <input type=text name=seconds size=10><br>
 <input type=submit value="submit this form">
</form>
<a href="example5.jsp">Reload this page</a>
</BODY>
</HTML>
```

Figure 7-13   Additional code added to example5.jsp

3. Save the file.

4. Load the page, using the following URL:
   http://localhost:8080/myapp/chapter07/example5.jsp

   The page is displayed as shown in Figure 7-14.

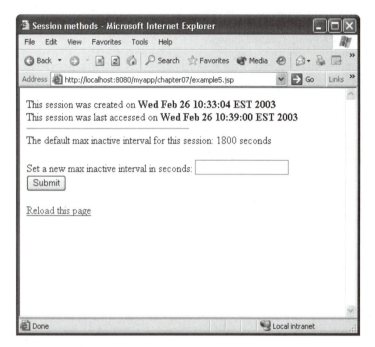

Figure 7-14 Session methods

Depending on whether this page is the first JSP page you requested in this browser window, or whether the current session has expired, the message telling you whether this session is newly created may or may not be displayed. If you load this page on the newly opened browser window, a new session begins and a message telling you so is displayed. In either case, regardless of whether it is new or not, the maxInactiveInterval is 1800 seconds. This value can be configured in the web.xml file in your Web application. The default value is 1800 seconds, which is 30 minutes. Whatever value you specified in web.xml will overwrite this default value.

 When you configure the maxInactiveInterval in the web.xml file, the value is in minutes.

The following example illustrates how to expire a session explicitly.

1. Open the data file example6-1.jsp. This page is used to bind string objects to the current session.

2. Add the code shaded in Figure 7-15.

```
<%@ page import="java.util.*" %>
<HTML>
<HEAD><TITLE>Binding objects to a session</TITLE></HEAD>
<BODY>
Please use the following form to bind a string object<br>
with an attribute in the session object.<br><br>
<form action=example6-1.jsp method=post>
 Attribute Name:<input type=text name=attributeName><br>
 String Value to be bound: <input type=text name=attribute><br><br>
 <input type=submit value="Submit">
</form>
<%
 String attrName = request.getParameter("attributeName");
 String attr = request.getParameter("attribute");
 if(attrName != null && attrName.length() != 0){
   session.setAttribute(attrName, attr);
 }else{
%>
 <hr>
 Please enter an attribute name and a string value and then submit the form.
<% } %>
<hr>
<a href="example6-2.jsp">Get These Bound String Objects</a>
</BODY>
</HTML>
```

Figure 7-15   Additional code added to example6-1.jsp

3. Open example6-2.jsp in the same folder. This page is used to retrieve bound string objects.

4. Add the code shaded in Figure 7-16.

```
<%@ page import="java.util.*" %>
<HTML>
<HEAD><TITLE>Getting bound objects</TITLE></HEAD>
<BODY>
<% if(session.isNew()){
   out.println("A new session begins<br><br>");
 }
%>
To get a bound object, please enter an attribute name<br>
and then submit the form.<br><br>
<form action=example6-2.jsp method=post>
 Attribute Name:<input type=text name=attributeName><br>
 <input type=submit value="Submit">
</form>
<%
```

Figure 7-16   Additional code added to example6-2.jsp

```
   String attrName = request.getParameter("attributeName");
   if(attrName != null){ %>
     <br>
     The attribute Name: <b><%= attrName %> </b><br>
     The bound object displayed as a string:
     <b><%= session.getAttribute(attrName) %></b>
<% } %>
<hr>
Click here to <a href="example6-3.jsp"> expire </a>current session
<br>Back to <a href="example6-1.jsp"> example6-1.jsp </a><br>
</BODY>
</HTML>
```

Figure 7-16   Additional code added to example6-2.jsp (continued)

5. Open a new document in your text editor, and type in the following code, which explicitly expires a session:

```
<%@ page import="java.util.*" %>
<HTML>
<HEAD><TITLE>Expiring a session</TITLE></HEAD>
<BODY>
The old session information was created on:
<%= new Date(session.getCreationTime()) %><br><br>
It is going to expire...<br><br>
<% session.invalidate(); %>
This session expired.<br><br>
Back to <a href="example6-2.jsp">example6-2.jsp</a>
</BODY>
</HTML>
```

6. Save it as **example6-3.jsp** in the folder C:\myjspapp\chapter07.

7. Load the page example6-1.jsp, using the following URL:
   http://localhost:8080/myapp/chapter07/example6-1.jsp

8. Enter an attribute name and a string value (for example, attribute name: username; string value: Joe Davis) and submit the form.

9. In Step 8, you bound a string object with an attribute in the session. Click the link on this page. The page example6-2.jsp is displayed. On this page, you can retrieve the string bound to an attribute in the session by specifying the attribute name. Enter the attribute name you entered in Step 8 and submit the form. The string value bound to this attribute is displayed.

10. Click the **expire** link to expire the current session. The message displayed on the example6-3.jsp page, as shown in Figure 7-17, tells you that the current session has expired.

11. Click the link to return to example6-2.jsp. The first line on this page says that a new session has begun (please think about why). Reenter the attribute name you entered in Step 8. This time a "null" value is displayed.

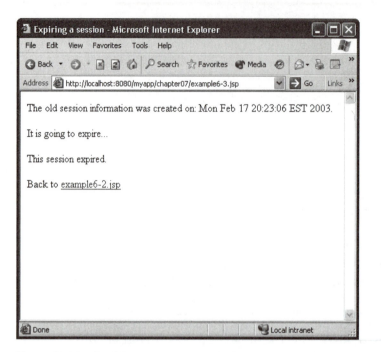

Figure 7-17 Expiring a session

The example above contains three pages: example6-1.jsp binds string objects to attributes in a session; example6-2.jsp retrieves the objects bound to the attributes of the session; example6-3.jsp expires the current session. All objects bound to attributes in a session can be accessed from any JSP pages in the same session. After a session expires, the objects bound to the attributes of the session are no longer available.

 Timeout can be changed by using setMaxInactiveInterval. The timeout periods used by these methods are defined in seconds. If the timeout period for a session is set to -1, the session will never expire.

When to Use the Session Object

Storing large amounts of data in the session object can be a problem for sites with a large user base. For example, if you store 5 KB of data in each user's session, and there are 1000 users with active sessions, this consumes 5 megabytes (MB) of memory (in some combination of physical memory and virtual memory). If you manage data for a million active sessions, then 5 gigabytes (GB) of memory are required. Based on the available hardware, then, the amount of data stored in the session has a direct impact on the number of simultaneous users that can practically be supported.

A common approach for reducing memory utilization of session data is to store only critical and frequently used data, for example, a username or an ID number, in the session. Actual session-specific (client-related) data are stored in some other repository, such as a database, which is accessed as needed, using the reference information residing in the session as the key for restoring it from the repository. For example, you can use the user ID to retrieve a user record from a database.

 Session tracking uses cookies by default to associate a session identifier with a unique user. If the browser does not support cookies, or if cookies are disabled, you can still enable session tracking using URL rewriting. URL rewriting is beyond the scope of this book.

COOKIES

7

A **cookie** is a small piece of textual information that a Web server sends to a browser and that the browser returns unchanged to the same Web site. The browser saves the cookie to a file on your hard drive. Information stored in cookies enables certain user conveniences, such as allowing visitors to store customizations made to the site's appearance, or storing previously entered user data such as IDs, passwords, and addresses.

Creating Cookies

You create a cookie by calling the Cookie constructor, which takes two string parameters: the cookie name, and the cookie's initial value. The syntax for creating a cookie takes the following form:

new Cookie("cookieName", "initialValue")

Neither the cookie name nor the cookie value should contain white space or any of the following characters:

[ ] ( ) = , " / ? @ : ;

Cookie Attributes

A cookie has a single value, but it may have optional attributes, including a comment that describes the purpose of the cookie, a maximum age, the domain to which a cookie belongs, and a version. Before sending a cookie to a client browser, you can set the attributes of the cookie by using one of the cookie methods.

You can use the following method to add a comment stating the purpose of the cookie:

setComment("purposeofCookie")

If a browser presents the cookie to a user, the cookie's purpose is described using this comment. To retrieve the comment attribute associated with a cookie, use the following syntax:

getComment()

This method returns the comment describing the purpose of the cookie. If this attribute has not been set, a null value is returned.

The following methods set and get the domain to which the cookie applies. Normally, the browser only returns cookies to the same domain that sent them. You can instruct the browser to return cookies to other hosts within the same domain name by using the setDomain method. The domain specified must begin with a dot (e.g., .a_domain_name.com).

setDomain("domain name")
getDomain()

The methods below get and set the maximum age of the cookie. These methods determine how much time (in seconds) should elapse before the cookie expires. The cookie will not be available after that many seconds have passed.

getMaxAge()
setMaxAge(lifetime_in_seconds)

A negative value, which is the default, indicates that the cookie lasts only for the current session (i.e., until the user quits the browser) and will not be stored on disk. Therefore, this kind of cookie is also called a **session cookie**. Specifying a value of zero instructs the browser to delete the cookie. All other cookies having a date associated with them are called **persistent cookies**. The getMaxAge method returns the maximum specified age of the cookie. If this attribute has not been set, a negative value is returned, indicating that it is a session cookie.

 A session cookie expires when the browser window is closed. A session may expire, but the session cookie will still be available as long as the browser is still open. Hands-on Project 7-5 illustrates the relationship between a session and a session cookie.

The following method returns the name of the cookie as a string. The name cannot be changed after it is created.

getName()

The following methods get and set the value of a cookie. An initial value is assigned to a cookie when it is created; you can change this value by calling the setValue method in your JSP page.

getValue()
setValue()

The following methods are used to get and set the path to which the cookie applies:

getPath()
setPath("pathString")

If you do not specify a path, the browser returns the cookie only to URLs in or below the directory containing the page that sent the cookie. For example, if the server sent a cookie from http://localhost:8080/myapp/chapter07/sendCookie.jsp, the browser would send the cookie back to http://localhost:8080/myapp/chapter07/cookie/getCookie.jsp, but not to http://localhost:8080/myapp/chapter04/getCookie.jsp or http://localhost:8080/myapp/getCookie.jsp. The setPath method can be used to allow the cookie to be sent to pages in other directories or its parent directories. For example, setPath("/") specifies that all pages on the server should receive the cookie. The path specified must include the page that sends the cookie. For example, if you send a cookie from the page http://localhost:8080/myapp/chapter07/a/sendCookie.jsp, you may specify a path of "/myapp/chapter07/", since "/myapp/chapter07/" includes "/myapp/chapter07/a/". That means you may specify a more general path than the current page, but not a more specific one.

Sending a Cookie to a Client

To send a cookie to a client browser, you use the response object. All cookies are sent to the client as headers of the response; they are added using the addCookie method of the response object. The syntax to add a cookie to the response header takes the following form:

response.addCookie(aCookie)

You can add as many cookies as you like by calling the addCookie method. All cookies are inserted into the response header and sent to the client browser.

Reading Cookies

All cookies are returned from the client as fields added to the HTTP request headers. To read the cookies returned from the client, you call the getCookies method of the request object. The syntax to get all cookies returned from a client takes the following form:

request.getCookies()

This method returns an array of cookie objects that have been sent to the client previously. If there is no cookie in the request, it returns a zero-length array. Once you have this array, you can use the getName() method to find the one you are looking for, and use the getValue() method to retrieve the cookie value.

 Cookies are not supported by all browsers. In addition, users can disable cookies in their browsers. Therefore, you should not rely on cookies in your Web application. If browsers do not support cookies, you can use URL rewriting or hidden fields.

The following example illustrates how to use cookies in your JSP pages. This example includes three JSP pages: example7-1.jsp creates cookies; example7-2.jsp lists the cookies; example7-3 deletes the cookies.

1. Open the data file example7-1.jsp, which is located in C:\myjspapp\Chapter07.

2. Add the code shaded in Figure 7-18 to create cookies.

```
<HTML>
<HEAD><TITLE>Creating cookies</TITLE></HEAD>
<BODY>
Use the following form to set cookies.<br><br>
<form action=example7-1.jsp method=post>
 Cookie Name:<input type=text name=cookieName><br>
 Cookie Value: <input type=text name=cookieValue><br>
 Set maxAge (in seconds): <input type=text name=cookieAge size=10>
 <br><br>
 <input type=submit value="Submit">
</form>
<%
 String cookieName = request.getParameter("cookieName");
 String cookieValue = request.getParameter("cookieValue");
 if(cookieName != null && cookieName.length() != 0){
   Cookie cookie = new Cookie(cookieName, cookieValue);
   int maxAge = 24*60*60; //default to one day
   try{
     maxAge=Integer.parseInt(request.getParameter("cookieAge"));
     cookie.setMaxAge(maxAge);
   }catch(Exception exc){}
   response.addCookie(cookie);
 }
%>
<a href="example7-2.jsp">List cookies</a><br>
<a href="example7-3.jsp">Delete cookies</a>
</BODY>
</HTML>
```

Figure 7-18   Additional code added to the example7-1.jsp page

3. Save the file.

4. Open the data file example7-2.jsp in the same folder.

5. Add the code shaded in Figure 7-19 to list all cookies.

```
<HTML>
<HEAD><TITLE>Listing cookies</TITLE></HEAD>
<BODY>
 <table border=1>
 <tr><th colspan=2 align=center>Cookie List</th></tr>
 <tr><th align=center>Cookie Name</td>
   <th align=center>Cookie Value</td>
 </tr>
```

Figure 7-19   Additional code added to example7-2.jsp

```
<%
 Cookie[] cookies = request.getCookies();
 for(int i=0; i<cookies.length; i++){
%>
 <tr><td align=center><%= cookies[i].getName() %></td>
   <td align=center><%= cookies[i].getValue() %></td>
 </tr>
<% } %>
</table><br>
<a href="example7-1.jsp">Create cookies</a><br>
<a href="example7-3.jsp">Delete cookies</a>
</BODY>
</HTML>
```

Figure 7-19   Additional code added to example7-2.jsp (continued)

7

6. Save the file.

7. Open the data file example7-3.jsp in the same folder.

8. Add the code shaded in Figure 7-20 to delete a cookie.

```
<HTML>
<HEAD><TITLE>Delete cookies</TITLE></HEAD>
<BODY>
<%
 String cookienametoremove = request.getParameter("removecookie");
 Cookie[] cookies = request.getCookies();
 if(cookienametoremove !=null){
    for(int i=0; i<cookies.length; i++){
     if(cookies[i].getName().equals(cookienametoremove)){
       cookies[i].setMaxAge(0);
       response.addCookie(cookies[i]);
       response.sendRedirect("example7-3.jsp");
       break;
      }
    }
 }
%>
<table border=1>
 <tr><th colspan=3 align=center>Cookie List</th></tr>
 <tr><th align=center>Cookie Name</td>
    <th align=center>Cookie Value</td>
    <th> Remove?</th>
 </tr>
<%
 for(intfi=0; i<cookies.length; i++){
%>
```

Figure 7-20   Additional code added to example7-3.jsp

```
<tr><td align=center><%= cookies[i].getName() %></td>
   <td align=center><%= cookies[i].getValue() %></td>
   <td><a href="example7-3.jsp?removecookie=<%= cookies[i].getName()%>">
     Remove?</a>
   </td>
</tr>
<% } %>
</table>
<a href="example7-1.jsp">Create cookies</a><br>
<a href="example7-2.jsp">List cookies</a>
</BODY>
</HTML>
```

Figure 7-20   Additional code added to example7-3.jsp (continued)

9. Save the file.

10. Load the page, using the following URL:
    http://localhost:8080/myapp/chapter07/example7-1.jsp

    The page is displayed as shown in Figure 7-21.

11. Before you create a cookie, click the **List Cookies** link on this page to reload the page. You should see a cookie called "JSESSIONID" and its value displayed. This cookie is discussed in the following section.

12. Create several cookies on this page. For example, username, e-mail, etc. To create a cookie, enter the cookie name and its value in their related input fields, and specify the max age before the cookie expires. Create cookies with different max ages so you can test that a cookie definitely expires when the time specified as max age elapses. For example, create three cookies with max ages 10, 100, and 1000 seconds, respectively.

13. Click the link on this page to list all cookies you created in Step 12. This page should look similar to Figure 7-22.

14. Wait for a while and reload this page; the cookies whose maxAge time has elapsed have expired. Try to create a cookie with maxAge set to 0. The cookie will never be displayed, because specifying a value of 0 maxAge instructs the browser to delete the cookie. So the cookie is deleted immediately after it is sent to the browser.

15. Click the **Delete cookies** link. The page displayed is similar to Figure 7-23.

16. To delete a cookie, simply click the corresponding **Remove** link on the page.

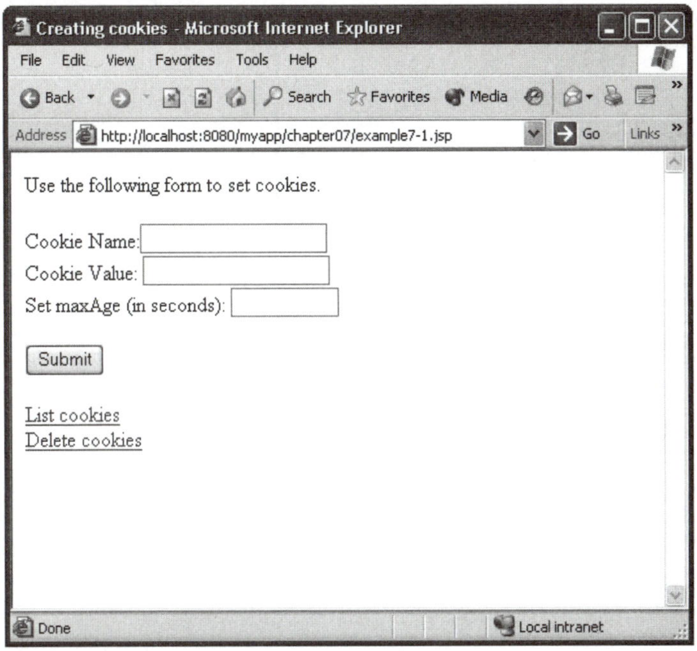

Figure 7-21   Creating cookies

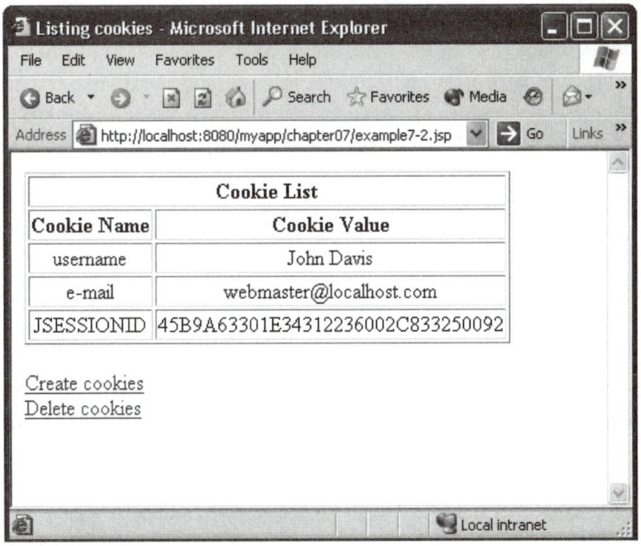

Figure 7-22   Listing cookies

![Delete cookies - Microsoft Internet Explorer window showing a Cookie List table. Address bar: http://localhost:8080/myapp/chapter07/example7-3.jsp]

Cookie List		
Cookie Name	Cookie Value	Remove?
username	John Davis	Remove?
e-mail	webmaster@localhost.com	Remove?
JSESSIONID	45B9A63301E34312236002C833250092	Remove?

Create cookies
List cookies

Figure 7-23   Deleting cookies

Every session gets a unique ID, and that ID is sent to the client. Two techniques are used by the JSP container to send the client the session ID, URL rewriting and cookies. In the first technique, the client appends some extra data on the end of each URL that identifies the session. This method is guaranteed to work but requires extra work for the JSP programmers. Using cookies is another approach for session tracking. But this approach also is limited because the user can choose not to accept cookies. In the second approach, a session cookie is created when a session starts. The JSP container names this session cookie as "JSESSIONID" and a value. The value assigned to the "JSESSIONID" cookie is the session ID of the session.

CHAPTER SUMMARY

❑ A Web application is a group of files, such as HTML/XML documents, Web components (servlets and JSP pages), and other resources that reside in either a directory structure or archived format known as a Web Archive (WAR) file.

❑ Each Web application has a single application object. The application object is accessible from all JSP pages and all clients who request these pages.

❑ You can store information that can be shared by all clients in the application object.

❑ A session begins when a client requests any JSP page for the first time. A session is not available once it expires or once the client closes the browser.

❑ You can store information in a session that can be accessed only by the client who owns the session.

❐ There are two kinds of cookies: session cookies and persistent cookies. Session cookies expire when the client closes the browser window. Persistent cookies exist for the time period specified in the maxAge attribute.

REVIEW QUESTIONS

1. Each Web application has ＿＿＿＿＿＿＿＿＿ application object(s).

   a. 0

   b. 1

   c. 2

   d. 3 or more

2. The application object in a Web application is shared by all application users. True or False?

3. The application variables created by the initialization parameters cannot be modified in JSP pages. True or False?

4. What value is assigned to the variable userName in the following JSP script segment?

   ```
   application.setAttribute("username", "Joe Davis");
   application.setAttribute("username", "John Kanet");
   application.setAttribute("username", "Peter Hunter");
   String userName= (String)application.getAttribute
   ("username");
   ```

   a. "Joe Davis"

   b. "John Kanet"

   c. "Peter Hunter"

   d. null

5. The default max inactive interval of a session is ＿＿＿＿＿＿＿＿＿ minutes in Tomcat.

   a. 0

   b. 10

   c. 20

   d. 30

6. Which of the following statements is/are true?

   a. A new session starts when a client visits a JSP page.

   b. A session expires immediately after a client exits the browser.

   c. A session is not available after the browser is closed.

   d. A new session begins when a client requests a JSP page for the first time.

7

7. The statement `session.setmaxInactiveInterval(60)` sets the max inactive interval of the session to:

   a. 1 minute

   b. 60 days

   c. 60 weeks

   d. 60 hours

8. If a client loads the same JSP page in three Internet Explorer browser windows, how many sessions might exist?

   a. 0

   b. 1

   c. 2

   d. 3

9. If a client loads the same JSP page in three Netscape browser windows, how many sessions might exist?

   a. 0

   b. 1

   c. 2

   d. 3

10. If an object has been bound to an attribute in a session, then this object can be accessed by:

    a. all clients from any JSP page

    b. all JSP pages requested by the client who owns the current session

    c. the page where this object is bound to an attribute in a session

    d. none of the above

11. The method session.getAttribute("attributeName") returns:

    a. a string

    b. an integer

    c. a character

    d. an object

12. The method session.getAttribute("anAttributeName") returns _____ if no object is bound under the specified attribute name.

    a. null

    b. an object

    c. an empty string

    d. the attribute name

13. A session cookie is _____ when the browser window is closed.

    a. deleted

    b. stored to the client computer

14. After a session expires, the objects bound to attributes in this session can still be accessed from a JSP page. True or False?

15. Which of the following statements creates a session cookie?

    a. `myCookie.setMaxAge(-1)`

    b. `myCookie.setMaxAge(0)`

    c. `myCookie.setMaxAge(100)`

    d. none of the above

16. Which of the following statements deletes the cookie on the client?

    a. `myCookie.setMaxAge(-1)`

    b. `myCookie.setMaxAge(0)`

    c. `myCookie.setMaxAge(100)`

    d. none of the above

17. If a cookie's maxAge has been set as follows: `setMaxAge(60)`, then the cookie remains on the client computer for _____ before it expires.

    a. 1 minute

    b. 60 hours

    c. 60 days

    d. 60 minutes

18. If a cookie is sent to the client from a JSP page under the directory /clients/createAccount/, then which of the following statements is true, assuming that the cookie path is not set in this JSP page? (choose all that apply)

    a. All JSP pages in the same directory can receive this cookie.

    b. All JSP pages in the directory /clients/ can receive this cookie.

    c. All JSP pages in the directory /clients/createAccount/checking/ can receive this cookie.

    d. none of the above

19. Which of the following statements is/are true?

    a. A persistent cookie expires when a client exits the browser.

    b. The same cookies can be accessed from more than one browser window.

    c. There may be more than one cookie in the current session.

    d. There may be more than one session object in the current session.

7

20. The method request.getCookies() returns:

    a. an array of cookie objects that have been sent to the client previously

    b. an enumeration object that contains all of the cookie objects that have been sent to the client previously

    c. a cookie object that has been sent to the client previously

    d. a null value

21. Cookies are supported by all browsers. True or False?

HANDS-ON PROJECTS

Project 7-1 Application Object

In this project, you will list all attribute names in an application object.

1. Open a new document in your text editor and type in the following code:

```
<%@ page import="java.util.*" %>
<HTML>
<HEAD><TITLE>Application attributes</TITLE></HEAD>
<BODY>
<%
  Enumeration enu = application.getAttributeNames();
  while(enu.hasMoreElements()){
%>
  <font face="Arial" size=-1 color=blue>
  <%= (String)enu.nextElement() %><br>
  </font>
<% } %>
</BODY>
</HTML>
```

2. Save the file as **project1.jsp** in the folder C:\myjspapp\chapter07.

3. Load the page, using the following URL:
   http://localhost:8080/myapp/chapter07/project1.jsp

   The page displayed is similar to Figure 7-24.

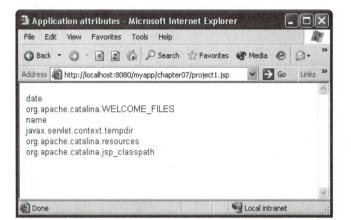

Figure 7-24   Attribute names in the application object

Project 7-2 Session ID

In this project, you will use session object methods to get the unique session ID.

1. Open a new document in your text editor, and type in the following code:

```
<HTML>
<HEAD><TITLE>Session ID</TITLE></HEAD>
<BODY>
<%  Cookie[] cookies = request.getCookies();
    Cookie sessionCookie = null;
    for(int i=0; cookies!=null && i<cookies.length; i++){
      if(cookies[i].getName().equals("JSESSIONID")){
          sessionCookie = cookies[i];
          break;
      }
    }
%>
<% if(sessionCookie == null ){ %>
    <a href="project2.jsp">Reload this page</a>
<% }else { %>
    Cookie Name: JSESSIONID<br>
    Cookie Value:<%= sessionCookie.getValue() %><br>
    Session ID: <%= session.getId() %>
<% } %>
</BODY>
</HTML>
```

2. Save the file as **project2.jsp** in the folder C:\myjspapp\chapter07.

3. Load the page, using the following URL:
   http://localhost:8080/myapp/chapter07/project2.jsp

4. Depending on whether a session exists, the page may be shown as in Figure 7-25 or Figure 7-26. If it is displayed as shown in Figure 7-25, click the link; then the page should be similar to Figure 7-26. Note that the sessionID is a unique value, so the ID displayed in your browser is different from this one. You see that the session cookie value is the same as the session ID.

Figure 7-25   Project2.jsp with a link displayed

Figure 7-26   Project2.jsp with the session ID displayed

Project 7-3 Automatically Filling Forms

In this project, you will create a cookie to store address information on the client computer, so that this information can be filled in automatically when necessary.

1. Open the data file project3.jsp, which is located in C:\myjspapp\chapter07.

2. Load the page, using the following URL:
   http://localhost:8080/myapp/chapter07/project3.jsp

The page is displayed as shown in Figure 7-27.

3. Add code to create four cookies to store address data when the form is filled out and submitted.

4. Add code to retrieve the cookies that store address data and fill in the address data with the data that is stored in the cookies when the page is reloaded.

5. Save the file.

6. Enter address data and submit the form.

7. Reload the page; the address data stored in the cookies should fill the address input fields.

8. Close the browser and reload the page. Again, all fields should be filled automatically.

7

Fill form automatically - Microsoft Internet Explorer

File Edit View Favorites Tools Help

Back · · Search Favorites Media

Address http://localhost:8080/myapp/chapter07/project3.jsp Go Links

Address Form

Address:
City:
State:
Zip Code:

Submit

Reload this page

Done   Local intranet

Figure 7-27   Address form

Project 7-4 Customize Pages

In Chapter 3, you created a page that allows clients to customize a Web page so that it is displayed according to their preferences. However, their preferences are not stored, and must be specified at every visit. In this project, you will use cookies to store these preferences.

1. Open the data file project4-1.jsp, which is located in C:\myjspapp\Chapter07.

2. Add code to project4-1.jsp to retrieve the data collected on the form in project4.html, and save the font preference in cookies.

3. Add code to project4-1.jsp to retrieve the font preferences stored in the cookies and display the message on the page, using the preferred font color and size.

4. Load the page project4.html, using the following URL:
   http://localhost:8080/myapp/chapter07/project4.html

   The page is displayed as shown in Figure 7-28.

5. Specify your preferred font then submit the form. Your font preferences should be stored in cookies, and the message on the page project4.jsp is displayed, using your font preferences.

Figure 7-28 Specifiying font preferences

Project 7-5 Session Cookies

In this project, you will create session cookies and test the availability of a session cookie after the client exits the browser.

1. Create a new document and save it as **project5–1.jsp** in the folder C:\myjspapp\chapter07.

2. Use Figure 7-29 as a guideline to design a form on this page.

3. Specify the action of the form so that the data collected on the form are processed in the same page.

4. Add code to create a session cookie based on the data collected on the form.

5. Provide a link to project5-2.jsp on this page (label the anchor **Get cookies**, as shown in Figure 7-29).

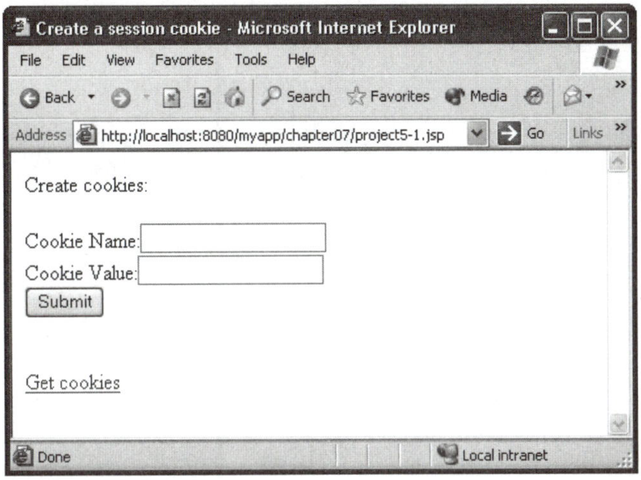

Figure 7-29   Creating session cookies

6. Create a new document and save it as **project5–2.jsp** in the folder C:\myjspapp\chapter07.

7. Use Figure 7-30 as a guideline to design a form on this page.

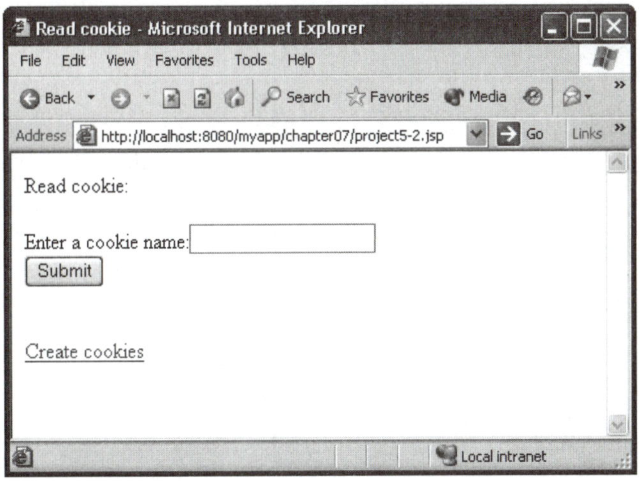

Figure 7-30   Reading session cookies

8. Specify the action of the form on this page so that the data collected on this form are processed on the same page.

9. Add code to retrieve the cookie based on the data provided on the form (the cookie name), and to then display the cookie value if the cookie exists (as in Figure 7-31); otherwise, it should display a message saying that the cookie does not exist (as in Figure 7-32).

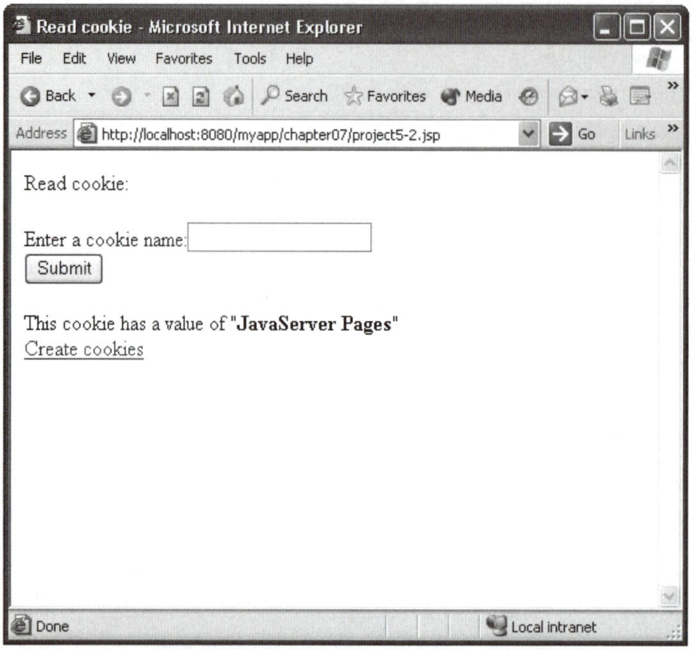

Figure 7-31   A cookie that exists

Figure 7-32   A cookie that does not exist

10. Provide a link to project5-1.jsp on this page, so you can navigate between these two pages.

11. Load page project5-1.jsp, using the following URL:
http://localhost:8080/myapp/chapter07/project5-1.jsp

12. Create cookies by providing cookie names and values.

13. Click the link on this page to display project5-2.jsp, where you retrieve the cookie values you created in Step 12.

14. Enter a cookie name and try to read the cookie. If the cookie (the name you specified) exists, its value is displayed; otherwise, a message is displayed on the page saying that the cookie does not exist.

15. Close the browser window.

16. Load the page project5-2.jsp, using the following URL:
http://localhost:8080/myapp/chapter07/project5-2.jsp

17. Try to read the cookie you created. You see that all cookies no longer exist. Because the cookies you created in Step 12 are all session cookies, they expire when the current session expires.

7

Project 7-6 Set Cookie Path

If the cookie path is not specified before it is sent to the client, the browser can send the cookie back to pages within the same directory or its subdirectories as the one in which the page that sent the cookie resides. To send the cookie to pages other than those specified above, you must set the cookie path before sending the cookie to the client. This project illustrates how to set a cookie path.

1. Open the data file project6.jsp, which is located in C:\myjspapp\chapter07.

2. Add code to create a cookie when the form is submitted. If the path check box is checked, you need to set the path for the cookie.

3. Save the file.

4. Load the page, using the following URL:
http://localhost:8080/myapp/chapter07/project6.jsp

The page is displayed as shown in Figure 7-33.

5. Create a cookie. You can set the path of this cookie to the root directory of the application. All pages will receive this cookie when it is returned from the browser. (In the next project, you will create another JSP page to verify this.)

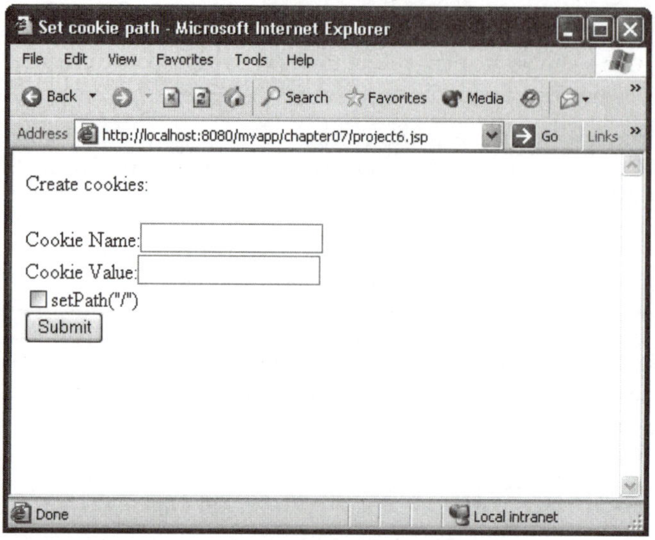

Figure 7-33 Setting the cookie path

Project 7-7 Read Cookies

In this project, you will test the cookie path set in Project7-6. You will create a JSP page and read the cookies set in Project 7-6. You must complete Project 7-6 before beginning this project.

1. Create a new document in your text editor, and save the file as **project7-7.jsp** in the folder C:\myjspapp (note that this is the root directory for this book).

2. Use Figure 7-34 as a guideline to design a form on this page.

3. Specify the action of the form so that the data collected on this page is processed on the same page.

4. Add code to read the cookie (based on the specified cookie name) and then display the cookie value if the cookie exists; otherwise, it should display a message saying that the cookie does not exist.

5. Load the page project6.jsp, using the following URL:
   http://localhost:8080/myapp/chapter07/project6/jsp

6. On the page project6.jsp, create a cookie without checking the setPath check box. Create another cookie with the setPath checkbox checked.

7. Load the page project7-7, using the following URL:
   http://localhost:8080/myapp/project7-7.jsp

8. After the page is displayed, try to read the two cookies you created in Step 6. When you try to read the cookie whose cookie path was not specified, the message says that the cookie does not exist. But you can read the other one, whose cookie path is set to the root directory.

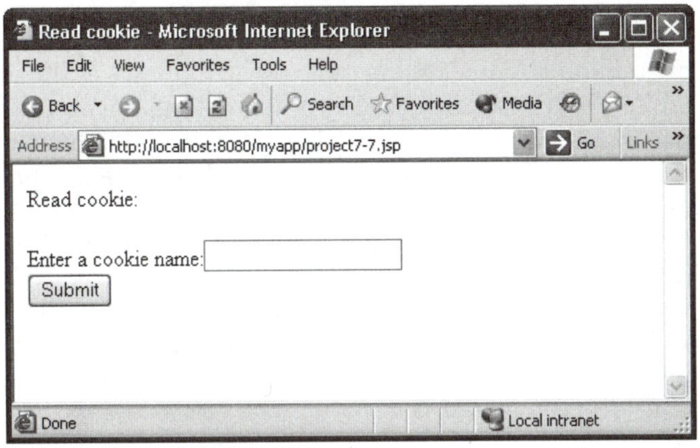

Figure 7-34   Reading cookies

CASE PROJECTS

SRAS: Auto-logout When a Session Expires

You have already designed the logon page for accessing the SRAS system. However, users can still access other pages in the SRAS application if they know the URLs. To secure all the pages, you must check whether the user has logged on before the requested page can be displayed. To do this, you must store all logon information, and make this information available to all pages in the SRAS application. Add the JSP script to your logon page that stores user IDs and passwords in a session object. In addition, you want to simplify the logon process by allowing users to store their user ID and password on their computer as cookies. These are retrieved when the logon page is requested. To do this Case Project, you need accomplish the following tasks:

1. Open the data file logon.jsp in the folder C:\myjspapp\chapter07\sras. Then add code to check whether the user ID has been stored in a cookie; if it has, the user ID automatically fills the User Name field on this page. You also need to add a check box to allow users to store their user ID in a cookie.

2. Open the data file main.jsp in the folder C:\myjspapp\chapter07\sras. Add code to create a cookie if and only if the user has checked the "Remember my ID on this computer" check box on the logon page. Then store the cookie on the client computer.

3. Open the data file checklogin.jsp in the folder C:\myjspapp\chapter07\sras. Add code to check whether the current session has expired. If it has, redirect the user to the logon page. (*Hint*: The user ID and password are bound to session attributes in main.jsp.)

Shopping Cart

A classic example of maintaining state among successive requests is the ubiquitous shopping cart application. The user browses a catalog of items, using forms to select items (and corresponding quantities) from multiple catalog pages to add them to a single shopping cart. Once the user is finished shopping, a checkout page is provided for confirming the order and supplying payment and shipping information. As a consultant, you have been asked by a company to develop a shopping cart system for its online bookstore to accomplish all the functions described above. For the sake of simplicity, suppose that this bookstore provides five books. Customers specify the book and the quantity they want to buy and add the book to the shopping cart, and they can view and delete items in the shopping cart. When they check out, the items, amount, subtotal, and grand total should be displayed on a page.

Tracking Client Preferred Web Page

The Weiwei Movie Store provides all kinds of movies. All movies are arranged in categories. Customers can browse the movie titles on the Internet. Since most customers have their favorite movie categories, the Weiwei Movie Store has hired you to improve its Web site to allow customers to specify their favorite categories. When the customer next visits the Web site, it automatically displays the customer's preferred categories. Create a Web site that uses cookies to store customers' favorite movie categories, so that a customer's preferred categories are displayed each time the customer visits.

JAVABEANS

In this chapter, you will:

- ◆ Survey the basics of the Java programming language
- ◆ Write JavaBeans
- ◆ Compile and install bean classes
- ◆ Use beans with action tags
- ◆ Get and set a bean's properties
- ◆ Connect beans with forms
- ◆ Use beans in scriptlets
- ◆ Write a file bean to read from and write to files

In this chapter, you will learn how to write, compile, and install a bean class; how to use beans to facilitate form processing and to implement business rules for your Web applications; and how to connect a bean with a form. By introducing JavaBeans into JSP scripts, you can develop reusable bean components that can be used in any of your JSP pages.

JAVA BASICS

JavaBeans are written in the Java programming language. While you can use JavaBeans in JSP scripts without Java programming experience, some knowledge of Java will help you better understand beans, and can even help you develop your own JavaBeans. This section provides enough Java basics to enable you to follow the code of the JavaBean classes presented in this book. If you are familiar with the Java programming language, you can safely skip this section.

As you learned earlier in this book, JSP is built on top of a servlet, which in turn is built on Java. So the programming basics introduced in Chapter 4 are "stolen" from Java. All the syntax you learned in Chapter 4 applies to Java as well as JSP.

Objects and Classes

The Java programming language is an object-oriented language. What this means is that everything in this language is an object, aside from primitive data types such as int, char, float, Boolean, etc. For each primitive data type there is a corresponding class in the package java.lang with which you can create an object for that type. To understand the difference between objects and primitive data types, take for example an actual object, such as your computer monitor. You can determine the characteristics of the monitor, for example the size, model, screen resolution, etc. In addition, you can determine what your monitor can do, for example display images, characters, and so on. The size, model, and screen resolution are called **attributes** or **properties** of the monitor, and what a monitor can do is called its **behaviors**. In fact all of the objects around you probably have some attributes and some behaviors. The attributes describe them, while the behaviors indicate what they can do. Some of the attributes, such as viewable size and model, cannot be modified, while others, such as the screen resolution, can be reset to a new value. An object cannot perform its "behaviors" automatically; it responds to some stimulus, such as an action or an environmental change. For example your monitor displays the Microsoft Word window when instructed to do so.

Object-oriented programming methodology allows you to simulate the functionality of real-world objects in your program. In object-oriented programming, you use data members to simulate attributes, and you use methods to simulate behaviors. Therefore, unlike the primitive data types introduced in Chapter 4, objects have attributes and/or behaviors.

In Java, the objects you create are based upon classes. A **class** is a template or blueprint for objects. A class consists of three parts:

- Data members to simulate attributes
- Methods to simulate behaviors
- Methods used to create objects from the class

The following is an example of a class.

```java
public class Circle{
  private float radius;
  private float area;
  public Circle(){
    radius=0.0f;
    area = 0.0f;
  }
  public Circle(float radius){
    this.radius = radius;
    area = 0.0f;
  }
  public void setRadius(float radius){
    this.radius = radius;
  }
  public void calculateArea(){
    area = radius*Math.PI;
  }
  public float getArea(){ return area;}
}
```

8

The code above defines a simple class called Circle. It has two data members: radius and area. Data members can be primitive data types or objects. The setRadius method sets the radius of the circle, the calculateArea method calculates the area of the circle, and the getArea method returns the area of the circle.

Variables defined in a method are local to that method, meaning that they can be referenced within this method only. If a method defines a variable with the same name as a data member variable, the data member variable is hidden in the method. To access a hidden data member, you precede the hidden variable name with the keyword **this** and the dot operator. In the example above, the parameter of the method setRadius has the same name as the data member of the class radius. So this.radius references the data member of the class, and radius (without the prefix this.) references the argument passed to the method.

There are two other special methods with the same name but different parameters. These two methods have no return type, and the name of the methods is the same as the class name. These methods are called **constructors**. Constructors of a class are used to create objects from the class. As mentioned in Chapter 4, a user-defined data type is called a class. The class Circle in the example above is actually a new data type, so you can create an object from the class as follows:

```java
Circle myCircle1 = new Circle();
Circle myCircle2 = new Circle(3.0);
```

Here you create, or instantiate, two objects from the Circle class. The object myCircle1 is created with the constructor with no argument, and myCircle2 is created with the constructor and an argument. The radius and area of the first circle are initialized to 0, and the radius of the second circle object is initialized to 3.0. After objects are created, you use dot notation to use or call their public methods. For example, to set the radius of myCircle1 to 4.5, use the code `myCircle1.setRadius(4.5);` To calculate the area, use `myCircle1.calculateArea();`, and so on.

To use this class, it must be saved as Circle.java (the filename is the same as the class name, and the file has the extension java).

 There are four access specifiers: public, package, protected, and private. Please refer to other Java programming books for details. *Java Programming* by Farrell (Course Technology) is a good resource.

Vector

Vector is one of the most frequently used classes in Java. Vector is a class packaged in the java.util package. The syntax for creating a Vector object takes one of the following forms:

Vector v1 = new Vector();
Vector v2 = new Vector(Collection c);
Vector v3 = new Vector(int initialCapacity);
Vector v4 = new Vector(int initialCapacity, int capacityIncrement);

There are several methods that you will use in this chapter. These methods are listed in Table 8-1.

Table 8-1   Vector methods

Method	Usage
addElement(Object o) or add(Object o)	Appends the specified object in the argument to the end of the vector.
elementAt(int index)	Returns the component at the specified index. The index of the first element is zero, the second element is 1, and so on.
contains(Object o)	Tests whether the specified object is a component in this vector. It returns a Boolean value.
indexOf(object o)	Searches for the first occurrence of the given argument, testing for equality using the equals method. It returns the index of the element in the vector if found, −1 otherwise.
InsertElementAt(Object o, int index)	Inserts the specified object as a component in this vector at the specified index.
size()	Returns the number of components in this vector as an int.

The elements added to a vector object must be objects. You cannot add a primitive data type to a vector object. The method elementAt returns an object. For example, the following code segment adds a string object to a vector:

```
Vector v = new Vector();
```

```
String message = "Hello World!";
v.add(message);
```

To retrieve the String object from the vector object, use the following code:

```
Object anObject = elementAt(0);
```

The component returned by this method is an object. To use this object as a string object, you must cast it back to the string object. You use the cast operator to cast an object as follows:

String s = (String)anObject;

Then you can use all methods associated with a string object to perform any manipulation on the string object.

WRITING JAVABEANS

JavaBeans bring component technology to JSP script. Object-oriented programming languages dominate the modern software application markets. Indeed, with object technology, most software is built by combining components, which are called classes in Java. With the JavaBeans API, you can create reusable, platform-independent, and most importantly, robust components. JavaBean components are known as beans. They are nothing but Java objects that follow some naming conventions. JavaBeans are commonly used in JSP script to facilitate form information processing and to implement business logic. Since beans are so important in implementing business rules, as a JSP developer you should be able to understand and use beans, although you may not be required to write the beans yourself.

A bean is just an instance of a Java class. A bean encapsulates its properties by declaring them private and provides public methods for reading and modifying its properties. In general, a bean provides two methods for each property: one to get the property and one to set the property. These **GET** and **SET** methods are also called **Accessors** or getters/setters. However, in order to access a bean's properties with action tags in JSP, the method names should follow a few simple naming conventions. For example, for a property named foo, which is of the type dataType, the GET method is called getFoo and returns an element of dataType; the SET method takes an argument of DataType and is called setFoo. In general, beans are Java classes that have public constructors with no arguments, and use public SET and GET methods to simulate properties. The GET method takes no arguments.

In the following example you create a very simple bean with one property:

1. Open a new document in your text editor, and type in the following code:

```
package com.jspbook.chapter08;
public class SimpleBean{
  private String message;
```

```
      public SimpleBean(){
        message = "Hi, there.";
      }
      public String getMessage(){ return message;}
      public void setMessage(String aMessage){
      message = aMessage;}
    }
```

2. Save the file as **SimpleBean.java** in the folder C:\myjspapp\chapter08.

Java classes are grouped in a collection called a **package**. In your application development, you may create many classes. These classes are grouped into a number of packages. Packages are directory structures used to organize classes. The first line of the code above defines a package named com.jspbook.chapter08. Later in this chapter, after this class is compiled, a class named SimpleBean.class can be found in the folder com\jspbook\chapter08.

The code `public class SimpleBean` starts a class definition. The class should be defined as public; otherwise, it can be used only by other classes in the same package. By convention, a class name should begin with a capital letter. If a name combines more than one word, the first letter of each word should be capitalized. The code `private String message` defines a property or instance variable or data member of the class. Every bean object contains one copy of each **instance variable**. A private property can only be accessed within the class definition. The code segment `public class SimpleBean(){ ... }` defines a public constructor with no argument. A constructor without an argument is also called a **default constructor**. To create and use a bean with action tags in JSP script, a default constructor must be provided. If no constructor is defined in your class, a default constructor is provided automatically. However, if any constructors are defined for a class, a default constructor is not created automatically; in this case, you must define a constructor with no argument in order to create a bean with action tags. You usually initialize instance variables within constructors. In the example above, you assign an initial value to the instance variable message. A private property cannot be accessed outside of the class. In order to access it, you need to provide a public method to do so. The code `public getMessage` is used to access the private property, and the code `public setMessage` is used to set the property with a new value.

Sun Microsystems specifies a convention for package naming. Every package name should start with your Internet domain name in reverse order. For example, if the domain is ebcity.com, you may use the package name com.ebcity.

Finally, the bean class must be saved with the same name as the class name, and must have the extension .java. So, the class in the above example must be saved as SimpleBean.java.

By convention, the first letter of a class name is capitalized, and the first letter of each following word is capitalized—for example, CalculateInterestRateBean. By contrast, the first letter of a method name is in lowercase.

COMPILING AND INSTALLING BEAN CLASSES

In previous chapters, you learned that in order to create objects from a class, the class must be available to the JSP engine. For example, to create a date object, you must make the class package java.util.Date available. To be available, the class must be somewhere in the CLASSPATH. A **CLASSPATH** is a directory where the JSP engine looks for the required classes. How you do this may vary among implementations, but most JSP containers provide some standard directories where new bean classes can be installed.

To install bean classes in Tomcat, you install all classes in the directory WEB-INF\classes under the root directory of your application. The source code can be saved anywhere. But for security reasons, you may want to store all your source files under the folder WEB-INF in a real application.

The class must be compiled and installed in the proper class path. When a class is compiled, the resulting class file (a file with the extension .class) is placed in the directory specified by the package statement. If the directory specified in the package does not exist, the compiler creates it. To compile a class in the Windows operating system, you use the following command:

```
javac –d classpath classFile
```

To compile a class in a package, the option –d is passed to the compiler to specify where to create (or locate, if these directories exist) all the directories in the package. The CLASSPATH is a directory where the JSP engine searches for the classes. In this text, the CLASSPATH is the directory C:\myjspapp\WEB-INF\classes. The classFile is the JavaBean file to be compiled. In the following exercise, you compile and install SimpleBean.java in the Windows operating system.

1. Open a DOS command window.

2. Use the following command to change the directory to the directory where SimpleBean.java is located:

   C:\windows\system32>cd c:\myjspapp\chapter08

3. Use the following command to compile and install the bean class.

   C:\myjspapp\chapter08>javac –d c:\myjspapp\WEB-INF\classes SimpleBean.java

The directory C:\myjspapp\WEB-INF\classes contains a directory called com, com contains a directory called jspbook, and jspbook contains a directory called chapter08. In the directory chapter08, you should find the file SimpleBean.class.

USING BEANS

Writing Java classes requires that you know the Java programming language. However, you need not know the Java programming language in order to use beans in your JSP scripts. With the action tags, you can use beans that are developed by other Java programmers. Most importantly, you can use beans as components in any JSP pages when you need them. In Chapter 11, you will create a data bean to facilitate the manipulation of a database.

JSP provides three basic tags for working with beans: one to bind a local variable to an existing bean or instantiate a new bean and make it available in the action tags and JSP script, one to get a property, and one to set one or more properties.

Instantiate a Bean Object

The simplest way to get a bean is to use the following code to load the bean.

```
<jsp:useBean id="bean_name" class="class_name" />
```

This action lets you create and load a JavaBean to be used in the JSP page. This usually means "instantiate an object of the class specified by the class attribute, and bind it to a variable with the name specified by the ID attribute." There are some other methods for instantiating and using beans, which you will learn about in Chapter 9. In the action tag above, "bean_name" is the name that refers to the bean. The bean name must be a valid Java identifier (a combination of letters, numbers, and other characters, which cannot begin with a digit), and it must be unique everywhere it is to be used. No two beans can have the same name in the same page. The bean name serves as a local variable reference to the bean object.

The class name is the name of a java class that defines the bean. You must specify the whole package name of the bean class. The execution of this action tag creates a new bean object and binds a local variable (the value of the ID attribute) to the object. The local variable is used to access the bean's properties.

Accessing Bean Properties

Once you have a bean, you can read the existing properties using the tag jsp:getProperty. The getProperty action tag takes the following syntax:

<jsp:getProperty name="bean_name" property="property_name" />

This tag retrieves the value of a bean property, converts it to a string, and inserts it into the output. The two required attributes are name and property. The "bean name" is the same name specified in the ID attribute when the bean is created, and the "property name" is the name of the property to get. In the following exercise you create a bean, then get a property of the bean.

1. Open a new document in your text editor, and type in the following code:

```
<HTML>
<HEAD><TITLE>Example1: Get bean property</TITLE></HEAD>
<BODY>
<jsp:useBean id="simpleBean" class="com.jspbook.
chapter08.SimpleBean"/>
<H1>
```

```
<jsp:getProperty name="simpleBean" property="message"/>
</H1>
</BODY>
</HTML>
```

2. Save it as **example1.jsp** in the folder C:\myjspapp\chapter08.

3. Load the page, using the following URL:
   http://localhost:8080/myapp/chapter08/example1.jsp

   The page is displayed as shown in Figure 8-1.

Figure 8-1   Getting bean properties

In this example, the first thing the JSP does is to get the bean. The execution of the code `<jsp:useBean id="simpleBean" class="com.jspbook.chapter08.Simple Bean"/>` creates a new bean object from the class specified in the class attribute, and binds this bean to the local variable specified in the ID attribute. Once the bean is loaded, the getProperty tag gets its property and inserts it into the output.

Set Bean Properties

Once you have a bean, you can modify its properties via the tag jsp:setProperty. The setProperty action tag takes the following form:

<jsp:setProperty name="bean_name" property="property_name"
value="a new property value" />

This tag assigns a new value to the specified property. In this tag, the "value" attribute specifies the new value to be assigned to the bean property. In the following exercise, you use this action tag to assign a new value to the bean property.

1. Open a new document in your text editor, and type in the following code:

```
<HTML>
<HEAD><TITLE>Example2: set and get bean property</TITLE>
</HEAD>
```

```
<BODY>
<jsp:useBean id="simpleBean"
class="com.jspbook.chapter08.SimpleBean"/>
<H3>The original property value:</H3>
<H1>
<jsp:getProperty name="simpleBean" property="message"/>
</H1>
<H3>Set a new property value.<H3>
<jsp:setProperty name="simpleBean" property="message"
value="Hello World!"/>
<H3>The new property value is:</H3>
<H1>
<jsp:getProperty name="simpleBean" property="message"/>
</H1>
</BODY>
</HTML>
```

2. Save this as **example2.jsp** in the folder C:\myjspapp\chapter08.

3. Load the page using the following URL:
   http://localhost:8080/myapp/chapter08/example2.jsp

   The page is displayed as shown in Figure 8-2.

Figure 8-2   Set and get a bean's property

In the above example, the tag `<jsp:setProperty name="simpleBean"property ="message" value="Hello World!"/>` sets the message property of the bean to a new value: "Hello World!", and then the getProperty tag is used to retrieve the new property value.

A property of a bean can be set as many times as you need. Each value of the property stays in effect until the next change. Each time you assign a new value to a property, the new value overwrites the old property value.

In the above example, the new value is hard-coded. Hard-coded values are fine for many purposes, but for beans to participate in dynamic pages, they must be capable of interacting with other dynamic elements. One way to accomplish this is to use an expression to set a property. The setProperty tag can accept as a value any expression that can be put in a <%= %> tag. In the following exercise, you will set a property from an expression.

1. Open a new document in your text editor, and type in the following code:

```
<HTML>
<HEAD>
<TITLE>Example3: Set a bean property with an
expression</TITLE>
</HEAD>
<BODY>
Enter a message and submit the form.<br>
<form action="example3.jsp" method="POST">
<input type=text name="message">
<input type=submit value="Submit">
</form>
</BODY>
</HTML>
```

2. Save the file as **example3.html** in the folder C:\myjspapp\chapter08.

3. Open a new document in your text editor, and type in the following code:

```
<HTML>
<HEAD><TITLE>Example3: Set a bean property with an
expression</TITLE></HEAD>
<BODY>
<% String message=request.getParameter("message"); %>
<jsp:useBean id="simpleBean"
class="com.jspbook.chapter08.SimpleBean"/>
Set a new property value with an expression.<br>
<jsp:setProperty name="simpleBean" property="message"
value="<%= message %>"/>
The new property value is:<br>
<H1>
<jsp:getProperty name="simpleBean" property="message"/>
</H1>
</BODY>
</HTML>
```

4. Save the file as **example3.jsp** in the folder C:\myjspapp\chapter08.

5. Load example3.html, using the following URL:
http://localhost:8080/myapp/chapter08/example3.html

8

6. Type a message, as shown in Figure 8-3, and click the **Submit** button.

The message is displayed on the new page, as shown in Figure 8-4.

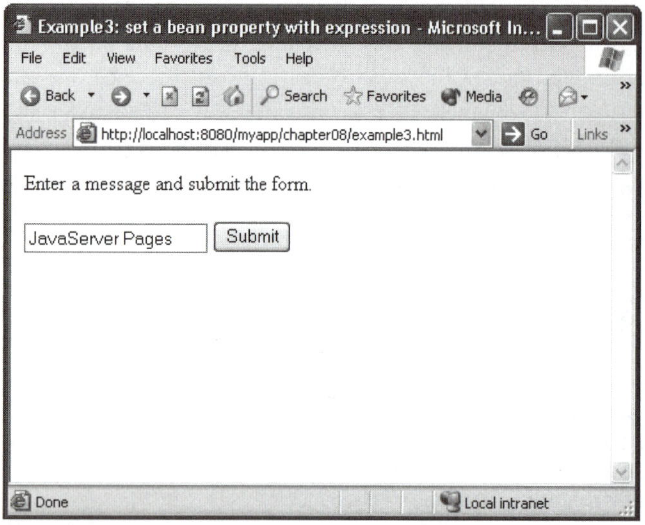

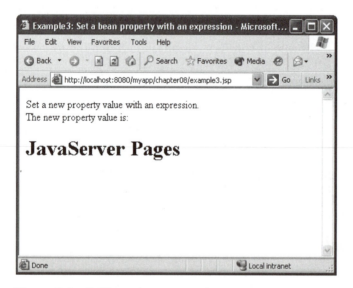

Figure 8-3   Setting a bean property form

Figure 8-4   Setting a bean property

In this example, a variable is defined on the example3.jsp page. The message you typed in example3.html is retrieved and assigned to the variable. This message is assigned to the bean's property by using an expression. You may wonder, why not assign the bean's property like this?

```
<jsp:setProperty name="simpleBean" property="message"
  value="<%= request.getParameter("message") %>"/>
```

It would be much simpler, because, using this method, you don't have to declare a variable. However, if you set a bean's property this way, you will get an exception in your JSP page. If you want to use request.getParameter to assign an attribute in JSP action tags, you have to use the escape character for the quotation marks inside the expression with backslashes. For instance, the above code could be modified as follows:

```
<jsp:setProperty name="simpleBean" property="message"
  value="<%= request.getParameter(\"message\") %>"/>
```

Without backslashes, the JSP page cannot be converted into a servlet, and the code will generate error messages instead.

BEANS AND FORMS

As you learned in previous chapters, dynamic Web pages are created in part with values that users provide via forms. Dynamic JSP pages often use these values to set the properties of JavaBeans. In the sections below, you will learn about the interaction between bean properties and form input parameters.

Setting Properties with Form Input Parameters

There is a simpler way to assign an input parameter to a bean than the method you learned above. JSP provides a shortcut. If, for example, a form provides an input parameter called foo, and if the bean has a property that is also called foo, to set the foo property of the bean with the form's foo input parameter, you use the following code:

```
<jsp:setParamter name="bean_name" property="foo"/>
```

In this case, the value assigned to the property is presumed to come from the form. In order for this technique to work, the bean must have a public setter method called setFoo, and this method takes a string object as an argument. This tag requires the match between the property name and the form's input parameter name. Sometimes the name of the form parameter and the name of the property do not match. In this case, you use another attribute, param, to specify the form's input parameter, as follows:

```
<jsp:setProperty name="bean_name" property="propertyName"
param="inputFieldName"/>
```

This tag uses the form input field called "inputFieldName" to set the bean's property called "propertyName".

In the following exercise, you will create a simplified calculator bean class to help to add two numbers. Then you will design a form to allow users to enter two numbers and use the bean object to process the form.

1. Open the data file CalcBean1.java, which is located in the folder C:\myjspapp\chapter08.

2. Add the code shaded in Figure 8-5.

```java
package com.jspbook.chapter08;
public class CalcBean1{
  private int value1;
  private int value2;
  private String value1S;
  private String value2S;
  private boolean value1_ok = false;
  private boolean value2_ok = false;

  public void setValue1(String value1){
    value1S = value1;
    try{
      this.value1 = Integer.parseInt(value1);
      value1_ok = true;
    }catch(Exception exc){}
  }
  public void setValue2(String value2){
    value2S = value2;
    try{
      this.value2 = Integer.parseInt(value2);
      value2_ok = true;
    }catch(Exception exc){}
  }

  public String getSum(){
    if(value1_ok && value2_ok)
      return "The sum of " + value1 + " and " + value2
          + " is " + (value1+value2);
    else {
      String tempS="The sum operation cannot be performed. Because <br>";
      if(!value1_ok)
        tempS += value1S + " is not a numeric value and <br>";
      if(!value2_ok)
        tempS += value2S + " is not a numeric value";

      return tempS;
    }
  }
}
```

Figure 8-5   CalcBean1.java

3. Save the file as **CalcBean1.java** in the folder C:\myjspapp\chapter08.

4. Open a DOS command window and change the directory to C:\myjspapp\chapter08.

5. At the DOS prompt, type the following command to compile and install the bean class:

javac –d c:\myjspapp\WEB-INF\classes CalcBean1.java

The calculator bean class has been installed. Now you are ready to use the calculator bean to add two numbers and output the result.

1. Open a new document in your text editor, and type in the following code:

```
<HTML>
<HEAD><TITLE>Example4: Simple calculator</TITLE></HEAD>
<BODY>
Enter two numbers and click the "Calculate" button.
<br><br>
<form action="example4.jsp" method="POST">
<input type=text name="value1" size=10 maxlength=9><br>
<input type=text name="value2" size=10 maxlength=9><br>
<input type=submit value="Calculate">
</form>
</BODY>
</HTML>
```

2. Save the file as **example4.html** in the folder C:\myjspapp\chapter08.

3. Open a new document in your text editor, and type in the following code:

```
<HTML>
<HEAD>
<TITLE>Example4: Simple calculator</TITLE>
</HEAD>
<BODY>
<jsp:useBean id="calcBean"
class="com.jspbook.chapter08.CalcBean1"/>
<jsp:setProperty name="calcBean" property="value1"/>
<jsp:setProperty name="calcBean" property="value2"/>
<jsp:getProperty name="calcBean" property="sum"/>
<br><br>
<a href="example4.html">Try again</a>
</BODY>
</HTML>
```

4. Save the file as **example4.jsp** in the folder C:\myjspapp\chapter08.

5. Load the page example4.html, using the following URL:
   http://localhost:8080/myapp/chapter08/example4.html

   The page is displayed as shown in Figure 8-6.

6. Enter two numbers and click the **Calculate** button. The sum of these two numbers is displayed on another page. Try to enter non-numeric values and click **Calculate**. A message is displayed on the page saying that the operation cannot be performed because the values you entered are not numeric values.

8

Figure 8-6 Simple calculator input form

In this example, the two values you entered in example4.html are passed to the second page, example4.jsp. In the page example4.jsp, a bean is created from the CalcBean1 class. The two values you entered on the first page are used to set the properties of the beans. The following tags assume that there are two input fields called "value1" and "value2" on the form:

```
<jsp:setProperty name="calcBean"
property="value1"/>
<jsp:setProperty name="calcBean" property="value2"/>
```

These form input fields are used to set the bean's properties accordingly. If a property name is not used as an input field name on the form, a null value is assigned to that property. After the bean's properties have been set, you use the following getProperty tag to display the sum of these two numbers.

```
<jsp:getProperty name="calcBean" property="sum"/>
```

You may notice that there is no property called sum in the CalcBean class. If there is no such property, how can you get it? Indeed, the getProperty action tag does not get any property directly. What the getProperty tag does is call the corresponding getter method. So, the above getProperty tag actually calls the getSum method of the bean object. In general, the execution of the action tag `<jsp:getProperty name="bean_name" property="foo"/>` calls the getFoo() method and inserts the value returned from this method in its output.

The action tag `<jsp:getProperty name="bean_name" property="bar"/>` does not imply that this bean has a property named "bar". But it does imply that the bean has a method called getBar.

The same rule applies to the setProperty tag. The execution of the tag `<jsp:setProperty name="bean_name" property="foo"/>` calls the setFoo method of the bean. If the method setFoo is not defined in the bean class, an exception occurs. The argument passed to the setter method is the value of the input field called "foo" on its corresponding form. Again, if the input field called "foo" is not found on the form, a null value is passed to the method.

 The action tag `<jsp:setProperty name="bean_name"property= "bar"/>` does not imply that this bean has a property named "bar". But it does imply that the bean has a method called setBar.

Bean properties can be of any data type, even though most JSP scripts deal with strings. The values you get from form input fields are always strings, and these strings are passed to beans' setter methods. If a bean's setter method expects an integer and is passed a string, an exception occurs. In most cases, the JSP engine attempts to convert the string to an appropriate data type. For example, if a method expects an integer, the JSP engine calls Integer.parseInt to try to convert the passed string to an integer value. If this automatic conversion fails—perhaps because a user entered a non-numerical value that cannot be converted into an integer—an exception occurs. Another, more robust approach is to convert strings to appropriate data types in the setter methods. This approach is used in the CalcBean class, where the properties value1 and value2 are integers, but their setter methods take strings as arguments. These strings are converted into integers within the setter methods.

To handle potential errors when converting strings to integers, there are two Boolean instance variables defined in this class. These Boolean variables are initially set to false. If a string value is successfully converted into an integer, its corresponding Boolean value is set to true, indicating that the string value has been converted to an integer and assigned to its corresponding property (instance variable). The getSum method uses these two Boolean instance variables to test whether the two values are ready. If so, the sum of these two numbers is returned; otherwise, a message is returned specifying the reason why the sum operation cannot be performed. If you instead allow the JSP engine to attempt an automatic conversion, and the automatic conversion fails, the setter method is not called and several exception messages are displayed. In the exercise below, you will write another calculator bean class that performs automatic conversion in its setter methods.

1. Open a new document in your text editor, and type in the following code:

```
package com.jspbook.chapter08;
public class CalcBean2{
  private int value1;
  private int value2;
  public void setValue1(int value1){
    this.value1 = value1;
  }
   public void setValue2(int value2){
```

8

```
        this.value2 = value2;
    }
    public String getSum(){
        return "The sum of " + value1 + " and " + value2 +
        " is " + (value1+value2);
    }
}
```

2. Save the file as **CalcBean2.java** in the folder C:\myjspapp\chapter08.

3. Open a DOS command window and change the directory to C:\myjspapp\chapter08.

4. Compile and install this bean class, using the following command under the DOS prompt:

   javac –d c:\myjspapp\WEB-INF\classes CalcBean2.java

5. The file example5.html is provided as a data file; this file is basically the same as example4.html, except that its action attribute is changed to example5.jsp.

6. Open the data file example5.jsp, which is located in the folder C:\myjspapp\chapter08.

7. Change the class attribute of the useBean tag to `com.jspbook.chapter08.CalcBean2`. Change the Try again hyperlink anchor to example5.html.

8. Save and close the file.

9. Load the page example5.html, using the following URL: http://localhost:8080/myapp/chapter08/example5.html

10. Enter two numbers and click the **Calculate** button. The sum of these two numbers is displayed. As long as you enter two numerical values, it works fine. However, if you enter a non-numerical value, the JSP engine cannot perform automatic conversion, and an exception is thrown. As a result, several exception messages are displayed.

As a reusable component, a JavaBean facilitates form processing and implements business logic, or the rules that govern data manipulation. In the above example, both example5.html and example5.jsp present user interfaces: one provides a form to collect data, and one displays the output. The data manipulation—specifically, the adding of two numbers—is implemented in CalcBean1. You don't need to worry about whether the values passed to CalcBean1 are valid numerical values or not; the bean itself handles everything. Using beans makes it easy to separate business logic from presentation.

There is one last version of the setProperty tag, which is the most powerful. This version looks through all the input fields provided by the form and all the methods provided by the bean, and links them together automatically. The tag takes the following form:

<jsp:setProperty name="bean_name" property="*"/>

If the form provides input field names called name1, name2, and so on, and the bean has methods called setName1, setName2, and so on, everything matches up perfectly, and all these methods are called automatically, as if you had written setProperty tags for all these properties. If a property (setter method) cannot find the match input field name on the form, it is ignored and no error occurs. The following example illustrates how to use this tag to connect a bean's properties with a form's input fields.

1. Open the data file example6.html in your text editor; this file is located in the folder C:\myjspapp\chapter08.

2. Add code to specify that the data collected on this form will be processed in example6.jsp.

3. Save and close the file.

4. Open a new document in your text editor, and type in the following code:

```
<HTML>
<HEAD><TITLE>Example6: Simple calculator</TITLE></HEAD>
<BODY>
<jsp:useBean id="calcBean"class="com.jspbook.chapter08.
CalcBean1"/>
<jsp:setProperty name="calcBean" property="*"/>
<jsp:getProperty name="calcBean" property="sum"/>
<br><br>
<a href="example6.html">Try again</a>
</BODY>
</HTML>
```

5. Save the file as **example6.jsp** in the folder C:\myjspapp\chapter08.

6. Load the page example6.html, using the following URL:
http://localhost:8080/myapp/chapter08/example6.html

7. Enter numbers and click the **Calculate** button. This example performs exactly like example4.html.

The only difference between these two examples is that different versions of the setProperty tag are used. In example6.html, the execution of the setProperty tag calls all setter methods of the bean, as long as the same property names can be found in the input field names on the form. Since there are two matched filenames on the form, value1 and value2, the setValue1 and setValue2 methods of the bean are called.

Working with Arrays

Sometimes multiple values are associated with one input field. In Chapter 6, you learned to get multiple values by using the getParameterValues method of the request object. You can also use a bean to get all the values associated with the same input field on a form, as in the following exercise.

8

1. Open a new document in your text editor, and type in the following code:

```
package com.jspbook.chapter08;
public class ArrayBean {
  private String[] values;
  public String getValuesString(){
    String tempS = "";
    if(values != null){
      for(int i=0; i<values.length; i++)
        tempS += values[i] + "<br>";
    }
    return tempS;

  public void setValues(String[] values){
    this.values = values;
  }
}
```

2. Save the file as **ArrayBean.java** in the folder C:\myjspapp\chapter08.

3. Open a DOS command prompt window, and change to the directory C:\myjspapp\chapter08.

4. Under the Dos prompt, use the following command to compile and install this Java class:

javac –d c:\myjspapp\WEB-INF\classes ArrayBean.java

5. Open a new document in your text editor, and type in the following code:

```
<HTML>
<HEAD><TITLE>Example7: Array processing</TITLE></HEAD>
<BODY>
<jsp:useBean id="arrayBean"
class="com.jspbook.chapter08.ArrayBean"/>
<jsp:setProperty name="arrayBean" property="values"
param="music"/>
Music type you listen to:<br>
<jsp:getProperty name="arrayBean"
property="valuesString"/>
<hr width=250 color=blue align=left>
<form action="example7.jsp" method="POST">
  What types of music do you listen to?<br>
  <input type=checkbox name=music value=Rock>Rock
  <input type=checkbox name=music value=Jazz>Jazz
  <input type=checkbox name=music
value=Classical>Classical
  <input type=checkbox name=music value=Pop>Pop
  <br><br>
  <input type=submit value="Submit">
</form>
</BODY>
</HTML>
```

6. Save the file as **example7.jsp** in the folder C:\myjspapp\chapter08.

7. Load the page, using the following URL:
http://localhost:8080/myapp/chapter08/example7.jsp

8. Select the music you listen to, and click the **Submit** button. The page displayed is similar to Figure 8-7.

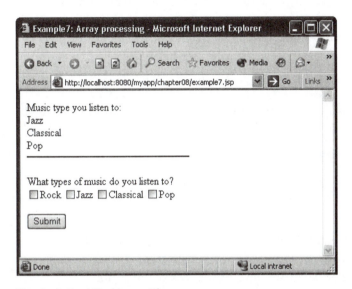

Figure 8-7   Working with an array

The ArrayBean class has a setter method that takes a String array as an argument. Since this method expects a String array, the execution of the setProperty tag gets all values associated with the music input field as an array, and this array is passed to the setter method. To display all of the elements of the String array of the bean, you need to call the getter method getValuesString to convert the string elements to a single string. Since the property name and the input field name on the form do not match, you use the param attribute to specify the input field name used to set the property of the bean.

BEANS AND SCRIPTLETS

To use a bean, a bean object must be created and bound to a variable. The execution of the tag <jsp:useBean id="bean_name" class="class_Path"/> locates or instantiates a bean object from the class, and binds the variable specified as "bean_name" to the bean object. After the variable "bean_name" has been bound to the bean object, you can use this variable as a reference to the bean object in your JSP script. Since the variable is a reference to the bean object, you can call all methods provided by the bean in your JSP scriptlets. In the following exercise, you will modify the calculator example to use a bean object in scriptlets.

1. Open the data file example8.html in your text editor; this file is located in the folder C:\myjspapp\chapter08.

2. Change the action attribute of the form to example8.jsp.

3. Save and close the file.

4. Open a new document in your text editor, and type in the following code:

```
<HTML>
<HEAD><TITLE>Example8: Simple calculator</TITLE></HEAD>
<BODY>
<jsp:useBean id="calcBean"
class="com.jspbook.chapter08.CalcBean1"/>
<%
  calcBean.setValue1(request.getParameter("value1"));
  calcBean.setValue2(request.getParameter("value2"));
%>
<%= calcBean.getSum() %>
<br><br>
<a href="example8.html">Try again</a>
</BODY>
</HTML>
```

5. Save it as **example8.jsp** in the folder C:\myjspapp\chapter08.

6. Load the page example8.html, using the following URL:
   http://localhost:8080/myapp/chapter08/example8.html

This simple calculator performs just as in previous examples. In this example, the tag `<jsp:useBean id="calcBean" class="com.jspbook.chapter08.CalcBea n"/>` instantiates a bean object and binds this object to the variable called "calcBean". This variable is used in the scriptlet as a reference to the bean object.

READING FROM AND WRITING TO A FILE

There are many situations in your Web application where you may need to read data from and write data to files. For example, an online news Web site might allow journalists to edit news online via the Internet by accessing files stored on the Web server. In this section, you will write a bean that can read data from and write data to a file. Then you will construct a bulletin board by using the bean.

1. Open the data file FileBean.java, which is located in the folder C:\myjspapp\chapter08.

2. Add the code shaded in Figure 8-8, which is a while loop to read data line by line from a file.

```
package com.jspbook.chapter08;

import java.io.*;

public class FileBean {
  private String file;
  public void setFile(String file){ this.file=file;}
  public void setData(String data){
    FileWriter fw = null;
    PrintWriter pw = null;
    try{
      fw = new FileWriter(file, true);
      pw = new PrintWriter(fw);
      pw.println(data);
      pw.flush();
      pw.close();
      fw.close();
    }catch(Exception exc){}
  }
  public String getData(){
    FileReader fr = null;
    BufferedReader br = null;
    String line = "";
    String tempS = "";
    try{
      fr = new FileReader(file);
      br = new BufferedReader(fr);
      line = br.readLine();
      while(line != null){
        tempS = tempS + line + "<br>";
        line = br.readLine();
      }
    }catch(Exception exc){}
    return tempS;
  }
}
```

8

Figure 8-8   File-reading bean

3. Save the file.

4. Open a DOS command prompt window, and change to the following directory: C:\myjspapp\chapter08.

5. Use the following command to compile and install the FileBean class:

javac −d c:\myjspapp\WEB-INF\classes FileBean.java

To perform file input and output operations, you use the package java.io.* to import all the required classes. This JavaBean class provides several methods that allow you to read data from, and write data to, files. You use the method setFile to set the file you are going to work with. The method setData writes data to a file, and the method getData reads data from a file. If you are not familiar with the Java programming language, don't worry. You can simply use the bean class provided here to perform file input and/or output operations. As long as you know how to use action tags, you do not need to know the details of how the file input and output are performed.

In the exercise below, you will use the file bean to build a bulletin board for your Web site.

1. Open a new document in your text editor, and type in the following code:

```
<HTML>
<HEAD><TITLE>Example9: Bulletin board</TITLE></HEAD>
<BODY>
<h2>Select Bulletin Board</h2>
<form action="example9.jsp" method="POST">
  <select name="topic">
  <option value="none">Select a topic
  <option value="JSP">Java Server Pages
  <option value="Tomcat">Tomcat Server
  <option value="Java">Java Programming
  </select><br><br>
  <input type=submit name="view" value="View
  bulletin"><br>
  <input type=submit name="post" value="Post bulletin">
</form>
</BODY>
</HTML>
```

2. Save the file as **example9.html** in the folder C:\myjspapp\chapter08.

3. Open the data file example9.jsp, which is located in the folder C:\myjspapp\chapter08.

4. Add the code shaded in Figure 8-9.

5. Save the file.

6. Load the page example9.html, using the following URL: http://localhost:8080/myapp/chapter08/example9.html

```
<HTML>
<HEAD><TITLE>Example9: Bulletin board</TITLE></HEAD>
<BODY>
<jsp:useBean id="fileBean" class="com.jspbook.chapter08.FileBean"/>
<%
  String topic = request.getParameter("topic");
  String vPath = "chapter08/"+topic+".txt";
  String filePath =
    getServletConfig().getServletContext().getRealPath(vPath);
  if(topic.equals("none")){
%>
Please select a topic.
<% } else {%>
  <jsp:setProperty name="fileBean" property="file"
      value="<%= filePath %>"/>
<%
    if(request.getParameter("view")!= null){
%>
    <jsp:getProperty name="fileBean" property="data"/>
<%  } %>
<%  if(request.getParameter("post") != null ) { %>
  <h2><%= topic %> Bulletin Board</h2>
  <form action="example9.jsp" method=post>
  <TextArea name=message cols=25 rows=5></TextArea>
  <input type=hidden name=topic value="<%= topic%>"><br>
  <input type=submit name=addBulletin value="post bulletin">
  </form>
<%  } %>
<% if(request.getParameter("addBulletin") != null &&
      !request.getParameter("message").equals("")) {
%>
<h2>Bulletin Saved!</h2>
<jsp:setProperty name="fileBean" property="data" param="message"/>
<jsp:setProperty name="fileBean" property="data"
    value="--------------------------------"/>
<% }%>
<%}%>
<br><br>
<a href="example9.html">Return to main Page</a>
</BODY>
</HTML>
```

Figure 8-9   Using FileBean

This page is displayed as shown in Figure 8-10.

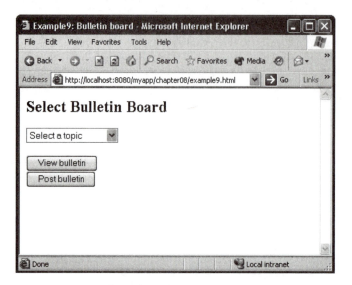

Figure 8-10   Bulletin board

7. Select a topic and click the **Post bulletin** button. A new page similar to Figure 8-11 is displayed. Enter a message and click the **Post bulletin** button to post a bulletin. The page shown in Figure 8-12 is displayed, indicating that the new bulletin has been added to the bulletin file. Click the link **Return to main page**, and repeat this step to add more bulletin messages.

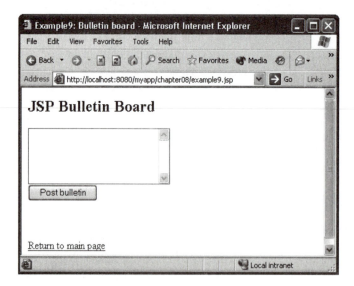

Figure 8-11   Posting a bulletin

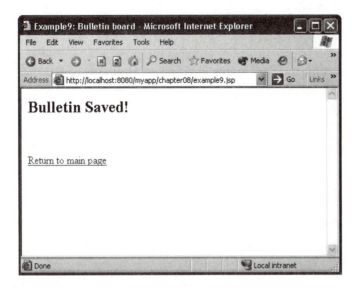

Figure 8-12   Saving the bulletin

8. To view bulletins, select a topic from the topic list, then click **View bulletin** to display messages that have been posted on the topic you selected. The page displayed is similar to the one shown in Figure 8-13.

In this example, you need not worry about how to read bulletins from a file and how to post bulletins. The file bean handles these for you. The file bean can be used in any JSP page to perform file input and output operations.

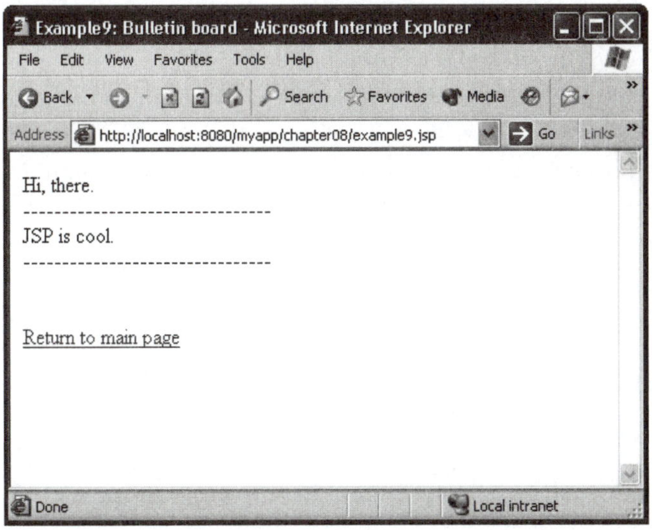

Figure 8-13   Viewing the bulletin

CHAPTER SUMMARY

❐ JavaBeans are instances of Java classes. They are commonly used in JSP script to facilitate form processing and the implementation of business logic.

❐ In general, a bean provides two methods for each property: one to get the property and one to set the property. In order to be able to get and set a bean's property, the getter and setter methods must follow certain naming conventions.

❐ A default constructor must be provided in order to instantiate a bean object with action tags.

❐ When you instantiate a bean object from a class, the class must be available to the JSP engine, so the class must be installed somewhere in the CLASSPATH where the JSP engine searches for the required classes.

❐ JSP provides three basic action tags for working with beans: one to bind a local variable to an existing bean object or instantiate a new bean object, one to get a property, and one to set one or more properties.

❐ Action tags provide a shortcut for setting a bean's properties with form input fields.

❐ Bean properties can be of any data type. If an argument passed to the setter method does not match the data type specified in the method definition, the JSP engine tries to convert that argument to an appropriate data type.

❐ The tag `<jsp:useBean id="bean_name" class="class_path"/>` binds a variable named "bean_name" to a bean object. This variable can be used in JSP scripts to reference the bean object.

❐ As a JSP developer, you can use the FileBean bean developed in this chapter to perform file input/output operations.

REVIEW QUESTIONS

1. To access a bean's property named foo, the getter method name should be:

   a. getFoo

   b. getfoo

   c. foo

   d. Foo

2. To set a bean's property named foo, the setter method name should be:

   a. setFoo

   b. setfoo

   c. foo

   d. Foo

3. A bean class can be installed anywhere in the local file system. True or False?

4. To use a bean with action tags, a default constructor must be provided. True or False?

5. Assume that a bean's method expects an integer as an argument. If you pass a string to this method, then which of the following statements is/are true?

    a. The JSP engine tries to convert the passed string to an integer before this method is called.

    b. An exception occurs, and this method is not called.

    c. If the string is a non-numerical value, an exception occurs and this method is not called.

    d. If the string is a numerical value, then this method is called.

6. Which of the following statements sets the bean's property named "value1" with the value of the input field named "lastName" on a form?

    a. `<jsp:setProperty name="bean_name" property="value1"/>`

    b. `<jsp:setProperty name="bean_name" property="value1" value="lastName"/>`

    c. `<jsp:setProperty name="bean_name" property="value1" param="lastName"/>`

    d. `<jsp:setProperty name="bean_name" property="*"/>`

7. Two beans can have the same bean name on the same page. True or False?

8. Assume that a bean's setter method is defined as follows: `void setFoo(int anInt){ … }`. When the tag `<jsp:setProperty name="beanName" property="foo" value="hello"/>` executes:

    a. an exception occurs and this method will not be called

    b. this method is called but an exception occurs later on

    c. this method is called successfully

    d. nothing happens

9. Assume that a bean's setter method is defined as follows: `void setFoo(String s){ … }`. When the tag `<jsp:setProperty name="beanName" property="foo" value="200"/>` executes:

    a. an exception occurs and this method will not be called

    b. this method is called but an exception occurs later on

    c. this method will be called

    d. nothing happens

8

10. If the execution of the action tag `<jsp:getProperty name="bean_name" property="foo"/>` does not result in an exception, which of the following statements is/are true?

a. The bean has a property called "foo".

b. The bean has a method called getFoo.

c. A string is inserted into the output stream.

d. There is an input field named foo on a form.

11. If the form that corresponds to the action tag `<jsp:setProperty name="bean_name" property="foo"/>` does not have an input field named "foo", then which of the following is/are true?

a. A null is passed to the setFoo method.

b. A null value is assigned to the foo property of the bean.

c. An exception occurs.

d. Nothing happens.

12. Which of the following scriptlets is equivalent to `<jsp:getProperty name="aBean" property="foo"/>`?

a. `<%= aBean.getFoo() %>`

b. `<% out.print(aBean.getFoo()); %>`

c. `<%= "foo" %>`

d. `<%= aBean.foo %>`

13. Which of the following scriptlets is/are equivalent to `<jsp:setProperty name="aBean" property="foo"/>`?

a. `<% aBean.setFoo(); %>`

b. `<% aBean.setFoo("foo"); %>`

c. `<% aBean.setFoo(request.getParameter("foo")); %>`

d. `<% aBean.setFoo(request.getParameterValues("foo")); %>`

14. Which of the following scriptlets is/are equivalent to `<jsp:setProperty name="aBean" property="foo" value="Hello"/>` ?

a. `<% aBean.setFoo("Hello"); %>`

b. `<% aBean.setFoo("foo"); %>`

c. `<% aBean.setFoo(request.getParameter("foo")); %>`

d. `<% aBean.setFoo(request.getParameterValues("foo")); %>`

15. Which of the following scriptlets is/are equivalent to `<jsp:setProperty name="aBean" property="foo" param="value1"/>`?

    a. `<% aBean.setFoo("value1"); %>`

    b. `<% aBean.setFoo("foo"); %>`

    c. `<% aBean.setFoo(request.getParameter("value1")); %>`

    d. `<% aBean.setFoo(request.getParameterValues("value1")); %>`

16. Assume that a bean has the following methods: getValue1, getValue2, setValue1, and setValue2, and that both of the setter methods take a string object as arguments. Then the tag `<jsp:setProperty name="aBean" property="*"/>` is equivalent to:

    a. `<% aBean.setValue1(request.getParameter("value1"));`
       `aBean.setValue2(request.getParameter("value2")); %>`

    b. `<% aBean.setValue1("value1"); aBean.setValue2("value2");`
       `%>`

    c. `<% aBean.setValue1("*"); aBean.setValue2("*"); %>`

    d. `<% aBean.setValues(*); %>`

17. The execution of the tag `<jsp:setProperty name="bean" property="foo"/>` can set another property of the bean, for example the "bar" property of the bean. True or False?

18. You cannot use an action tag to call a getter method that returns an array. True or False?

19. Regarding a bean class, which of the following statements is/are true?

    a. If no constructor is provided, a default constructor is provided by the JSP engine.

    b. If any constructor is defined in the class, no default constructor is provided automatically.

    c. The default constructor takes no argument.

    d. Constructors have no return type.

20. To instantiate a bean with an action tag, which of the following statements is/are correct?

    a. The default constructor is called.

    b. The constructor with an argument is called.

    c. A local variable specified as ID attribute is bound to the bean object.

8

HANDS-ON PROJECTS

Project 8-1 Letter Grade Conversion Bean

In Chapter 4, you created a JSP page that outputs a letter grade according to a numerical value. In this project, you will write a bean to encapsulate the rule for converting a number to a corresponding letter grade, and then use this bean in a JSP page.

1. Open the data file GradeBean.java, which is located in the folder C:\myjspapp\chapter08.

2. Add the code shaded in Figure 8-14, which converts a number to its corresponding letter grade.

```java
package com.jspbook.chapter08;
public class GradeBean {
  private String grade;
  private boolean validGrade = false;
  private String message;
  public void setGrade(String grade){
    try{
      int value = Integer.parseInt(grade);
      if(value>=90) this.grade="A";
      else if(value >= 80) this.grade ="B";
      else if(value >=70) this.grade = "C";
      else if(value >= 60) this.grade = "D";
      else this.grade = "F";
      validGrade = true;
    }catch(Exception exc){
      validGrade = false;
      message = "The grade is not valid:<br>" + exc.toString();
    }
  }
  public String getGrade(){
    if(validGrade)
      return grade;
    else
      return message;
  }
}
```

Figure 8-14   English language version of a simple procedural billing program

3. Save the file.

4. Open a DOS command prompt window, and change the directory, using the following command: **cd c:\myjspapp\chapter08**.

5. Use the following command to compile and install the bean class:

   javac −d c:\myjspapp\WEB-INF\classes GradeBean.java.

6. Create a new document in your text editor, and save the file as **project1.jsp** in the folder C:\myjspapp\chapter08.

7. Add code to use the GradeBean class to convert a number to its corresponding letter grade.

8. Load the page, using the following URL:
   http://localhost:8080/myapp/chapter08/project1.jsp

   The page is displayed as shown in Figure 8-15.

9. Type a grade on the page, then click the **Get letter grade** button. The corresponding grade should be displayed.

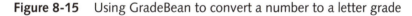

Figure 8-15   Using GradeBean to convert a number to a letter grade

Project 8-2 Payroll System

You are hired to develop an online payroll system that allows users to determine their gross pay based on the hours worked in a week. To calculate gross pay, the company uses the following rules: it pays "straight time" for the first 40 hours worked by each employee, and "time and a half" for all hours worked in excess of 40. The maximum number of hours an employee may work in one week is 65. The hourly rates for employees are 30 dollars for managers and 20 dollars for staff. You will write a bean to implement the business rules, then use this bean to calculate and display gross pay based on employee input.

1. Open the data file PayBean.java.

2. Add the code shaded in Figure 8-16, which determines the rate based on employment type.

```
package com.jspbook.chapter08;

public class PayBean {
  private String position;
  private boolean validData = false;
  private String message;
  private double payment;
  public void setPosition(String position){
    this.position = position;
  }
  public void setHours(String hours){
    try{
      double workHours = Double.parseDouble(hours);
      int rate =0;
      if(workHours>=0 && workHours <=65.0){
        if(position.equals("manager"))
          rate = 30;
        else
          rate = 20;
        if(workHours <=40.0)
          payment = rate*workHours;
        else
          payment = rate*40 + rate*(1.5)*(workHours - 40);
        validData = true;
      }else{
        validData = false;
        message = "The hours: " + hours + " is not valid";
      }
    }catch(Exception exc){
      validData = false;
      message = "Calculation cannot be performed:<br>" + exc.toString();
    }
  }
  public String getPayment(){
    if(validData)
      return "Payment is: $" + payment;
    else
      return message;
  }
}
```

Figure 8-16   PayBean.java

3. Save the file.

4. Open a DOS command window and change the directory, using the command:
   cd c:\myjspapp\chapter08.

5. Compile and install the bean class, using the following command:
   javac –d c:\myjspapp\WEB-INF\classes PayBean.java.

6. Use Figure 8-17 as a guideline to design a new JSP page named project2.jsp in the folder C:\myjspapp\chapter08.

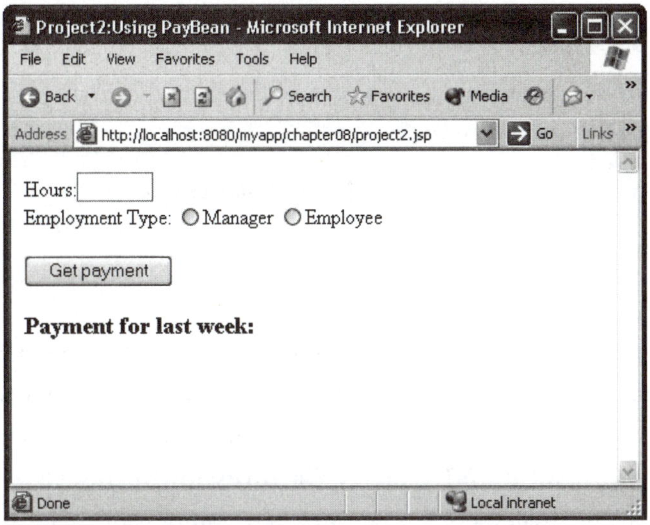

Figure 8-17   Calculating gross pay

7. Load the page, using the following URL:
   http://localhost:8080/myapp/chapter08/project2.jsp

   The page is displayed as shown in Figure 8-17.

8. Enter the number of hours worked and select employment type, then click **Get payment**. The payment for the last week should be displayed.

Project 8-3 Sales Commission

A car dealer pays its salespeople on a commission basis. Salespeople receive $320 per week plus 2 % of their gross sales for that week. In this project, you will write a bean to implement this logic. After the bean is installed, you will design a page to use the bean to help salespersons to calculate earnings.

1. Open a new document in your text editor, and type in the following code:

```
package com.jspbook.chapter08;
public class CommissionBean {
  private boolean validData = false;
  private String message;
  private double commission;
  public void setGrossSales(String sales){
    try{
      double grossSales = Double.parseDouble(sales);
      commission = 320 + grossSales *0.02;
      validData = true;
    }catch(Exception exc){
      validData = false;
```

```
            message = "Calculation cannot be performed:<br>" +
            exc.toString();
        }
    }
    public String getEarning(){
      if(validData)
        return "Commission is: $" + commission;
      else
        return message;
    }
}
```

2. Save the file as CommissionBean.java in the folder C:\myjspapp\chapter08.

3. Open a DOS command window and change the directory to C:\myjspapp\chapter08.

4. Compile and install the class, using the following command:

   java –d c:\myjspapp\WEB-INF\classes CommissionBean.java.

5. Create a JSP page to help salespeople calculate their commissions. This page
   should provide an input field to allow salespeople to input their gross sales, and a
   Submit button to submit the form. Then a bean is used to calculate the commission, and the result is displayed on the page. Use Figure 8-18 as a guideline. The
   figure shown is based on $40,000 in gross sales for that week.

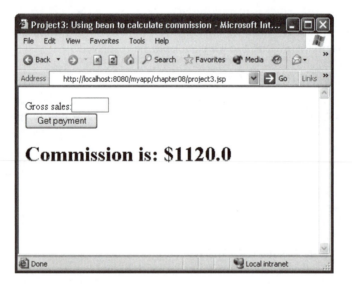

Figure 8-18   Calculating earnings

Project 8-4 Using FileBean to Update a Guestbook Web Page

In this project, you will use the FileBean class developed in this chapter to update and
read from a Web site guestbook.

1. Design an HTML page, as shown in Figure 8-19. Save this file as project4.html in the folder C:\myjspapp\chapter08. Corresponding to the labels shown in Figure 8-19, name the input fields Name, E-mail Address, Company, Comments, and Sign in, respectively.

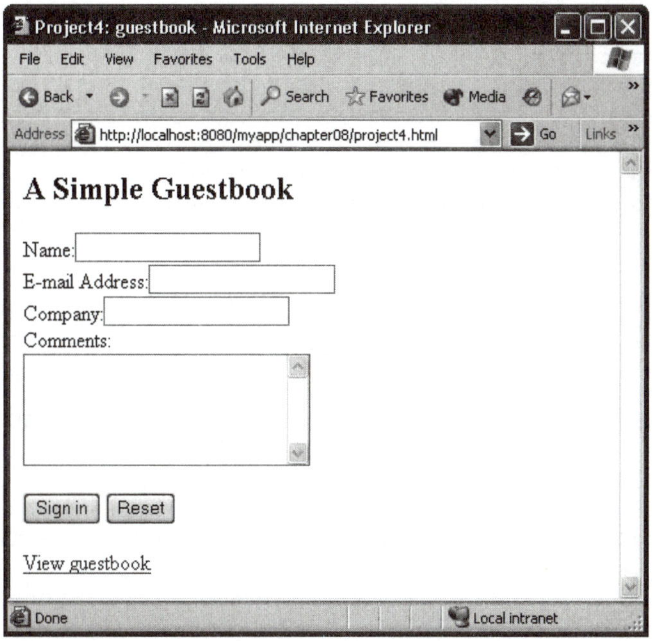

Figure 8-19   Sign-in form

2. Specify in the HTML file that the data collected on the form will be processed in the file project4.jsp when the Sign in button is clicked.

3. Specify in the HTML file that the link View guestbook directs the user to project4_view.jsp, which displays all guests who have signed the guestbook.

4. Open a new document in your text editor, and type in the following code:

```
<HTML>
<HEAD><TITLE>Project4: Sign-in guestbook</TITLE></HEAD>
<BODY>
<% String vPath = "/chapter08/guestbook.txt";
   String rPath =
     getServletConfig().getServletContext().getRealPath
     (vPath);
%>
<jsp:useBean id="guestbook"
class="com.jspbook.chapter08.FileBean"/>
<jsp:setProperty name="guestbook" property="file"
    value="<%= rPath%>"/>
```

```
<jsp:setProperty name="guestbook" property="data"
param="name"/>
<jsp:setProperty name="guestbook" property="data"
param="email"/>
<jsp:setProperty name="guestbook" property="data"
param="company"/>
<jsp:setProperty name="guestbook" property="data"
param="comments"/>
<jsp:setProperty name="guestbook" property="data"
   value="---------------------------------"/>
<h2>Thanks for signing in to the guestbook</h2>
<a href="project4.html">Sign-in</a><br><br>
<a href="project4-view.jsp">View guestbook</a>
</BODY>
</HTML>
```

5. Save the file as **project4.jsp** in the folder C:\myjspapp\chapter08.

6. Open a new document in your text editor, and type in the following code:

```
<HTML>
<HEAD><TITLE>Project4: View guestbook</TITLE></HEAD>
<BODY>
<% String vPath = "/chapter08/guestbook.txt";
   String rPath =
      getServletConfig().getServletContext().getRealPath
(vPath);
%>
<h2>Guestbook</h2>
<jsp:useBean id="guestbook"
class="com.jspbook.chapter08.FileBean"/>
<jsp:setProperty name="guestbook" property="file"
     value="<%= rPath%>"/>
<jsp:getProperty name="guestbook" property="data"/>
<br><br>
<a href="project4.html">Sign-in</a><br><br>
</BODY>
</HTML>
```

7. Save the file as **project4-view.jsp** in the folder C:\myjspapp\chapter08.

8. Load page project4.html, using the following URL:
   http://localhost:8080/myapp/chapter08/project4.html

   The page is displayed as shown in Figure 8-19.

9. Enter information and click the **Sign in** button. The page project4.jsp is displayed, as shown in Figure 8-20, which indicates that the guest data has been saved to the guestbook file.

   Click the **View guestbook** link, and the page displays all signed-in guests, as in Figure 8-21.

Figure 8-20   Sign in to the guestbook

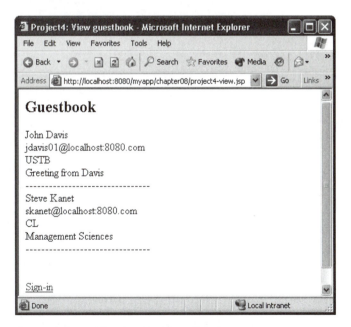

Figure 8-21   Viewing the guestbook

Project 8-5 Generic File Bean

In this project, you will write a JavaBean with the following requirements: a setter method to set its property, named file; a getLine method to read one line from the file; a method to test whether there are more lines in the file to read; and a setline method to append new data to the end of the file.

1. Open the data file FileBean2.java, which is located in the folder C:\myjspapp\chapter08.

2. Add the code shaded in Figure 8-22 to read lines from a file.

```java
package com.jspbook.chapter08;

import java.io.*;

public class FileBean2 {
  private String file;
  private FileReader fr = null;
  private BufferedReader br = null;
  public void setFile(String file){ this.file=file;}
  public void setLine(String data) throws IOException{
    PrintWriter pw = null;
    pw = new PrintWriter(new FileWriter(file, true));
    pw.println(data);
    pw.flush();
    pw.close();
  }

  public String getLine() throws IOException{
    if(br==null){ //prepare to open the file
      br = new BufferedReader(new FileReader(file));
    }
    String line =null;
    line = br.readLine();
    if(line==null) {br.close(); br=null;}
    return line;
  }
}
```

Figure 8-22   FileBean2.java

3. Save the file.

4. Open a DOS command window and change the directory, using the command: **cd c:\myjspapp\chapter08**.

5. Compile and install the bean class, using the command: **javac –d c:\myjspapp\chapter08 FileBean2.java**.

6. Open the data file **project5.html**, which is located in the folder C:\myjspapp\chapter08.

7. Specify that the data collected on this page will be processed in project5-1.jsp.

8. Save and close the file.

9. Open data file **project5-1.jsp**, which is located in the folder C:\myjspapp\chapter08.

10. Add the code shaded in Figure 8-23 to retrieve the data collected on project5.html, and set the line property of the bean with the data.

```
<HTML>
<HEAD><TITLE>Project5: Birthday list</TITLE></HEAD>
<BODY>
<% String vPath = "/chapter08/birthday.txt";
   String rPath =
     getServletConfig().getServletContext().getRealPath(vPath);
%>
<% String data = request.getParameter("name") + " " +
       request.getParameter("birthday");
%>
<jsp:useBean id="birthday" class="com.jspbook.chapter08.FileBean2"/>
<jsp:setProperty name="birthday" property="file"
    value="<%= rPath%>"/>
<jsp:setProperty name="birthday" property="line"
    value="<%= data%>"/>
<h2>Thanks for signing in to the birthday list</h2>
<a href="project5.html">Sign-in</a><br><br>
<a href="project5-2.jsp">View birthday list</a>
</BODY>
</HTML>
```

Figure 8-23   Project5-1.jsp

11. Save and close the file.

12. Open the data file project5-2.jsp, which is located in the folder C:\myjspapp\chapter08.

13. Add the code shaded in Figure 8-24 to read the family members' birthday list from a file and display it on the page.

14. Save and close the file.

15. Load the page project.html, using the following URL: http://localhost:8080/myjsp/chapter08/project5.html

16. You may add a few family members' birthdays, and you can also view the birthday list.

```
<HTML>
<HEAD><TITLE>Project5: Birthday list</TITLE></HEAD>
<BODY>
<% String vPath = "/chapter08/birthday.txt";
    String rPath =
      getServletConfig().getServletContext().getRealPath(vPath);
%>
<jsp:useBean id="birthday" class="com.jspbook.chapter08.FileBean2"/>
<jsp:setProperty name="birthday" property="file"
    value="<%= rPath%>"/>
<h2>Birthday list for family.</h2>
<% String line=null;
    while((line=birthday.getLine())!=null){
      out.println(line +"<br>");
    }
%>
<a href="project5.html">Sign-in</a><br><br>
</BODY>
</HTML>
```

Figure 8-24   Project5-2.jst

Project 8-6 Create a Bean to Validate Customer Input Data

In this project, you will write a simple bean to validate an input field based on the following rules:

❑ The value must begin with a character

❑ The length of the value must be between 5 and 15 characters.

❑ The value cannot contain spaces.

❑ All characters are in uppercases; if not, the bean will change them to uppercase.

❑ If a value is valid (passes all the above rules), the bean provides a method to return this valid value; otherwise, an empty string should be returned.

  1. Open the data file ValidatingBean.java in the folder C:\myjspapp\chapter08.

  2. Add the code shaded in Figure 8-25 to implement the validating rules specified above.

  3. Save the file.

  4. Open a DOS command window and change the directory, using the command:

    cd c:\myjspapp\chapter08.

```
package com.jspbook.chapter08;

public class ValidatingBean {
  private String data;
  private String message;
  public void setData(String data){
    //check whether the value begins with digit
    try{
      Integer.parseInt(data.substring(0,1));
      this.data="";
      message = "This value begins with a digit!";
      return;
    }catch(Exception exc){}
    this.data = data.toUpperCase();
    if(data.length() <5 || data.length()>15){
      message = "The number of the characters is " + data.length()+".";
      this.data = "";
      return;
    }
    if(this.data.indexOf(" ") != -1){
      message = "The data contains spaces.";
      this.data = "";
    }else{
      message = "The data is OK.";
    }
  public String getData(){
    return data;
  }
  public String getMessage(){
    return message;
  }
}
```

Figure 8-25   ValidatingBean.java

5. Compile and install bean classes, using the command:

   java –d c:\myjspapp\WEB-INF\classes ValidatingBean.java

6. Open a new document in your text editor and save the file as **project6.jsp** in the folder C:\myjspapp\chapter08.

7. Add code to create a bean instance from the bean class ValidatingBean.

8. Add code to design a form on this page with a text input field. Use this input field to set the "data" property of the bean.

9. Specify the action of the form so that the data collected on the form will be processed in the same page.

10. Add code to get the message and data properties of the bean.

11. Save the file.

12. Open the page, using the following URL:
    http://localhost:8080/myapp/chapter08/project6.jsp

    The page is displayed as shown in Figure 8-26.

13. Enter a value and click **Validation** to verify the validating rules.

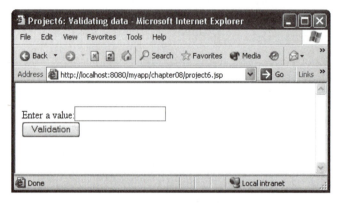

Figure 8-26   Validation with JavaBean

Project 8-7 Truth Table Bean

In this project, you will write a bean to display the truth table for a logical operator. This project is similar to Project 4-3 in Chapter 4, but in this project the main logic of the truth table is implemented in the bean class.

1. The TruthTableBean.java file is provided in the folder C:\myjspapp\chapter08. Compile and install the bean class.

2. Create a JSP page using the TruthTableBean to display truth tables. If you do not know how to design a truth table, you should review Project 4-3 in Chapter 4.

CASE PROJECTS

SRAS: Update Student Profile

In the Student Records Access System, only the faculty is allowed to add courses. A JavaBean class called AddCourseBean.java has been provided in the folder C:\myjspapp\chapter08\sras. In this project, you are required to modify the file addcourse.jsp (which is provided as a data file in the folder C:\myjspapp\chapter08\sras) so that the AddCourseBean is used to add courses to the database. Please note that you must compile and install the JavaBean class properly before you use it in the JSP file.

Library Search Bean

The XYZ entertainment company has hired you to develop a Web site to extend their business over the Internet. This company carries music CDs. You must provide a page to allow clients to view all available music, or search for a particular kind of music. You must create and implement a JavaBean to accomplish this. All data is stored in a text file containing the name of the performer or composer and the title. Each record takes one line in the file, and the performer and title are separated by a tab. Clients can also search for music written by a performer or composer.

Advanced Bulletin Board

In this project, you will enhance the bulletin board that you created in this chapter so that the webmaster is allowed to delete bulletins on the Internet. Modify the FileBean class to accomplish this task.

8

9

SCOPES OF VARIABLES AND JAVABEANS

> **In this chapter, you will:**
> ♦ Learn the difference between variable scope and variable duration
> ♦ Learn the difference between variables defined in declarations and variables defined in scriptlets
> ♦ Create and use page scope, session scope, and application scope variables
> ♦ Create and use page scope, request scope, session scope, and application scope beans

In the previous chapter, you learned how to write JavaBean classes and how to use JavaBeans to process forms and implement business rules. Thus far all the beans you have seen can only be referenced on the page on which they are instantiated. In this chapter, you will learn about variable and bean scopes. Specifically, you will learn how to define and use beans in four different scopes, namely, page scope, request scope, session scope, and application scope.

VARIABLE SCOPE

You already know how to use variables to store information, and how to use that information in your JSP scripts. Variables have many attributes, among them duration and scope. **Variable duration** is the period during which the variable exists in memory. Some variables exist briefly, some are repeatedly created and destroyed, and others exist after your Web application starts. The **scope of a variable** refers to where a variable can be referenced in your JSP scripts. Some variables can be referenced from any JSP pages in your Web application, some can be referenced within the same session, and others can be referenced only from limited portions of a JSP page. Duration and scope are two different attributes of variables. A variable may still exist in memory even if it is not referenced in a program.

Page Scope Variables

You can declare variables in a declaration or in scriptlets. Variables defined in a declaration are created when the servlet that defines them is loaded into memory, and continue to exist throughout the execution of the Web application. Variables defined in scriptlets are created when the program control reaches their declarations; they exist throughout the execution of the JSP page, and they are destroyed when the execution of the page is finished. Both variable declarations have the same **page scope**, because they can be referenced only on the page in which they are defined, but the variable durations are different. Variables defined in declarations continue to exist much longer than those defined in scriptlets. When a JSP page is requested for the first time, the page is compiled into a servlet and the servlet is loaded into memory. The variables defined in declarations are created when the servlet is loaded into memory, and these variables remain in memory until the servlet is unloaded from memory. The variables defined in scriptlets exist only during the execution of the page. The following example demonstrates the durations of variables defined in declarations and scriptlets.

1. Open a new document in your text editor, and type in the following code:

```
<HTML>
<HEAD><TITLE>Example1: page scope</TITLE></HEAD>
<BODY>
The variables defined in a <b>declaration</b> have
<b><u>instance scope</u></b>
<br>
&lt;%! int counter1 = 0; %&gt;
<%! int counter1 = 0; %><br><br>
The variables defined in <b>scriptlets</b> have
<b><u>local scope</u></b>
<br>
&lt;% int counter2 = 0; %&gt;
<% int counter2 = 0; %><br><br>
```

```
The current value of counter1: <b><%= counter1++ %></b>
<br><br>
The current value of counter2: <b><%= counter2++ %></b>
</BODY>
</HTML>
```

2. Save the file as **example1.jsp** in the folder C:\myjspapp\chapter09.

3. Load the page, using the following URL:
   http://localhost:8080/myapp/chapter09/example1.jsp

4. Reload the page by clicking the **Refresh** button on the browser toolbar. A page similar to the one shown in Figure 9-1 is displayed.

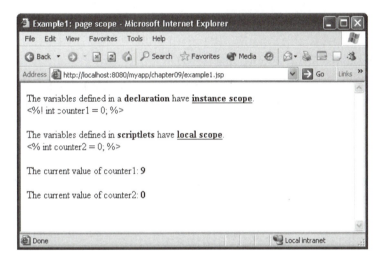

Figure 9-1   Declaring variables

In this example, counter1 increments by 1 every time this page is reloaded, while the value in counter2 remains the same. This is because counter1 is defined in a declaration, and is created and initialized when the corresponding servlet is loaded into memory. The same variable is accessed on the successive requests for the page. Counter2 is defined in scriptlets; it is created and initialized every time the page is requested, and destroyed when the execution of the page is finished.

If two variables, one defined in a declaration and one defined in scriptlets, have the same name, the variable defined in a declaration is "hidden" from the point where a variable with the same name is defined in scriptlets. The following example illustrates how the variable defined in scriptlets hides the one defined in a declaration.

1. Open a new document in your text editor, and type in the following code:

```
<HTML>
<HEAD><TITLE>Example2: hiding variable</TITLE></HEAD>
```

```
<BODY>
A variable defined in a<b>declaration</b>.
<br>
&lt;%! int counter = 0; %&gt;
<%! int counter = 0; %><br><br>
A variable with the same name as above defined in <b>
scriptlets</b>.
<br>
&lt;% int counter = 0; %&gt;
<% int counter = 0; %><br><br>
The current value of the counter: <b><%= counter++ %></b>
</BODY>
</HTML>
```

2. Save the file as **example2.jsp** in the folder C:\myjspapp\chapter09.

3. Load the page, using the following URL:
   http://localhost:8080/myapp/chapter09/example2.jsp

4. Reload the page several times. The counter value remains unchanged. This is because the variable defined in scriptlets hides the variable defined in a declaration. Therefore the counter value displayed is the one defined in scriptlets, not the one defined in a declaration.

Even though variables defined in declarations and scriptlets have different durations, they have the same page code. These variables can be referenced only from the page in which they are defined.

Session and Application Scope Variables

Page scope variables can be referenced only from the page in which they are defined. Other types of variables can be referenced from more than one JSP page or even from any JSP pages within a Web application. A session object is available throughout a session. As discussed in Chapter 7, you can store information in a session object by binding objects with attributes set to the session object. Objects bound to the attributes of the session object are retrievable from any JSP page in the same session. These attributes of the session object serve as session variables, and they are tied to the current session only. Because they can be referenced only within the same session, they have **session scope**. These objects cannot be referenced after the session expires or becomes inactive (for example, a client closes the browser window before the session expires). Some variables can be referenced through the entire Web application. These variables have **application scope**. There is only one application object in a Web application, and it is shared throughout the entire Web application, so all objects associated with the application object are shared. The following example illustrates the use of variables with different scopes.

1. Open a new document in your text editor, and type in the following code:

```
<%
 String existingID =
  (String)session.getAttribute("userID");
 if(existingID == null){
    //if the user id has not been assigned, assign one
    Object existingCounter =
     application.getAttribute("counter");
    if( existingCounter == null){
       existingCounter = new Integer(1000);
       application.setAttribute("counter",
existingCounter);
    }
    int counter =
     ((Integer)(existingCounter)).intValue();
    counter++;
    existingID = counter + "";
    application.setAttribute("counter", new Integer
(counter));
    session.setAttribute("userID", existingID);
 }
%>
Your User ID: <b><%= existingID%></b><br>
```

2. Save the file as **getID.jsp** in the folder C:\myjspapp\chapter09.

3. Open a new document in your text editor, and type in the following code:

```
<HTML>
<HEAD><TITLE>Example3: session and application scope
</TITLE></HEAD>
<BODY>
<%@ include file="getID.jsp" %>
</BODY>
</HTML>
```

4. Save the file as **example3.jsp** in the folder C:\myjspapp\chapter09.

5. Load the page example3.jsp, using the following URL:
http://localhost:8080/myapp/chapter09/example3.jsp

In this example, the included file getId.jsp is used to get a unique user ID. The code: `String existingID = (String)session.getAttribute("userID")` is used to get the user ID bound to the "userID" attribute of the session variable. If no object is bound to the attribute, it returns null, which indicates that this is a new user and a new user ID needs to be created and assigned to the user. The code segment: `Object existingCounter = application.getAttribute("counter")` tests whether an object has been bound to the "counter" attribute of the application object. If not, a null value is returned, and an initial value is bound to the attribute. To bind a variable to an attribute of session or application objects, the variable must be an object,

9

so the int primitive data type is converted to an Integer object, and then the Integer object is bound to the counter attribute of the application object. An Integer object provides a method called intValue to get its corresponding int value. After the counter value is assigned to a user, the counter value increments by one and then the new value is bound to the counter attribute of the application object.

 Primitive data values cannot be bound to attributes of session or application objects. To be bound, these primitive data values have to be converted to their corresponding objects.

The session object has session scope. All objects bound to the session object are available as long as the current session is still available. In this example, after a user ID is assigned to a user, you can reference it from other JSP pages in the same session. On the other hand, the application object is available throughout the entire Web application. Therefore, all objects bound to the application object can be referenced from all JSP pages in the same Web application.

JAVABEAN SCOPE

In Chapter 8, you learned how to instantiate a JavaBean object, and how to use the bean object in your JSP scripts. A bean object can have one of the following scopes: page scope, request scope, session scope, or application scope. The syntax for specifying the scope of a bean object has the following form:

<jsp:useBean id="bean_name" class="class_name" scope="bean_scope"/>

Each scope specifies how long a bean exists in memory and where the bean object can be referenced.

Page Scope JavaBeans

Page scope is the default scope for JavaBeans. It's the scope used in all examples you have seen so far. Page scope bean objects are available only to action tags or scriptlets within the page in which they are instantiated. These bean objects disappear as soon as the current page is finished. To explicitly specify page scope, use the following syntax:

<jsp:useBean id="bean_name" class="class_name" scope="page"/>

A page scope bean object may be modified as often as desired within the page, but all these changes are lost when the page is closed.

To illustrate the different scopes of a bean, the following JavaBean class is used in future exercises in this chapter. Please follow the steps to create, compile, and install the bean class in an appropriate CLASSPATH.

1. Open a new document in your text editor, and type in the following code:

```
package com.jspbook.chapter09;
public class Counter{
 private int counter=0;
 public int getCounter(){ return ++counter;}
}
```

2. Save the file as **Counter.java** in the folder C:\myjspapp\chapter09.

3. Open a DOS command window and the change directory, using the command:

cd c:\myjspapp\chapter09

4. Compile and install the bean class, using the following command:

javac –d c:\myjspapp\WEB-INF\classes Counter.java

The counter bean has one property called counter, which is initialized to zero, and a getter method to get the counter property. Before the getter method returns the counter value, it increments the counter first. This simple bean is used to track the number of hits on a Web page.

In the following exercise, you will test a page scope bean.

1. Open a new document in your text editor, and type in the following code:

```
<HTML>
<HEAD><TITLE>Example4: page scope bean</TITLE></HEAD>
<BODY>
A counter bean with page scope.<br><br>
<jsp:useBean id="counterBean"
 class="com.jspbook.chapter09.Counter" scope="page"/>
This page has been accessed
<b><jsp:getProperty name="counterBean"
  property="counter"/></b>
time(s).
<br><br>
<a href="example4.jsp">Reload this page</a>
</BODY>
</HTML>
```

2. Save the file as **example4.jsp** in the folder C:\myjspapp\chapter09.

3. Load the page, using the following URL:
http://localhost:8080/myapp/chapter09/example4.jsp

4. Reload the page several times; the same counter value is displayed, as shown in Figure 9-2.

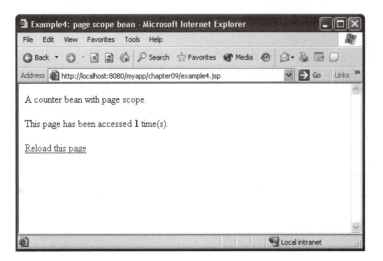

Figure 9-2   Page scope bean

In this example, the bean is instantiated with page scope, and the getProperty action tag is used to modify the counter value and get the counter value after modification. However, because the bean has page scope, the bean object is gone after the request for this page has been processed. So each time this page is requested, a new bean object is created, and the bean is destroyed.

 Page scope has the shortest lifetime among the four scopes. A page scope bean is repeatedly created upon request and destroyed after the execution of the page.

Request Scope JavaBeans

Request scope bean objects have the same lifetime as the request object. This may seem no different from page scope, since presumably the request object lasts exactly as long as the page it requested. In most cases, when a client requests a JSP page, the server processes the request and outputs to the client. In this case, there is no difference between page and request scopes. However, you can separate requests using the JSP forward tag. To forward a request to another page, use the following syntax:

<jsp:forward page="relativeURL"/>

This action tag lets you forward the request to another page. It has a single attribute, page, which consists of a relative URL. The forward action stops the processing of the current page and continues processing the same request on the new target page. The page attribute can be dynamically assigned upon a request for the page as follows:

<jsp:forward page="<%= someJavaExpression %>" />

The forward action passes the same request to the new target page. Therefore, the bean object is also available to the target page. In the following example, you will create a request scope bean object and use it from the pages involved in the same request scope.

1. Open a new document in your text editor, and type in the following code:

```
<HTML>
<HEAD><TITLE>Example5-1: request scope bean</TITLE></HEAD>
<BODY>
<jsp:useBean id="counterBean"
 class="com.jspbook.chapter09.Counter" scope="request"/>
<jsp:getProperty name="counterBean" property="counter"/>
<jsp:forward page="example5-2.jsp"/>
</BODY>
</HTML>
```

2. Save the file as **example5-1.jsp** in the folder C:\myjspapp\chapter09.

3. Open a new document in your text editor, and type in the following code:

```
<HTML>
<HEAD><TITLE>Example5-2: request scope bean</TITLE>
</HEAD>
<BODY>
A counter bean with request scope.<br><br>
<jsp:useBean id="counterBean"
 class="com.jspbook.chapter09.Counter" scope="request"/>
This page has been accessed
<b><jsp:getProperty name="counterBean"
 property="counter"/></b>time(s).
</BODY>
</HTML>
```

4. Save the file as **example5-2.jsp** in the folder C:\myjspapp\chapter09.

5. Load the page example5-1.jsp, using the following URL:
http://localhost:8080/myapp/chapter09/example5-1.jsp

The page is displayed as shown in Figure 9-3.

When the page example5-1.jsp is initially requested, a request scope bean is created and its property is obtained via the getProperty action. However, the execution of the forward action forwards the request to example5-2.jsp, and the new target page continues processing the same request. Since the bean created in the old target page example5-1.jsp is a request scope bean, the bean object is available within the same request. So the new target page does not create a new bean object. Instead, the bean object created in the old target page is used. The counter property increments by 1 in the original target page, so the getProperty action in the new target page returns 2. That is why you see the page displayed as shown in Figure 9-3. After processing the target page, the bean object is out of scope and is destroyed. So reloading this page returns the same result.

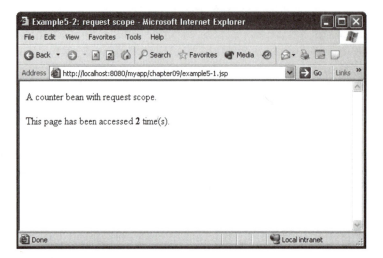

Figure 9-3   Forwarding request

 Since the browser is not aware that more than one page is involved with the forward action, the URL remains unchanged. Therefore, reloading the page by clicking the Refresh button reloads the original requested page.

 The forward action stops the processing of the original target page, and forwards the request to the new target page. Any content buffered on the output stream is discarded when the request is forwarded to a new target page.

When you use the forward action, the target page processes the same request; therefore, all information encapsulated in the request is also available to the forwarded page.

In the following exercise, you will see that the information encapsulated in the request object is processed in the new target page.

1. Open a new document in your text editor, and type in the following code:

```
<HTML>
<HEAD><TITLE>Example6: forward request</TITLE></HEAD>
<BODY>
The following information is first sent to <br>
<u>example6-1.jsp</u>, then forwarded to <u>
example6-2.jsp</u>.
<br><br>
<form action="example6-1.jsp" method="POST">
 Message:<input type=text name=message><br>
 <input type=submit value="Submit">
</form>
</BODY>
</HTML>
```

2. Save the file as **example6.html** in the folder C:\myjspapp\chapter09.

3. Open a new document in your text editor, and type in the following code:

```
<HTML>
<HEAD><TITLE>Example6-1: forward request</TITLE></HEAD>
<BODY>
The request is processed in this page.<br><br>
The message retrieved is:<b>
<%= request.getParameter("message")%>
</b>
<jsp:forward page="example6-2.jsp"/>
</BODY>
</HTML>
```

4. Save the file as **example6-1.jsp** in the folder C:\myjspapp\chapter09.

5. Open a new document in your text editor, and type in the following code:

```
<HTML>
<HEAD><TITLE>Example6-2: forward request </TITLE></HEAD>
<BODY>
The message retrieved from the request object is:<b>
<%= request.getParameter("message")%>
</b>
<br><br>
The original request is processed in example6-2.jsp.
</BODY>
</HTML>
```

6. Save the file as **example6-2.jsp** in the folder C:\myjspapp\chapter09.

7. Load the page example6.html, using the following URL:
   http://localhost:8080/myapp/chapter09/example6.html

   The page is displayed as shown in Figure 9-4.

8. Enter a message and submit the form. A page similar to the one shown in Figure 9-5 is displayed.

The data collected in the form is originally sent to example6-1.jsp and processed there. But the processing is forwarded to another page with the following action tag. So the request object is passed and processed in the new target page specified as the page attribute in the forward action tag. However, since the browser is unaware that the request was forwarded to another page, the URL remains unchanged.

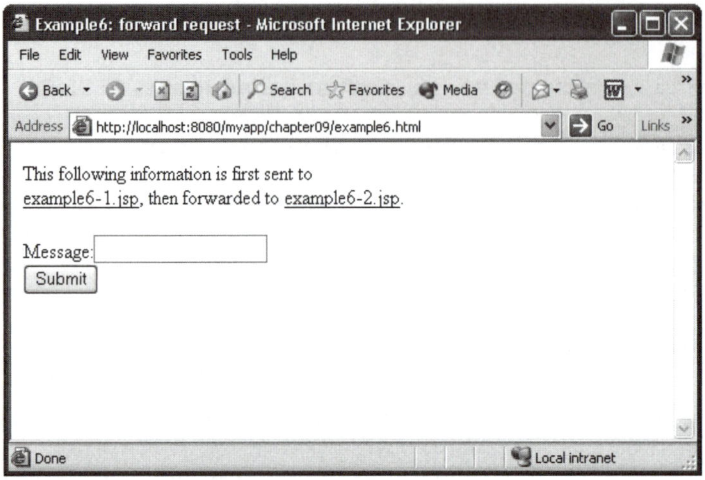

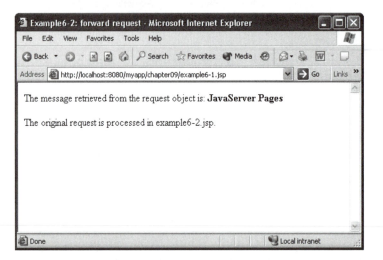

Figure 9-4   Forwarding a request

Figure 9-5   Processing the request in the new target page

Session Scope JavaBeans

Session scope bean objects have the same lifetime as the session object. Like session scope variables, these beans can be referenced throughout the session in which they are created. In the following exercise, you will create a session scope bean, and the same session bean object is referenced throughout the current session.

1. Open a new document in your text editor, and type in the following code:

```
<HTML>
<HEAD><TITLE>Example7: session scope bean</TITLE></HEAD>
```

```
<BODY>
A counter bean with session scope.<br><br>
<jsp:useBean id="counterBean"
 class="com.jspbook.chapter09.Counter" scope="session"/>
This page has been accessed
<b><jsp:getProperty name="counterBean"
  property="counter"/></b>
time(s).
<br><br>
<a href="example7.jsp">Reload this page</a>
</BODY>
</HTML>
```

2. Save the file as **example7.jsp** in the folder C:\myjspapp\chapter09.

3. Load the page, using the following URL:
http://localhost:8080/myapp/chapter09/example7.jsp

4. Click the **Reload this page** link to reload the page several times. The page should look like the one shown in Figure 9-6.

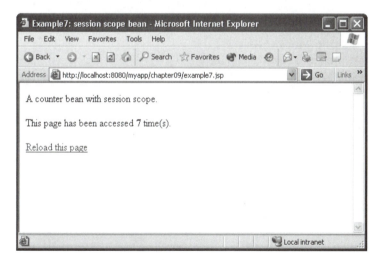

Figure 9-6 Session scope bean

A session scope bean is instantiated only once in a session. When a page having a session bean is requested, the JSP container determines whether a bean has been created in the current session. If a bean has been created, the existing bean is used. Therefore, a session scope bean is instantiated once, and the bean can be referenced throughout the current session. In the example above, a session scope bean is instantiated when the page is requested for the first time. All subsequent requests for this page use the same bean as long as the current session is active. Unlike the page scope bean, the session scope bean can be referenced from any JSP page in the same session.

You use jsp:setProperty to give values to properties of beans that have been created earlier. You have done this outside of the jsp:useBean element as follows:

```
<jsp:useBean id="beanName" class="className"
scope="beanScope"/>
...
<jsp:setProperty name="beanName"
property="someProperty" />
```

In this case, jsp:setProperty is executed regardless of whether a new bean is instantiated or an existing bean is found. In fact, the jsp:setProperty action tag can appear inside the body of a jsp:useBean element, as follows:

```
<jsp:useBean id="beanName" scope="beanScope">
 <jsp:setProperty name="myName" property="someProperty"s />
</jsp:useBean>
```

Here, jsp:setProperty is executed only if a new object is instantiated. The following example illustrates when the setProperty action is executed.

1. Open a new document in your text editor, and type in the following code:

```
package com.jspbook.chapter09;
import java.util.*;
public class MessageBean{
 private Date creationDate;
 private String message;
 public MessageBean(){
   creationDate = new Date();
 }
 public void setMessage(String message){
   this.message = message;
 }
 public String getMessage(){ return message;}
 public String getCreationDate(){
   return creationDate.toString();
 }
}
```

2. Save the file as **MessageBean.java** in the folder C:\myjspapp\chapter09.

3. Open a DOS command window and change the directory, using the following command:

cd c:\myjspapp\chapter09

4. Compile and install bean class using the following command:

javac -d c:\myjspapp\WEB-INF\classes MessageBean.java

5. Open a new document in your text editor, and type in the following code:

```
<HTML>
<HEAD><TITLE>Example8: Session Scope bean and setProperty
</TITLE></HEAD>
<BODY>
<jsp:useBean id="messageBean"
 class="com.jspbook.chapter09.MessageBean" scope=
"session">
 <jsp:setProperty name="messageBean" property="message"
 value="Set property within useBean tags."/>
</jsp:useBean>
This bean was created on:
<jsp:getProperty name="messageBean" property=
"creationDate"/>
<br><br>
<jsp:getProperty name="messageBean" property="message"/>
<jsp:setProperty name="messageBean" property="message"
 value=""/>
<br><br>
<a href="example8.jsp">Reload this page</a>
</BODY>
</HTML>
```

6. Save the file as **example8.jsp** in the folder C:\myjspapp\chapter09.

7. Load the page, using the following URL:
   http://localhost:8080/myapp/chapter09/example8.jsp

   The page is displayed as shown in Figure 9-7.

8. Reload the page. Then the page is displayed as shown in Figure 9-8.

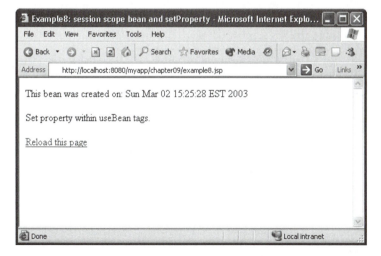

Figure 9-7   Setting properties within useBean tags

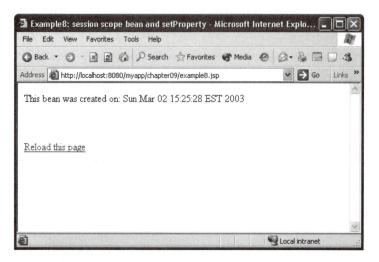

Figure 9-8   Setting properties using the setProperty action

In this example, the JavaBean class has two properties: creationDate and message. When a bean object is created, the creationDate property is set to the current date. The setMessage method sets the message property. Two getter methods are provided to get creationDate and message. When the page example8.jsp is requested for the first time in the current session, a session scope bean is created, and the setProperty action in the body of the useBean action is executed. The message "Set property with useBean tags" is displayed as long as the creationDate property is displayed. Then setProperty is used to set the message with an empty string again. On successive requests, since the bean has been created and loaded in memory, the useBean action is not executed anymore; therefore, the setProperty action in the body of useBean is not executed. Instead, the setProperty method outside of the useBean tag is executed, and the get "message" property returns the message set in the previous request for this page—in this case, it always is an empty string. In fact, the same bean is used as long as the current session is active.

In the following example, you will design a shopping cart for an online bookstore. The shopping cart is implemented using a session bean. This example includes a JavaBean class and three pages. The JavaBean class is used to create the shopping cart bean. An HTML page provides the list of items; one JSP page processes items in the shopping cart, and another handles the checkout process.

1. Open the data file ShopCart1.java, which is located in C:\myjspapp\chapter09.

2. Add the code shaded in Figure 9-9 to complete the setItemArray method.

3. Save the file.

4. Open a DOS command window and change the directory, using the command:

   cd c:\myjsapapp\chapter09

```
package com.jspbook.chapter09;
/**
 * This class has three private data members: A string array stores the book
 * titles, an integer array stores the quantity of each book that has been
 * added to the shopping cart, and a double array stores the price information
 * for each item.
 */
public class ShopCart1{
  private String[] titles = {"Java Programming","Java Server Pages",
                              "Java Servlet Programming"};
  private int[] items = new int[3];
  private double[] prices = {45.69, 50.66, 55.69};

  /**
   * Create a method to add items to the shopping cart. The parameter is a
String
   * array obtained from an item list form from which a shopper selects
   * items.
   */
  public void setItemsArray(String[] item){
    if(item == null) return;
    for(int i=0; i<item.length; i++){
      try{
        int index = Integer.parseInt(item[i]);
        items[index]++;
      }catch(Exception exc){}
    }
  }
  /**
   * a method to allow shoppers to remove items from the shopping cart.
   * If an item is removed from the cart, the total of the item is set to zero.
   */
  public void resetItem(int index){
    items[index] = 0;
  }
  /**
   * getter methods to access the private data members
   */
  public String[] getTitles(){ return titles;}
  public int[] getItems(){
    return items;
  }
  public double[] getPrices(){
    return prices;
  }
}
```

Figure 9-9   ShopCart1.java

5. Compile and install the shopping cart JavaBean, using the following command:

javac –d c:\myjspapp\WEB-INF\classes ShopCart1.java

6. Open data file example9.html, which is located in the folder C:\myjspapp\chapter09.

7. Add the code shaded in Figure 9-10 to specify that the data collected on this page will be processed in example9-1.jsp.

```
<HTML>
<HEAD>
<TITLE>Example9: shopping cart</TITLE>
</HEAD>
<BODY>
<h2>An Online Book Store</h2>
Check the items then click the Add button to add items to the shopping cart.
<br><br>
<form action=example9-1.jsp method=post>
<input type="checkBox" name=items value="0">
  <i><b>Java Programming</b></i>
Unit Price: $45.69<br>
<input type="checkBox" name=items value="1">
  <i><b>Java Server Pages</b></i> Unit Price: $50.66<br>
<input type="checkBox" name=items value="2">
  <i><b>Java Servlet Programming</b></i> Unit Price: $55.69<br><br>
<input type=submit value="Add">
</form>
</BODY>
</HTML>
```

Figure 9-10   Example9.html

8. Save the file.

9. Open a new document in your text editor to use the shopping cart. Save the file as **example9-1.jsp** in the folder C:\myjspapp\chapter09. This page is used to add items to the shopping cart, display items that have been added to the shopping cart, or remove items from the shopping cart.

10. Add the basic HTML tags and the useBean action tag to create a shopping cart session scope bean, as follows:

```
<HTML>
<HEAD><TITLE>Example9: adding or removing items</TITLE>
</HEAD>
<BODY>
<jsp:useBean id="cart"
 class="com.jspbook.chapter09.ShopCart1"
      scope="session"/>
<jsp:setProperty name="cart" property="itemsArray"
 param="items"/>
```

11. Add the following code segment to remove an item from the shopping cart:

```
<%
 String action = request.getParameter("remove");
 if( action != null){
  cart.resetItem(Integer.parseInt(action));
 }
%>
```

12. Add a table and column names to display the item information, as follows:

```
<h2>Items in shopping cart:</h2>
<table>
<tr>
 <th>Item</th>
 <th>Quantity</th>
 <th>Unit Price</th>
 <th>Subtotal</th>
 <th> </th>
</tr>
```

13. Add the code below to use the cart bean object to get the items that have been added to the cart. Then a loop is used to display each item in the table.

```
<%
 int[] items = cart.getItems();
 double[] prices = cart.getPrices();
 String[] titles = cart.getTitles();
 double total = 0;
 for(int i=0; i<items.length; i++){
  if(items[i]>0){
    total += prices[i]*items[i];
%>
   <tr><td><%= titles[i] %></td>
     <td align=center><%= items[i] %></td>
     <td align=center>$<%= prices[i]%></td>
     <td align=center>$<%= prices[i]*items[i]%></td>
     <td><a href=example9-1.jsp?remove=<%= i%>>Remove
</a></td>
   </tr>
 <%}%>
<%}%>
```

14. Add the code below to display the total price and add links to allow shoppers to add more items or check out.

```
<tr><td colspan=3 align=right>Total</td>
  <td colspan=2 align=left>$<%= total%></td>
</tr>
<tr><td colspan=5 align=center>
  <a href="example9.html">Add more items</a>  
  <a href="example9-2.jsp">Checkout</a>
  </td>
```

```
</tr>
</table>
</BODY>
</HTML>
```

15. Save the file.

16. Open a new document in your text editor, and save it as **example9-2.jsp** in the folder C:\myjspapp\chapter09. This page is used for processing the shopping cart.

17. Add the basic HTML tags and the useBean action as shown below. Note that a session scope bean called "cart" already exists, so it is used in this page.

```
<HTML>
<HEAD><TITLE>Example9-
2: processing shopping cart</TITLE></HEAD>
<BODY>
<jsp:useBean id="cart"
class="com.jspbook.chapter09.ShopCart1" scope="session"/>
```

18. Add the code to get item information from the shopping cart bean and calculate and display the total charge, as follows:

```
<%
 int[] items = cart.getItems();
 double[] prices = cart.getPrices();
 double total = 0;
 for(int i=0; i<items.length; i++){
  if(items[i]>0){
   total += prices[i]*items[i];
  }
 }
%>
<h2>
Total payment:$<%= total%><br>
Thank you for shopping with us.
</h2>
```

19. Add the code below to expire the current session, so the shopping cart cannot be referenced further. A link is provided to allow shoppers to continue shopping; when a user clicks this link, a new shopping cart bean is created, because the current cart cannot be referenced after the current session expires.

```
<% session.invalidate(); %>
<br><br>
<a href="example9.html">continue shopping</a>
</BODY>
</HTML>
```

20. Save the file.

21. Load the page example9.html, using the following URL:
http://localhost:8080/myapp/chapter09/example9.html

The page is displayed as shown in Figure 9-11.

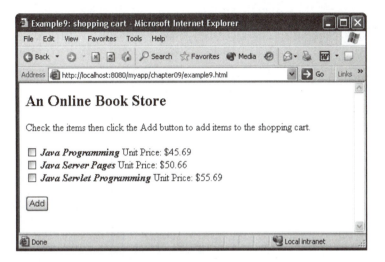

Figure 9-11 Using the shopping cart

22. Check the items on the form, and click the **Add** button to add them to the shopping cart. A page similar to the one shown in Figure 9-12 is displayed.

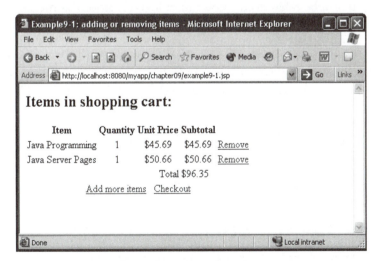

Figure 9-12 Adding items to the shopping cart

23. You may add more items to or remove items from the shopping cart before checking out. Click **Checkout**, and a page similar to the one shown in Figure 9-13 is displayed, showing the total payment. After you check out, a new session begins when you return to the shopping page.

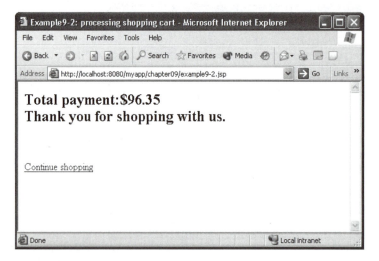

Figure 9-13   Checking out

Application Scope JavaBeans

A session scope bean can be referenced across multiple pages as long as the session where the bean was created is still active. Compared to page or request scope beans, session scope beans have longer lifetimes. Page scope, request scope, and session scope beans are associated with a single user, and cannot be shared across all users. The **application scope** bean, which persists across all users and all pages, is created once and exists throughout the execution of the Web application. In the following example, you will create a page that tracks the number of hits across all users throughout the execution of the Web application.

1. Open a new document in your text editor, and type in the following code:

```
<HTML>
<HEAD><TITLE>Example10: application scope bean</TITLE>
</HEAD>
<BODY>
A counter bean with application scope.<br><br>
<jsp:useBean id="counterBean"
 class="com.jspbook.chapter09.Counter" scope=
"application"/>
This page has been accessed
<b><jsp:getProperty name="counterBean" property="counter"
/></b>time(s).
```

```
<br><br>
<a href="example10.jsp">Reload this page</a>
</BODY>
</HTML>
```

2. Save the file as **example10.jsp** in the folder C:\myjspapp\chapter09.

3. Load the page, using the following URL:
   http://localhost:8080/myapp/chapter09/example10.jsp

4. Reload the page several times, then close the browser window and reload the page using the URL specified in Step 3. You should see the page-hit number increase by one each time you access the page.

In the above example, the counter bean is created when a user requests the page for the first time. Since the bean has application scope, it stays in memory and the same bean is used on successive requests from all users. So the counter bean reflects the total number of hits on this page by all users.

If the session scope bean has the same name as an application scope bean, then the application scope bean is "hidden" from the point where the session scope bean is referenced. In the following example, you will create a session scope bean and an application scope bean to demonstrate that an application bean is hidden by a session bean with the same name.

1. Open the data file example11-1.jsp.

2. Add the code shaded in Figure 9-14 to instantiate a session bean.

```
<HTML>
<HEAD>
<TITLE>Example11-1: creating a session bean</TITLE>
</HEAD>
<BODY>
A session scope bean was created on this page.<br><br>

<jsp:useBean id="messageBean"
 class="com.jspbook.chapter09.MessageBean" scope="session">
 <jsp:setProperty name="messageBean" property="message"
 value="This is the session scope bean "/>
</jsp:useBean>

<h1>
<jsp:getProperty name="messageBean" property="message"/>
</h1>
<br>
<a href="example11-1.jsp">Reload example11-1.jsp</a><br>
<a href="example11-2.jsp">Load example11-2.jsp</a>
</BODY>
</HTML>
```

Figure 9-14   Example11-1.jsp

3. Save the file.

4. Open the data file example11-2.jsp.

5. Add the code shaded in Figure 9-15 to instantiate an application scope bean.

6. Save the file.

```
<HTML>
<HEAD>
<TITLE>Example11-2: creating an application bean</TITLE>
</HEAD>
<BODY>
An application scope bean was created on this page.<br><br>

<jsp:useBean id="messageBean"
 class="com.jspbook.chapter09.MessageBean" scope="application">
 <jsp:setProperty name="messageBean" property="message"
 value="This is the application scope bean"/>
</jsp:useBean>

<h1>
<jsp:getProperty name="messageBean" property="message"/>
</h1>
<br>
<a href="example11-1.jsp">Load example11-1.jsp</a><br>
<a href="example11-2.jsp">Reload example11-2.jsp</a>
</BODY>
</HTML>
```

Figure 9-15   Example11-2.jsp

7. Load the page example11-2.jsp, using the following URL:
   http://localhost:8080/myapp/chapter09/example11-2.jsp

   The page is displayed as shown in Figure 9-16, which shows that the application scope bean is referenced.

8. Click the link **Load example11-1.jsp**. The page is displayed as shown in Figure 9-17, which shows that the session scope bean is referenced.

9. Load example11–2.jsp again. You should see the page displayed as shown in Figure 9–18, which shows that the session bean is referenced, even though an application scope bean was created on this page.

Figure 9-16   Application scope bean

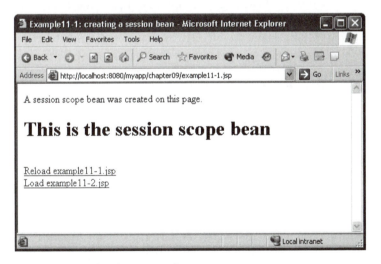

Figure 9-17   Session scope bean

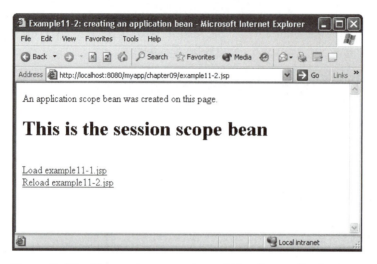

Figure 9-18   The session scope bean hides the application scope bean

You have to load example11-2.jsp first in order to see the message from the application scope bean. When the page is requested for the first time, an application scope bean is created, and this bean remains in memory throughout the execution of the Web application. Click the link on this page to load the page example11-1.jsp. In this page, a session scope bean is created when the page is requested for the first time in the current session. Click the link to load example11-2.jsp again; the message from the session scope bean is displayed, as shown in Figure 9-18. Since these two beans have the same name, when example11-2.jsp is requested after the session scope bean is created, the application scope bean is hidden. So the session scope bean is referenced, instead of the application scope bean.

 To prevent an application scope bean from being hidden by a session scope bean, use different names for each bean.

CHAPTER SUMMARY

❏ Variables defined in declarations and scriptlets have page scope. Variables defined in scriptlets have shorter duration. They are created when the page is requested and destroyed after the execution of the page. Variables defined in declarations are created when the corresponding servlets are loaded into memory. They stay in memory until the servlets are unloaded from memory.

❏ Session scope variables are available to all pages in the current session, and they are destroyed when the current session expires.

❏ Application scope variables are available across all users throughout the entire execution of the Web application.

❑ Page scope beans have the shortest lifetime. They are created with the execution of the useBean action, and destroyed after execution of the page.

❑ Request scope beans have the same lifetime as the request object.

❑ The forward action forwards a request object to a new target page. All buffered content on the original target page is discarded.

REVIEW QUESTIONS

1. A variable defined in scriptlets has what scope?

   a. page scope

   b. request scope

   c. session scope

   d. application scope

2. A variable defined in a declaration has what scope?

   a. page scope

   b. request scope

   c. session scope

   d. application scope

3. Which of the following statements regarding variables defined in scriptlets is true?

   a. They are destroyed after the execution of the page.

   b. They can be referenced in the request scope.

   c. They are created once.

4. Which of the following statements regarding variables defined in declarations is true?

   a. They are destroyed after the execution of the page.

   b. They can be referenced in the request scope.

   c. They have a longer lifetime than those defined in scriptlets.

5. A JSP page contains the following code:

   ```
   <% int num = 1; %>
   <%= num++%>
   ```

   At the 10th request for this page, the number displayed on the page is:

   a. 1

   b. 2

   c. 10

   d. 11

9

6. What is the output of the following code?

```
<%! int num = 10; %>
<% int num = 20; %>
<%= num %>
```

a. 10

b. 20

c. 30

d. none of the above

7. What is the output of the following code?

```
<% int num = 10; %>
<%! int num = 20; %>
<%= num %>
```

a. 10

b. 20

c. 30

d. none of the above

8. Which of the following statements is/are correct?

a. Variables in session scope are destroyed when the browser window is closed.

b. Variables in session scope cannot be referenced when the browser window is closed.

c. A variable cannot be in different sessions.

d. none of the above

9. A page scope bean is created every time the page is requested, and it is destroyed after the execution of the page. True or False?

10. Which of the following scopes has the shortest lifetime?

a. page scope

b. request scope

c. session scope

d. application scope

11. Which of the following statements about the forward action tag is/are correct?

a. It causes the original request object to be forwarded to a new target page.

b. It causes the contents buffered to the output stream in the original target page to be discarded.

c. When it's called, none of the contents generated in the original target page are sent to the client.

d. none of the above

12. The default scope in the useBean action tag is _____.

   a. page scope

   b. request scope

   c. session scope

   d. application scope

13. If a request is not separated by the forward action, then the request scope bean in the page has the same scope as a bean in _____.

   a. page scope

   b. session scope

   c. application scope

   d. none of the above

14. A session scope bean can be referenced _____.

   a. by all users

   b. from all pages in the Web application

   c. from all pages in the same session

   d. none of the above

15. All changes made to a page scope bean are lost when the page is closed. True or False?

16. An application scope bean is instantiated how many times?

   a. 1

   b. 2

   c. 3

   d. many times

17. If a session scope bean and an application scope bean with the same name have been created, then which of the following statements is/are correct?

   a. The bean in application scope can still be referenced.

   b. The application scope bean cannot be referenced.

   c. The session scope bean cannot be referenced.

   d. The session scope bean can be referenced.

18. An application scope bean is destroyed _____. (Choose all that apply.)

   a. when the Web server is shut down

   b. when the current session expires

   c. when the browser window is closed

   d. when a client turns off the computer

19. JavaBeans exist on the _____.

   a. client computer

   b. Web server

20. A bean may still exist in memory, even though it cannot be referenced. True or False?

HANDS-ON PROJECTS

Project 9-1 Poll

In this project, you will design a Web page to conduct a poll online. Two variables are defined in a declaration. They are used to store the poll results from all participants.

1. Open the data file project1.jsp, which is located in the folder C:\myjspapp\chapter09.

2. Add code beneath the form tags in this file (after line 12) to perform the following tasks:

   ❏ Define two variables of int data type in a declaration, name the variables as countYes and countNo, and initialize them to zero.

   ❏ Retrieve the data collected on the form, that is, the value of the radio button named answer. If the value is Yes, increment countYes by 1; if the value is No, increment countNo by 1.

3. Save the file.

4. Load the page, using the following URL:
http://localhost:8080/myapp/chapter09/project1.jsp

5. Vote and submit the page several times. A page similar to Figure 9-19 is displayed.

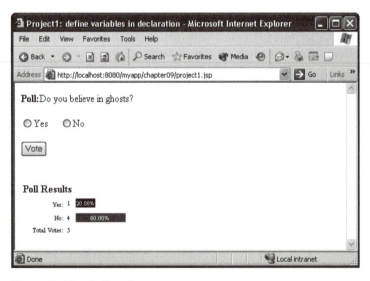

Figure 9-19   Poll online

Project 9-2 Poll Bean

In Project 9-1, you used variables defined in a declaration to store the poll results. In this project, you will write a JavaBean to perform the same computational tasks.

1. Open the data file PollBean.java, which is located in the folder C:\myjspapp\ chapter09.

2. Add the code shaded in Figure 9-20 to perform the computational task based on the vote result.

9

```java
package com.jspbook.chapter09;
import java.math.*;
public class PollBean{
  private String answer;
  private int countYes =0;
  private int countNo = 0;
  private int total = 0;
  public void setAnswer(String s){
    if(s !=null){
        if(s.equals("yes")){
          countYes++;
          total++;
        }else if(s.equals("no")){
          countNo++;
          total++;
        }
     }
  }
  public int getCountYes(){ return countYes;}
  public int getCountNo(){return countNo;}
  public int getWidthYes(){
    return total==0?1:countYes*100/total;
  }
  public int getWidthNo(){
    return total==0?1:countNo*100/total;
  }
  public String getPercentYes(){
    if(total == 0) return "";
    BigDecimal bdYes = new BigDecimal(countYes*100.0/total);
    return bdYes.setScale(2,2)+"%";
  }
   public String getPercentNo(){
    if(total == 0) return "";
    BigDecimal bdNo = new BigDecimal(countNo*100.0/total);
    return bdNo.setScale(2,2)+"%";
  }
  public int getTotal(){ return total;}
}
```

Figure 9-20   PollBean.java

3. Save the file.

4. Open a DOS window and change the directory, using the following command:

   cd c:\myjspapp\chapter09

5. Compile and install the bean as you learned in this chapter.

Project 9-3 Poll Using PollBean

In this project, you will use a bean to redesign the poll Web page developed in Project 9-1. To do this project, you must first complete Project 9-2.

1. Open the data file project3.jsp, which is located in the folder C:\myjspapp\chapter09.

2. Add code right below the form tags on this page to instantiate a bean from the PollBean class, assign the bean ID the value pollBean, and set the bean in application scope.

3. Add code to set the answer property of the bean with the value of the radio button on the form.

4. Save the file.

5. Load the page, using the following URL:
   http://localhost:8080/myapp/chapter09/project3.jsp

6. Vote and submit the page several times. You should see that it works the same as project1.jsp.

Project 9-4 Variable Duration and Scope

In this project, you will use both a variable defined in a declaration and an application scope bean to track the hits on a Web page.

1. Open a new document in your text editor, and save it as **project4.jsp** in the folder C:\myjspapp\chapter09.

2. Add code to define a variable and initialize it to zero in a declaration.

3. Add code to use the variable defined in Step 2 to track the number of hits on this page, and display the total hits (see Figure 9-21).

4. Add code to use the Counter JavaBean (developed in this chapter) in application scope to track the total hits on this page and display the total hits.

5. Save the file.

6. Load the page, using the following URL:
   http://localhost:8080/myapp/chapter09/project4.jsp

7. Reload the page several times; you should see a page similar to Figure 9-21. The variable and the bean show the same number of hits.

8. Open project4.jsp (if it is closed), change the <BODY> tag to <body>, or add a space at the end of the file, and save the page.

9. Reload the page. Notice that the bean accumulates the total hits on the page correctly, but the variable counts from 1 again.

10. Explain what you observed in Step 9.

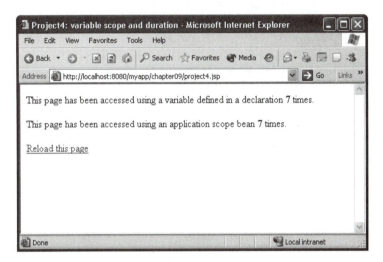

Figure 9-21 Tracking page hits

Project 9-5 Creating a Function in a Declaration

In this project, you will write a function in a declaration and use the function to validate an input field on the page.

1. Open the data file project5.jsp, which is located in the folder C:\myjspapp\chapter09.

2. Add the code shaded in Figure 9-22 to use the function to validate userID.

3. Save the file.

4. Load the page, using the following URL:
   http://localhost:8080/myapp/chapter09/project5.jsp

5. Enter a string containing spaces, and click the **Submit** button; note that the same page is displayed. Enter a string without spaces; note that a message is displayed thanking you for the valid user ID.

```
<HTML>
<HEAD>
<TITLE>Project5: define and use the function</TITLE>
</HEAD>
<body>
<%!
  public boolean validateUserID(String id){
    if(id == null || id.equals("")) return false;
    return id.indexOf(" ") == -1;
  }
%>
<% if(validateUserID(request.getParameter("userID"))){ %>
    <h2>Thank you for the valid user ID.</h2>
<% }else{%>
    <h2>Please enter a user ID without spaces.</h2>
    <form action="project5.jsp" method=post>
      <input type=text name="userID"><br>
      <input type=submit value="Submit">
    </form>
<%} %>
</BODY>
</HTML>
```

Figure 9-22   Project5.jsp

Project 9-6 Transfer Form Data with a Session Scope Bean

In this project, you will use a session scope bean to transfer data between forms on different pages. If a field on a form has been filled and submitted, then the field is automatically filled when a user revisits the page.

1. Open the data file DataBean.java, which is located in the folder C:\myjspapp\chapter09.

2. Add the code shaded in Figure 9-23.

```
package com.jspbook.chapter09;

import java.util.*;

public class DataBean{
  private Vector fields = new Vector();
  private Vector values = new Vector();
  public Vector getFields(){ return fields;}
  public Vector getValues(){ return values;}
  public String getValue(String field){
    for(int i=0; i<fields.size(); i++){
      if(field.equals((String)fields.elementAt(i)))
          return (String)values.elementAt(i);
    }
    return "";
  }
  public void addData(String field, String value){
    if(fields.contains(field)){
      int index = fields.indexOf(field);
      if(value !=null && !value.equals("")){
        values.removeElementAt(index);
        values.insertElementAt(value,index);
      }
    }else if(value != null && !value.equals("")){
      fields.addElement(field);
      values.addElement(value);
    }
  }
}
```

Figure 9-23   DataBean.java

3. Save the file.

4. Open a DOS window and change the directory, using the following command:

   cd c:\myjspapp\chapter09

5. Compile and install the bean class, using the following command:

   javac –d c:\myjspapp\WEB-INF\classes DataBean.java

6. Open the data file project6-1.jsp, which is located in the folder C:\myjspapp\chapter09.

7. Add the code shaded in Figure 9-24.

8. Save the file.

9. Open the data file project6-2.jsp in the same folder.

```
<%@ page import="java.util.*"%>
<HTML>
<HEAD>
<TITLE>
Project6: using a session scope bean to transfer form data
</TITLE>
</HEAD>
<body>
<jsp:useBean id="dataBean" class="com.jspbook.chapter09.DataBean"
  scope="session"/>
<%
  Enumeration enu = request.getParameterNames();
  while(enu.hasMoreElements()){
    String field = (String)enu.nextElement();
    String value = request.getParameter(field);
    dataBean.addData(field,value);
  }
%>
Get ID and password for access to the online course system.<br><br>
<form name="signinForm" action="project6-2.jsp" method=post>
<table  border=0>
  <tr><td align=right>
      <font face=Arial size=-1 >User ID:</font>
      </td>
      <td ><input type=text name="userID"
            value="<%= dataBean.getValue("userID")%>" size=15 >
          <font face=Arial size=-1><b>@ ebcity.com</b> </font>
      </td>
  </tr>
  <tr><td><font face=Arial size=-2> </font></td>
      <td><font face=Arial size=-2>(examples: "weiwei" or "myfriend")
          </font></td>
  </tr>
  <tr><td align=right><font face=Arial size=-1 >Password:</font></td>
      <td ><input type=password name="password"
          value="<%= dataBean.getValue("password")%>" size=20></td>
  </tr>
  <tr><td colspan=2 align=center>
      <input type=submit value=Next >
      </td>
</table>
</form>
</BODY>
</HTML>
```

Figure 9-24   Project6-1.jsp

10. Add the code shaded in Figure 9-25.

11. Save the file.

12. Open the data file project6-3.jsp in the same folder.

```
<%@ page import="java.util.*"%>
<HTML>
<HEAD><TITLE>Project6: store data in a session scope bean</TITLE></HEAD>
<body>
<jsp:useBean id="dataBean" class="com.jspbook.chapter09.DataBean"
  scope="session"/>
<%
  Enumeration enu = request.getParameterNames();
  while(enu.hasMoreElements()){
    String field = (String)enu.nextElement();
    String value = request.getParameter(field);
    dataBean.addData(field,value);
  }
%>
Fill in the following information:<br><br>
<form name="signinForm" action="project6-2.jsp" method=post>
<table border=0>
  <tr><td align=right><font face=Arial size=-1 >First Name:</font></td>
      <td ><input type=text name="firstName"
          value="<%= dataBean.getValue("firstName")%>" size=10 >   
      <font face=Arial size=-1 >Last Name: </font>
      <input type=text name="lastName"
        value="<%= dataBean.getValue("lastName")%>" size=10 ></td>
  </tr>
  <tr>
    <td align=right><font face=Arial size=-1 >Address:</font></td>
    <td><input type=text name=address
        value="<%= dataBean.getValue("address")%>" size=30></td>
  </tr>
  <tr>
    <td align=right><font face=Arial size=-1 >City:</font></td>
    <td><input type=text name=city
        value="<%= dataBean.getValue("city")%>" size=30></td>
  </tr>
  <tr><td align=right><font face=Arial size=-1 >State:</font></td>
      <td ><input type=text name="state"
        value="<%= dataBean.getValue("state")%>" size=10 >   
      <font face=Arial size=-1 >zip code: </font>
      <input type=text name="zipCode"
        value="<%= dataBean.getValue("zipCode")%>" size=10 ></td>
  </tr>
  <tr><td colspan=2 align=center>
    <a href="project6-1.jsp">Back</a>    
    <a href="project6-3.jsp">Display data</a>    
    <input type=submit value=Submit>
    </td>
</table>
</form>
</BODY>
```

Figure 9-25   Project6-2.jsp

13. Add the code shaded in Figure 9-26.
14. Save the file.

```
<%@ page import="java.util.*"%>
<HTML>
<HEAD>
<TITLE>Project6: displaying data stored in the session scope bean</TITLE>
</HEAD>
<body>
<jsp:useBean id="dataBean" class="com.jspbook.chapter09.DataBean"
  scope="session"/>
<table>
  <tr><th colspan=2 align=center>Data Collected<hr></th></tr>
  <% Vector fields = dataBean.getFields();
     Vector values = dataBean.getValues();
     for(int i=0; i<fields.size(); i++){
        String f = (String)fields.elementAt(i);
        String v = (String)values.elementAt(i);
     %>
     <tr><td><%= f%></td>
         <td><%= v%></td>
     </tr>
     <%}%>
     <tr><td colspan=2><hr></td></tr>
     <tr><td><a href="project6-1.jsp">Back to project6-1.jsp</a></td>
         <td><a href="project6-2.jsp">Back to project6-2.jsp</a></td>
     </tr>
</table>
</BODY>
</HTML>
```

Figure 9-26 Project6-3.jsp

15. Load the page project6-1.jsp, using the following URL:
    http://localhost:8080/myapp/chapter09/project6-1.jsp

    The page is displayed as shown in Figure 9-27.

16. Fill in the form and click the **Next** button to submit the form; note that the page project6-2.jsp is displayed, as shown in Figure 9-28. Fill out the form and submit it. The data collected are stored in the session bean. Click the link **Display data**; the page displayed is similar to Figure 9-29. You should see that all the data you entered are displayed.

17. Use the link on the page project6-3.jsp to go back to either project6-1.jsp or project6-2.jsp. Notice that the form is filled automatically with previously entered data. You can modify the data and resubmit the form.

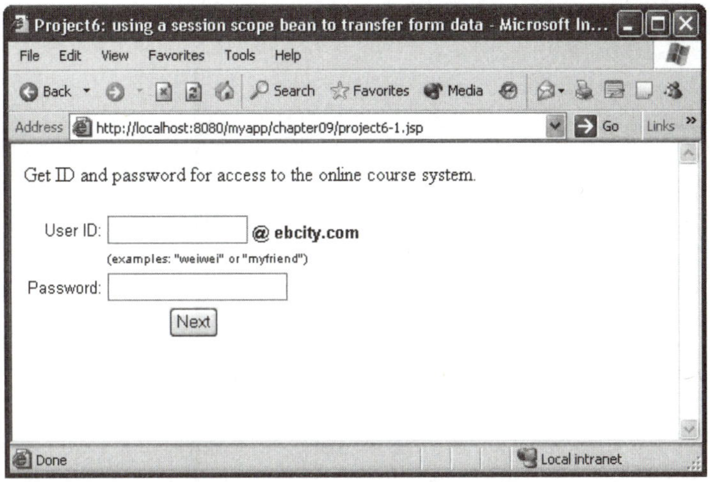

Figure 9-27   Using a session bean to transfer data

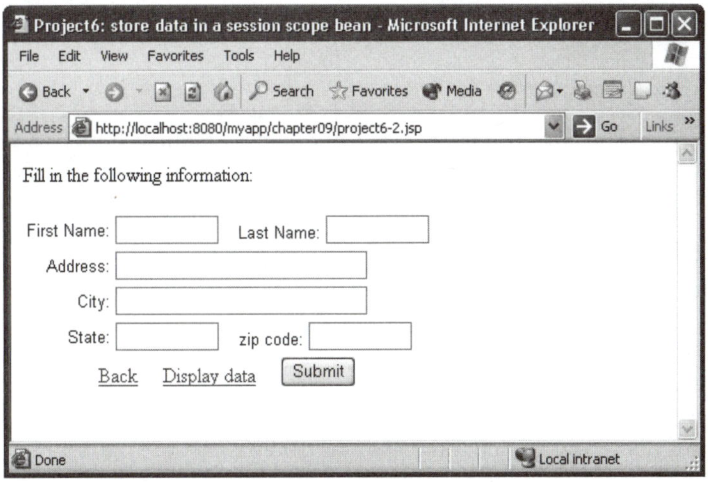

Figure 9-28   Storing data in a session scope bean

![Project6: displaying data stored in the session scope bean - Microsoft Internet Explorer browser window showing Address http://localhost:8080/myapp/chapter09/project6-3.jsp]

Data Collected

password	clemson
userID	jdavis
firstName	John
address	215A Newcastle Drive
city	Clemson
zipCode	29634
state	SC
lastName	Davis

Back to project6-1.jsp Back to project6-2.jsp

Figure 9-29   Displaying data stored in a session scope bean

Project 9-7 File Viewer

Weiwei IBC Company provides Internet-based file management systems. In this project, you will design a page allowing customers to view the file list in a directory.

1. Compile and install the FileViewer.java JavaBean class. This file is located in the folder C:\myjspapp\chapter09.

2. Open the data file project7.jsp, which is located in the same folder.

3. Add the code shaded in Figure 9-30.

4. Save the file.

5. Load the page project7.jsp, using the following URL:
   http://localhost:8080/myapp/chapter09/project7.jsp

   A page similar to Figure 9-31 is displayed.

```
<HTML>
<HEAD>
<TITLE>Project7: file viewer</TITLE>
</HEAD>
<BODY>
<jsp:useBean id="fv" class="com.jspbook.chapter09.FileViewer"/>
<%
String vPath = "chapter09";
String rPath =
  getServletConfig().getServletContext().getRealPath(vPath);
%>
<jsp:setProperty name="fv" property="myDir" value="<%= rPath%>"/>
<%
while(fv.nextFile()){
  if(fv.isDir()){%>
  <img src="images/folder.gif" border=0><%= fv.getFileName()%><br>
  <%}else{%>
  <%= fv.getFileName()%>    <%= fv.getFileSize()%><br>
  <%}%>
<%}%>
</BODY>
</HTML>
```

Figure 9-30   Project7.jsp

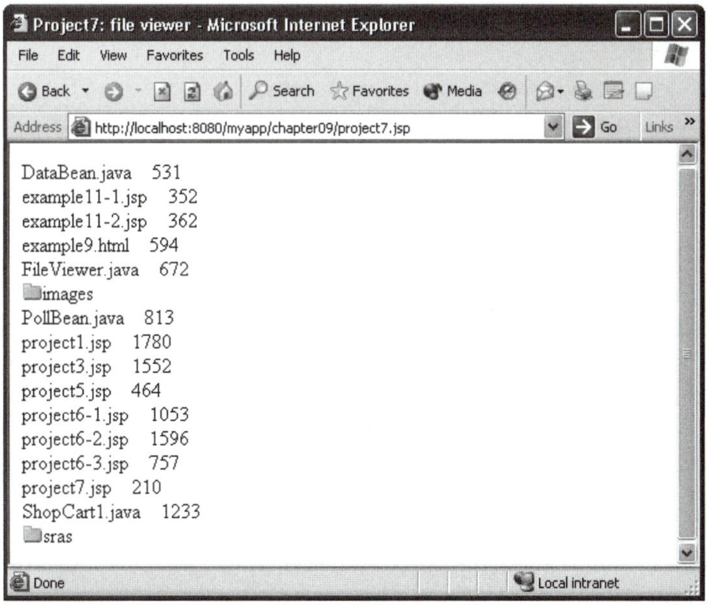

Figure 9-31   File viewer

CASE PROJECTS

SRAS: Track the Last Added Course

As you learn more about JSP, you are continuously improving the SRAS system. In this project, you are provided with a JavaBean class called LastAddedCourseBean.java, which is located in the folder C:\myjspapp\chapter09\sras. You are required to use this bean to track the last added course by a faculty member, so that when the faculty member revisits the addcourse.jsp page, the last added course data are filled in on the form. To do this project, you need to compile the LastAddedCoursebean.java properly. Then, you must create a session bean in the addcourse.jsp file and use the data stored in the bean to fill out the input fields on the form. (*Note:* The login IDs are 1, 2, and 3, and the password is "password.")

EBCity

EBCity provides various products for Web-based learning environments. The manager wants to add an online test system to the Web. You are hired to design this system. The requirements for the system are as follows:

- Five questions are displayed on each page. That means if there are 20 questions on a test, the questions appear over four pages.
- All answers are saved into a session bean before an examinee submits the test for grading.
- After the test is submitted, the bean is cleared either by expiring the current session or by deleting answers from the bean.
- Examinees can go back and modify their answers.

To complete this Case Project, you need to develop a JavaBean class to carry answers from one page to another. To create the grading system, you simply display all answers after an examinee submits answers for grading.

Shopping Cart

You are working for an online store; they are currently developing a Web site so customers can shop online. You are required to design a shopping cart bean that can be customized as follows:

1. The bean can store the following information:
   - Item name
   - Price
   - Quantity
   - Subtotal for each item
   - Total for all items
   - Other features of items, for example, color, size, weight, and so forth.
2. Item names can be determined within the JSP page instead of hard-coded.
3. The price of each item can be customized in a JSP page.
4. New features about products can be added dynamically.

10

MORE ADVANCED JSP

In this chapter, you will:

♦ Learn the difference between forwarding and redirecting

♦ Declare and use methods in JSP pages

♦ Handle exceptions to make your Web applications more robust

♦ Create and use custom JSP tag libraries

♦ Manipulate JSP content using custom tags

In previous chapters, you learned how to use JavaBeans to perform computational tasks in JSP. JSP technology also allows you to develop new custom
tags that use an HTML-like syntax. A custom tag encapsulates much of the
computational tasks and can be used by a Web developer even without requiring knowledge of Java. In this chapter, you will learn how to develop and use
a custom tag. In addition, you will learn how to involve another page while
processing a request, how to define a method in a declaration, and how to
handle exceptions.

HTTP FORWARD AND REDIRECT

In most of the examples discussed so far, there are one or two pages involved in processing a request: the requesting page and the requested page. To invoke another page, you can forward or redirect to another page. You have already learned how to forward a request to a new target page. With the forward action, the original request can be forwarded to another page and processed there, so that all the information encapsulated in the request object is available in the new target page. For example, if a form is submitted to a JSP page but the page forwards the request to another JSP page, then the form information (all input fields) is available in the new target page. Since the forwarding occurs on the server, the client browser is not aware that the request has been forwarded to another page, so the URL shown in the browser remains unchanged.

When you redirect a Web page, the Web server tells the browser to make a new request, so the URL shown in the browser changes to the URL of the new page. Since the browser makes a new request, request scope objects are not available after a redirect action (that is, all information associated with the original request is gone).

The redirect action requires more communication between the browser and the Web server. Therefore it takes more time than forwarding a page. To redirect a request, you use the response object as follows:

```
<% response.sendRedirect("relativeURL"); %>
```

The following exercise illustrates the difference between these two methods. This example includes three pages.

1. Open a new document in your text editor, and type in the following code:

```
<HTML>
<HEAD>
<TITLE>Example1: forward or redirect a request </TITLE>
</HEAD>
<BODY>
Type a message into the input field and click the<br>
Forward or Redirect button.<br><br>
<form action=example1-1.jsp method=post>
 <input type=text name="message"><br>
 <input type=submit name="action" value="Forward"><br>
 <input type=submit name="action" value="Redirect"><br>
</form>
</BODY>
</HTML>
```

2. Save the file as **example1.html** in the folder C:\myjspapp\chapter10.

3. Open a new document in your text editor, and type in the following code:

```
<HTML>
<HEAD>
<TITLE>Example1: forward or redirect</TITLE>
</HEAD>
<BODY>
<%
 String action = request.getParameter("action");
 if(action.equals("forward")){
%>
 <jsp:forward page="example1-2.jsp"/>
<%}else if(action.equals("redirect")){%>
 <% response.sendRedirect("example1-2.jsp"); %>
<% } %>
</BODY>
</HTML>
```

4. Save the file as **example1-1.jsp** in the folder C:\myjspapp\chapter10.

5. Create a new document in your text editor, and type in the following code:

```
<HTML>
<HEAD>
<TITLE>Example1: forward or redirect</TITLE>
</HEAD>
<BODY>
Can I get the message in the original request?<br><br>
The message: <%= request.getParameter("message") %>
</b><br><br>
<a href="example1.html">Back</a>
</BODY>
</HTML>
```

6. Save the file as **example1-2.jsp** in the folder C:\myjspapp\chapter10.

7. Load the page example1.html, using the following URL:
   http://localhost:8080/myapp/chapter10/example1.html

   The page is displayed as shown in Figure 10-1.

8. Type a message into the input box and click the **Forward** button. A page similar to Figure 10-2 is displayed.

10

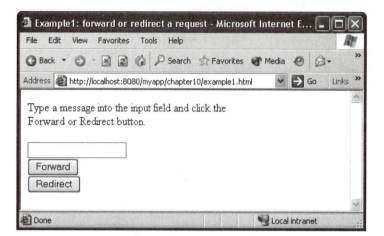

Figure 10-1 Forwarding or redirecting a request

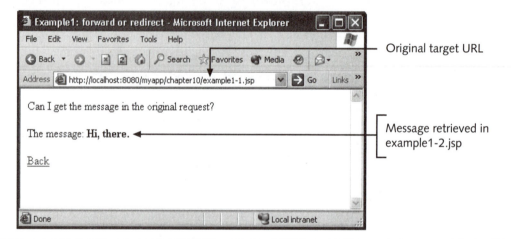

Figure 10-2 Forwarding a request

9. Go back to example1.html and type a message again, but click the **Redirect** button this time. A page similar to Figure 10–3 is displayed.

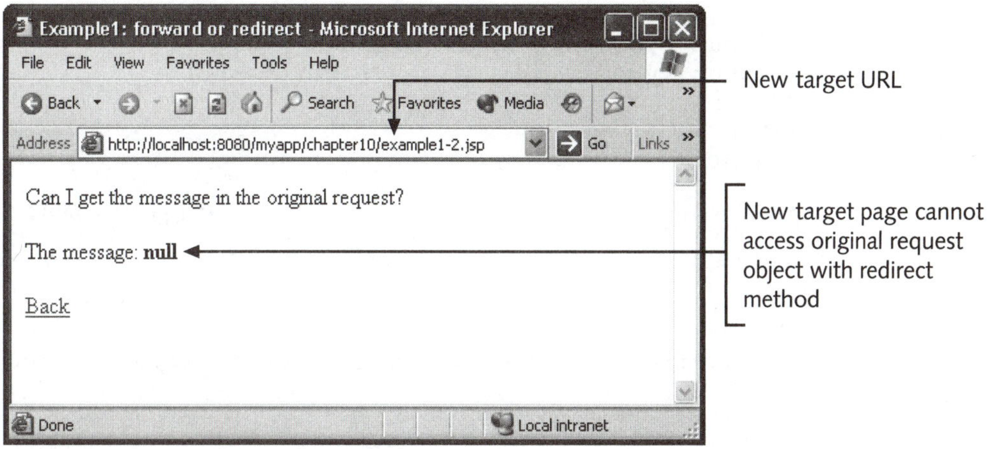

Figure 10-3   Redirecting a request

On the first page, example1.html, the action attribute is set to example1-1.jsp, so the initial target page is example1-1.jsp. There are two submit buttons on the form: one is labeled Forward and the other one is labeled Redirect. If the name attribute of a submit button is set and it is clicked, as with other input fields on the form, the name/value pair of this submit button can be retrieved. The two submit buttons on the form have the same name. Depending on which submit button you click, you get its corresponding value by using the `getParameter("action")` method on the target page. When a button is clicked, the page example1-1.jsp processes the request. If the Forward button is clicked, the original request is sent to example1-2.jsp, where the message you entered is retrieved and displayed on this page, and the URL shows the original requested file. If the Redirect button is clicked, the Web server tells the browser to make a new request. Since in the new request the message field does not exist, a null value is displayed, and the URL shows the newly requested file.

When you use redirect, all information associated with the original request object is lost. You can avoid this problem by passing information in the query string, as illustrated in the following example.

1. Open a new file in your text editor, and type in the following code:

```
<HTML>
<HEAD>
<TITLE>Example2: redirecting a request </TITLE>
</HEAD>
<BODY>
Type a message into the input field and then submit the
form<br><br>
```

```
<form action=example2-1.jsp method=post>
 <input type=text name="message"><br>
 <input type=submit value="Submit"><br>
</form>
</BODY>
</HTML>
```

2. Save the file as **example2.html** in the folder C:\myjspapp\chapter10.

3. Open a new document in your text editor, and type in the following code:

```
<HTML>
<HEAD>
<TITLE>Example2: using a query string with redirecting
</TITLE>
</HEAD>
<BODY>
<%
 String message = request.getParameter("message");
 response.sendRedirect("example2-2.jsp?message="
+message);
%>
</BODY>
</HTML>
```

4. Save the file as **example2-1.jsp** in the folder C:\myjspapp\chapter10.

5. Create a new document in your text editor, and type in the following code:

```
<HTML>
<HEAD>
<TITLE>Example2: retrieving a query string</TITLE>
</HEAD>
<BODY>
The message is :
<b><%= request.getParameter
("message") %></b>
</BODY>
</HTML>
```

6. Save the file as **example2-2.jsp** in the folder C:\myjspapp\chapter10.

7. Load the page example2.html, using the following URL:
   http://localhost:8080/myapp/chapter10/example2.html

8. Type in a message and click the **Submit** button. The message is displayed on the redirected page.

When you use the forward method, and the user clicks the Refresh button on the Internet Explorer Toolbar, the information is resent to the original target page. In a shopping cart application, like the one you saw in Chapter 9, this causes any items previously added to the shopping cart to be added again. To prevent this unexpected result, you can use redirect instead. (This problem does not occur in Netscape Navigator.)

Forwarding or redirecting a page to itself results in an infinite loop.

DECLARING METHODS

A method declaration consists of five parts: method access specifier, return type, method name, method parameter list, and method body. For example, look at the following code:

```
public int smallest(int x, int y, int z){
  int temp = x;
  if(y < temp )
   temp = y;
  if(z < temp)
   temp = z;
  return temp;
}
```

This code defines a method named smallest. This method has a public access specifier; it returns an int value; it takes three integers as parameters and returns the smallest one among the three arguments. To call a method, you simply use the method name and provide the required arguments. For example, to get the smallest number among the three numbers 3, 40, and 23, you call the above method as follows: smallest (3,40,23) and it returns 3. In the following example, you will define a method that determines the larger number between two numbers.

1. Open a new document in your text editor.

2. Add basic HTML tags as follows:

```
<HTML>
<HEAD>
<TITLE>Example 3: Function</TITLE>
</HEAD>
<BODY>
```

3. Type the following code to define a method called max that takes as parameters two integers and returns an int value:

```
<%!
  int max(int num1, int num2){
   if(num1>num2)
    return num1;
   else
    return num2;
  }
%>
```

10

4. Add the following code to create a form and input fields:

```
<form action="example3.jsp" method="POST">
 Number 1:<input type=text name=number1 size=10
maxlength=9><br>
 Number 2:<input type=text name=number2 size=10
maxlength=9><br>
 <input type=submit value="Submit">
</form>
```

5. Add the following code to get the values entered into the input fields:

```
<%
 String number1 = request.getParameter("number1");
 String number2 = request.getParameter("number2");
```

6. Add the following code to declare two integer values. Convert the string values to integers and assign them to these two int variables.

```
int n1, n2;
 if(number1 != null){
  n1 = Integer.parseInt(number1);
  n2 = Integer.parseInt(number2);
%>
```

7. Add the following code to call the max method and display the result:

```
The larger one between <%= number1%> and <%= number2%>
is :
  <%= max(n1, n2)%>
<% } %>
</BODY>
</HTML>
```

8. Save the file as **example3.jsp** in the folder C:\myjspapp\chapter10.

9. Load the page, using the following URL:
   http://localhost:8080/myapp/chapter10/example3.jsp

10. Enter two numbers and submit the form. A page similar to Figure 10-4 is displayed. Notice that the max method determines which of the numbers you entered is the larger one.

You can place methods anywhere in your JSP page.

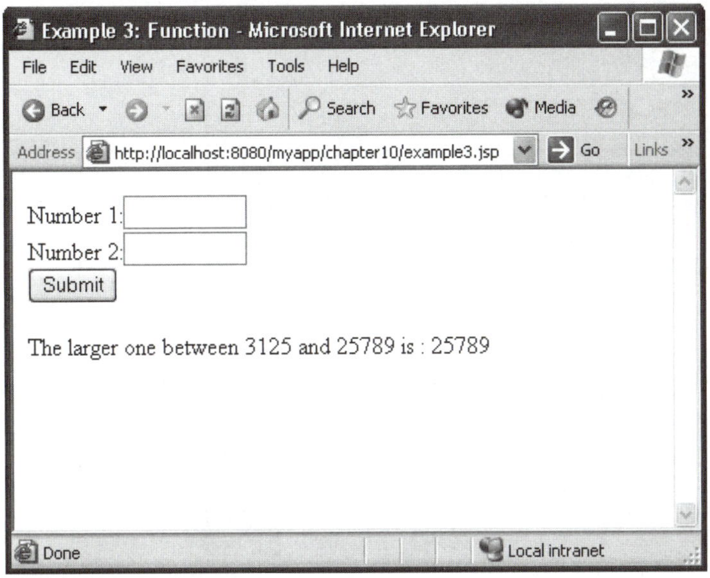

Figure 10-4   Defining and using a function

EXCEPTION HANDLING

There are many types of errors that can arise when you are developing applications. These errors can be categorized into two groups: syntax errors and runtime errors. Each programming language defines rules for the writing of applications. These rules are called syntax. If you do not follow these rules, you will not be able to compile the code. This kind of error is called a **syntax error**. Since these errors can be detected at compile time, they are also called **compile-time errors**. As you have already learned, JSP pages are compiled into corresponding servlets and are loaded into memory. If there are any syntax errors, the JSP pages cannot be converted into servlets, and errors detected by the server are displayed. For example, the page shown in Figure 10-5 contains a syntax error and cannot be displayed in the browser properly.

The error messages you saw were generated by the JSP container when it tried to convert the JSP into a servlet.

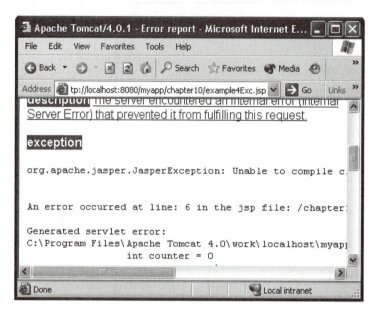

Figure 10-5   JSP syntax error

Runtime errors occur during the execution of a program, for a variety of reasons. For example, the user enters a non-numerical value when a numerical value is expected; the program attempts to write data to a file, but the disk is full; a number is divided by zero in the program, and so on. When a runtime error occurs, the JSP container raises an exception, as you will see in the following exercise.

1. Open a new document in your text editor, and type in the following code:

```
<HTML>
<HEAD><TITLE>Example 4: runtime error</TITLE></HEAD>
<BODY>
<form action="example4.jsp" method="POST">
 Enter a numerical value:
<input type=text name=number size=10 maxlength=9>
 <input type=submit value=submit>
</form>
<%
 String numS =  request.getParameter("number");
 if(numS != null){
   double number = Double.parseDouble(numS);
%>
   <hr width=200 align=left>
   The number you entered is : <%= number %>
 <% } %>
</BODY>
</HTML>
```

2. Save the file as **example4.jsp** in the folder C:\myjspapp\chapter10.

3. Load the page, using the following URL:
http://localhost:8080/myapp/chapter10/example4.jsp

4. After the page is displayed (which means the page is successfully converted to a servlet and loaded into memory), enter a numerical value and submit the form. The numerical value is converted to a double number and displayed on the page.

5. Enter a non-numerical value and submit the form. A page similar to Figure 10-6 is displayed, which indicates that a runtime error has occurred.

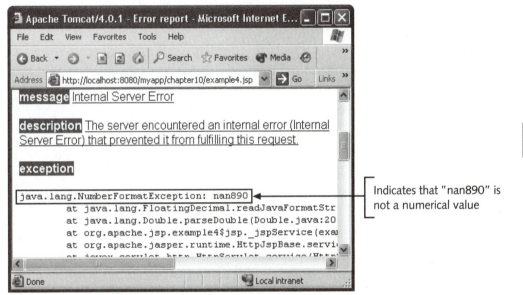

Figure 10-6   Runtime error

In this page, a user is supposed to enter a numerical value in the input box. The program retrieves the value and parses the value into a double number. The method `Double.parseDouble("aNumericalValue")` expects a numerical value as parameter. If a non-numerical value is passed to this method, the method call cannot be executed and an error occurs. When a runtime error occurs, the JSP container raises an exception. An exception is an instance of a class derived from the Throwable class. Subclasses of Throwable are contained in various packages. For example, errors related to number format are included in the package java.lang.NumberFormatException (which is imported automatically).

You can handle JSP exceptions within the same JSP page, or in another JSP page. You can use the errorPage attribute to specify a JSP page that processes any exceptions that are not handled in the current page. You learned how to handle exceptions in another JSP page in Chapter 5.

Handling Exceptions Within the Same Page

To handle an exception within the same page, you need to enclose in a **try** block the code that may generate an exception. The try block is immediately followed by zero or more **catch** blocks. Each catch block specifies the type of exception it can catch and the code that deals with that exception. After the last catch block, an optional **finally** block provides code that always executes, regardless of whether or not an exception occurs. The following example illustrates how to handle an exception within the same page.

1. Open the data file example5.jsp, which is located in the folder C:\myjspapp\chapter10.

2. Add the code shaded in Figure 10-7.

```
<HTML>
<HEAD>
<TITLE>Example 5: Handling exceptions within the same page</TITLE>
</HEAD>
<BODY>
<form action="example5.jsp" method="POST">
 Enter a numerical value:
 <input type=text name=number size=10 maxlength=9>
 <input type=submit value=Submit>
</form>
<%
 String numS = request.getParameter("number");
 if(numS != null){
   try{
     double number = Double.parseDouble(numS);
%>
     <hr width=200 align=left>
     The number you entered is : <%= number %>
<% } catch(NumberFormatException nfexc){ %>
     An exception is raised: <%= nfexc.toString() %><br>
     <b>Please enter a numerical value!</b>
   <%}finally{%>
     <br><font color=red>The finally block is executed anyway!</font>
   <%}%>
<% }%>
</BODY>
```

Figure 10-7   Example5.jsp

3. Save the file in the folder C:\myjspapp\chapter10.

4. Load the page, using the following URL:
   http://localhost:8080/myapp/chapter10/example5.jsp

5. Enter a numerical value and submit the form. A page similar to Figure 10-8 is displayed. The number is displayed, followed by the content generated from the finally block.

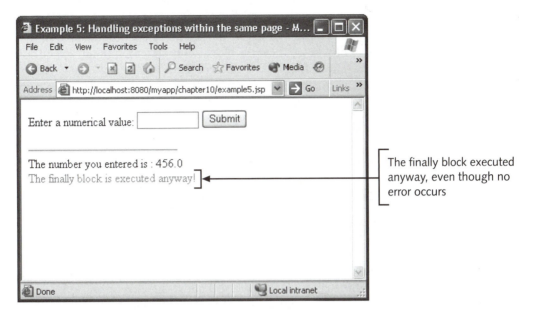

Figure 10-8   Example5.jsp without error

6. Enter a non-numerical value and submit the form. An exception is raised, and a page similar to Figure 10-9 is displayed. The exception message indicates that a NumberFormatException occurs. The content generated from the finally block is also displayed.

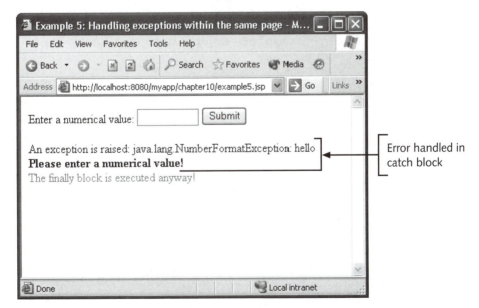

Figure 10-9   Example5.jsp with runtime error

In this example, since the code `double number = Double.parseDouble(numS);` generates an exception if you enter a non-numerical value, it is included in the try block. Following the try block is a catch block, which catches an exception of type NumberFormatException. If this type of exception occurs, the code within this catch block is executed. The finally block is executed regardless of whether or not an exception occurs.

If several types of exceptions might occur in a try block, you need a catch block for each type of exception. If you are not sure what types may occur, you can specify one catch block with a type of Exception. Then this catch block catches all types of exceptions.

Exception Handling and Request Scope

If you handle an exception in a different page, what is the scope of the page that handles the exception? The page where an exception occurs and the page where the exception is handled have request scope. To handle exceptions in another page, you set the errorPage attribute in the page directive. If an exception occurs during execution, the page specified in the errorPage attribute is invoked to handle the exception, and the same request is passed to the page that handles the exception. Therefore, a bean can be created in request scope and shared between these pages. In the following example, you will create a bean with request scope to handle exceptions in another page.

1. Open a new document in your text editor, and type in the following code:

```
<HTML>
<HEAD>
<TITLE>Example 6: Exception and scope</TITLE>
</HEAD>
<BODY>
<form action="example6-1.jsp" method="POST">
 <input name=message>
 <input type=submit value=Submit>
</form>
</BODY>
</HTML>
```

2. Save the file as **example6.html** in the folder C:\myjspapp\chapter10.

3. Create a new document in your text editor, and type in the following code:

```
<%@ page errorPage="example6-2.jsp"%>
<HTML>
<HEAD>
<TITLE>Example 6: Exception and scope</TITLE>
</HEAD>
<BODY>
<jsp:useBean id="counterBean"class=
   "com.jspbook.chapter09.Counter"
    scope="request"/>
```

```
Counter Value:<b>
<jsp:getProperty name="counterBean" property="counter"/>
</b>
<%-- let's purposely raise an exception --%>
<%= 12/0 %>
</BODY>
</HTML>
```

4. Save the file as **example6-1.jsp** in the folder C:\myjspapp\chapter10.

5. Create a new document in your text editor, and type in the following code:

```
<%@ page isErrorPage="true"%>
<HTML>
<HEAD><TITLE>Example 6: Exception and scope</TITLE></HEAD>
<BODY>
<jsp:useBean id="counterBean"
 class="com.jspbook.chapter09.Counter"
 scope="request"/>
Counter Value:<b>
<jsp:getProperty name="counterBean" property="counter"/>
</b>
<br><br>
The following exception occurs:<br>
<%= exception.toString() %>
<br><br>
The input field value can be retrieved in the
error-handling page.<br>
Message:<font face="Arial" size=1>
<%= request.getParameter("message")%></font>
</BODY>
</HTML>
```

6. Save the file as **example6-2.jsp** in the folder C:\myjspapp\chapter10.

7. Load the page example6.html, using the following URL:
   http://localhost:8080/myapp/chapter10/example6.html

8. Enter a message, for example, **Hi, there!**, and submit the form. A page similar to Figure 10-10 is displayed.

In the above example, if an exception occurs in the page example6-1.jsp, example6-2.jsp is invoked to process the exception. Since the original target page (example6-1.jsp) and the exception-handling page (example6-2.jsp) process the same request, the input field of the form can be retrieved via the getParameter method of the request object. After you enter a message in the message input field and submit the form, a request is sent to example6-1.jsp, and the useBean action tag creates a bean object on that page. The code <%= 12/0 %> raises an exception, and the request is directed to example6-2.jsp. Since a bean object in the request scope is created in the original target page, the error-handling page uses the same bean object, which is why the counter value is 2.

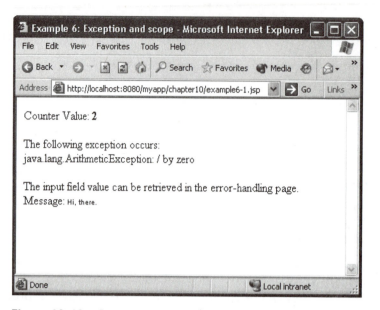

Figure 10-10   Request scope and exception handling in another page

 In order to access the implicit exception object, the isErrorPage attribute in the page directive must be set to true.

CREATING CUSTOM JSP TAG LIBRARIES

Throughout this text, you have used action tags in your JSP scripts. You can also create your own action tags, called **custom tags**. Custom tags allow you to add a vast range of new functionality to JSP.

JSP Custom Tags

JSP custom tags are merely Java classes that implement certain required interfaces. As with action tags, you can use custom tags in your JSP pages, using XML syntax. Custom tags have a starting tag and an ending tag. They may or may not have a body. For example, you use the following action tag to create a bean:

```
<jsp:useBean id="beanName" class="classPath"/>
```

Similarly, you can create a custom tag that is used as follows:

```
<jspbook:hello name="Davis" />
```

In the above examples, jsp and jspbook are called tag prefixes; useBean and hello are tag names; id, class, and name are attributes. A tag may or may not have attributes. These tags do not have bodies, so they are called bodyless tags. The following sample custom tag contains a body:

```
<jsp:useBean id="beanName" class="classPath" >
  <jsp:setProperty name="beanName" property="property1"
       value="aValue"/>
</jsp:useBean>
```

The body of a tag can be a string, a JSP script expression, or a nested tag, as in the above example. Figure 10-11 shows the elements within action tags.

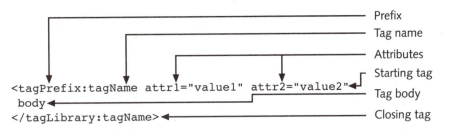

Figure 10-11 Action tag elements

The action tag `<tagLibrary:tagName attr1="value1"/>` is shorthand for `<tagLibrary:tagName attr1="value1"></ tagLibrary:tagName>`.

JSP Custom Tag Components

To create and use custom tags, you need to define three separate components:

- Tag handler class
- Tag library descriptor file
- JSP pages

The tag handler class defines the tag's behavior; it is an object invoked by the JSP engine to evaluate a custom tag during the execution of a JSP page that uses the tag. The tag library descriptor is a collection of custom actions that maps the XML element names to the tag implementation; the JSP file tests and uses the tag library.

The Tag Handler Class

A tag handler class is a Java class that implements one of two specialized interfaces. It is used to encapsulate the functionality of a JSP page. Specifically, a tag handler class must implement the javax.servlet.jsp.tagext.Tag or the javax.servlet.jsp.tagext.BodyTag interfaces, which contain methods that access the request and page information, as well as methods that are called when the starting and ending tags are encountered. These interfaces contain a number of methods that need to be implemented in the tag handler classes, regardless of whether you need them or not. The BodyTag interface extends the Tag interface by defining additional methods that allow a tag handler to access its body. Table 10-1 lists the methods in the Tag interface, and Table 10-2 lists the additional methods defined in the BodyTag interface. To minimize the effort involved in defining a tag handler class, two abstract classes are provided. They are TagSupport and BodyTagSupport. You do not need to worry about the details of these two abstract classes; you may simply define a tag handler class by extending one of them.

Table 10-1   Methods in the Tag interface

Method	Description
setPageContext(PageContext pc)	Invoked before doStartTag, to set the page context
setParent(Tag parent)	Invoked before doEndTag, to pass a tag handler a reference to its parent tag
getParent()	Returns a tag instance that is the parent tag
doStartTag()	Invoked when the starting tag is encountered; returns either EVAL_BODY_INCLUDE or SKIP_BODY
doEndTag()	Invoked after returning from doStartTag when the ending tag is encountered; returns either EVAL_PAGE or SKIP_PAGE
release()	Invoked when the tag handler is no longer needed, to perform any cleanup necessary

Table 10-2   Additional methods defined in the BodyTag interface

Method	Description
setBodyContent(BodyContent bc)	Invoked before processing the body; not invoked if the method doStartTag returns SKIP_BODY
doInitBody()	Invoked after the setBodyContent method, to prepare for evaluation of the body; not invoked if the method doStartTag returns SKIP_BODY
doAfterBody()	Invoked after doBodyInit(); not invoked if the method doStartTag returns SKIP_BODY. Returns either EVAL_BODY_PAGE or SKIP_BODY. It is repeatedly invoked as long as the doAfterBody() evaluation returns EVAL_BODY_TAG.

Your tag handler extends one of the abstract classes. To make your tag handler function, you need to overwrite a few methods. In the following example, you will define a simple tag handler by extending the TagSupport class, and output messages by overwriting the doStartTag method.

As with JavaBeans, you need to compile and install the tag handler classes in the WEB-INF/classes directory for your application.

1. Open a new document in you text editor, and type in the following code:

```
package com.jspbook.chapter10;
import java.io.*;
import javax.servlet.jsp.*;
import javax.servlet.jsp.tagext.*;
public class ExampleTag extends TagSupport{
 public int doStartTag(){
   try{
     JspWriter out = pageContext.getOut();
     out.println("<h1>Custom Tag in JSP</h1>");
   }catch(IOException ioexc){}
   return SKIP_BODY;
 }
}
```

2. Save the file as **ExampleTag.java** in the folder C:\myjspapp\chapter10.

3. Open a DOS command window and change the directory by using the following command:
   cd c:\myjspapp\chapter10

4. Use the following command to compile and install the tag handler class:
   javac −d c:\myjspapp\WEB-INF\classes ExampleTag.java

10

Tag Library Descriptor

Once you define a tag handler, the next task is to associate it with a particular XML tag name. You accomplish this task by means of a tag library descriptor (TLD) file. In the following steps, you will create a minimal TLD file for a library with just one custom action element.

1. Open a new document in your text editor, and add the following general description for the TLD file. This general description remains the same in all TLD files in this book.

```
<?xml version="1.0" encoding="ISO-8859-1" ?>
<!DOCTYPE taglib
    PUBLIC "-//Sun Microsystems, Inc.//DTD JSP Tag
Library 1.1//EN"
    "http://java.sun.com/j2ee/dtds/
web-jsptaglibrary_1_1.dtd">
```

2. Add a tag library by specifying the library version, JSP version, and custom tag prefix.

```
<taglib>
 <tlibversion>1.0</tlibversion>
 <jspversion>1.1</jspversion>
 <shortname>example</shortname>
```

3. Enter the code below to add a tag name; map the tag name to a tag handler by specifying the tagclass, which gives the fully qualified class name of the tag handler.

```
<tag>
 <name>message</name>
 <tagclass>com.jspbook.chapter10.ExampleTag</tagclass>
</tag>
</taglib>
```

4. Save the file as **myfirsttaglib.tld** in the folder C:\myjspapp\chapter10.

The extension of the TLD file can be anything, or even no extension at all. By convention, a TLD file has the extension of .tld. TLD files can be saved in any directory in the Web application, but they are usually saved in the directory WEB-INF\tlds\. For convenience, all TLD files created in this chapter are stored in the folder C:\myjspapp\chapter10.

The same comment format is used in the descriptor file as in HTML.

Using a Custom Tag

Once you have a tag handler class and a tag library descriptor, you are ready to write a JSP page to make use of the tag. The following example illustrates how to use the custom tag you created.

1. Open a new document in your text editor, and type in the following code:

```
<%@ taglib uri="/chapter10/myfirsttaglib.tld"
prefix="example" %>
<HTML>
<HEAD>
<TITLE>tag lib example</TITLE>
</HEAD>
<BODY>
<example:message />
</BODY>
</HTML>
```

2. Save the file as **example7.jsp** in the folder C:\myjspapp\chapter10.

3. Load the page, using the following URL:
http://localhost:8080/myapp/chapter10/example7.jsp

The page is displayed as shown in Figure 10-12.

Figure 10-12   Custom tag example

Before you can use your custom tag, you need to specify the taglib directive. The syntax of the taglib directive takes the following form:

<%@ taglib uri="URLReferringToTheTagLib" prefix="prefixOfTheTag" %>

Both uri and prefix attributes are required. The code **<example:message />** uses the prefix example and the tag name message. This custom tag invokes the doStartTag method you defined in the tag handler class. Calling this method writes "<h1>Custom Tag in JSP</h1>" to the output stream.

Adding Attributes to a Custom Tag

A custom tag may have optional or mandatory attributes. The syntax of a custom tag that has attributes takes the following form:

<tagprefix:tagname attribute1="value1" attribute2="value2" … />

or

<tagprefix:tagname attribute1="value1" attribute2="value2" … >

body

</tagprefix:tagname>

To add an attribute in a custom tag, you follow the same convention as for the setter methods in the tag handler class in JavaBeans. For example, use of an attribute called attribute1 simply results in a call to a method called setAttribute1 in your tag handler class.

To make your tag function, you need to overwrite a few methods of the class it extends. Typically, you overwrite three methods if your tag handler class extends the tagSupport class. The two frequently overwritten classes are doStartTag and doEndTag. The doStartTag method is called when the starting tag is encountered; the doEndTag method is called when the ending tag is encountered. If a tag provides attribute support, the corresponding setter methods are called before the doStartTag method. In the following example, you will add attribute support to a tag and indicate when the setter methods and overwritten methods are called.

1. Open the data file AttributeTag.java, which is located in the folder C:\myjspapp\chapter10.

2. Add the code shaded in Figure 10-13 to add two attributes.

```java
package com.jspbook.chapter10;
import java.io.*;
import javax.servlet.*;
import javax.servlet.jsp.*;
import javax.servlet.jsp.tagext.*;
public class AttributeTag extends TagSupport{
  private String attr1;
  private String attr2;
  public void setAttr1(String value1){
   attr1 = value1;
   helper("setAttr1");
   }
  public void setAttr2(String value2){
   attr2 = value2;
   helper("setAttr2");
  }
  public int doStartTag(){
   helper("doStartTag");
   return SKIP_BODY;
  }
  public int doEndTag(){
   helper("doEndTag");
   return SKIP_PAGE;
  }
  private void helper(String methodName){
   try{
     JspWriter out = pageContext.getOut();
     out.println("<h2>" + methodName+ " is called</h2>");
   }catch(IOException ioexc){}
  }
}
```

Figure 10-13   AttributeTag.java

3. Save the file as **AttributeTag.java** in the folder C:\myjspapp\chapter10.

4. Open a DOS command window and change the directory, using the following command:
   cd c:\myjspapp\chapter10

5. Use the following command to compile and install the tag handler class:
   javac −d c:\myjspapp\WEB-INF\classes AttributeTag.java

This tag handler class has two attributes, attr1 and attr2, and overwrites doStartTag and doEndTag. A private helper class is provided to output a message indicating which method is called. The next step is to map the tag handler to the custom tag, as follows.

1. Open the data file mytaglib.tld, which is located in the folder C:\myjspapp\chapter10.

2. Add the code shaded in Figure 10-14.

```xml
<?xml version="1.0" encoding="ISO-8859-1" ?>
<!DOCTYPE taglib
    PUBLIC "-//Sun Microsystems, Inc.//DTD JSP Tag Library 1.1//EN"
    "http://java.sun.com/j2ee/dtds/web-jsptaglibrary_1_1.dtd">
<!-- a tag library descriptor -->
<taglib>
 <tlibversion>1.0</tlibversion>
 <jspversion>1.1</jspversion>
 <shortname>jspbook</shortname>
 <tag>
  <name>test</name><!-- tag name -->
 <!-- tag handler-->
<tagclass>com.jspbook.chapter10.AttributeTag</tagclass>
  <attribute>
   <name>attr1</name>
   <required>true</required><!-- required -->
  </attribute>
  <attribute>
   <name>attr2</name>
   <required>false</required><!-- optional -->
  </attribute>
 </tag>

 <!-- add more tags here -->
</taglib>
```

Figure 10-14   Mytaglib.tld

3. Save and close the file.

To add attribute support for a custom tag, you must declare the attribute tag inside the tag element by means of an **attribute** element, and two nested elements, <name> and

\<required\>, must be provided between \<attribute\> and \</attribute\>. The following code adds two attributes to the \<test\> tag:

```
<attribute>
    <name>attr1</name>
    <required>true</required><!-- required -->
</attribute>
<attribute>
    <name>attr2</name>
    <required>false</required><!-- optional -->
</attribute>
```

The nested tag \<required\> specifies whether or not an attribute is required. If a true value is set, that means this attribute must be provided in the custom tag; otherwise, it is optional. In the above example, the attr1 is mandatory, and the attr2 is optional.

In the following exercise, you will write a JSP page that makes use of the custom tag.

1. Open a new document in your text editor, and type in the following code:

```
<%@ taglib uri="/chapter10/mytaglib.tld"
prefix="jspbook" %>
<HTML>
<HEAD>
<TITLE>Tag lib example</TITLE>
</HEAD>
<BODY>
<jspbook:test attr1="value1" attr2="value2" />
</BODY>
</HTML>
```

2. Save the file as **example8.jsp** in the folder C:\myjspapp\chapter10.

3. Load the page, using the following URL:
   http://localhost:8080/myapp/chapter10/example8.jsp

   The page is displayed as shown in Figure 10-15.

In this example, since doStartTag returns SKIP_BODY, if you provide a body for this custom tag, the body content is ignored. In the following exercise, you will add a body to this custom tag to see whether the body content is displayed:

1. Open a new document in your text editor, and type in the following code:

```
<%@ taglib uri="/chapter10/mytaglib.tld"
prefix="jspbook" %>
<HTML>
<HEAD>
<TITLE>Tag lib example</TITLE>
</HEAD>
<BODY>
<jspbook:test attr1="value1" attr2="value2">
 <h2>The body content is evaluated</h2>
</jspbook:test>
</BODY>
</HTML>
```

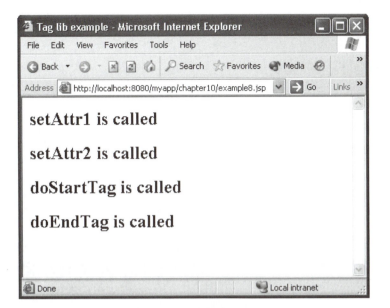

Figure 10-15   Sequence of method calls

2. Save the file as **example9.jsp** in the folder C:\myjspapp\chapter10.

3. Load the page, using the following URL:
   http://localhost:8080/myapp/chapter10/example9.jsp

The page displayed is the same as example8.jsp. Because doStartTag returns SKIP_BODY, the body content in the custom tag is ignored. In order for the body content to be evaluated, doStartTag should return EVAL_BODY_INCLUDE. If you modify the AttributeTag handler class by changing the return value of the doStartTag method to EVAL_BODY_INCLUDE, recompile and install the handler class, and then reload example9.jsp, the body content is displayed on the page.

Table 10-3   Return values for tag handlers implementing the TagSupport class

Method	Return Value	Description
doStartTag	EVAL_BODY_INCLUDE	Instructs the JSP engine to evaluate the tag's body and any child tags
	SKIP_BODY	Instructs the JSP engine to ignore the body
doEndTag	EVAL_PAGE	Instructs the JSP engine to evaluate the rest of the page
	SKIP_PAGE	Instructs the JSP engine to terminate evaluation of the page

Table 10-3 lists possible return values of the doStartTag and doEndTag methods and their usage. What happens if you want to access the body content or want to evaluate the body content more than once? To solve this problem, the tag handler class should extend the BodyTagSupport class, instead of the TagSupport class.

Manipulating the Tag Body

To manipulate the tag body, a tag handler class should extend the BodyTagSupport class and overwrite some methods to make it function. A tag handler class extending BodyTagSupport usually extends one or all of the three methods doStartTag, doEndTag, and doAfterTag. To evaluate the tag body, the doStartTag method must return EVAL_BODY_TAG. Then the body content can be accessed and processed in the doAfterBody method. To repeatedly evaluate the body content, you simply specify the return value of the doAfterBody method with EVAL_BODY_TAG. Table 10-4 lists the possible return values of several methods.

Table 10-4 Return values for the tag handler implementing the BodyTagSupport class

Method	Return Value	Description
doStartTag	EVAL_BODY_TAG EVAL_BODY_BUFFERED	Instructs the JSP engine to evaluate both the tag's body and any child tags
	SKIP_BODY	Instructs the JSP engine to ignore the body
doAfterBody	EVAL_BODY_AGAIN	Instructs the JSP engine to process the body again
	SKIP_BODY	Lets the processing continue to the doEndTag() method
doEndTag	EVAL_PAGE	Instructs the JSP engine to evaluate the rest of the page
	SKIP_PAGE	Instructs the JSP engine to terminate evaluation of the page

If the doAfterBody method always returns EVAL_BODY_AGAIN, it will result in an infinite loop.

In the following example, you will access the body content in the method doAfterBody, and you will see the order when these overwritten methods are called.

1. Open the data file ProcessBodyTag.java, which is located in the folder C:\myjspapp\chapter10.

2. Add the code shaded in Figure 10-16 to overwrite the doAfterBody method.

```
package com.jspbook.chapter10;
import java.io.*;
import javax.servlet.*;
import javax.servlet.jsp.*;
import javax.servlet.jsp.tagext.*;
public class ProcessBodyTag extends BodyTagSupport{
 private String attr1;
 private String attr2;
 public void setAttr1(String value1){
  attr1 = value1;
  helper("setAttr1");
  }
 public void setAttr2(String value2){
  attr2 = value2;
  helper("setAttr2");
 }
 public int doStartTag(){
  helper("doStartTag");
  return EVAL_BODY_ BUFFERED;
 }
 public int doAfterBody(){
  BodyContent bc = getBodyContent();
  String bcs = bc.getString(); //get the body
  try{
    JspWriter out = bc.getEnclosingWriter();
    out.println("Body content is retrieved from the doAfterBody <br>");
    out.println("method within the tag handler. The body content is <br>");
    out.println("sent to the output stream:<br>");
    out.println("<font size=1 face=Arial color=red>"+bcs+"</font>");
    out.println("<h2>doAfterBody is called</h2>");
  }catch(IOException ioexc){}
  return SKIP_BODY;
 }
 public int doEndTag(){
  helper("doEndTag");
  return SKIP_PAGE;
 }
 private void helper(String methodName){
  try{
    JspWriter out = pageContext.getOut();
    out.println("<h2>" + methodName+ " is called</h2>");
  }catch(IOException ioexc){}
 }
}
```

Figure 10-16 ProcessBodyTag.java

3. Save the file as **ProcessBodyTag.java** in the folder C:\myjspapp\chapter10.

4. Open a DOS command window and change the directory, using the following command:
cd c:\myjspapp\chapter10

5. Use the following command to compile and install the tag handler class:
   javac –d c:\myjspapp\WEB-INF\classes ProcessBodyTag.java

Once you have defined and installed the tag handler class, you need to create a TLD file. A tag library may contain many custom tags. In the following steps, you will add a tag entry to the mytaglib.tld file.

1. Open the file mytaglib.tld in your text editor, and add the following code right before the comment <!-- add more tags here --> in the file:

```
<!-- tag for ProcessBodyTag handler -->
 <tag>
  <name>processbody</name><!-- tag name -->
  <!--tag handler-->
  <tagclass>com.jspbook.chapter10.ProcessBodyTag</tagclass>
  <!-- tag handler -->

<attribute>
   <name>attr1</name>
   <required>true</required><!-- required -->
  </attribute>
  <attribute>
   <name>attr2</name>
   <required>false</required><!-- optional -->
  </attribute>
 </tag>
```

2. Save and close the file.

Now you can create a JSP page that makes use of this tag.

1. Open a new document in your text editor, and type in the following code:

```
<%@ taglib uri="/chapter10/mytaglib.tld"
prefix="jspbook" %>
<HTML>
<HEAD>
<TITLE>Tag lib example</TITLE>
</HEAD>
<BODY>
<jspbook:processbody attr1="value1" attr2="value2" >
This is the body content
</jspbook:processbody>
</BODY>
</HTML>
```

2. Save the file as **example10.jsp** in the folder C:\myjspapp\chapter10.

3. Load the page, using the following URL:
   http://localhost:8080/myapp/chapter10/example10.jsp

   The page is displayed as shown in Figure 10-17.

Figure 10-17   Processing the body content

If you want the body content to be evaluated repeatedly in certain circumstances, you can change the return value of the doAfterBody method.

In the tag handler class, getBodyContent() returns an instance of the BodyContent class. The BodyContent class has three important methods:

- getEnclosingWriter, which returns the JspWriter being used by doStartTag and doEndTag
- getReader, which returns a Reader that can read the tag's body
- getString, which returns a String containing the entire tag body

In fact, since all JSP content, including response and request objects, can be accessed in tag handler classes, you can manipulate JSP contents in tag handlers, as in JSP scripts.

Manipulate JSP Content with Custom Tags

Unlike JavaBeans, custom tags can manipulate JSP content. Custom tags can obtain information about their environment. They automatically get access to all information about the request, the response, and all the variables in the JSP pages. Therefore, you can use the request object to get the information encapsulated in the request, or use the response to add a cookie, and so on.

To access the request object, you simply use getRequest to obtain a reference to the request object from the automatically defined pageContext field of the TagSupport class, as follows:

```
HttpServletRequest req = (HttpServletRequest)pageContext.get
Request();
```

In the exercise below, you will develop a custom tag. This tag will optionally evaluate tag body and page content after the custom tag, depending on the request time information, which is a field value on a form.

You need to define a tag handler class first. This tag handler class overwrites both the doStartTag and doEndTag methods. Inside both methods, a reference to the request object is obtained via the pageContext field, and you use the getParameter method of the request object to get a parameter value sent in the request. Depending on the parameter value, doStartTag returns either SKIP_BODY or EVAL_BODY_INCLUDE; doEndTag returns either SKIP_PAGE or EVAL_PAGE.

1. Open the data file AccessRequest.java, which is located in the folder C:\myjspapp\chapter10.

2. Add the code shaded in Figure 10-18.

```
package com.jspbook.chapter10;
import java.io.*;
import javax.servlet.http.*;
import javax.servlet.jsp.*;
import javax.servlet.jsp.tagext.*;
public class AccessRequest extends TagSupport{
 public int doStartTag(){
  HttpServletRequest req =
       (HttpServletRequest)pageContext.getRequest();
  String s = req.getParameter("skipBody");
  if(s.equals("yes"))
     return SKIP_BODY;
  else
     return EVAL_BODY_INCLUDE;
 }
 public int doEndTag(){
  HttpServletRequest req =
       (HttpServletRequest)pageContext.getRequest();
  String s = req.getParameter("skipPage");
  if(s.equals("yes"))
     return SKIP_PAGE;
  else
     return EVAL_PAGE;
 }
}
```

Figure 10-18   AccessRequest.java

3. Save the file.

4. Open a DOS command window and change the directory, using the following command:
   cd c:\myjspapp\chapter10

5. Compile and install the tag handler class, using the following command:
   java –d c:\myjspapp\WEB-INF\classes AccessRequest.java

6. Open the file mytaglib.tld in your text editor, and add the following tag entry right before the line <!-- add more tags here --> :

```
<!-- tag for AccessRequest handler -->
 <tag>
  <name>accessRequest</name><!-- tag name -->
  <tagclass>com.jspbook.chapter10.AccessRequest
</tagclass>
 </tag>
```

7. Save and close the file.

8. Open a new document in your text editor, and type in the following code:

```
<HTML>
<HEAD>
<TITLE>Example 11: Access request object in custom tag
</TITLE>
</HEAD>
<BODY>
<form action="example11.jsp" method=post>
 <input type=radio name=skipBody value=yes checked>Skip
body
 <input type=radio name=skipBody value=no >Evaluate body
<br><br>
 <input type=radio name=skipPage value=yes checked>Skip
page
 <input type=radio name=skipPage value=no >Evaluate page
<br><br>
 <input type=submit value=Submit>
</form>
</BODY>
</HTML>
```

9. Save the file as **example11.html** in the folder C:\myjspapp\chapter10.

10. Open a new document in your text editor, and type in the following code:

```
<%@ taglib uri="/chapter10/mytaglib.tld"
prefix="jspbook" %>
<HTML>
<HEAD>
```

10

```
<TITLE>Example 11: Access request object in custom tag
</TITLE>
</HEAD>
<BODY>
<a href="example11.html">Try again.</a><br><br>
<jspbook:accessRequest>
 This is the body content
</jspbook:accessRequest>
<br><br>
Content after the custom tag.
</BODY>
</HTML>
```

11. Save the file as **example11.jsp** in the folder C:\myjspapp\chapter10.

12. Load page example11.html, using the following URL:
    http://localhost:8080/myapp/chapter10/example11.html

    The page is displayed as shown in Figure 10-19.

13. Make your selection and submit the form. Depending on the value you select on the form, the tag body and the page content after the custom tag will or will not be evaluated. For example, if you choose to evaluate body and page, then the page is displayed as shown in Figure 10-20.

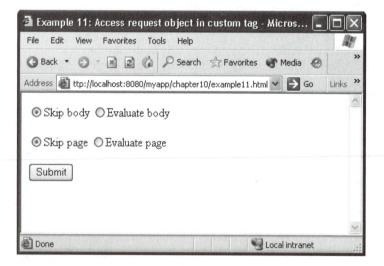

Figure 10-19 Custom tag and request object

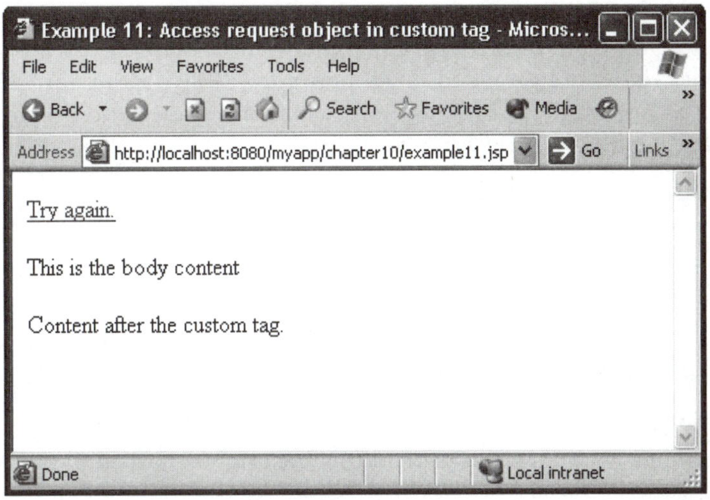

Figure 10-20   Accessing the request object in the custom tag

CHAPTER SUMMARY

❑ To invoke another page when processing a request, the request can be either forwarded or redirected to another page.

❑ When a request is forwarded, all involved pages are in the same request scope; therefore, the same request object is shared among the pages. When a request is redirected, the Web server forces the browser to make a new request. Therefore, the original request object is gone and cannot be accessed from the redirected page. To access the information associated with the original request, you can convert this information to a query string sent with the new request.

❑ A method declaration consists of five parts: method access specifier, return type, method name, method parameter list, and method body. You can declare and use methods anywhere in your JSP pages.

❑ All programs are subject to syntax errors and runtime errors. Syntax errors are detected during compile time, while runtime errors occur during the execution of the program.

❑ Runtime errors are called exceptions. An exception must be handled; otherwise, your program will abort. An exception can be handled either in the same page where the exception occurs or in another JSP page, which you must specify as errorPage in the page directive.

❑ JSP technology allows you to introduce custom tags. A custom tag contains three components: the tag handler class, a tag library descriptor file, and a JSP page to make use of the custom tag.

◻ A tag handler class must extend the Tag interface and implement all methods provided in the interface. To minimize the effort involved in defining a tag handler class, two abstract classes are provided, TagSupport and BodyTagSupport. Therefore, a tag handler class can simply extend one of the abstract classes and only overwrite the methods that need to be overwritten.

◻ Unlike JavaBeans, custom tags can access and manipulate JSP content.

REVIEW QUESTIONS

1. If a request is sent to page1.jsp, and page1.jsp forwards the request to page2.jsp, and page2.jsp forwards it to page3.jsp, then _____.

   a. the request object processed in page3.jsp is the same as that in page1.jsp

   b. the request object processed in page3.jsp is the same as that in page2.jsp

   c. both a and b

   d. none of the above

2. If a request is sent to page1.jsp, and page1.jsp redirects it to page2.jsp, and page2.jsp redirects it to page3.jsp, then _____.

   a. the request object processed in page3.jsp is the same as that in page1.jsp

   b. the request object processed in page3.jsp is the same as that in page2.jsp

   c. both a and b

   d. none of the above

3. When redirecting to a new page, the browser makes a new request. True or False?

4. If a request is sent to page1.jsp, and page1.jsp forwards the request to page2.jsp, and page2.jsp forwards it to page3.jsp, then how many requests are sent from the browser?

   a. 1

   b. 2

   c. 3

   d. 0

5. If a request is sent to page1.jsp, and page1.jsp redirects it to page2.jsp, and page2.jsp redirects it to page3.jsp, then how many requests are sent from the browser?

   a. 0

   b. 1

   c. 2

   d. 3

6. In Question 1, if all three pages contain the following code:

```
<jsp:useBean id="counter" class="someValidClassPath"
scope="request"/>
```

then which of the following statements is true?

   a. All pages reference the same bean instance.

   b. All pages reference different bean instances.

7. Variables declared in declarations are created every time the page in which they are declared is requested. True or False?

8. In a declaration, you can _____. (Choose all that apply.)

   a. declare variables

   b. define methods

   c. access the request object

   d. use the out object

9. The compiler can detect _____ at translation time.

   a. syntax errors

   b. runtime errors

10. Which of the following are logic errors?

   a. syntax errors

   b. runtime errors

10

11. You provide an input field on a form in a page. If a user enters the value "101" and submits the form, the request is processed and no error occurs; if the user enters "hi" and submits the form, an error message is displayed. This error is a

_____ .

   a. syntax error

   b. runtime error

12. You can handle an exception in the same page by using a try/catch block. That means the code inside the try block must throw an exception during runtime. True or False?

13. In exception-handling code, if you provide a finally code block after a try code block, which of the following statements is correct?

   a. The finally block is not executed if no exception occurs in the try block.

   b. The finally block is executed if and only if an exception occurs in the try block.

   c. The finally block is executed regardless of whether or not an exception occurs in the try block.

   d. none of the above

14. To handle an exception in another page, the errorPage attribute of the page directive must be set to the page where the exception will be handled. True or False?

15. In order for a JSP page to serve as an errorPage to handle exceptions that occur in other pages, the isErrorPage attribute of the page directive must be set to true on the page. True or False?

16. A tag handler may extend which of the following classes? (Choose all that apply.)

    a. TagSupport

    b. BodyTagSupport

    c. Vector

    d. a and b

    e. a and c

17. A setter method in a tag handler is called the _____.

    a. before doStartTag

    b. after doStartTag

    c. after doEndTag

    d. none of the above

18. When the starting tag is encountered, which of the following methods is called?

    a. doEndTag

    b. doStartTag

    c. doAfterBody

    d. none of the above

19. A tag handler extends the TagSupport class. If you want the body content to be evaluated, then you must overwrite the doStartTag method, and this method must return _____.

    a. SKIP_BODY

    b. EVAL_BODY_INCLUDE

    c. EVAL_BODY_TAG

    d. none of the above

20. A tag handler extends BodyTagSupport. To repeatedly evaluate the body content, the doAfterBody method must be overwritten, and this method must return _____.

    a. EVAL_BODY_BUFFERED

    b. SKIP_BODY

    c. EVAL_BODY_INCLUDE

    d. none of the above

HANDS-ON PROJECTS

Project 10-1 Passing All Information as a Query String with Redirecting

In this project, you will use the skills you learned in previous chapters to get all field names and their corresponding values. Then you will send this information as a query string, using redirecting; information is retrieved in the redirected page.

1. Use Figure 10-21 as a guide to design an HTML page.

Project1: Redirecting a request - Microsoft Internet Explorer

File   Edit   View   Favorites   Tools   Help

Back ▼   ⟳   ☑ ☒ ⌂   ⌕ Search   ☆ Favorites   ⬤ Media   ⟲

Address   http://localhost:8080/myapp/chapter10/project1.html   ⮕ Go   Links

Fill in the fields and then click Submit.

Name: [   ]
Address: [   ]
City: [   ]
State: [   ]
Zip Code: [   ]
[Submit]

Done   Local intranet

Figure 10-21   Redirecting example

2. Specify the action attribute of the form so that the data collected on this page will be processed in project1-1.jsp.

3. Save this file as **project1.html** in the folder C:\myjspapp\chapter10.

4. Create a new document in your text editor, and save the file as **project1-1.jsp** in the folder C:\myjspapp\chapter10.

5. Add code to retrieve data collected in project1.html and convert it into a query string, then redirect to project1-2.jsp and append the query string to the redirected URL.

6. Save and close the file.

7. Create a new document in your text editor, and save it as **project1-2.jsp** in the folder C:\myjspapp\chapter10.

8. Add code to retrieve the data in a query string and display it on this page.

9. Save and close the file.

10. Load the page project1.html, using the following URL:
    http://localhost:8080/myapp/chapter10/project1.html

    The page is displayed as shown in Figure 10-21.

11. Fill in the form and submit it. The information is retrieved in project1-1.jsp and converted into a query string, then the page redirects to project1-2.jsp, and the information is sent as a query string, which is retrieved and displayed on the redirected page. A page similar to Figure 10-22 is displayed.

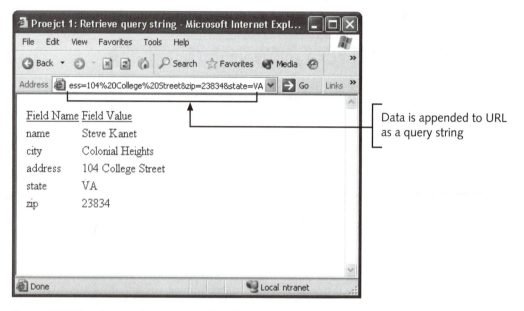

Figure 10-22   Query string and redirecting

Project 10-2 Reloading Issues Caused by Forwarding

After forwarding, reloading the page will resend the information. This project illustrates the information is resent with refreshing in Internet Explorer. In this project, you will design a pseudo-shopping cart that allows customers to select an item from a drop-down list and add the item to a shopping cart, then displays the number of each item in the shopping cart.

1. Use Figure 10-23 as a reference to design an HTML page, and save it as **project2.html** in the folder C:\myjspapp\chapter10.

2. Specify that the data collected on this page will be processed in project2-1.jsp.

3. Save and close the file.

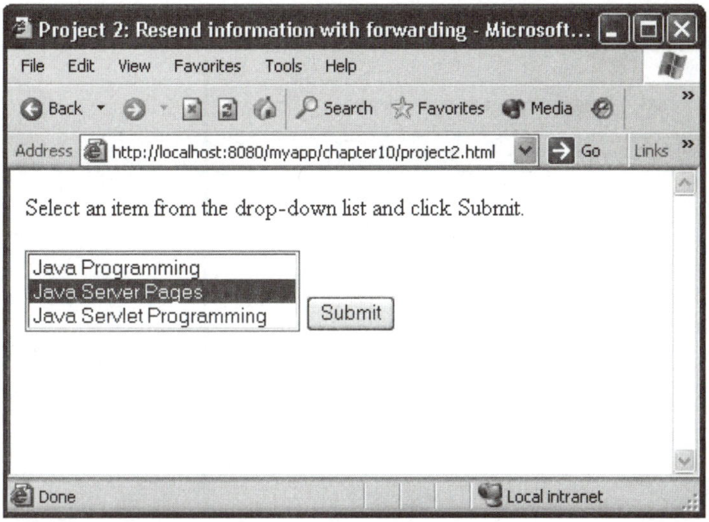

Figure 10-23   Item list

4. Create a new document in your text editor, and save it as project2-1.jsp in the folder C:\myjspapp\chapter10.

5. Add code to forward the request to project2-2.jsp.

6. Save and close the file.

7. Create a new document in your text editor, and save it as **project2-2.jsp** in the folder C:\myjspapp\chapter10.

8. Add code to retrieve data encapsulated in the request object. Based on what item is selected in project2.html, you need to increment the number of the corresponding item by 1, and display the number of each item in the shopping cart (see Figure 10-24).

9. Load the page project2.html, using the following URL:
   http://localhost:8080/myapp/chapter10/project2.html

   The page is displayed as shown in Figure 10-23.

10. Select an item from the drop-down list and submit the form. The request is sent to project2-1.jsp, where the same request is forwarded to project2-2.jsp and processed there. A page similar to Figure 10-24 is displayed.

11. Click the **Refresh** button (Reload in Netscape Navigator). A message window is displayed asking whether you want to resend the information. Click **Retry** (OK in Netscape) to resend the information, and you will see that the previously added item is added again.

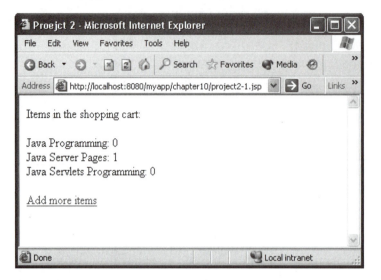

Figure 10-24   Data processed in the new target page

Project 10-3 Improved Shopping Cart

In Chapter 9, you created a shopping cart for an online bookstore. But there is a problem with the shopping cart. When a user selects an item and submits the form, the item is added to the shopping cart, and the page displays the item. However, if the user refreshes the page, the same item is added to the shopping cart again. In this project, you will create a shopping cart that corrects this problem and prevents an item from being added again when a user refreshes the page. This project contains five files: project3.html, project3-1.jsp, project3-2.jsp, project3-3.jsp, and project3-4.jsp. They are all provided as data files except project3-1.jsp. These files are contained in the folder C:\myjspapp\chapter10.

1. Create a new document in your text editor, and save it as **project3-1.jsp** in the folder C:\myjspapp\chapter10.

2. Add code to instantiate a JavaBean from class ShopCart1, which was installed in Chapter 9. Assign the ID cart to this bean, and specify that the bean has session scope.

3. Add code to the page project3-1.jsp to set the property itemsArray, using the items check boxes.

4. Add code to redirect to project3-2.jsp.

5. Save and close the file.

6. Load the page project3.html, using the following URL:
   http://localhost:8080/myapp/chapter10/project3.html

7. Select an item and submit the form. The selected item should be added to the shopping cart. Notice that if you refresh the page, the content of the shopping cart does not change.

Project 10-4 Exception Handling in an errorPage Page

In this project, you will handle an exception in another page.

1. Open the data file project4-1.jsp, which is located in the folder C:\myjspapp\chapter10.

2. Add the code shaded in Figure 10-25 to specify that runtime errors will be handled in project4-2.jsp.

```
<%@ page errorPage="project4-2.jsp" %>
<HTML>
<HEAD>
<TITLE>Project 4: Handle an exception in another page</TITLE>
</HEAD>
<BODY>
<form action="project4-1.jsp" method="POST">
 Enter a numerical value:
  <input type=text name=number size=10 maxlength=9>
 <input type=submit value=submit>
</form>
<%
 String numS =  request.getParameter("number");
 if(numS !=null){
  double number = Double.parseDouble(numS);
%>
  <hr width=200 align=left>
  The number you entered is : <%= number %>
 <%}%>
</BODY>
</HTML>
```

Figure 10-25   Project4-1.jsp

3. Save and close the file.

4. Open a new document in your text editor, and type in the following code:

```
<%@ page isErrorPage="true" %>
The following exception has occurred:<br>
<%= exception.toString() %><br><br>
<a href="project4-1.jsp">Try again</a>
```

5. Save the file as **project4-2.jsp** in the folder C:\myjspapp\chapter10.

6. Load the page project4-1.jsp, using the following URL:
http://localhost:8080/myapp/chapter10/project4-1.jsp

7. Enter a numerical value and submit the form. The number you enter is displayed on the page. If you enter a non-numerical value, an exception is raised and the exception is processed in another page.

10

Project 10-5 AddCookie Custom Tag Handler

In this project, you will create a custom tag handler that helps to add a cookie.

1. Open the data file AddCookieTag.java, which is located in the folder C:\myjspapp\chapter10.

2. Add the code shaded in Figure 10-26 to create a cookie.

```java
package com.jspbook.chapter10;
import java.io.*;
import javax.servlet.http.*;
import javax.servlet.jsp.*;
import javax.servlet.jsp.tagext.*;
public class AddCookieTag extends TagSupport{
 private String name;
 private String value;
 private String maxAgeString;
 private int maxAge = 60*60*24;
 public void setName(String name){
  this.name = name;
  }
 public void setValue(String value){
  this.value = value;
 }
 public void setMaxAgeString(String age){
  maxAgeString = age;
  try{
    maxAge = Integer.parseInt(maxAgeString) * 60;
  }catch(Exception exc){
    maxAge = 60*60*24; //if exception occurs, default to one day
  }
 }
 public int doEndTag(){
  HttpServletResponse res =
        (HttpServletResponse)pageContext.getResponse();
  Cookie cookie = new Cookie(name,value);
  cookie.setMaxAge(maxAge);
  cookie.setPath("/"); //make cookie accessible from all
                       // directories in the application
  res.addCookie(cookie);
  return EVAL_PAGE;
 }
}
```

Figure 10-26 AddCookieTag.java

3. Save and close the file.

4. Open a DOS command window and change the directory, using the following command:
   cd c:\myjspapp\chapter10

5. Compile and install the tag handler class, using the following command:
   java −d c:\myjspapp\WEB-INF\classes AddCookieTag.java

6. Open mytaglib.tld in your text editor, and add the following tag entry right before the line <!-- add more tags here -->:

```
<!-- tag for AddCookieTag handler -->
 <tag>
  <name>addCookie</name><!-- tag name -->
  <tagclass>com.jspbook.chapter10.AddCookieTag</tagclass>
  <attribute>
   <name>name</name>
   <required>true</required><!-- required -->
  </attribute>
  <attribute>
   <name>value</name>
   <required>true</required><!-- required -->
  </attribute>
  <attribute>
   <name>maxAgeString</name>
   <required>false</required><!-- optional -->
  </attribute>
 </tag>
```

7. Save and close the file.

Note that in the AddCookieTag tag handler, the doEndTag method returns EVAL_BODY, so the content after the ending tag will be processed.

Project 10-6 Using the AddCookieTag Custom Tag

In this project, you will make use of the custom tag you developed in Project 10-5.

1. Open the data file project6-1.jsp, which is located in the folder C:\myjspapp\chapter10.

2. Add the code shaded in Figure 10-27 to use the custom tag to create a cookie.

```
<HTML>
<HEAD>
<TITLE>Project 6: Use custom tag to add cookie</TITLE>
</HEAD>
<BODY>
<%@ taglib uri="/chapter10/mytaglib.tld" prefix="jspbook" %>
<jspbook:addCookie name="chapter10"
    value="Introduction to Custom Tag" maxAgeString="10"/>
A cookie has been created. Click here to
<a href="project6-2.jsp">Read this cookie</a>
</BODY>
</HTML>
```

Figure 10-27   Project6-1.jsp

3. Save and close the file.

4. Create a new document in your text editor, and save it as **project6-2.jsp** in the folder C:\myjspapp\chapter10.

5. Add code to retrieve the cookie created in project6-1.jsp, and display the cookie name and its value on this page.

6. Save and close the file.

7. Load the page project6-1.jsp, using the following URL:
   http://localhost:8080/myapp/chapter10/project6-1.jsp

   The page is displayed as shown in Figure 10-28.

8. Click the link on this page to read the cookie added with the custom tag. The page is displayed as shown in Figure 10-29.

Figure 10-28   Creating a cookie with a custom tag

Figure 10-29   Reading a cookie

10

CASE PROJECTS

SRAS: Course List

One of the features of the SRAS system is that it allows users to view all available courses. You are required to use custom tags to perform this task. The tag handler CourseListTag.java file is provided, and is located in the folder C:\myjspapp\chapter10\sras. To use this custom tag, you need to perform the following tasks:

1. Compile and install the custom tag handler.
2. Modify the custom tag file mytaglib.tld, which is located in the folder C:\myjspapp\chapter10, to add an entry to the tag library descriptor.
3. Modify courselist.jsp to use the custom tag to list all courses in the database.

Encoding HTML Tags

You are hired by XYZ News to maintain its daily news Web site. Design a Web page to allow reporters to edit and post news online. All news is stored in text format files. These files are loaded and content is sent to clients in HTML format. Basically, the editing tool is a textarea field on a form, and the content entered in the textarea field is saved to a file. The problem is that if the content contains an HTML-specific tag, the content will not be displayed properly. For example, the content <Weather Report> will not be displayed. To solve this problem, write a custom tag to replace all characters with special meaning in HTML (', ", <, >, and &) with their corresponding HTML character entities (', ", <, >, and &). Then your custom tag will be used as follows:

```
<jspbook:encodingHTML file="filename"/>
<!--read file and display content properly-->
```

or

```
<jspbook:encodingHTML >
  <body content>
</jspbook:encodingHTML>
<!--the body content will be displayed properly-->
```

Then you need to compile and install the custom tag. After you have created and installed the custom tag properly, design a JSP page to test the custom tag you created.

11

DATABASES WITH JSP

In this chapter, you will:

♦ Learn basic database and DBMS concepts

♦ Use SQL to manipulate databases via your JSP Web applications

♦ Use the JDBC or JDBC-ODBC bridge to connect to databases from JSP pages

♦ Create tables and insert data into tables via JSP pages

♦ Get data from tables via JSP pages

♦ Use forms to add data to a table

Many companies organize data—for example, inventory or customer information—in what are called databases. The most common type of commercial database is a relational database. Many Web sites allow their customers to interact with their databases via the Internet, for example to update their personal information, or to facilitate e-commerce. In this chapter, you will learn about databases and database management systems (DBMS), and you will learn how to manipulate a database using the SQL language. Then you will learn how to connect to a database and issue SQL statements and commands from a JSP page.

A QUICK INTRODUCTION TO DATABASES

A **database** is a collection of data items related to some enterprise. For example, a database might contain checking account information in a bank, product items information in an online store, student records in a college, and so on. There are many kinds of databases.

Relational databases store information in simple structures called tables. Most commercial databases today are relational databases. Table 11-1 shows a sample table containing product information for an online store. The data in a table is organized into rows and columns. The rows in the table are called **records**. A record contains information about a given entity. An **entity** is a distinct object—for example, a person's name, a product, or an event. Each row in Table 11-1, for instance, contains information about a specific product. The columns in the table contain fields. A **field** contains a single, specific piece of information within a record. So, a record is a group of related fields. In Table 11-1, each record has four fields: item number, item name, unit price, and inventory.

Table 11-1   Sample Database Table

Item Number	Item Name	Unit Price	Inventory
100	Camera	$267.99	13
101	Washer	$489.56	8
102	TV	$189.99	29

Each field in a database has a **data type**, which indicates what kind of data is stored in the field. For example, in Table 11-1, Item Number and Inventory contain numbers, Item Name contains text, and Unit Price contains currency. The data stored in each field should be consistent with the data type of the field. For example, the inventory field stores the inventory level of a product, so the data in the inventory field should be a number. Most databases handle data types that are very similar to the data types you learned about in Chapter 4, such as integers, characters, strings, dates, floats, and so on.

Creating Database Tables

To create a table, you need to specify at least the following two things:

- Table name
- Fields and their data types

The table name identifies the table. A database can consist of many tables. You use the name of a table to reference the table and to manipulate data in that table. You specify what kind of information will be stored in a table by providing field names and associated data types. For example, to create a table to store bank customers' savings account information, you would include fields for the account number, client name, and account balance. You could name these fields accNumber, name, and balance, respectively. The accNumber field is a number, the name field is text, and the balance field is a number. The data stored in each field should be consistent with the data type of the field. Table 11-2 shows the table with three records.

Table 11-2 Savings Account Data

accNumber	Name	Balance
100	Nichols Steve	2500.59
101	Anderson Kanet	6880.10
200	Gomez Ashton	5692.20

 Do not use spaces in a table name or a field name. Although some databases allow you to do so, you might have problems when you attempt to use these names in your applications.

Suppose you want to store product information in a table, including product ID, product name, model, price, and manufacturer's information. The manufacturer's information includes manufacturer's name, street address, city, state, Zip code, and phone number. You could incorporate all this data in one table, so that each product record contains the product ID, product name, price, and the manufacturer's street address, city, state, Zip code, and phone number. If a single manufacturer provides 50 different products, that manufacturer's data would be recorded in this table 50 times. It is much more efficient to use two tables, one for the products and one for the manufacturers. The two tables could be linked via some common fields in both tables. For example, you might design these two tables as shown in Tables 11-3 and 11-4.

11

Table 11-3 Product Table

productID	ProductName	Model	Price	ManufacturerID
100	Washer	D1	356.99	1
101	Washer	D3	289.89	1
102	Washer	D6	525.59	1
103	Washer	D6	459.89	2
200	TV	S2	255.68	2

Table 11-4 Manufacturer Table

ManufacturerID	Name	Address	City	State	Zip	Phone
1	Weiwei Co.	Edward Rd.	Petersburg	VA	23806	(804) 1234567
2	XYZ Co.	Central	Clemson	SC	29634	(804) 7654321

To link these two tables, an additional field, manufacturerID, is included in both tables. For example, to get information about the manufacturer for productID 100 (washer), you can get the manufacturerID, which is 1, and then use this ID to get the manufacturer's information from the Manufacturer table.

Primary Keys in a Table

The first field in Table 11-3 is productID. This is a code assigned to each product in the table. Unlike other fields in this table, these IDs are unique; that is, no two products are assigned the same ID. Such a field is used as a **unique identifier**. This simply means that a given product ID appears in only a single record in the table. For example, only one record exists in which the productID is 100. A unique identifier is also called a **primary key**. Thus, the productID field is the primary key for the Product table. For the Manufacturer table, manufacturerID is the primary key.

A database is an organized collection of associated data. To manage a database, you need a **database management system (DBMS)**. A DBMS is a collection of software that creates, manages, and controls access to databases. Most DBMSs run structured query language (SQL) to manipulate databases.

A Quick Introduction to SQL

SQL, pronounced either "ess queue ell" or "sequel," is a computer language designed to process relational databases. SQL includes both a **data definition language (DDL)** and a **data manipulation language (DML)**. DDL commands, such as CREATE TABLE and ALTER TABLE, operate on the tables. DDL is used to define a table's columns, add or delete columns, and delete tables. DML, which includes commands such as INSERT INTO, UPDATE, DELETE, and SELECT, operates on the entries or records in the tables. DML is used to insert, update, delete, and retrieve data in a table.

Data Types

Columns (fields) within a table are assigned a given data type, such as CHARACTER (or CHAR), REAL, and INTEGER. The data type indicates the kind of data allowed in a column. Table 11-5 lists the data types that most databases support.

Table 11-5   Data Types Supported in Most Databases

Data Type	Sample Data	Description
CHAR(length)	Newcastle Dr.	For nonnumeric data. Fixed length.
VARCHAR(length)	Newcastle Dr.	For nonnumeric data. Variable length (listed length indicates maximum).
INTEGER	123456	For whole-number data between -2^{31} and $+2^{31}-1$
SMALLINT	31	For whole-number data between -2^{15} and $+2^{15}-1$
FLOAT	2.6E+10	For very large or very small numbers
DATE	11/16/2001	For dates. Implementations vary in different databases.

There are many other data types not included in this table. And you need to be aware that some data types are implemented differently in different databases.

Creating and Dropping Tables

Many DBMSs provide a graphical user interface **(GUI)** or wizards to facilitate database manipulation. Using the GUI and/or wizards, you can issue SQL commands to manipulate a database even without knowing how to write SQL commands. For example, in Microsoft Access 2000, you can create tables in Design view or you can use wizards; you can insert and update data using forms; you can create queries in Design view or by using wizards, and so on. In this section, you will learn how to write SQL commands, instead of using the interfaces provided by a DBMS.

The syntax for creating a table has the following form:

CREATE TABLE tableName (field1 dataType, field2 dataType, ...)

SQL syntax is case insensitive. Therefore, CREATE TABLE is equivalent to CrEaTe tAbLe. By convention, all SQL keywords, such as CREATE and TABLE, are in uppercase. It is recommended that you follow this convention, even though it is not required.

To create a table, you use the keywords CREATE TABLE followed by a table name, followed by field names and their data types. Field names and data types are separated with at least one space. All fields and their data types are placed within parentheses.

You can specify a primary key for your table. Creating a primary key takes the following syntax:

CREATE TABLE tableName (field1 dataType PRIMARY KEY, field2 dataType, ...)

To specify a field as the primary key, you use the keyword PRIMARY KEY following dataType.

To drop a table, use the following syntax:

DROP TABLE tableName

This command deletes the specified table from the database.

The following command creates a table called student, containing three fields.

```
CREATE TABLE student (
    id integer PRIMARY KEY,
    firstName varchar(15),
    lastName varchar(15));
```

The field id is specified as the primary key, so no duplicate values can be entered in this field. The fields firstName and lastName have the data type varchar with a maximum length of 15.

11

The following command deletes this table from the database:

```
DROP TABLE student;
```

Inserting Data into a Table

After a table has been created, you can issue SQL commands to insert records into the table, delete records from the table, or update records in the table.

The syntax to insert a record into a table is as follows:

INSERT INTO TABLE tableName VALUES (value1, value2, ...)
or
INSERT INTO TABLE tableName (field1, field2, ...) VALUES (value1, value2, ...)

The first form inserts values into the fields in the order in which they are defined in the table. That means value1 will be inserted into the first field, value2 into the second field, and so on. This form requires you to provide values for all fields in the table. For example, the fields in the student table are defined in the following order: id, firstName, and lastName. Therefore, the SQL command:

```
INSERT INTO student VALUES (200, 'John', 'Kanet');
```

inserts 200 into the id field, 'John' into the firstName field, and 'Kanet' into the lastName field.

The second form specifies the destination fields for the inserted values. This allows you to insert values into specific fields without necessarily populating the entire table, since some fields can have null values. The above command can be rewritten as follows:

```
INSERT INTO student (lastName, firstName, id) VALUES
('Kanet', 'John', 200);
```

You may have noticed that the character values are placed within single quotation marks. This is required for almost all DBMSs. Although double quotation marks work in some DBMSs, for example in Microsoft Access, it is recommended that you use single quotation marks.

You don't need to assign values to all fields in order to insert a record into a table. For example, in the student table, only the ID (which is the primary key) is required. You can insert a record into this table by providing the ID only, and all omitted fields are assigned NULL values.

If a field is a primary key, you must provide a valid value for it when you insert a record into the table. But how do you make other fields required? The SQL implementations for this are different in different DBMSs. In Microsoft Access and Oracle, you can use the following SQL command to specify that both firstName and lastName are required fields.

```
CREATE TABLE student2 (id INTEGER PRIMARY KEY,
                firstName char(15) NOT NULL,
                lastName char(15) NOT NULL));
```

Consider the following table data:

ID	First name	Last name
100	John	Davis
101	Mike	Kanet

You can use the following command to insert these two records into the student table:

```
INSERT INTO student VALUES(100, 'John', 'Davis');
INSERT INTO student (id, lastName, firstName) VALUES(101,
'Kanet', 'Mike');
```

Updating Table Data

Some Web sites frequently access and update their associated databases. For example, a checking account is updated after each online transaction; an online bookstore updates its inventory each time an item is sold, and so on. To update data in a table, you use the following syntax:

UPDATE tableName SET field1=value1, fiedl2=value2, ... WHERE conditions

The WHERE clause gives the condition for selecting which rows (records) are to be updated in the table identified as tableName. The SET keyword is followed by the list of fields to be updated. If the WHERE clause is omitted, all rows in the table are updated.

Conditions in a WHERE clause are similar to conditional statements in JSP. You can construct condition statements using comparison operators and logical operators. You can use the six comparison operators (=, <> for not equal, <, >, <=, >=) as well as the three logical operators (AND, OR, and NOT) to create compound conditions or to negate a condition. You can also use parentheses as in JSP to group conditions.

Deleting Records from a Table

To delete records (rows) from a table, use the following syntax:

DELETE FROM tableName WHERE conditions

This deletes all rows that satisfy the WHERE clause in the statement. If there is no WHERE clause, then all rows in the table are deleted.

Retrieving Data

To get data from tables, you need to issue queries. The basic structure of a query is as follows:

SELECT field1, field2, ...
FROM tableName
WHERE conditions

The SELECT clause lists the fields retrieved in the query result, separated by commas. The FROM clause lists one or more table names to be used by the query. All fields listed in the SELECT or WHERE clauses must be found in one and only one of the tables listed in the FROM clause. The WHERE clause contains conditions for selecting rows from the tables listed in the FROM clause. The data retrieved is from the rows that satisfy the condition (and are therefore selected). If the WHERE clause is omitted, all rows are selected. For example, to get all washer models and prices in the product table (Table 11-3), you can use the following query:

```
SELECT model, price
FROM product
WHERE productName = 'Washer';
```

Execution of this SQL command gets the model and price information for all washers in the product table. The following query gets model and price data for all products in the table.

```
SELECT model, price
FROM product
```

Suppose you cannot remember the exact spelling of "Washer." Is it "Washer" or "Washor"? **Wildcard characters**, special symbols that represent any character or combination of characters, make it easier to use inexact spelling in a query. Two wildcards are frequently used in databases: % and _ (underscore). The percent symbol (%) represents any collection of characters, including zero characters. The underscore (_) represents any individual character. Therefore, h_t represents the letter h, followed by any single character, followed by the letter t, for instance hit or hot; and h%t represents the letter h, followed by any collection of characters, followed by the letter t, as in hot, heat, or hello cat.

 The two wildcards used in Microsoft Access are * (asterisk) and ? (question mark). But if you access a Microsoft Access database from a JSP page, you use the wildcards % and _, because the JDBC-ODBC bridge handles the query.

To use a character string in a SQL statement, you need to place it within single quotation marks. To use wildcards, you need to begin the conditional statement with the special word LIKE. For example, the following SQL command gets data for all products whose names begin with "Wash" followed by any number of characters:

```
SELECT model, price FROM product WHERE productName LIKE
'Wash%';
```

A SELECT statement selects rows from one or more tables according to specified criteria. It produces output containing one or more columns for each row selected. If you want all the fields' information for selected rows, you do not need to specify all fields; instead you can use the asterisk to achieve this, as follows:

SELECT * FROM tableName WHERE conditions;

A SQL statement may involve more than one table. For example, how can you get price and manufacturer information about the model D1 washer? The price information resides in the product table, while the manufacturer information resides in the manufacturer table. You can easily get the price information from the product table. To get the manufacturer information, you need to get the manufacturer ID from the product table, and then use the manufacturer ID to get manufacturer information from the manufacturer table. The following code shows how to achieve this in SQL:

```
SELECT product.price, manufacturer.name
FROM product, manufacturer
WHERE product.manufacturerID = manufacturer.manufacturerID;
```

Again, the SELECT clause is followed by the desired fields list. But the field names are preceded with table names. If a field can be found in more than one table listed in the FROM clause, you to need specify which table by using the table name, followed by a dot, followed by the field name. Otherwise, you do not have to use the table name. The FROM clause lists all involved tables. The WHERE clause specifies how the involved tables are linked and/or other criteria for selecting data.

Sorting Retrieved Data

If you want table data retrieved in a particular order, you need to use the ORDER BY clause. The ORDER BY clause sorts data to meet user needs. The use of the ORDER BY clause has the following form:

```
SELECT field1, field2, ... FROM tableName  WHERE conditions
ORDER BY sort_field1 DESC, sort_field2, ...
```

To sort data according to certain fields, you list the fields in the ORDER BY clause and specify the sort order. The keyword DESC following a field name sorts the data from the field in descending order. If a sort order is not provided for a field in the ORDER BY clause, the default order is ascending order. To explicitly specify ascending order, you use the keyword ASC. If more than one field is listed in the ORDER BY clause, then the data is first sorted according to the first sort field, then the second sort field, and so on. For example, to get all student names in the student table, sorted by last name then first name in ascending order, you can use the following SQL statement:

```
SELECT firstName, lastName FROM student ORDER BY lastName,
firstName;
```

11

DATABASE ACCESS FROM JSP

You can access a variety of relational databases from your JSP Web pages. For most relational databases, you use the Java database package (java.sql.*) either via a JDBC connection or via a JDBC to ODBC bridge if the database requires an ODBC driver. **Open Database Connectivity (ODBC)** is a technology developed by Microsoft to allow generic access to database systems on the Windows platform and some UNIX platforms. **Java Database Connectivity (JDBC)** is a technology developed by Sun to allow access to virtually any database system from JSP pages. To access databases from JSP pages, you must execute the following seven steps:

1. Load the JDBC driver.

2. Define the connection URL.

3. Establish the connection.

4. Create the statement object.

5. Execute a query or update.

6. Process the results.

7. Close the connection.

Each of these steps is covered in the sections below.

Loading the JDBC Driver

The first step in using JDBC is to obtain a JDBC driver for the specific database. The driver acts as the bridge between the JDBC classes (the classes used in JSP and JavaBeans to access a database) and the database itself. The **driver** is a piece of software that knows how to talk to the DBMS. To load a driver, all you need to do is to load the appropriate class. The syntax to load a driver takes the following form:

Class.forName("fully qualified class name");

For example:

```
Class.forName("sun.jdbc.odbc.JdbcOdbcDriver");
Class.forName("oracle.jdbc.driver.OracleDriver");
Class.forName("org.mysql.Driver");
Class.forName("org.gjt.mm.mysql.Driver");
```

To load a driver, the driver class must be somewhere in the CLASSPATH. The JdbcOdbcDriver driver comes with JDK. You make other drivers available by putting them in the CLASSPATH. You can put these driver classes under the WEB-INF/classes directory.

The database driver must be loaded before the program can connect to the database. If the driver specified can't be found in the CLASSPATH, the ClassNotFoundException occurs.

 Many drivers for different databases can be loaded and made available at the same time, which allows a JSP page to use more than one database simultaneously.

Defining the Connection URL

Once a driver has been loaded, you can make a connection to a database. To make a connection, you need to specify the location of the database server. URLs referring to databases use the JDBC protocol followed by a specific subprotocol and the name of the database. For some subprotocols, you may need to specify the database server host name and port number, username and password, etc. The URLs are different in different databases.

For the JDBC:ODBC bridge connection, the URL has the following syntax:

Jdbc:odbc:data_source_name

The subprotocol odbc indicates that the connection will use JDBC to connect to a Microsoft ODBC data source. ODBC is a technology developed by Microsoft to allow access to disparate database systems on the Windows platform.

For MySQL databases, the URL takes the following form:

jdbc:mysql://hostname:port/dbname

The subprotocol mysql indicates that your program will use the mysql driver to connect to the database.

For Oracle databases, the URL has the following form:

jdbc:oracle:thin:@ hostname:port :dbName;

The subprotocol oracle indicates that the connection is made through the Oracle driver.

Establishing the Connection

To manipulate a database, you must create a connection to the database server. To make the actual network connection, you need to pass the URL, the database username, and the password to the getConnection method of the DriverManager class, as follows:

Connection conn = DriverManager.getConnection(connURL,username, password);

If the connection is successful, the getConnection method returns the connection. Then the connection makes available a Statement object, which actually issues queries.

Creating the Statement Object

A Statement object is used to send queries and commands to the database. The syntax for making a statement takes the following form:

Statement stm = conn.createStatement();

The following section shows how to use the Statement object to issue queries to the database.

11

Executing a Query or Command

Once you have a Statement object, you can use it to send SQL queries or commands to the database. The Statement object has two methods: the executeUpdate() method for table updating, creating, modifying, and so on; and the executeQuery() method for retrieving data from a table. The executeUpdate() method returns an integer indicating how many rows were affected, and the executeQuery() method returns a ResultSet object containing the selected rows from a table in the database.

For example, to create a table by using the Statement object stm, you can issue the following command to the database:

```
stm.executeUpdate("CREATE TABLE product (productID char(5),
    name varchar(15))";
```

This creates a table named product with two columns.

Processing ResultSets

The executeQuery method of a Statement object returns a ResultSet object. The ResultSet object contains the selected rows based on the query. This object provides methods that allow you to retrieve the data and use it in your JSP page. The simplest way to handle the results is to process them one row at a time, using the resultSet's next method to move through the table a row at a time. The ResultSet returned from the execution of a query maintains a cursor pointing to the position right before the first row (if there are any rows selected). When the next method is called, if there are more rows after the position pointed to by the current cursor, the method call returns true, and the cursor moves to the next row; if there are no more rows, it returns false. Within a row, ResultSet provides various getXXX methods that take a column index or column name as an argument and return the results as a variety of different Java data types specified as XXX in the getXXX method. For example, if a field called ssn has the data type of integer, you can use getInt("ssn"), and it returns the ssn as an int in your JSP scripts. If the data type of a field—say, lastName—is char or varchar in the database, you should use getString("lastName") to get the data. If you want to process all columns as strings in your JSP scripts, you can simply use the getString method for all columns, regardless of the actual column type. If you use the version that takes a column index, note that columns are indexed starting at 1, not at 0 as with arrays, vectors, and most other data structures in the Java programming language.

For example, suppose a table, called employee, has two columns: firstName and lastName. The following code segment illustrates how to process the ResultSet:

```
String query = "select * from employee";
ResultSet rst = stm.executeQuery(query);
while(rst.next()){
        out.println(rst.getString("firstName") + "<br> +
rst.getString("lastName");
}
```

Closing the Connection

You may explicitly close a connection by calling the close method of a connection object. Since you may have three objects when you access a database via JSP, to close the connection, you should close these objects in the following order:

1. Close ResultSet

2. Close Statement

3. Close Connection

JDBC EXAMPLE

In this section, you will use a JDBC-ODBC bridge to connect to a Miscrosoft Access database in your JSP page. First, you will learn how to open a connection with your DBMS, and then, since JDBC sends your SQL code to your database, you will use the connection to create a table, insert data into the table, and retrieve data from the table. To connect to a database, the database must be created first. Since you will use the odbc subprotocol to connect to the database, the database must be registered as an ODBC data source in advance.

Creating a Microsoft Access Database

To create a Microsoft Access database, execute the following steps:

1. Start Microsoft Access.

2. Create a blank Access database.

3. Save it as **product.mdb** in the folder C:\myjspapp\chapter11.

4. Close the Microsoft Access window.

Now you must register the database as an ODBC data source so you can access the database from JSP Web pages.

Registering the Database as an ODBC Data Source

This section shows you how to set up an ODBC data source on Microsoft Windows XP and Windows 2000 systems. To connect to the database with the odbc subprotocol, an ODBC data source must be registered with the system via the ODBC Data Source in the Windows Control Panel.

1. Open your Control Panel. (Click **Switch to Classic View** if you are working in Microsoft Windows XP and are not already using Classic View.) Open the folder Administrative Tools. You should see Data Sources (ODBC) in the list. Double-click **Data Sources (ODBC)** to display the ODBC Data Source Administrator dialog box, as shown in Figure 11-1. Select the **System DSN** tab if it is not already selected.

11

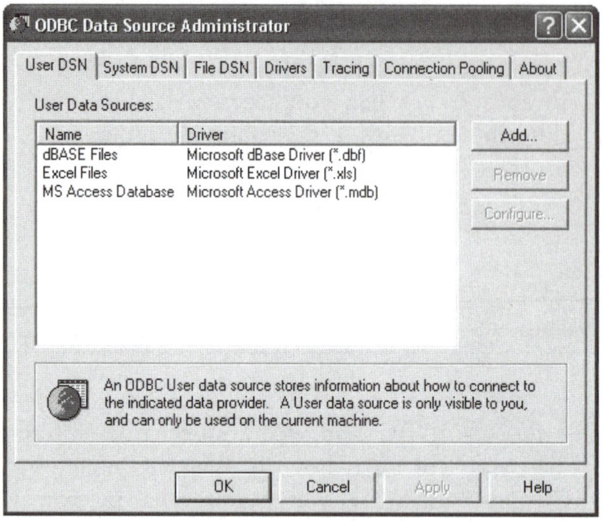

Figure 11-1   ODBC Data Source Administrator dialog box

2. Click the **Add** button to open the Create New Data Source dialog box, as shown in Figure 11–2. From the driver name list, select the driver **Microsoft Access Driver (*.mdb)**, then click the **Finish** button.

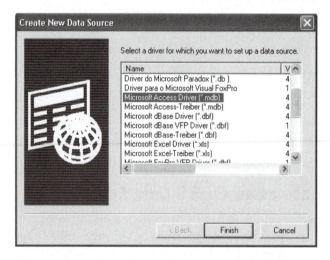

Figure 11-2   Create New Data Source dialog box

3. The ODBC Microsoft Access Setup dialog box opens, as shown in Figure 11-3. In the Data Source Name field, enter **productDSN**. Then click the **Select** button to select the database you created above. Locate the file product.mdb in the folder C:\myjspapp\chapter11, select the file, click **OK**, then click **OK** to return to the ODBC Data Source Administrator dialog box.

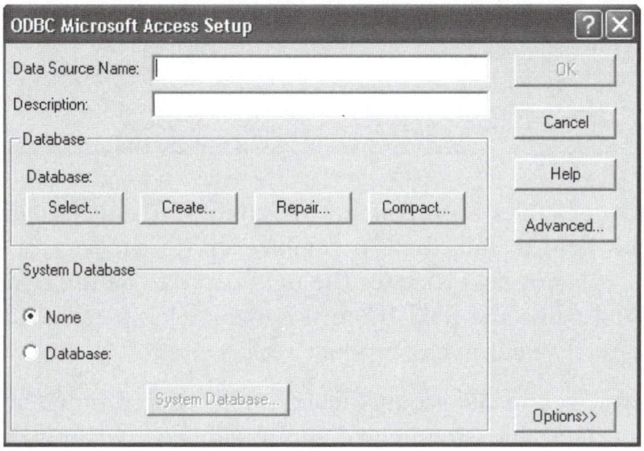

Figure 11-3   ODBC Microsoft Access Setup dialog box

Creating Tables

First, you will create two tables in the Access database. The product table contains the information about products sold by the online store; the manufacturer table contains information about the manufacturers of these products. The product table includes the fields id for product ID, name for product name, model, price, and manufacturerID; the manufacturer table includes id for manufacturer ID, name, address, city, state, zipCode, and phone. Table 11-6 and Table 11-7 list the field names and data types for the product table and manufacturer table, respectively.

Table 11-6   Product Table

Field Name	Data Type	Description
id	char(3)	Unique product ID; serves as primary key
name	varchar(15)	Product name
model	char(5)	Model series number
price	float	Unit price of product
manufacturerID	integer	Manufacturer's ID; links this table to the manufacturer table

Table 11-7 Manufacturer Table Description

Field Name	Data Type	Description
manufacturerID	integer	Unique manufacturer ID, serves as primary key
name	varchar(15)	Manufacturer name
address	varchar(20)	Manufacturer address
city	varchar(20)	City
state	varchar(15)	State
zipCode	char(5)	Zip code
phone	varchar(15)	Manufacturer's contact phone number

The product and manufacturer tables both contain the column manufacturerID, which means that you can use this field to link these two tables and to get data based on the information in both tables. It is not necessary for the field name to be the same in order to link two tables. You could name the field ID in the manufacturer table, and still use it to link to the manufacturerID field in the product table.

The column id is the primary key in the product table, and as such, it uniquely identifies each of the products sold in the online store. The column manufacturerID is the primary key in the manufacturer table. The column manufacturerID in the product table is called a **foreign key**, because it is the primary key in another table.

The following SQL statements create product and manufacturer tables:

```
CREATE TABLE product(id char(3) PRIMARY KEY,
            name varchar(15),
            model varchar(5),
            price float,
            manufacturerID integer)
CREATE TABLE manufacturer(manufacturerID integer PRIMARY
KEY,
            name varchar(15),
            address varchar(20),
            city varchar(20),
            state varchar(15),
            zipCode char(5),
            phone varchar(15))
```

Since you can connect to the database using JDBC, you can issue these SQL commands in a JSP page. The following exercise shows you how to create these two tables from within a JSP page.

1. Open the data file example1.jsp, which is located in the folder C:\myjspapp\ chapter11.

2. Add the code shaded in Figure 11-4 to make a connection to the database and to create a Statement object to execute SQL commands.

```jsp
<%@ page import="java.sql.*" %>
<%
 String url = "jdbc:odbc:productDSN";
 String username="";
 String password="";
 Connection   conn=null;
 String classPath = "sun.jdbc.odbc.JdbcOdbcDriver";
 try{
    Class.forName(classPath);
    conn = DriverManager.getConnection(url,username,password);
 }catch(Exception exc){
    out.println(exc.toString());
 }
%>
<%
    Statement stm= conn.createStatement();
    String query1, query2;
    query1="CREATE TABLE product(id char(3) PRIMARY KEY,"+
        "name varchar(15), model varchar(5), price float,"+"
        " manufacturerID integer)";
    query2="CREATE TABLE manufacturer(id integer PRIMARY KEY,"+
        "name varchar(15),address varchar(20), city varchar(20),"+
        "state varchar(15), zipCode char(5), phone varchar(15))";
    try{
    stm.executeUpdate(query1);
    stm.executeUpdate(query2);
    out.println("Two tables were successfully created.");
    }catch(Exception exc){
    out.println("These tables exist already");
    }
    stm.close();
    conn.close();
%>
```

Figure 11-4   Example1.jsp

3. Save and close the file.

4. Load the page, using the following URL:
   http://localhost:8080/myapp/chapter11/example1.jsp

   The page is displayed as shown in Figure 11-5.

5. Open the database product.mdb to verify that the two tables were created, then close the database.

11

Figure 11-5 Creating tables

Execution of this JSP page creates two tables in the product.mdb database. Loading this page again results in an exception during the execution of the executeUpdate method of the Statement object, because the page attempts to create a table that already exists.

Entering Data into Tables

Now that you have created two tables in the product.mdb database, you are ready to add data to them. The data to be added to the product table are shown in Table 11-3, and the data to be added to the manufacturer table are shown in Table 11-4.

The following SQL statement inserts a record into the product table.

```
INSERT INTO product VALUES('100','Washer','D1',356.99,1)
```

In the following exercise, you will add data to tables from a JSP page.

1. Open the data file example2.jsp, which is located in the folder C:\myjspapp\ chapter11.

2. Add the code shaded in Figure 11-6 to add two more records to the product table.

3. Save and close the file.

```
<%@ page import="java.sql.*" %>
<%
 String url = "jdbc:odbc:productDSN";
 String username="";
 String password="";
 Connection  conn=null;
 String classPath = "sun.jdbc.odbc.JdbcOdbcDriver";
 try{
    Class.forName(classPath);
    conn = DriverManager.getConnection(url,username,password);
   }catch(Exception exc){
    out.println(exc.toString());
  }
%>
<%
  Statement stm=null;
  try{
  stm= conn.createStatement();
  //adding data to product table
  stm.executeUpdate("INSERT INTO product "+
          "VALUES('100','Washer','D1',356.99,1)");
  stm.executeUpdate("INSERT INTO product "+
          "VALUES('101','Washer','D3',289.89,1)");
  stm.executeUpdate("INSERT INTO product "+
          "VALUES('102','Washer','D6',525.59,1)");
  stm.executeUpdate("INSERT INTO product "+
          "VALUES('103','Washer','D6',459.89,2)");
  stm.executeUpdate("INSERT INTO product "+
          "VALUES('200','TV','S2',255.68,2)");
  out.println("<h2>Five records were added to "+
          "the product table.</h2>");
  //adding data to manufacturer table
  stm.executeUpdate("INSERT INTO manufacturer "+
          "VALUES(1,'Weiwei Co','Edward Rd',"+
          "'Petersburg','Virginia','23806',"+
          "'(804) 123-4567')");
  stm.executeUpdate("INSERT INTO manufacturer "+
          "VALUES(2,'XYZ Co','Central','Clemson',"+
          "'South Carolina','29634',"+
          "'(864) 123-4567')");
  out.println("<h2>Two records were added to "+
          "the manufacturer table.</h2>");
 }catch(Exception exc){ out.println(exc.toString());}
 stm.close();
 conn.close();
%>
```

Figure 11-6   Example2.jsp

4. Load the page, using the following URL:
http://localhost:8080/myapp/chapter11/example2.jsp

The page is displayed as shown in Figure 11-7.

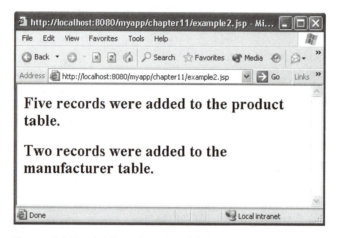

Figure 11-7   Adding data to tables

Since the SQL statements do not fit on one line on the page, each insert statement is split into several strings concatenated by a plus sign (+). Execution of this page for the first time adds five records to the product table and two records to the manufacturer table. You can verify this by opening the database product.mdb and opening the product and manufacturer tables. You should see the records in these tables.

Getting Data from Tables

Now that the product and manufacturer tables contain records, you can write SELECT statements to access their data.

The following sample code illustrates how to get all columns from the product table. To display all columns, you can use one of the following SQL statements:

```
SELECT * FROM product
```

or

```
SELECT id, name, model, price, manufacturerID FROM product
```

In this exercise, you will retrieve all data from the product table and display it in an HTML table.

1. Open the data file example3.jsp, which is located in the folder C:\myjspapp\chapter11.

2. Add the code shaded in Figure 11-8 to retrieve and display data on the page.

```
<%@ page import="java.sql.*" %>
<%
 String url = "jdbc:odbc:productDSN";
 String username="";
 String password="";
 Connection  conn=null;
 String classPath = "sun.jdbc.odbc.JdbcOdbcDriver";
 try{
    Class.forName(classPath);
    conn = DriverManager.getConnection(url,username,password);
   }catch(Exception exc){
    out.println(exc.toString());
  }
%>
<%
  Statement stm=null;
  ResultSet rst=null;
  stm= conn.createStatement();
  String query = "SELECT * FROM product";
  rst = stm.executeQuery(query);
%>
<table>
<tr>
 <th>ID</th><th>Name</th><th>Model</th><th>Price</th>
<th>ManufacturerID</th>
</tr>
<% while(rst.next()){ %>
<tr>
    <td align=center> <%= rst.getString("id")%> </td>
    <td align=center> <%= rst.getString("name")%> </td>
    <td align=center> <%= rst.getString("model") %> </td>
    <td align=center> $<%= rst.getFloat("price") %> </td>
    <td align=center> <%= rst.getInt("manufacturerID") %> </td>
</tr>
<%}%>
</table>
<%
  rst.close();
  stm.close();
  conn.close();
%>
```

Figure 11-8   Example3.jsp

3. Save and close the file.

4. Load the page, using the following URL:
   http://localhost:8080/myapp/chapter11/example3.jsp

   The page is displayed as shown in Figure 11-9.

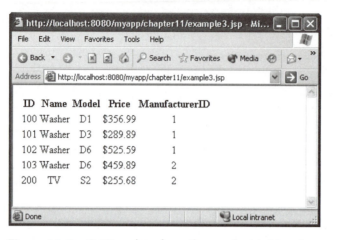

Figure 11-9 Getting data from the product table

The executeQuery statement retrieves all data from the product table, and the retrieved data are stored in the ResultSet object. The next method of the ResultSet object is used to get the selected rows one by one. For each row, the getXXX method is used to get the value for each column, and the value is displayed in the HTML table. Then the next method of the ResutlSet method returns false, indicating that all selected rows have been processed, and the while loop ends.

In the data displayed in Figure 11-9, the last column is the manufacturer's ID. To provide more information regarding the manufacturer, you can display the manufacturer's name and contact phone number. You can write a SQL statement to get this information from both the product and manufacturer tables as follows:

```
SELECT product.*, manufacturer.name, manufacturer.phone
FROM product, manufacturer
WHERE product.manufacturerID =
manufacturer.manufacturer.ID
```

In the following exercise, you will issue a SQL query from a JSP page.

1. Open the data file example4.jsp, which is located in the folder C:\myjspapp\ chapter11.

2. Add the code shaded in Figure 11-10.

3. Save the file.

```
<%@ page import="java.sql.*" %>
<%
 String url = "jdbc:odbc:productDSN";
 String username="";
 String password="";
 Connection  conn=null;
 String classPath = "sun.jdbc.odbc.JdbcOdbcDriver";
 try{
    Class.forName(classPath);
    conn = DriverManager.getConnection(url,username,password);
   }catch(Exception exc){
    out.println(exc.toString());
  }
%>
<%
  Statement stm=null;
  ResultSet rst=null;
  stm= conn.createStatement();
  String query = "SELECT product.id, product.name,product.model,"+
     "product.price, manufacturer.name as mname,"+
     "manufacturer.phone FROM product, manufacturer " +
     "WHERE product.manufacturerID=manufacturer. manufacturerID";
  rst = stm.executeQuery(query);
%>
<table>
<tr>
 <th>ID</th><th>Name</th><th>Model</th><th>Price</th>
 <th>Manufacturer Name</th><th>Manufacturer Phone</th>
</tr>
<% while(rst.next()){ %>
<tr>
    <td align=center><%= rst.getString("id")%></td>
    <td align=center><%= rst.getString("name")%></td>
    <td align=center><%= rst.getString("model") %></td>
    <td align=center>$<%= rst.getFloat("price") %></td>
    <td align=center><%= rst.getString("mname") %></td>
    <td align=center><%= rst.getString("phone") %></td>
</tr>
<%}%>
</table>
<%
  rst.close();
  stm.close();
  conn.close();
%>
```

Figure 11-10   Example4.jsp

4. Load the page, using the following URL:
   http://localhost:8080/myapp/chapter11/example4.jsp

The page is displayed as shown in Figure 11-11.

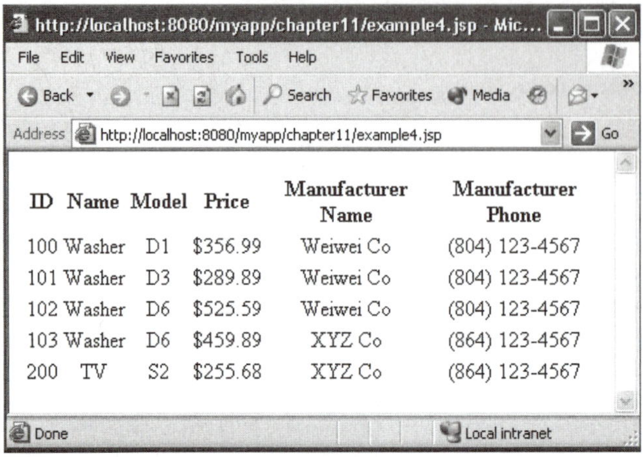

Figure 11-11   Getting data from both the product and manufacturer tables

In the query, the columns include two fields called name, one for the product name, and the other one for the manufacturer name. If the same column name is selected from more than one table, you must assign an alias to one of the columns, so that no two columns in the selected rows have the same column name. In this example, the manufacturer name is assigned the alias mname, and this alias is used in the getXXX method.

Using Forms to Interact with the Database

So far, the SQL statements you have worked with have been hard-coded. But a working Web application must allow customers to interact with the database. For example, for customers to use an online banking system, each customer must have an ID and a password, which are typically stored in a table. A logon page allows customers to enter their ID and password, and then the ID and password are looked up in the table to check whether a match can be found. In the following example, you will create a form that enables a user to add a new product to the product table.

1. Open the data file example5.jsp, which is located in the folder C:\myjspapp\ chapter11.

2. Add the code shaded in Figure 11-12. This code retrieves the data collected on the form provided in the data file example5.html (which is located in C:\myjspapp\chapter11), and then inserts this data into the product table.

3. Save and close the file.

```
<%@ page import="java.sql.*" %>
<%
 String url = "jdbc:odbc:productDSN";
 String username="";
 String password="";
 Connection  conn=null;
 String classPath = "sun.jdbc.odbc.JdbcOdbcDriver";
 try{
    Class.forName(classPath);
    conn = DriverManager.getConnection(url,username,password);
   }catch(Exception exc){
    out.println(exc.toString());
  }
 Statement stm=null;
 String id = request.getParameter("id");
 String name=request.getParameter("name");
 String model=request.getParameter("model");
 String priceS=request.getParameter("price");
 String midS=request.getParameter("mid");
 float price=0;
 int mid=0;
 try{price = Float.parseFloat(priceS);}catch(Exception exc){}
 try{mid = Integer.parseInt(midS);}catch(Exception exc){}
 stm= conn.createStatement();
 String query = "INSERT INTO product VALUES('"+id+"', '" +
                name +"', '"+ model + "'," + price +", "+ mid + ")";
 try{
   stm.executeUpdate(query);
   out.println("The data was added to the table successfully!");
 }catch(Exception exc){
   out.println("Inserting data failed!");
 }
 stm.close();
 conn.close();
%>
<br><br><a href="example5.html">Add more record</a>
```

Figure 11-12   Example5.jsp

4. Load the page example5.html, using the following URL:
   http://localhost:8080/myapp/chapter11/example5.html

   The page is displayed as shown in Figure 11-13.

5. Fill out the form and click the **Submit** button; a record should be added to the product table.

Figure 11-13   Adding a record to the product table

In this example, instead of being hard-coded, the values to be added into the product table are actually collected from the form on the page example5.html. All product information collected on the form is retrieved in the page example5.jsp, and the data are used to construct a SQL command. Since the price column in the table has the data type float, you parse a string value to its corresponding float value; the manufacturerID column has an integer data type in the table, so the value is parsed into a corresponding integer value. The parsing is not required, as long as the fields are not included in single quotation marks. But for the char or varchar data type, the values must be included within single quotation marks. Consider the following example:

```
String query1 = "INSERT INTO product VALUES(" +
    "'303', 'TV', 'S90', 234.89, 2)";
String query2 = "INSERT INTO product VALUES(" +
    "'303', 'TV', 'S90', '234.89', '2')";
```

The values of query1 and query2 are identical, even though the price in query1 has a float data type and the manufacturerID is an integer, and in query2 they are all strings.

> To add records to a table, the values for char or varchar data types must be placed within single quotation marks.

CHAPTER SUMMARY

❏ A database is a collection of related data. A relational database stores data in simple structures called tables.

❏ The data in a table are organized into rows and columns. A row contains a record, and a column contains pieces of information in a record.

❏ Primary keys in a table uniquely identify a record. Therefore no two records in a table can have the same value in the primary key field.

❏ SQL is a computer language designed to process relational databases. You can use SQL to create and modify tables, to insert data into tables, to update data in tables, to delete data from tables, and to get data from tables.

❏ JDBC makes it possible to connect to a database from a JSP page and issue a SQL command to manipulate the database from a JSP page.

❏ You can create and modify tables, insert data into tables, update data in tables, delete data from tables, and get data from tables from a JSP page.

REVIEW QUESTIONS

1. A group of related fields is called a _____.

   a. form

   b. record

   c. relational database

   d. table

2. A collection of related tables is called a _____.

   a. relational database

   b. field

   c. record

   d. table

3. If no two records in a table have the same value for a field, then this field is most likely to be used as a _____.

   a. unique key

   b. foreign key

   c. primary key

11

4. If a field in one table is used as a primary key in another table, then this field is called a _____.

   a. unique key

   b. foreign key

   c. primary key

5. There are three columns in a table called item. The three fields are f1, f2, and f3, and they all have the same data type, integer. If you want to insert three integers, v1, v2, and v3 in a record as follows: v1 to the f1 field, v2 to f2, and v3 to f3, which of the following statements do you use?

   a. `INSERT INTO item VALUES(v1, v3, v2)`

   b. `INSERT INTO item VALUES(v3, v2, v1)`

   c. `INSERT INTO item (f1, f2, f3) VALUES(v1, v2, v3)`

   d. `INSERT INTO item (f3, f2, f1) VALUES(v3, v2, v1)`

6. In Question 5, assume that f2 and f3 are not required fields. Which of the following statements work(s) without raising an exception? (Select all that apply.)

   a. `INSERT INTO item VALUES(v1, v3, v2)`

   b. `INSERT INTO item VALUES(v1, v2)`

   c. `INSERT INTO item (f1, f3) VALUES(v1, v2, v3)`

   d. `INSERT INTO item (f1, f3) VALUES(v1, v2)`

7. If a field has the data type char or varchar, then the value provided for that field in an INSERT SQL statement must be placed within single quotation marks. True or False?

8. In Microsoft Access, which of the following wildcard characters represents any number and any combination of characters?

   a. *

   b. %

   c. ?

   d. _ (underscore)

9. In Microsoft Access, which of the following wildcard characters represents any single character?

   a. *

   b. %

   c. ?

   d. _ (underscore)

10. The text W_t can represent which of the following? (Select all that apply.)

    a. wet

    b. wit

    c. what

    d. WET

    e. Wheat

    f. wt

11. The text W%t can represent which of the following? (Select all that apply.)

    a. wet

    b. wit

    c. what

    d. WET

    e. Wheat

    f. wt

12. For most relational databases, which of the following packages must be imported in order to connect and process a database?

    a. java.io.*;

    b. java.util.*;

    c. javax.servlet.jsp.*;

    d. java.sql.*;

13. To connect to a database from a JSP page, which of the following must you do first?

    a. create a Statement object

    b. get a ResultSet object

    c. load the JDBC driver

    d. define the connection URL

14. The driver class for a database must be stored somewhere in the CLASSPATH. True or False?

15. To create a table in a database, which of the following methods of a Statement object should be used?

    a. executeQuery()

    b. executeUpdate()

16. To close a connection to a database, which of the following sets of steps is correct?

    a. 1. close ResultSet 2. close Statement 3. close Connection

    b. 1. close Connection 2. close Statement 3. close ResultSet

11

17. To use JDBC-ODBC to access Microsoft Access database, the database must be registered as an ODBC data source. True or False?

18. Which of the following conditions should be used in the WHERE clause in order to select all records from a table where the name field in the table meets the following criteria: the name begins with the character "S" and ends with the character "h" and must contain at least one character "m"?

    a. WHERE name LIKE 'S*m*h'

    b. WHERE name = 'Smith'

    c. WHERE name LIKE 'S%m%h%'

    d. WHERE name LIKE 'S%m%h'

19. The following code segment defines and initializes a string variable:

    ```
    <% String value1 = "Introduction to JSP"; %>
    ```

    Which of the following segments inserts a SQL statement in JSP?

    a. `stm.executeUpdate("INSERT INTO books (name)`
       `VALUES(value1)");`

    b. `stm.executeUpdate("INSERT INTO books (name)`
       `VALUES("`

                        `+ value1 + ")");`

    c. `stm.executeUpdate("INSERT INTO books (name)`
       `VALUES(' "`

                        `+ value1 + "')");`

    d. `stm.executeUpdate("INSERT INTO books (name)`
       `VALUES('value1')");`

20. If more than one row contains the same value in a particular column, then which of the following statements is correct?

    a. The column can be used as a primary key in the table.

    b. The column may be a foreign key.

    c. none of the above

HANDS-ON PROJECTS

Project 11-1 Registering a Database

To use JDBC-ODBC to connect to a database, the database must be registered as an ODBC data source first. In this project, you will register a given Microsoft Access database as an ODBC data source.

1. The Access database buyer.mdb is provided as a data file in the folder C:\myjspapp\ chapter11.

2. Open your Control Panel, and from the folder list, open the folder **Administrative Tools**. You should see Data Sources (ODBC) in the list. Double-click **Data Sources (ODBC)** to open the ODBC Data Source Administrator dialog box. Select the **System DSN** tab if it is not already selected.

3. Click the **Add** button to open the Create New Data Source dialog box. From the driver name list, select the driver **Microsoft Access Driver (*.mdb)**, then click the **Finish** button.

4. The ODBC Microsoft Access Set Up dialog box opens. In the Data Source Name field, enter **customerDSN**. Then click the **Select** button and select the database **buyer.mdb**, which is located in the folder C:\myjspapp\chapter11. Click **OK** twice to go back to the ODBC Data Source Administrator dialog box. Click **OK** to close the dialog box.

Now you have set the ODBC data source. You will use this data source name to access this database in the following projects.

Project 11-2 Create Tables

In this project, you will set up tables for the customer database. You are going to create two tables, customer and purchase. You will use the data file table.txt to create tables and insert data into the tables. The data file contains the SQL commands to create these two tables and insert data into the tables. Table 11-8 shows the structure of the customer table, and Table 11-9 shows the structure of the purchase table. Note that you must have completed Project11-1 before you can complete this project.

Table 11-8   Customer Table

Column Name	Data Type	Description
custid	integer	Customer ID, primary key
custname	varchar(20)	Customer name
custaddr	varchar(15)	Customer address
zipcode	char(5)	Zip code
phone	char(8)	Customer phone number

Table 11-9   Purchase Table

Column Name	Data Type	Description
purchnum	integer	Purchase number, primary key
custnum	integer	Customer ID
purchdate	date	Purchase date

1. Open the data file project2.jsp, which is located in the folder C:\myjspapp\chapter11.

2. Add the code shaded in Figure 11-14 to make a connection to the customer database using the DSN you created in Project 11-1.

11

```
<%@ page import="java.sql.*,java.io.*" %>
<%
 String action = request.getParameter("action");
 if(action == null){%>
 <a href="project2.jsp?action=setuptable">Set up table</a>
 <%}else if(action.equals("setuptable")){
 String url = "jdbc:odbc:customerDSN";
 String username="";
 String password="";
 Connection  conn=null;
 String classPath = "sun.jdbc.odbc.JdbcOdbcDriver";
 try{
    Class.forName(classPath);
    conn = DriverManager.getConnection(url,username,password);
  }catch(Exception exc){
    out.println(exc.toString());
  }
%>
<%  Statement stm= conn.createStatement();
 try{
    String vPath = "/chapter11/table.txt";
    String file =null;
    file =
     getServletConfig().getServletContext().getRealPath(vPath);
    BufferedReader br = new BufferedReader(new FileReader(file));
    String query= br.readLine();
    while(query != null){
      stm.executeUpdate(query);
      query = br.readLine();
    }
    out.println("Tables were set up successfully.");
    out.print("<br><a href=\"project2.jsp?action=setuptable\">");
    out.println("Try to set up table again</a>");
    br.close();
  }catch(Exception exc){
    out.println(exc.toString());
  }
    stm.close();
    conn.close();
}%>
```

Figure 11-14   Project2.jsp

3. Save and close the file.

4. Load the page, using the following URL:
   http://localhost:8080/myapp/chapter11/project2.jsp

5. Click the link **Set up tables**, and a page indicating that the tables were set up successfully is displayed.

6. Click the link **Try to set up tables again**, and a page indicating that an exception has occurred is displayed.

7. Open the buyer database; you should see that two tables were created and that several records were inserted into these two tables.

Project 11-3 Viewing Data from a Customer Database

In this project, you will use JSP to access the customer database and display all customer information in an HTML table.

1. Open a new document in your text editor. Import the java.sql package and provide all connection information.

2. Add code to load the database driver in the connection information.

3. Add code to create a Statement object and execute a query to get the ResultSet, as follows:

```
<%  Statement stm= conn.createStatement();
    String query= "SELECT * FROM customer";
    ResultSet rst = stm.executeQuery(query);
%>
```

4. Add code to process the ResultSet and display the data in an HTML table, then close the connection.

5. Save the file as **project3.jsp**, and then close the file.

6. Load the page, using the following URL:
   http://localhost:8080/myapp/chapter11/project3.jsp

   A page similar to Figure 11-15 is displayed.

11

```
http://localhost:5059/myapp/chapter11/project3.jsp - Mic...
File  Edit  View  Favorites  Tools  Help
Back    ⬤  ⬤  Search  Favorites  Media
Address   http://localhost:8080/myapp/chapter11/project3.jsp        Go
```

ID	Name	Address	Zip code	Phone
1	David Joe	215 Newcastle D	21354	323-1212
2	Weiwei Inc.	300 Blvd	56354	856-2356
3	John Kanet	236 Miami Ave	12475	635-1254
4	Aimily Davis	12 Central Ave	39586	723-5623
5	David Harward	236 Senica	74125	393-9612
6	Brown Wong	102 Sunshine Av	52134	574-1219
7	Susan Yong	405 Sweetwater	30124	452-1292
8	Eric Deitel	453 West Falls	86123	786-1516

Done   Local intranet

Figure 11-15   Data retrieved from the customer database

Project 11-4 Viewing Data from Customer and Purchase Tables

You have two tables in the buyer database now. The purchase table records the purchases made by each customer. In this project, you will display purchase dates for a particular customer.

1. Create a new document in your text editor, and save it as **project4-1.jsp** in the folder C:\myjspapp\chapter11.

2. Add code to import the necessary class to connect to the customer.mdb database from JSP, and then provide the connection information to the customer database.

3. Add code to create a Statement object, and execute the query to get the customer name and IDs from the customer table.

4. Add code to display all customer names in a drop-down list (a select field; use IDs as option values and names as labels). The HTML code generated by this page should look like Figure 11-16.

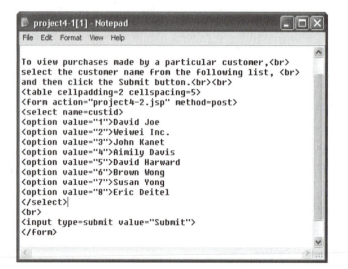

Figure 11-16   HTML code generated by executing project4-1.jsp

5. Add code to specify that the data collected on this page will be processed in project4-2.jsp.

6. Save the file.

7. Open the data file project4-2.jsp, which is located in the folder C:\myjspapp\chapter11.

8. Add the code shaded in Figure 11-17 to retrieve and display purchase dates.

```
<%@ page import="java.sql.*" %>
<%
 String url = "jdbc:odbc:customerDSN";
 String username="";
 String password="";
 Connection  conn=null;
 String classPath = "sun.jdbc.odbc.JdbcOdbcDriver";
 try{
    Class.forName(classPath);
    conn = DriverManager.getConnection(url,username,password);
   }catch(Exception exc){
    out.println(exc.toString());
  }
%>
<%
  Statement stm= conn.createStatement();
  String custid=request.getParameter("custid");
  String query = "SELECT custname FROM customer "+
                 "WHERE custid="+custid;
  ResultSet rst=stm.executeQuery(query);
  rst.next();
%>
The customer:<b><%= rst.getString("custname") %></b>
made purchase(s) on the following date(s):<br><br>
<% query= "SELECT purchdate FROM purchase "+
          "WHERE custnum=" + custid;
%>
<% rst = stm.executeQuery(query); %>
<% while(rst.next()){%>
<%= rst.getDate("purchdate") %><br>
<%}%>
<%
    rst.close();
    stm.close();
    conn.close();
%>
<br>
<a href="project4-1.jsp">Back</a>
```

Figure 11-17   Project4-2.jsp

9. Save and close the file.

10. Load the page project4–1.jsp, using the following URL:
    http://localhost:8080/myapp/chapter11/project4-1.jsp

    The page is displayed as shown in Figure 11-18.

11. Select a name from the drop-down list and click the **Submit** button. A page similar to Figure 11-19 is displayed.

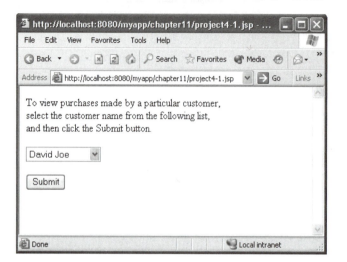

Figure 11-18 Customer list

Figure 11-19 Purchase dates

Project 11-5 Using Wildcards

In this project, you will use a wildcard to get information about customers whose first name is David.

1. Create a new document in your text editor, and save it as **project5.jsp** in the folder C:\myjspapp\chapter11.

2. Add code to import the java.sql package, and provide all information to make a database connection to the customer.mdb database from a JSP page.

3. Add the following code to create a Statement object and query the database to get the ResultSet. The query gets all data from the customer table where the customer first name is David, so the wildcard % is used in the WHERE clause.

```
<% Statement stm= conn.createStatement();
String query = "SELECT custname, custaddr, zipcode, "+
               "phone FROM customer "+
               " WHERE custname LIKE 'David%'";
ResultSet rst=stm.executeQuery(query);
%>
```

4. Add code to display the selected rows that satisfy the specified condition.

5. Add the code to close the connection.

6. Save and close the file.

7. Load the page, using the following URL:
http://localhost:8080/myapp/chapter11/project5.jsp

The page is displayed as shown in Figure 11-20.

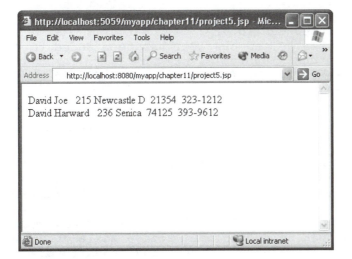

Figure 11-20   Using a wildcard in a WHERE clause

Project 11-6 Adding a Customer to the Customer Table

In this project, you will design a page that allows users to add records to the customer table.

1. Create a new document in your text editor, and save it as **project6.jsp** in the folder C:\myjspapp\chapter11.

2. Add code to import the java.sql package, and provide connection information.

3. Add the following code to create a Statement object and get the maximum custid number in the customer database. The custid for the next customer should be

larger than the maximum custid in the table. The function MAX is used to get the maximum value for the specified column passed as an argument.

```
<% Statement stm= conn.createStatement();
 String query = "SELECT MAX(custid) FROM customer";
 ResultSet rst=stm.executeQuery(query);
 int maxID = 1;
 if(rst.next()){ maxID = rst.getInt(1); }
%>
```

4. Add the following code to insert a record into the table:

```
<% String custname = request.getParameter("custname");
   String custaddr = request.getParameter("custaddr");
   String zipcode = request.getParameter("zipcode");
   String phone = request.getParameter("phone");
   maxID++;
   if(custname != null && !custname.equals("")){
     query = "INSERT INTO customer VALUES("+ maxID +", '"+
             custname + "', '"+ custaddr + "', '" +
zipcode + "','"
             + phone +"')";
     stm.executeUpdate(query);
     out.println("A new customer has been added to "+
             "customer table.<br><br>");
     out.println("<a href=project6.jsp>add more
customer</a>");
   }else{%>
```

5. Add the following code to provide a form to allow users to enter data for a new customer:

```
<form action="project6.jsp" method=post>
 custID[system assigned]:<%= maxID %><br>
 customer Name:<input name="custname" size=16 maxlength=
20><br>
 address:<input name="custaddr" size=16 maxlength=15><br>
 zip code:<input name="zipcode" size=6 maxlength=5><br>
 phone:<input name="phone" size=9 maxlength=8><br>
 <input type=submit value="submit the form"><br>
</form>
<% }%>
```

6. Add code to close the connection.

7. Save the file.

8. Load the page, using the following URL:
   http://localhost:8080/myapp/chapter11/project6.jsp

   The page is displayed as shown in Figure 11-21.

9. Enter data and submit the form to add a record to the customer table.

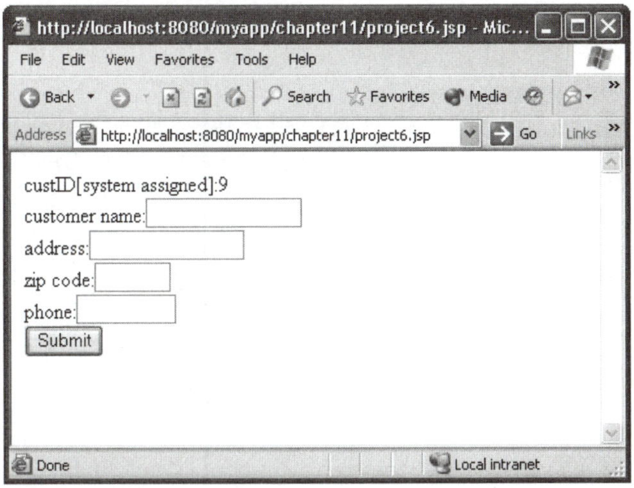

Figure 11-21   Adding a record to the customer table

In this project, the new customer ID is assigned by the system automatically, ensuring that the custid cannot be duplicated.

CASE PROJECTS

SRAS: Course Search

In this project, you will create a page called coursebyfaculty.jsp, which allows a user to look up courses taught by a particular faculty member. This page should function as follows:

1. When you click the link to the page coursebyfaculty.jsp, a page similar to Figure 11-22 is displayed. In this page, you will write code to connect to the faculty table in the sras.mdb and display faculty information in a SELECT element.

2. When you select a faculty member from the list and click the Submit button, a page similar to Figure 11-23 is displayed. To perform this task, you need to use the faculty information selected from the list to query the course table.

11

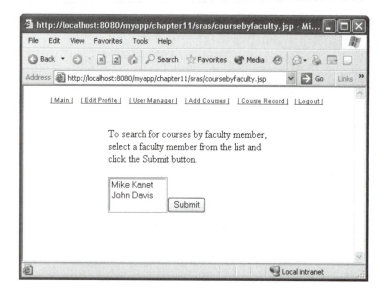

Figure 11-22   Searching for courses by faculty member

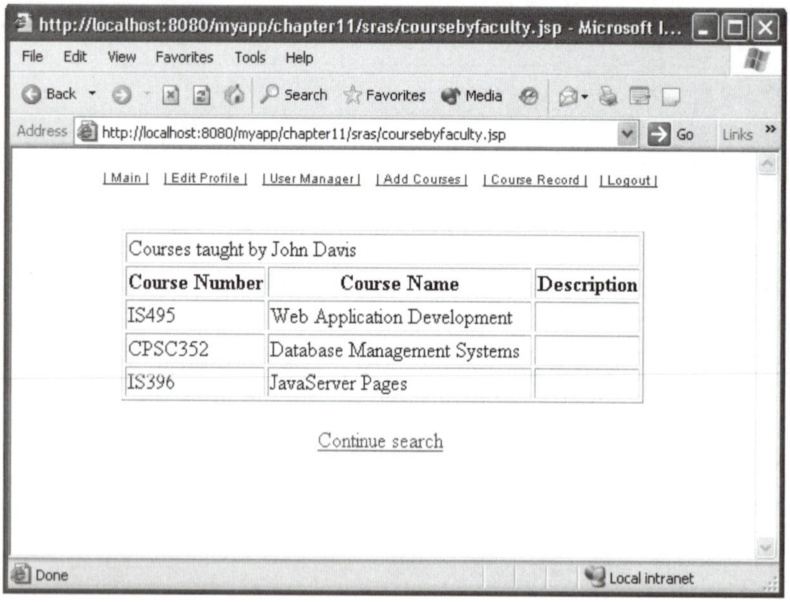

Figure 11-23   Courses taught by John Davis

SRAS: Student List

The SRAS system allows faculty and administrators to view student lists in the form of an ML table. Please add code to the file studentlist.jsp, which is located in C:\myjspapp\chapter11\sras, so that it displays all students in the database in an HTML table (similar to the one shown in Figure 11-24).

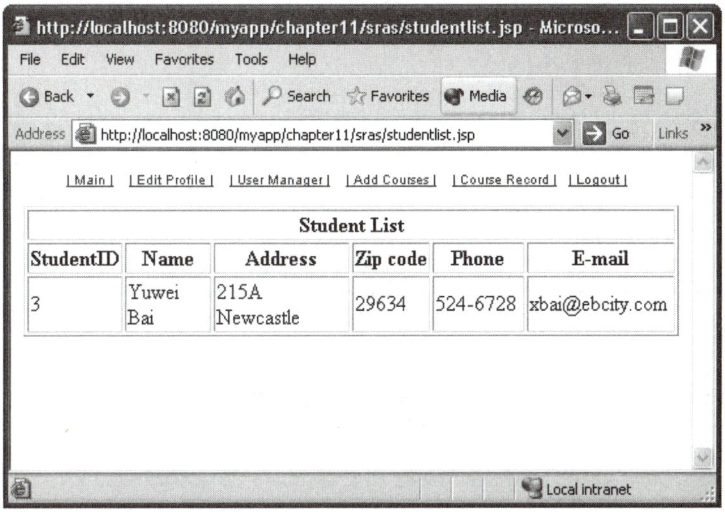

Figure 11-24   Student list

SRAS: Faculty Contact Information

The SRAS allows users to look up faculty contact information. In this project, you will add code to facultyinfo.jsp (which is located in C:\mjspapp\chapter11\sras) to display faculty contact information as follows:

1. When you click FacultyContactInfo, the link to the faculty.info.jsp page, a page displays all faculty members in the database similar to the one shown in Figure 11-25.

2. When you select a faculty member from the list and click the **Submit** button, a page similar to Figure 11-26 is displayed.

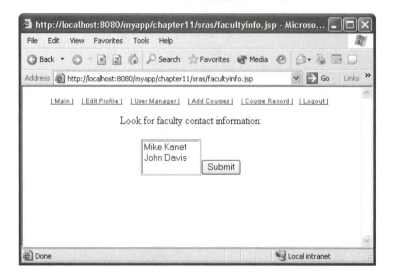

Figure 11-25   Faculty list

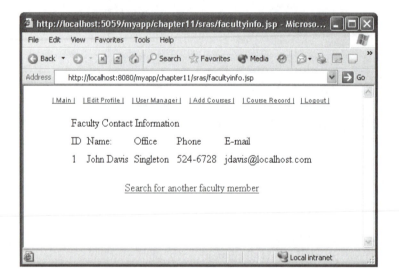

Figure 11-26   Faculty contact information

Designing a Database

In Chapter 5, an SRAS database was provided for you. In this project, you will create a database similar to the SRAS database. Name the database **SRAS2**, and create the tables shown below.

Student Table

Column Name	Data Type	Required	Description
studid	varchar(10)	yes	Student ID, primary key
fname	varchar(15)	yes	First name
lname	varchar(15)	yes	Last name
address	varchar(20)	no	Student address
zipcode	char(5)	no	Zip code
phone	char(8)	no	Student phone number
email	varchar(50)	no	Student e-mail address

Faculty Table

Column Name	Data Type	Required	Description
facultyid	varchar(10)	yes	Faculty ID, primary key
fname	varchar(15)	yes	First name
lname	varchar(15)	yes	Last name
office	varchar(20)	no	Faculty office
phone	char(8)	no	Faculty phone number
email	varchar(50)	no	Faculty e-mail address

Course Table

Column Name	Data Type	Required	Description
coursenum	varchar(10)	yes	Course number, primary key
coursename	varchar(35)	yes	Course name
description	varchar(100)	no	Course description
facultyid	varchar(10)	yes	Faculty ID

User Table

Column Name	Data Type	Required	Description
userid	varchar(10)	yes	User ID
password	varchar(10)	yes	Password
userlevel	integer	yes	Admin 1, Faculty 2, Student 3

11

Course Taken Table

Column Name	Data Type	Required	Description
coursenum	varchar(10)	yes	Course number
studid	varchar(10)	yes	Student ID
facultyid	varchar(10)	yes	Faculty ID
grade	varchar(3)	no	Grade

As shown above, there are five tables in this database: student, faculty, course, user, and course taken. You can add records to the student, faculty, and course tables independently. There are some constraints to updating the course taken and user tables. In the course taken table, the data for all three fields *must* be from the student, faculty, and course tables. That means all data in this table must be found in the corresponding tables that are linked through common fields. For example, the coursenum in the course taken field must be found in the course table; the studid must be found in the student table; the facultyid must be found in the faculty table. You cannot update only the user table. When you add records to the student and faculty tables, you need to add an entry to the user table at the same time.

Based on the rules described above, create a JSP page that adds at least one record each to the faculty and user tables.

12

ADDING POWER TO DATABASE ACCESS WITH JSP

In this chapter, you will:

♦ Create more powerful query statements using the SQL operators IN and BETWEEN

♦ Access database metadata from a JSP page

♦ Control transactions to ensure database integrity

♦ Create and use beans to access a database

In the previous chapter, you learned how to access a database and issue SQL commands in JSP to allow users to interact with your database via your Web pages. In this chapter, you will learn how to use the IN and BETWEEN operators to add power to your SQL queries, how to get information about a database, and how to use transaction control to preserve data integrity. You will also learn how to write JavaBeans to access and process a database.

ADDING POWER TO YOUR QUERIES

You have already learned how to query a database to retrieve data from tables and how to use logical operators, such as OR and AND to combine more than one condition, or NOT to negate a logical expression. For example, you might use the following SQL commands to list all customers with the Zip code 23834, 23806, or 29639:

```
SELECT customerName FROM customer
WHERE zipcode='23834' OR zipcode='23806' OR zipcode='29634'
```

The code above uses the OR operator to combine these conditions. In this example, though, the Zip codes must be known in advance. What about a scenario in which the Zip codes are from another query, and so are unknown? In this case you cannot hard code the conditions as in the above example. To accommodate such situations, you can use the SQL operators IN and BETWEEN.

The IN Operator

The **IN** operator is used to determine whether a field's value falls within a specified range of values. The use of the IN operator takes the following form:

SELECT column_list FROM table_name
WHERE a_column_name IN (value1, value2, …)

Consider the buyer database you created in Chapter 11. Suppose you want to list all customers who have the Zip code 21354, 12475, or 39586. You could use the OR operator to make the query, but it would be a rather clumsy query, as follows:

```
SELECT * FROM buyer
WHERE zipcode = '21354'
      OR zipcode = '12475'
      OR zipcode = '39586'
```

If you use the IN operator, the query is short and concise.

```
SELECT * FROM customer
WHERE zipcode IN ('21354', '12475', '39586')
```

The series of values to be looked up is placed within single quotation marks. Note that some database implementations require the single quotation marks, while others do not. Microsoft Access requires the data type match for the listed values. Therefore, if the column data type is char, or varchar, or date, these listed values should be placed within single quotation marks.

The series values listed within the IN operator can be the result of another nested query. For example, to list all purchases made by the customer named Weiwei Co., you can use the following SQL query:

```
SELECT * FROM purchase
WHERE   custnum IN
        ( SELECT custid FROM customer
        WHERE custname = 'Weiei Co.')
```

The BETWEEN Operator

The **BETWEEN** operator is used to determine whether a column's value is between one value and another. The use of the BETWEEN operator takes the following form:

SELECT column_list FROM table_name
WHERE a_column_name BETWEEN value1 AND value2

This operator checks a column for values within a given range. For example, to find all purchases made during the period from August 20, 2003 through August 20, 2004, you can apply the BETWEEN operator in the query as follows:

```
SELECT * FROM purchase
WHERE purchdate BETWEEN #2003-08-20# AND #2004-08-20#
```

The BETWEEN operator is inclusive.

In most databases, the date value is placed within single quotation marks without the # (pound sign).

METADATA

Metadata in a database is data about the database itself—for example, information about the tables, the columns in a table, the column data type, and so on. JDBC allows you to access information about the whole database as well as information about a table within a database. In the following sections, you will learn how to get database information using the DatabaseMetaData object, and table information using the ResultSetMetaData object.

Database Metadata

Once a connection to a database has been set up, you can use the following method of the established connection object to get a reference to the DatabaseMetaData object:

DatabaseMetaData dbmd = conn.getMetaData();

The DatabaseMetaData object provides many methods you can use to get information about the database. Many of the methods return lists of information in the form of ResultSet objects. You can use the ResultSet methods, such as getString and getInt, to retrieve the data from these ResultSet objects. Not all database drivers support all methods specified in the DatabaseMetaData API. If a driver does not support a metadata method, a SQLException will be thrown. Therefore, in the case of methods that return a ResultSet, either a ResultSet is returned or a SQLException is thrown.

A Metadata method can return an empty ResultSet.

The information you can obtain about the database includes the database driver name and version, the database you are using (for example, Microsoft Access), the number of tables, the table names, and so on. This section focuses on one of the most frequently used methods, getTables, which you can use to get information about the tables in the database.

The getTables method of a DatabaseMetaData object has the following form:

getTables(String catalog, String schemaPattern, String tableNamePattern, String[] types)

12

This method returns a ResultSet object containing information about the tables in the database. Each row in the ResultSet contains information about one table in the database. The ResultSet contains one column called TABLE_NAME that you can use to get table names. To get table names, you do not need to worry about all the parameters passed to the method. You can simply pass null values to the catalog, schemaPattern, and tableNamePattern parameters, and pass a String array to specify the table types. For example, the following code returns a ResultSet containing table information:

```
String[] types={"TABLE"};
ResultSet rst = dbmd.getTables(null, null, null, types);
```

The following exercise illustrates how to get the name of a DBMS and the database table names.

1. Open a new document in your text editor. Add the following code to make the connection to the database:

```
<%@ page import="java.sql.*" %>
<% String url = "jdbc:odbc:customerDSN";
String usernamedb="";
String passworddb="";
Connection  conn=null;
try{
 Class.forName("sun.jdbc.odbc.JdbcOdbcDriver");
 conn= DriverManager.getConnection(url,usernamedb,
 passworddb);
 }catch(Exception exc){
  out.println(exc.toString());
}
```

2. Add the following code to get a reference to the DatabaseMetaData object:

```
DatabaseMetaData dbmd=conn.getMetaData();
```

3. Add the following code to call the getTables method to get a reference to a ResultSet object:

```
String[] types={"TABLE"};
ResultSet rst = dbmd.getTables(null,null,null,types);
```

4. Add the following code to get the database product name:

```
String productName = dbmd.getDatabaseProductName();
%>
```

5. Add the following code to process the ResultSet object and display information in an HTML table:

```
<table border=1>
<tr><th colspan=2>Database Information</th></tr>
<tr><td>Database</td><td><%= productName%></td></tr>
<tr><td><b>Tables</b></td>
  <td>
```

```
<% while(rst.next()){ %>
  <%= rst.getString("TABLE_NAME")%><br>
<%}%>
  </td>
</tr>
</table>
```

6. Add the following code to close the connection:

```
<% rst.close(); conn.close(); %>
```

7. Save the file as **example1.jsp** in the folder C:\myjspapp\chapter12.

8. Load the page, using the following URL:
http://localhost:8080/myapp/chapter12/example1.jsp

The page is displayed as shown in Figure 12-1.

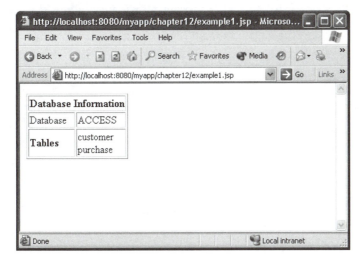

Figure 12-1   Database metadata

As shown in Figure 12-1, the database is Microsoft Access, and the database contains two tables, namely customer and purchase.

The ResultSetMetaData Object

As long as you know a table's name, which you can get from the DatabaseMetaData object, you can get information about the types and properties of the columns in the table by using the ResultSetMetaData object. To use the ResultSetMetaData object, you need to create a ResultSet object first, and use the getMetaData method of the ResultSet object to obtain a reference to the ResultSetMetaData object. The following code fragment creates the ResultSet object rst, and then creates the ResultSetMetaData object rsmd:

```
ResultSet rst = stm.executeQuery("select * from customer");
ResultSetMetaData rsmd = rst.getMetaData();
```

The ResultSetMetaData object rsmd contains information about selected columns from the customer table. There are many methods you can use to get information about columns, such as the number of columns returned, an individual column's suggested display size, column names, column types, and so on. A few of the most useful methods are: getColumnCount(), which returns the number of columns in this ResultSet object; getColumnName(int column), which returns the designated column's name, and takes a parameter which is the column number; and getColumnDisplaySize(int column), which indicates the designated column's normal maximum width in characters. In the following exercise, you will display all of the customer table's column names and data types.

1. Open the data file example2.jsp, which is located in the folder C:\myjspapp\chapter12.

2. Add the code shaded in Figure 12-2 to get information about the table.

```
<%@ page import="java.sql.*" %>
<% String url = "jdbc:odbc:customerDSN";
String usernamedb="";
String passworddb="";
Connection  conn=null;
try{
  Class.forName("sun.jdbc.odbc.JdbcOdbcDriver");
  conn= DriverManager.getConnection(url,usernamedb,passworddb);
  }catch(Exception exc){
   out.println(exc.toString());
  }
Statement stm= conn.createStatement();
ResultSet rst = stm.executeQuery("select * from customer");
ResultSetMetaData rsmd = rst.getMetaData();
int num=rsmd.getColumnCount();
%>
<table border=1>
<tr><th colspan=3>Column Information in Customer Table</td></tr>
<tr><th>Column Name</th>
    <th>Data Type</th><th>Display Size</th>
</tr>
<% for(int i=1;  i<=num;i++){%>
    <tr>
       <td> <%= rsmd.getColumnName(i)%> </td>
       <td> <%= rsmd.getColumnTypeName(i)%> </td>
       <td> <%= rsmd.getColumnDisplaySize(i)%> </td>
    </tr>
<%}%>
</table>
<% rst.close(); stm.close(); conn.close(); %>
```

Figure 12-2   Additional code added to example2.jsp

3. Save and close the file.

4. Load the page, using the following URL:
http://localhost:8080/myapp/chapter12/example2.jsp

The page is displayed as shown in Figure 12-3.

Column Information in Customer Table

Column Name	Data Type	Display Size
custid	INTEGER	11
custname	VARCHAR	20
custaddr	VARCHAR	15
zipcode	CHAR	5
phone	CHAR	8

Figure 12-3   Column data

> **Note**
> Column reference numbers begin with 1; that is, 1 represents the first column, 2 the second column, and so on.

USING TRANSACTIONS

You have already learned how to issue a SQL statement to update database records. To update multiple tables, you have to issue a SQL statement to each table. If the execution of SQL statements is successful, the updates or changes immediately take effect in the database. But there are times when you do not want one statement to take effect unless another one also succeeds. For example, in the SRAS database, there is a user table that stores user ID, password, and user level. To add a new student to the system, two tables must be updated, the student table and the user table. In this case, there are two actions involved: adding a record to the student table and adding a record to the user table. If both tables are not updated successfully, then it's important that neither of the tables is changed, or the database data will be inconsistent. For example, if the update to the student table succeeds, but the update to the user table fails, a student is added to the student table, but the user table remains unchanged. When the new user tries to log on to the system, the user ID and password will be looked up in the user table, and the user will not be found.

12

To solve this problem, you can use a transaction. A **transaction** is a set of one or more statements that are executed together as a unit, so either all of the statements are executed, or none of the statements is executed. Within a transaction, you can actually control when each statement is executed, and when all actions take effect, or you can even abort the whole transaction (leaving the database unchanged).

Auto-Commit Mode

When a connection to a database is created, it is by default in auto-commit mode. When a database is in **auto-commit mode**, each individual SQL statement is treated as a transaction, and the execution of the SQL statement immediately affects the database. In order to allow two or more statements to be grouped into a transaction, you need to disable auto-commit mode. To disable or enable auto-commit mode, you use the setAutoCommit method of a connection object. This method takes the following form:

conn.setAutoCommit(boolean_value)

To disable auto-commit, pass a false value to this method, as follows:

conn.setAutoCommit(false)

You can change the auto-commit mode in your JSP code. For example, the following code sets all transactions to be committed automatically (assume conn is an active connection):

conn.setAutoCommit(true)

Committing a Transaction

If auto-commit is set to false, all transactions are incomplete until the SQL statements are either committed or aborted. When a statement is committed, any change made by the SQL statement is reflected in the database; when a statement is aborted, the database remains unchanged. To commit a SQL statement, use the following syntax:

```
conn.commit()
```

When this method is called, all uncommitted SQL statements are committed, and all changes are made to the database.

Aborting a Transaction

Aborting a SQL statement takes the following syntax:

```
conn.rollBack()
```

Calling this method aborts a transaction and leaves the database unchanged within the current transaction. Therefore, you can use the auto-commit mode combined with the commit and rollback methods. For example, assume you try to execute two statements as a unit; if either of them raises an exception, you can call the rollback method to abort the transaction and to restart it.

Transaction Control Example

Before you can complete the exercise below, you need to register the database as an ODBC data source, which you learned about in the previous chapter. The steps to register a database as an ODBC data source are as follows:

1. Open your Control Panel. (Click **Switch to Classic View** if you are working in Microsoft Windows XP and not already using Classic View.) Then open the folder Administrative Tools. You should see Data Sources (ODBC) in the list. Double-click **Data Sources (ODBC)** to display the ODBC Data Source Administrator dialog box, as shown in Figure 12-4. Select the **System DSN** tab, if it is not already selected.

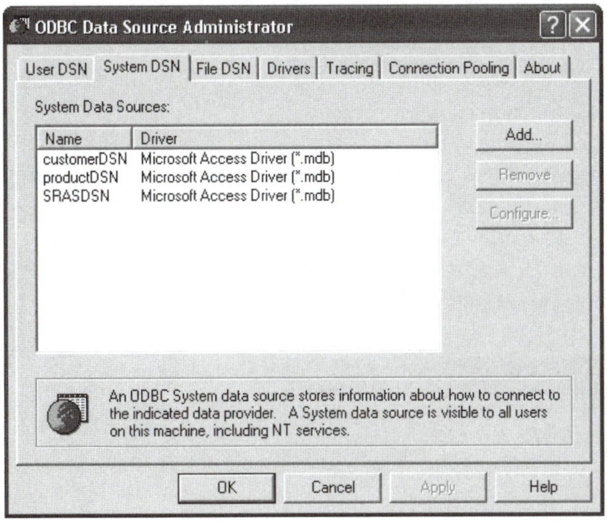

Figure 12-4   ODBC Data Source Administrator dialog box

2. Click the **Add** button to open the Create New Data Source dialog box, as shown in Figure 12-5. From the driver name list, select the driver **Microsoft Access Driver (*.mdb)**, then click the **Finish** button.

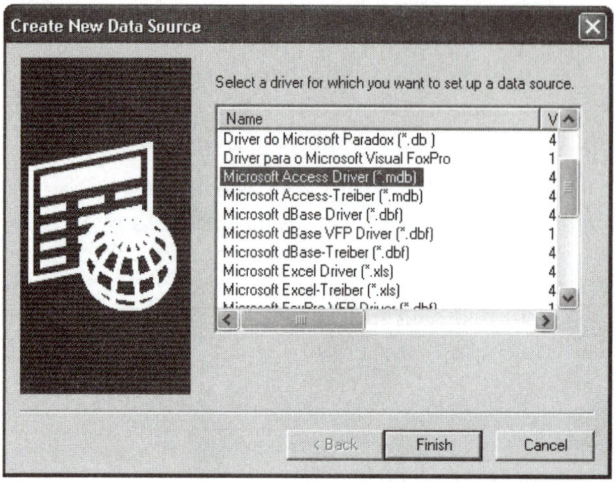

Figure 12-5   Create New Data Source dialog box

3. The ODBC Microsoft Access Setup dialog box opens, as shown in Figure 12-6. In the Data Source Name field, enter **employeeDSN**. Then click the **Select** button, navigate to the folder C:\myjspapp\chapter12, select the file **employee.mdb**, and click **OK** twice to return to the ODBC Data Source Administrator dialog box. Click **OK**.

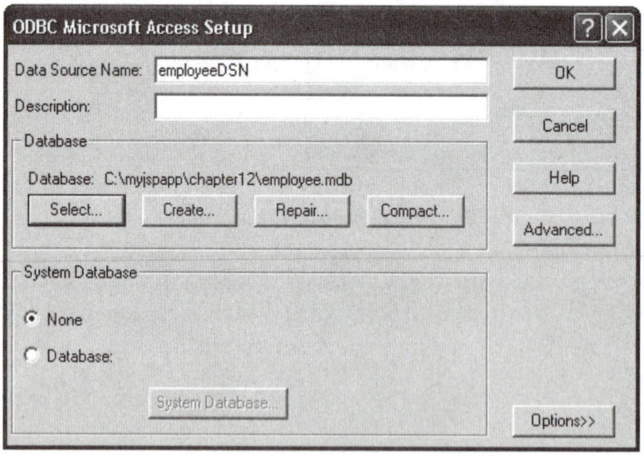

Figure 12-6   ODBC Microsoft Access Setup dialog box

This database consists of three tables: employee, administrator, and account. You may open this database and examine the table structures in table design view. The account table keeps employee IDs and passwords for all users in both the employee and administrator tables. Employee ID serves as the primary key in all tables. Therefore, to add a new employee to the employee table, you need to update the account table also. In the following exercise, you will do this by creating two SQL statements that are controlled as a single transaction.

1. Open the data file example3-1.jsp, which is located in the folder C:\myjspapp\chapter12.

2. Add the code shaded in Figure 12-7 to display all employees in the employee table.

```
<%@ page import="java.sql.*" %>
<%  String url = "jdbc:odbc:employeeDSN";
    String usernamedb="";
    String passworddb="";
    Connection  conn=null;
    Statement stm=null;
    try{
      Class.forName("sun.jdbc.odbc.JdbcOdbcDriver");
      conn= DriverManager.getConnection(url,usernamedb,passworddb);
    }catch(Exception exc){
      out.println(exc.toString());
    }
%>
<center>
<a href="example3-2.jsp">Add new employee</a>  
</center>
<br><br>
<%stm = conn.createStatement();
  ResultSet rst = stm.executeQuery("SELECT * FROM employee");
%>
<table align=center border=1>
<tr><th>EmployeeID</th><th>Name</th><th>Address</th>
    <th>Zip Code</th><th>Phone</th><th>E-mail</th>
</tr>
<% while(rst.next()){%>
<tr>
   <td><%= rst.getString("empid")%></td>
   <td ><%= rst.getString("fname")+" "+rst.getString("lname")%></td>
   <td width=100><%= rst.getString("address")%> </td>
   <td><%= rst.getString("zipcode")%> </td>
   <td><%= rst.getString("phone")%> </td>
   <td width=100><%= rst.getString("email")%> </td>
</tr>
 <%}%>
</table>
<% if(rst !=null){rst.close();}
   stm.close();
   conn.close();
%>
```

Figure 12-7   Additional code added to example3-1.jsp

3. Save and close the file.

4. Open the data file example3-2.jsp, which is located in the folder C:\myjspapp\chapter12.

12

5. Add the code shaded in Figure 12-8 to specify that the data collected on this page will be processed in example3-3.jsp.

```
<center>
 <a href="example3-1.jsp">View employee</a>
</center><br>
<form method=post action="example3-3.jsp">
<table align=center cellpadding=2>
<tr><td colspan=2><font size=1 face=Arial>
    * indicates that field is required</font>
    </td>
</tr>
<tr><td align=right>Employee ID:*</td>
    <td><input name=empid size=12 maxlength=10></td>
</tr>
<tr><td align=right>First Name:*</td>
    <td><input name=fname size=16 maxlength=15></td>
</tr>
<tr><td align=right>Last Name:*</td>
    <td><input name=lname size=16 maxlength=15></td>
</tr>
<tr><td align=right>Address:</td>
    <td><input name=address size=21 maxlength=20></td>
</tr>
<tr><td align=right>Zip Code:</td>
    <td><input name=zipcode size=6 maxlength=5></td>
</tr>
<tr><td align=right>Phone:</td>
  <td><input name=phone size=9 maxlength=8></td>
</tr>
<tr><td align=right>E-mail:</td>
  <td><input name=email size=25 maxlength=50></td>
</tr>
<tr><td align=center colspan=2>
  <input type=submit value="Add employee"> 
      <input type=reset>
</td>
</tr>
</table>
</form>
```

Figure 12-8   Additional code added to example3-2.jsp

6. Save and close the file.

7. Open the data file example3-3.jsp, which is located in the folder C:\myjspapp\chapter12.

8. Add the code shaded in Figure 12-9 to change the auto-commit code to control transactions.

```
<%@ page import="java.sql.*" %>
<%  String url = "jdbc:odbc:employeeDSN";
    String usernamedb="";
    String passworddb="";
    Connection  conn=null;
    Statement stm=null;
    try{
      Class.forName("sun.jdbc.odbc.JdbcOdbcDriver");
      conn= DriverManager.getConnection(url,usernamedb,passworddb);
    }catch(Exception exc){
      out.println(exc.toString());
    }
%>
<center><a href="example3-1.jsp">View employee</a></center><br>
<%
   String empid=request.getParameter("empid");
   String fname=request.getParameter("fname");
   String lname=request.getParameter("lname");
   String address=request.getParameter("address");
   String zipcode=request.getParameter("zipcode");
   String phone=request.getParameter("phone");
   String email=request.getParameter("email");
   String query1=null;
   String query2=null;
   query1 = "INSERT INTO employee VALUES( '" + empid+"','"+
            fname+"','"+lname+"','"+address+"', '"+zipcode +
            "','"+phone+"','"+email+"')";
   query2 = "INSERT INTO account VALUES('"+empid+"','password')";
   conn.setAutoCommit(false);
   stm = conn.createStatement();
   try{
    stm.executeUpdate(query1);
    stm.executeUpdate(query2);
    conn.commit();
    out.println("<center><h2>A new employee has been added.</h2>");
    out.println("<a href=example3-2.jsp>Add more</a></center>");
   }catch(Exception exc){
     conn.rollback();
     conn.setAutoCommit(true);
   %>
     <script>
     alert("Transaction failed! Modify data and try again.");
      window.history.back(-1);
     </script>
  <%}%>
<%
  if(stm != null){ stm.close();}
  conn.close();
%>
```

Figure 12-9   Additional code added to example3-3.jsp

9. Save and close the file.

12

10. Load the page exmple3-1.jsp, using the following URL:
http://localhost:8080/myapp/chapter12/example3-1.jsp

A page similar to Figure 12-10 is displayed.

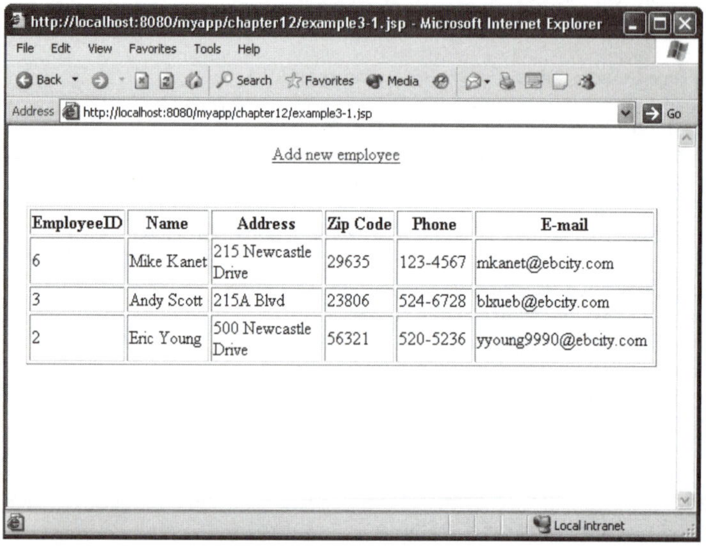

Figure 12-10   Employee list

11. Click **Add new employee**, and the page is displayed as shown in Figure 12-11.

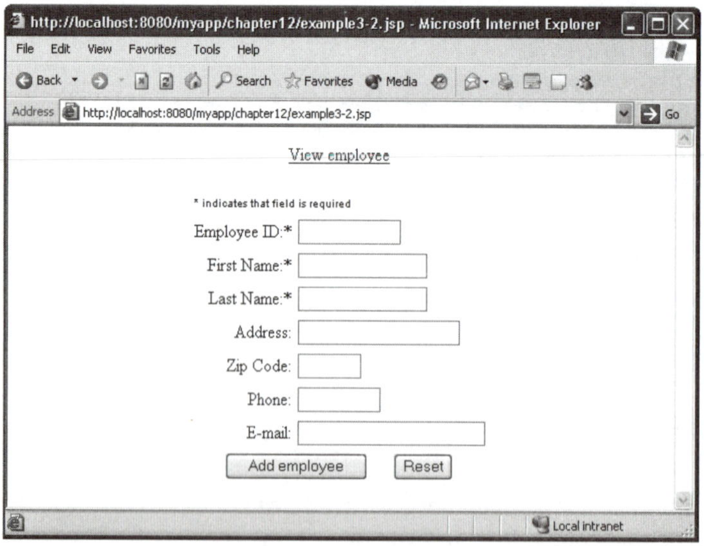

Figure 12-11   Add new employee

12. Enter at least all required fields (marked with *), then click **Add new employee** to add a new employee to the database. The page is displayed as shown in Figure 12-12.

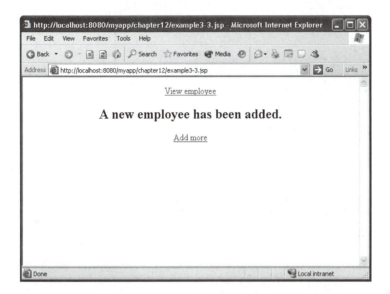

Figure 12-12   A new record added to the employee table

13. Click **View employee** to view the employee list. You should see that the new record you entered in Step 12 was added to the database.

14. Repeat Steps 11 and 12 to add a new record, but leave at least one required field blank. The page is displayed as shown in Figure 12-13, showing that the transaction failed.

12

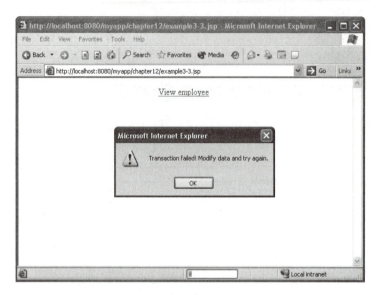

Figure 12-13   Transaction failed

In this example, you can view all employees or add a new employee. In the page example3-3.jsp, the auto-commit mode is set to false, so if an exception occurs when you try to add a new employee, the transaction is aborted. As illustrated in the above example, to add a new employee, you have to enter data in the first three fields (they are required); if you leave any of them blank, an exception occurs during the transaction, and the rollback method is called in the catch block, aborting the transaction.

What happens if you try to assign a new employee with an ID that appears in the administrator table? Without transaction control, you would be allowed to add this employee to the employee table, but when you tried to update the account table, since the ID already existed, an exception would be thrown and the transaction would be aborted. That means the employee's information would not be added to the account table. With transaction control, the two SQL statements are committed as one transaction; if an exception occurs, the transaction is aborted, neither of the two tables is changed, and database integrity is preserved.

BEANS AND DATABASES

You have already used JavaBeans to create reusable components for your Web applications. In this section, you will create beans to facilitate database processing. Specifically, you will create a connection bean to connect to a database, a database metadata bean to get database meta-information, a table information bean that helps to get table information, and a bean that helps to execute SQL statements and displays results.

Database Connection Bean

To access a database via JSP, you must first create a connection. Instead of writing JSP code to connect to a database on each JSP page that accesses the database, you could create a bean to make the connection to a database. In the following steps, you will write a database connection bean and install the bean class.

1. Open the data file DBConnection.java, which is located in the folder C:\myjspapp\chapter12.

2. Add the code shaded in Figure 12-14 to load the driver and make the connection to the database.

```java
package com.jspbook.chapter12;
import java.sql.*;
public class DBConnection{
  static String dbdriver;
  static String connURL;
  static String dbusername="";
  static String dbpassword="";
  static Connection  connection=null;
  public String getDbdriver(){return dbdriver;}
  public String getConnURL(){ return connURL;}
  public String getDbusername(){return dbusername;}
  public String getDbpassword(){return dbpassword;}
  public void setDbdriver(String dbdriver){
    this.dbdriver=dbdriver;
  }
  public void setConnURL(String url){connURL=url;}
  public void setDbusername(String dbusername){
    this.dbusername=dbusername;
  }
  public void setDbpassword(String dbpassword){
    this.dbpassword=dbpassword;
  }
  public static Connection getConnection(){
    if(connection ==null){
      try{
        Class.forName(dbdriver);
        connection=DriverManager.getConnection(
          connURL,dbusername,dbpassword);
      }catch(Exception exc){ connection=null; }
    }
    return connection;
  }
}
```

Figure 12-14   DBConnection.java

3. Save and close the file.

4. Open a DOS command prompt window and change the directory, using the following command:

cd c: \myjspapp\chapter12

5. Compile and install the bean class, using the following command:

javac–d c:\myjspapp\WEB-INF\classes DBConnection.java

6. Close the DOS command window, using the command exit.

Notice that all data members are declared as static variables. The getConnection() method is also defined as a static member. That means you can use this static method without instantiating the object from the class. Since a static method cannot access a nonstatic data member, all data members are declared as static. The setter methods are used to set the database driver, connection URL, and database username and password. The getConnection() method returns an established connection. This method first checks whether or not a connection to the database has been made; if not, it loads the driver and builds the connection, and then returns the connection. This bean can be used in your JSP pages to connect to the database.

Database MetaData Bean

In the exercise below, you will create a bean to get information about a database, as you did in example1.jsp; this bean can easily be reused to get information about another database.

1. Open the data file DBMetaDataBean.java, which is located in the folder C:\myjspapp\chapter12.

2. Add the code shaded in Figure 12-15 to make a connection to a database.

```
package com.jspbook.chapter12;
import java.sql.*;

public class DBMetaDataBean{
  public String getTables() throws SQLException{
    Connection conn = DBConnection.getConnection();
    DatabaseMetaData dbmd=conn.getMetaData();
    String[] types={"TABLE"};
    ResultSet rst = dbmd.getTables(null,null,null,types);
    String productName = dbmd.getDatabaseProductName();
    StringBuffer sb= new StringBuffer();
    sb.append("<table border=1>\n");
    sb.append("<tr><th colspan=2>"+
        "Database Information</th></tr>\n");
    sb.append("<tr><td>Database</td><td>"+
       productName+"</td></tr>\n");
    sb.append("<tr><td><b>Tables</b></td>\n");
    sb.append("<td>");
    while(rst.next()){
      sb.append(rst.getString("TABLE_NAME")+"<br>");
    }
    sb.append("</td>\n</tr>\n</table>\n");
    if(rst!=null) rst.close();
    return sb.toString();
  }
}
```

Figure 12-15   DBMetaDataBean.java

12

3. Save and close the file.

4. Open a DOS command window, and use the following command to change the directory:

   cd c:\myjspapp\chapter12

5. Compile and install the bean class, using the following command:

   javac −d c:\myjspapp\WEB-INF\classes −classpath c:\myjspapp\WEB-INF\classes DBConnection.java DBMetaDataBean.java

 The above Command is different than the JavaBean compile commands you've used so far, because in addition to using the classes installed with the Java API, the DBMetaDataBean also uses the DBConnection.java class, which you created earlier in this chapter.

6. Close the DOS command window.

This class has only one method: getTables(). To get database information, a connection to that database must be created first. The static method of the DBConnection class is called to return a connection that has been established already. Then a Statement object is created, and you use this Statement object to get information about the database, as you did in example2.jsp. In this method, a StringBuffer object is used to facilitate string processing. This object maintains a buffer so you can append a string to the buffer, and the toString() method of the StringBuffer object returns all appended strings.

Table Information Bean

In the following exercise, you will create a bean that can be used to display database table information.

1. Open the data file TableInfoBean.java, which is located in the folder C:\myjspapp\chapter12.

2. Add the code shaded in Figure 12-16.

```java
package com.jspbook.chapter12;
import java.sql.*;
public class TableInfoBean{
  private String tableName;
  public String getTableName(){ return tableName;}
  public void setTableName(String tableName){
    this.tableName = tableName;}
  public String getTableInfo() throws SQLException{
    if(tableName==null || tableName.equals("")) return "";
    Connection conn = DBConnection.getConnection();
    Statement stm= conn.createStatement();
    ResultSet rst =
      stm.executeQuery("select * from "+ tableName);
    ResultSetMetaData rsmd = rst.getMetaData();
    int num=rsmd.getColumnCount();
    StringBuffer sb = new StringBuffer();
    sb.append("<table border=1\n");
    sb.append("<tr><th colspan=3>Column Information in ");
    sb.append(tableName + " table</td></tr>\n");
    sb.append("<tr><th>Column Name</th><th>Data Type</th>");
    sb.append("<th>Display Size</th></tr>\n");
    for(int i=1; i<=num;i++){
      sb.append("<tr><td>" +
        rsmd.getColumnName(i) + "</td>\n");
      sb.append("<td>" +
        rsmd.getColumnTypeName(i) + "</td>\n");
      sb.append("<td>" +
        rsmd.getColumnDisplaySize(i) + "</td>\n");
      sb.append("</tr>\n");
    }
    sb.append("</table>\n");
    if(rst != null) rst.close();
    if(stm != null) stm.close();
    return sb.toString();
  }
}
```

Figure 12-16 TableInfoBean.java

3. Save and close the file.

4. Open a DOS command window, and use the following command to change the directory:

   cd c:\myjspapp\chapter12

5. Compile and install the bean class, using the following command:

   javac −d c:\myjspapp\WEB-INF\classes −classpath c:\myjspapp\WEB-INF\classes DBConnection.java TableInfoBean.java

6. Close the DOS command window.

The setter method is used to set the table name whose column information will be retrieved. The getTableInfo() method is used to get a table's information, and it returns the information as a string that displays the table information in an HTML table. Therefore, to get a table's information, you simply specify a table name by using the setProperty action tag, and then use the getProperty action tag to display the table's information in an HTML table format.

Data-Processing Bean

You can write a JavaBean to help you to process database data. In the following exercise, you will write a bean that helps to get data from a database and displays the data in an HTML table.

1. Open the data file DBBean.java, which is located in the folder C:\myjspapp\chapter12.

2. Add the code shaded in Figure 12-17 to make a connection to the database and query the database, as well as to get metadata.

12

```
package com.jspbook.chapter12;
import java.sql.*;
public class DBBean{
  private Statement stm = null;
  private ResultSet rst = null;
  private String tableName;
  public String getTableName(){ return tableName;}
  public void setTableName(String tableName){
    this.tableName = tableName;}
  public String getData() throws SQLException{
    if(tableName==null || tableName.equals("")) return "";
    Connection conn = DBConnection.getConnection();
    Statement stm= conn.createStatement();
    ResultSet rst =
      stm.executeQuery("select * from "+ tableName);
    ResultSetMetaData rsmd = rst.getMetaData();
    int num=rsmd.getColumnCount();
    StringBuffer sb = new StringBuffer();
    sb.append("<table border=1>\n");
    sb.append("<tr><th colspan="+num+">Records in table: ");
    sb.append(tableName + "</th></tr>\n");
    sb.append("<tr>");
    for(int i=1; i<=num;i++){
      sb.append("<th>" + rsmd.getColumnName(i) + "</th>\n");
    }
    sb.append("</tr>\n");
    while(rst.next()){
      sb.append("<tr>\n");
      for(int i=1; i<=num; i++){
        sb.append("<td>"+rst.getString(i)+" </td>\n");
      }
      sb.append("</tr>\n");
    }
    sb.append("</table>\n");
    rst.close();
    stm.close();
    return sb.toString();
  }
}
```

Figure 12-17   DBBean.java

3. Save and close the file.

4. Open a DOS command window, and use the following command to change the directory:

   cd c:\myjspapp\chapter12

5. Use the following command to compile and install the bean class:

javac –d c:\myjspapp\WEB-INF\classes –classpath c:\myjspapp\WEB-INF\classes DBConnection.java DBBean.java

6. Close the DOS command window.

Again, a setter method is used to set the table from which you retrieve data. Since the column names are unknown, you use the ResultSetMetaData object to get the number of columns and the column names. In this case, it is easy to get column data using the column index, instead of the column name.

Using JDBC Beans

You have created several JavaBeans to access and process databases. In this section, you will use these beans to connect to a database, get database metadata, and process data in the database.

Connecting to a Database

Because the connection is always obtained in the same way, you can save the database connection code in a file and simply include this file where you need to make a connection to a database. The following code illustrates how to use the database connection bean to connect to a database.

1. Open a new document in your text editor, and type in the following code:

```
<%-- create a bean in application scope, so the bean
is shared in the whole Web application --%>
<jsp:useBean id="dbconnection"
  class="com.jspbook.chapter12.DBConnection"
  scope="application">
<jsp:setProperty name="dbconnection"
  property="dbdriver"
  value="sun.jdbc.odbc.JdbcOdbcDriver"/>
<jsp:setProperty name="dbconnection"
  property="connURL" value="jdbc:odbc:employeeDSN"/>
<jsp:setProperty name="dbconnection"
  property="dbusername" value=""/>
<jsp:setProperty name="dbconnection"
  property="dbpassword" value=""/>
</jsp:useBean>
```

2. Save the file as **dbconnection.jsp** in the folder C:\myjspapp\chapter12.

This JSP page creates a database connection bean in application scope. That means this bean is created only once and then can be shared among all JSP pages in the Web application. It connects to the employee database you use in this chapter via a JDBC-ODBC bridge. After the connection has been established, you can create a Statement object and query the database.

12

Getting Database Metadata

In the following exercise, you will use the database metadata bean to get information about the employee database.

1. Open a new document in your text editor, and type in the following code:

```
<%@include file="dbconnection.jsp" %>
<jsp:useBean id="mb" class="com.jspbook.chapter12.
DBMetaDataBean"/>
<jsp:getProperty name="mb" property="tables"/>
```

2. Save the file as **example4.jsp** in the folder C:\myjspapp\chapter12.

3. Load the page, using the following URL:
http://localhost:8080/myapp/chapter12/example4.jsp

The page is displayed as shown in Figure 12-18.

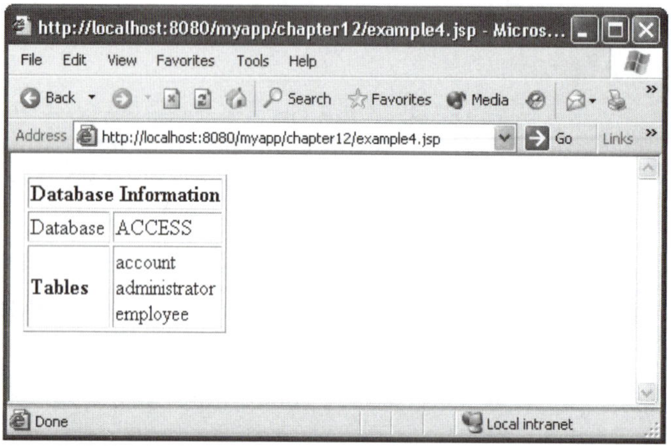

Figure 12-18   Tables in the database employee.mdb

In this page, the include directive is used to include the file dbconnection.jsp, which enables the connection to the database, and a bean is instantiated in the request scope. The getProperty action calls the getTables() method of the bean, which returns the database information and displays the information in an HTML table.

Obtaining Table Data

In the following exercise, you will select a table from the database and then display the table information in an HTML table.

1. Open a new document in your text editor, and type in the following code:

```
<%@include file="dbconnection.jsp" %>
<form action="example5.jsp" method="POST">
```

```
<select name="tableName">
 <option value="Employee">Employee Table
 <option value="Administrator">Administrator Table
 <option value="Account">Account Table
</select>
 <input type=submit value="Get table information">
</form>
<jsp:useBean id="mb"
       class="com.jspbook.chapter12.TableInfoBean"/>
<jsp:setProperty name="mb" property="tableName"/>
<jsp:getProperty name="mb" property="tableInfo"/>
```

2. Save the file as **example5.jsp** in the folder C:\myjspapp\chapter12.

3. Load the page, using the following URL:
   http://localhost:8080/myapp/chapter12/example5.jsp

4. Select a table and click **Get table information**. The selected table's information is displayed as shown in Figure 12-19.

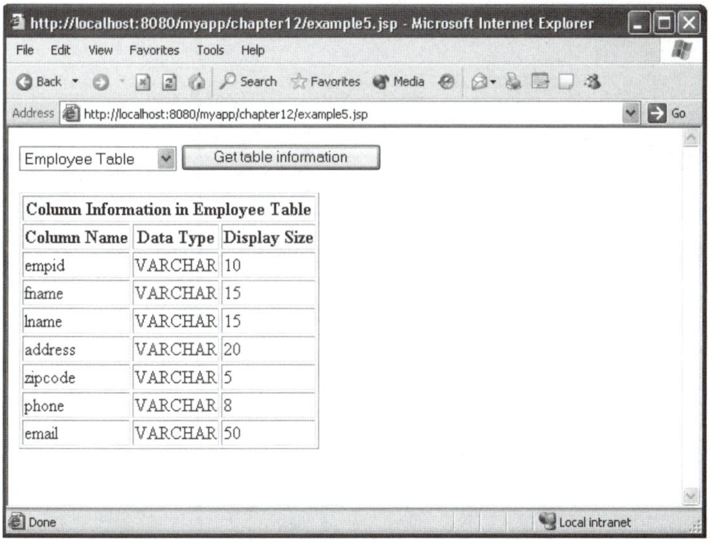

Figure 12-19   Using the table data bean to display table metadata

Displaying Data in a Table

In the following exercise, you will use the table data bean to access a database and display data from the selected table.

1. Open a new document in your text editor, and type in the following code:

```
<%@include file="dbconnection.jsp" %>
<form action="example6.jsp" method="POST">
```

```
<select name="tableName">
 <option value="Employee">Employee Table
 <option value="Administrator">Administrator Table
 <option value="Account">Account Table
</select>
 <input type=submit value="Get records">
</form>
<jsp:useBean id="mb"
      class="com.jspbook.chapter12.DBBean"/>
<jsp:setProperty name="mb" property="tableName"/>
<jsp:getProperty name="mb" property="data"/>
```

2. Save the file as **example6.jsp** in the folder C:\myjspapp\chapter12.

3. Load the page, using the following URL:
   http://localhost:8080/chapter12/example6.jsp

4. Select a table from the drop-down list and click the **Get records** button. The records in the selected table should be displayed, as shown in Figure 12-20.

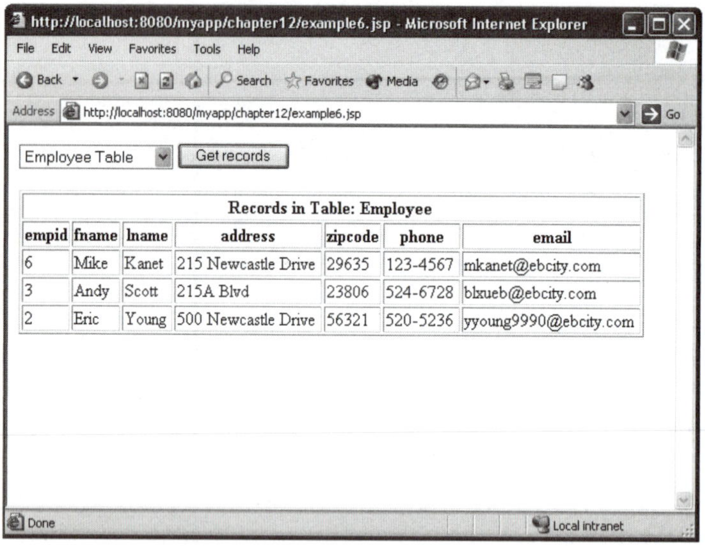

Figure 12-20 Using a bean to process data

CHAPTER SUMMARY

▫ The IN and BETWEEN operators can make your SQL queries simple and concise. The IN operator is used to determine whether a column's value is within a series of values. The BETWEEN operator is used to determine whether a column's value is between one value and another.

❑ Metadata is data about the database itself—for example, database name, database version, tables in the database, columns in a table, and so on. You can use the DatabaseMetaData object to get information about a database. A ResultSetMetaData object can be used to get information about a table.

❑ A transaction is a set of one or more statements that are executed together as a unit. You can use transactions in JSP to control how and when the execution of a SQL statement takes effect on a database.

❑ You can develop reusable components, JavaBeans, to access and process a database. You can use beans to connect to a database, get metadata, and process records in tables.

REVIEW QUESTIONS

1. To find customers who are from South Carolina, Virginia, or Florida, which of the following operators is most appropriately, used in a WHERE clause?

   a. OR

   b. AND

   c. IN

   d. BETWEEN

2. To find all transactions on a savings account occurring between January 25, 2002 and March 25, 2002, which of the following operators is most appropriately, used in a WHERE clause?

   a. OR

   b. AND

   c. IN

   d. BETWEEN

3. Which of the following WHERE clauses in a SQL statement can be replaced with a single IN operator?

   a. name='Joe Steve' OR zipcode='23834' OR major='MIS'

   b. name='Joe Steve' OR zipcode='23834' OR zipcode='23806'

   c. name='Joe Steve' AND (zipcode='23834' OR zipcode='23806')

   d. zipcode='29634' OR zipcode='23834' OR zipcode='23806'

4. Which of the following WHERE clauses in a SQL statement can be replaced with a single BETWEEN operator?

   a. purchdate='2002-01-25' OR purchdate='2002-02-25'

   b. purchdate<='2002-01-25' OR purchdate>='2002-02-25'

   c. purchdate>='2002-01-25' OR purchdate<='2002-02-25'

   d. purchdate>'2002-01-25' OR purchdate<'2002-02-25'

12

5. Which of the following objects can be used to get information about a database?

   a. connection object

   b. Statement object

   c. ResultSet object

   d. none of the above

6. Which of the following objects can be used to get the database name (Access, Oracle, and so on) directly?

   a. connection

   b. ResultSet

   c. Statement

   d. DatabaseMetaData

7. Which of the following objects can be used to get database column names directly?

   a. ResultSetMetaData

   b. ResultSet

   c. Statement

   d. DatabaseMetaData

8. To get metadata about a database, a connection to that database must be established first. True or False?

9. If a database driver does not support a metadata method, calling this method returns an empty ResultSet. True or False?

10. Look at the following SQL statement:

```
ResultSet rst = stm.executeQuery("SELECT fname, lname FROM
customer");
ResultSetMetaData rsmd = rst.getMetaData();
```

   Assume stm is an active Statement object reference. Then rsmd contains all columns' information in the customer table. True or False?

11. A transaction consists of a single SQL statement. True or False?

12. The execution of an UPDATE or INSERT SQL statement will make changes on a database. True or False?

13. When the auto-commit mode is set to true, you can still control several SQL statements so that they are executed as a single transaction. True or False?

14. When the auto-commit mode is set to true, the execution of a SQL statement immediately takes effect on the database. True or False?

15. When a connection to a database is created, the auto-commit mode is set to true by default. True or False?

16. Which of the following statements is the most accurate?

    a. The execution of a SQL statement takes effect on a database immediately.

    b. The execution of a SQL statement takes effect on a database immediately, if the auto-commit mode is set to true.

    c. A transaction contains two or more SQL statements.

    d. A transaction can contain two or more SQL statements if the auto-commit mode is set to true.

17. To use the rollBack method of a connection object, you must:

    a. group two SQL statements together

    b. set the auto-commit mode to true

    c. set the auto-commit mode to false

    d. call the rollBack() method after the connection is closed

18. Look at the following code:

    ```
    conn.setAutoCommit(false);
    stm.executeUpdate("UPDATE employee SET salary=salary*1.2");
    conn.rollBack();
    ```

    Assume that conn is an active connection and stm is an active statement. The execution of the above code will result in which of the following?

    a. The salary field of the first record in the table is increased by 1.2 times.

    b. All salary fields in the table are increased by 1.2 times.

    c. The salary field of the last record in the table is increased by 1.2 times.

    d. The data in the employee table is unchanged.

19. Look at the following code:

    ```
    conn.setAutoCommit(false);
    stm.executeUpdate("UPDATE employee SET salary=salary*1.2");
    conn.commit();
    ```

    Assume that conn is an active connection and stm is an active statement. The execution of the above code will result in which of the following?

    a. The salary field of the first record in the table is increased by 1.2 times.

    b. All salary fields in the table are increased by 1.2 times.

    c. The salary field of the last record in the table is increased by 1.2 times.

    d. The data in the employee table is unchanged.

20. If there is an uncommitted transaction, you must call either the commit() method to commit the transaction or the rollBack() method to abort the transaction, before you can change the auto-commit mode from false to true without raising a SQLException. True or False?

HANDS-ON PROJECTS

Project 12-1 Registering the Database

Register the database eventManagement.mdb, which is located in the folder C:\myjs-papp\chapter12, as an ODBC data source called eventManagementDSN. You must register this database before completing the rest of the Hands-on projects. This database consists of four tables: events, eventType, attendees, and registration. The first two tables store event information, and the last two tables store information about who registered which events.

Project 12-2 IN Operator

In this project, you will use the IN operator to list all attendees whose Zip code is either 23834 or 29634.

1. Create a new document in your text editor, and add code to connect to the evenManagement database.

2. Add code to create a ResultSet with the following SQL statement:

   ```
   SELECT * FROM attendees WHERE postalcode IN ('23834',
   '29634')
   ```

3. Add code to process the ResultSet and display the data in an HTML table.

4. Save the page as **project2.jsp** in the folder C:\myjspapp\chapter12.

5. Load the page, using the following URL:
   http://localhost:8080/myapp/chapter12/project2.jsp.

   The page is displayed as shown in Figure 12-21.

Figure 12-21   SQL statement with IN operator

Project 12-3 The BETWEEN Operator

In this project, you will use the BETWEEN operator to list all events held between January 1, 2003 and August 1, 2005.

1. Open a new document in your text editor, and save it as **project3.jsp** in the folder C:\myjspapp\chapter12.

2. Add code to set the import attribute of the page directive properly to make the package "java.sql.*" available in this page.

3. Add code to make a connection to the database eventManagement.mdb.

4. Add code to create a ResultSet object with the following SQL query:

```
"SELECT * FROM events WHERE eventDate "+
    "BETWEEN #2003-01-1# AND #2005-08-1#";
```

5. Use Figure 12-22 as a reference to process the ResultSet and display the events in an HTML table.

6. Add code to close the connection.

7. Save and close the file.

8. Load the page, using the following URL:
   http://localhost:8080/myapp/chapter12/project3.jsp

   The page should be displayed as shown in Figure 12-22.

12

Address http://localhost:8080/myapp/chapter12/project3.jsp

				Event Information	
id	Event name	Type ID	Location	Date	Description
100	E-commerce Programming with JSP	1	Singleton Hall	2003-12-01 00:00:00	Design and develop dynamic Web pages with Java, JavaBeans and EJB. Use UML to build Web application architectures, and build a complete business information system for the Web using client- and server-side scripting.
101	Christmas Party	3	101 Sirrine Hall	2003-12-23 00:00:00	This event begins at 7:30PM. Refreshments will be provided.
102	Visiting Weiwei Co.	4	215A Newcastle Drive	2004-02-05 00:00:00	Visit Weiwei Company. Manager Dr. Young will give a speech.

Figure 12-22 Using the BETWEEN operator

Project 12-4 Database Metadata

In this project, you will use the connection object to obtain information from the eventManagement database.

1. Create a new document in your text editor, and add code to make the connection to the eventManagement database.

2. Add code to create the DatabaseMetaData object, and use this object to retrieve information about the database, including database name and database table names.

3. Add code to display the information in an HTML table.

4. Save the file as **project4.jsp** in the folder C:\myjspapp\chapter12.

5. Load the page, using the URL:
   http://localhost:8080/myapp/chapter12/project4.jsp

   The page should be displayed as shown in Figure 12-23.

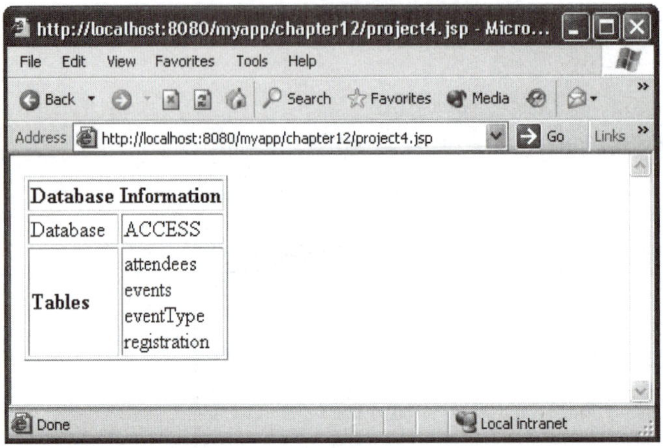

Figure 12-23 Getting metadata from the database

Project 12-5 Adding a New Record to the Attendee Table

In this project, you will provide pages to enable a new user to register in the database.

1. Use Figure 12-24 as a reference to create an HTML page to collect user data, including user ID, first name, last name, title, company name, address, city, state, Zip code, phone number, and fax number. Specify that the data will be processed in the page project5.jsp.

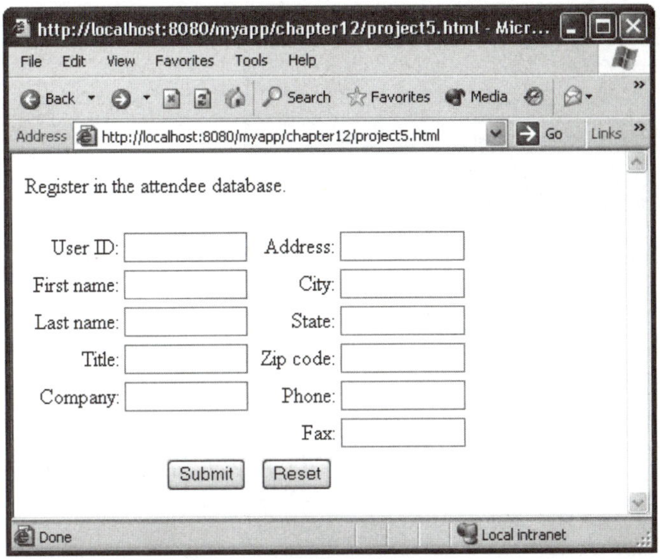

Figure 12-24   New record form

2. Save the file as **project5.html** in the folder C:\myjspapp\chapter12.

3. Create another file to process the data collected in the page project5.html, as follows:

   ❏ Add code to make connection to the database.

   ❏ Retrieve the data collected in the page project5.html.

   ❏ Build a SQL query statement.

   ❏ Use a SQL command to insert a new record into the attendees table.

4. Save the page as **project5.jsp** in the folder C:\myjspapp\chapter12.

5. Load the page project5.html, using the following URL:
   http://localhost:8080/myapp/chapter12/project5.html

6. Enter data into the form and submit the form. If no errors occur, a new entry should be added into the attendees table and a page like the one shown in Figure 12-25 should be displayed.

Figure 12-25 Adding a new record to the database

Project 12-6 Registering for an Event

In this project, you will design pages to allow users to register for events. The first page provides a drop-down list that lists all available events, and a text input field. To register for an event, a user selects an event from the list, enters a user ID in the input field, and then submits the form. The registration data is processed in the page project6-2.jsp. To register for an event, the user must exist in the attendees table. If the user ID is not found, then the user is prompted to register in the attendees table before registering for the event.

1. Open the data file project6-1.jsp, which is located in the folder C:\myjspapp\chapter12.

2. Add code to insert option items into the select field with the ResultSet. Each option takes the eventID as its value, and the eventName as its label. (*Hint*: Use a loop structure to navigate the ResultSet.)

3. Save and close the file.

4. Open a new document in your text editor, and save it as **project6-2.jsp** in the folder C:\myjspapp\chapter12.

5. Add code to perform the following tasks:

   ❏ Connect to the eventManagement.mdb database.

   ❏ Retrieve the form data submitted from the page project6-1.jsp.

   ❏ Test whether eventID and userID are valid; if not, alert the user and display the page project6-1.jsp, to allow the user to provide valid data on that page.

❑ Add the following code to query the database:

```
String query="SELECT * FROM attendees "+
          WHERE attendeeid='"+userID+"'";
stm = conn.createStatement();
ResultSet rst = stm.executeQuery(query);
```

❑ Test whether the ResultSet contains any records. If not, ask the user to register in the attendee table. If the user decides to register, direct the user to project5.html; otherwise, direct the user to project6-1.jsp.

❑ If the ResultSet is not empty, it means that the user is a registered user. Use the following query to update the registration table:

```
rst.close();
query = "INSERT INTO registration VALUES ('"+
      eventID+"','"+userID+"')";
stm.executeUpdate(query);
out.println("<h2>Thanks for registering!</h2>");
```

❑ Add code to close the connection.

6. Save and close the file.

7. Load the page project6-1.jsp, using the following URL:
   http://localhost:8080/myapp/chapter12/project6-1.jsp

A page similar to Figure 12-26 is displayed.

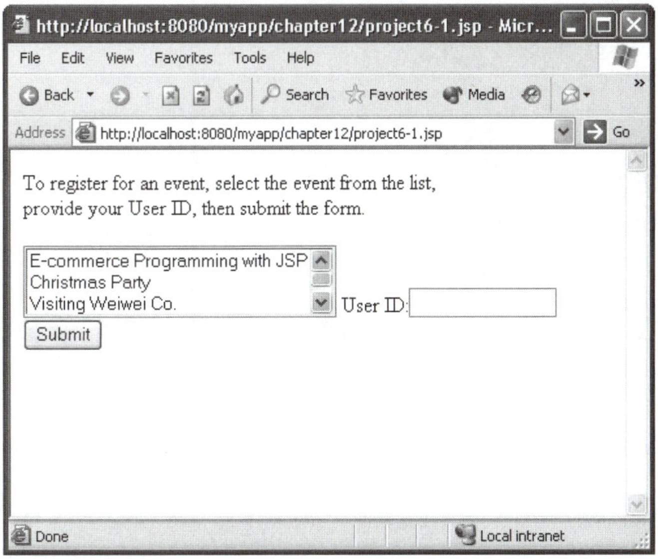

Figure 12-26 Registering for an event

8. Select an event from the available event list, and enter a user ID in the input field. Then submit the form to register for the selected event.

9. If the user ID is found in the attendees table, your registration should be successful, and a greeting message should be displayed. If the user ID is not found, you will be prompted to register in the attendees table. After you register in the attendees table, you can use your newly assigned user ID to register for events.

CASE PROJECTS

SRAS: Course Registration

You have almost completed the SRAS system, except for two pages: one for students to register for courses, and one for students to drop courses. As you know, when a user logs on to the system, the main page displayed by the system depends on the user's privileges. For a student, the main page is shown in Figure 12-27.

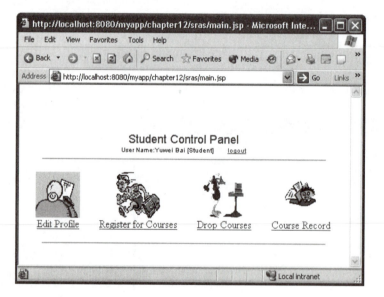

Figure 12-27   Main page for a student

In this project, you are required to add code to make the enrollcourse.jsp page function in the following way:

1. When a student accesses this page, the page displays all available courses in a drop-down list (a select field), as shown in Figure 12-28. Note that the courses the student has already registered for should not be on the list.

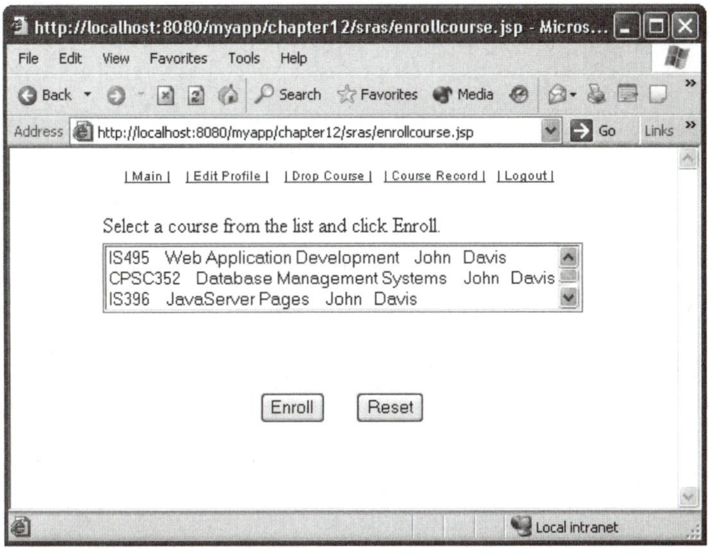

Figure 12-28   Course list

2. To register for a course, a student selects a course from the drop-down list and clicks the Enroll button. Then the coursetaken table is updated to reflect the new enrollment. The record includes studid, facultyid, coursenum, and grade (which is set to "ip," representing "in process"). Then this page displays the messages shown in Figure 12-29.

12

Figure 12-29   Registering for a new course

SRAS: Dropping Courses

You are required to complete the page dropcourse.jsp (which is located in the folder C:\myjspapp\chapter12\sras) so that it works as follows:

- List all courses that the student is registered for, as shown in Figure 12-30.

- To drop a course, select a course from the drop-down list and click the Drop course button. To accomplish this, you must update the coursetaken table. After a course is dropped, the page displays a message saying so, and provides a link to allow the student to drop another course.

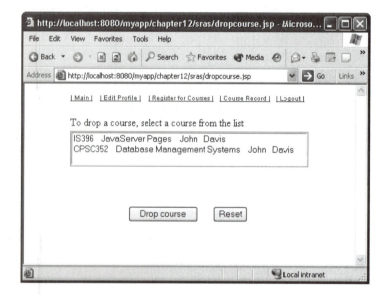

Figure 12-30   Dropping courses

APPENDIX
SUMMARY OF JSP 1.2 ELEMENTS

COMMENTS

There are two types of comments in a JSP page: HTML comments, which are sent to the client, and JSP comments, which are not sent to the client. The HTML comment syntax is as follows:

<!-- HTML comments ... -->

HTML comments are not interpreted by the JSP container, but are simply passed to the client as plain HTML.

JSP comments are used to document JSP code, and they are not sent to the client. JSP comments are completely ignored by the JSP container. JSP comments have one of the following forms:

<%-- comments --%>

or

<% /* comments */ %>

or

<% //comment %>

DECLARATIONS

You must declare variables and methods before you use them in a JSP page. You declare variables and methods as follows:

```
<%! int i=0; %>
<%! int max(int x, int y){
        if(x>y) return x;
        else return y;
    }
%>
```

EXPRESSIONS

A JSP expression inserts the value of the expression as a string into the output stream to the client. The syntax for a JSP expression is:

<%= expression %>

SCRIPTLETS

A scriptlet is a code fragment that gets executed at request-processing time. A scriptlet can contain any number of variable declarations and JSP statements. For example:

```
<%    String lname = request.getParameter("lname");
      out.println(lname);
%>
```

INCLUDE DIRECTIVE

When you use the include directive to include a static file in a JSP page, the file is included when the JSP page is translated into its corresponding servlet. Any modification made to the included file is not reflected in the JSP page until the page is recompiled into its corresponding servlet.

<%@ include file="relativePath" %>

INCLUDE ACTION

When you use the include action to include a file, the file is included each time the JSP page is requested. Therefore, any modification made to the included file is reflected in the page when it is requested next time.

<jsp:include page="relativePath" flush="true" />

PAGE DIRECTIVE

The page directive specifies a number of attributes that apply to an entire JSP page. Each of these attributes may be used independently. They may all appear in the same page directive, or each may be placed in a separate one.

```
<%@ page
  [ language="java" ]
  [ extends="superClassName" ]
  [ import="{package.class|package.*}, ..." ]
  [ session="true|false" ]
```

```
[ buffer="none|8kb|sizekb" ]
[ autoFlush="true|false" ]
[ isThreadSafe="true|false" ]
[ info="text" ]
[ errorPage="relativeURL" ]
[ contentType="{mimeType [ ; charset=characterSet ]" |
   "text/html ; charset=ISO-8859-1}" ]
[ isErrorPage="true|false" ]
[ pageEncoding="characterSet | ISO-8859-1" ]
%>
```

(*Note*: Not all attributes are discussed in this book.)

TAGLIB DIRECTIVE

The taglib directive loads a set of custom tags that can be used in the JSP page. It takes the following syntax:

<%@ taglib uri="URIReferringToTheTagLibrary" prefix="tagPrefix" %>

REQUEST FORWARD

The forward action forwards the request to another page. All pages involved in the forwarding action have the same request scope, which means that the same request object is accessible from all involved JSP pages. The forward action takes the following syntax:

<jsp:forward page="relativeURL"/>

PLUGIN ACTION ELEMENT

The <jsp:plugin> action element causes the execution of an applet or bean. Its use is beyond the scope of this book.

USEBEAN ACTION

The UseBean action tag makes a bean available for use in a JSP page. It takes the following syntax:

<jsp:useBean id="beanName" class="className"/>

The "class name" is the name of a Java class that defines the bean. You must specify the whole package name of the bean class. The execution of this action tag creates a new bean object and binds the variable (the value of the ID attribute) to the object. This variable is used to reference the bean object.

SETPROPERTY TAG

This tag assigns a new value to the specified property. It takes the following syntax:

`<jsp:setProperty name="beanName" property="propName"  value="a new value" />`

In this tag, the "value" attribute specifies the new value to be assigned to the bean property.

GETPROPERTY TAG

This tag retrieves the value of a bean property, converts it to a string, and inserts it into the output stream. It takes the following syntax:

`<jsp:getProperty name="bean_name" property="property_name" />`

The two required attributes are name and property. The "bean name" is the same name specified in the ID attribute when the bean is created, and the "property name" is the name of the property to retrieve.

Index

Sun Microsystems, Inc.
Binary Code License Agreement
Java™ 2 SDK, Standard Edition 1.4.0

READ THE TERMS OF THIS AGREEMENT AND ANY PROVIDED SUPPLEMENTAL LICENSE TERMS (COLLECTIVELY "AGREEMENT") CAREFULLY BEFORE OPENING THE SOFTWARE MEDIA PACKAGE. BY OPENING THE SOFTWARE MEDIA PACKAGE, YOU AGREE TO THE TERMS OF THIS AGREEMENT. IF YOU ARE ACCESSING THE SOFTWARE ELECTRONICALLY, INDICATE YOUR ACCEPTANCE OF THESE TERMS BY SELECTING THE "ACCEPT" BUTTON AT THE END OF THIS AGREEMENT. IF YOU DO NOT AGREE TO ALL THESE TERMS, PROMPTLY RETURN THE UNUSED SOFTWARE TO YOUR PLACE OF PURCHASE FOR A REFUND OR, IF THE SOFTWARE IS ACCESSED ELECTRONICALLY, SELECT THE "DECLINE" BUTTON AT THE END OF THIS AGREEMENT.

1. LICENSE TO USE. Sun grants you a non-exclusive and non-transferable license for the internal use only of the accompanying software and documentation and any error corrections provided by Sun (collectively "Software"), by the number of users and the class of computer hardware for which the corresponding fee has been paid.

2. RESTRICTIONS. Software is confidential and copyrighted. Title to Software and all associated intellectual property rights is retained by Sun and/or its licensors. Except as specifically authorized in any Supplemental License Terms, you may not make copies of Software, other than a single copy of Software for archival purposes. Unless enforcement is prohibited by applicable law, you may not modify, decompile, or reverse engineer Software. You acknowledge that Software is not designed, licensed or intended for use in the design, construction, operation or maintenance of any nuclear facility. Sun disclaims any express or implied warranty of fitness for such uses. No right, title or interest in or to any trademark, service mark, logo or trade name of Sun or its licensors is granted under this Agreement.

3. LIMITED WARRANTY. Sun warrants to you that for a period of ninety (90) days from the date of purchase, as evidenced by a copy of the receipt, the media on which Software is furnished (if any) will be free of defects in materials and workmanship under normal use. Except for the foregoing, Software is provided "AS IS". Your exclusive remedy and Sun's entire liability under this limited warranty will be at Sun's option to replace Software media or refund the fee paid for Software.

4. DISCLAIMER OF WARRANTY. UNLESS SPECIFIED IN THIS AGREEMENT, ALL EXPRESS OR IMPLIED CONDITIONS, REPRESENTATIONS AND WARRANTIES, INCLUDING ANY IMPLIED WARRANTY OF MERCHANTABILITY, FITNESS FOR A PARTICULAR PURPOSE OR NON-INFRINGEMENT ARE DISCLAIMED, EXCEPT TO THE EXTENT THAT THESE DISCLAIMERS ARE HELD TO BE LEGALLY INVALID.

5. LIMITATION OF LIABILITY. TO THE EXTENT NOT PROHIBITED BY LAW, IN NO EVENT WILL SUN OR ITS LICENSORS BE LIABLE FOR ANY LOST REVENUE, PROFIT OR DATA, OR FOR SPECIAL, INDIRECT, CONSEQUENTIAL, INCIDENTAL OR PUNITIVE DAMAGES, HOWEVER CAUSED REGARDLESS OF THE THEORY OF LIABILITY, ARISING OUT OF OR RELATED TO THE USE OF OR INABILITY TO USE SOFTWARE, EVEN IF SUN HAS BEEN ADVISED OF THE POSSIBILITY OF SUCH DAMAGES. In no event will Sun's liability to you, whether in contract, tort (including negligence), or otherwise, exceed the amount paid by you for Software under this Agreement. The foregoing limitations will apply even if the above stated warranty fails of its essential purpose.

6. Termination. This Agreement is effective until terminated. You may terminate this Agreement at any time by destroying all copies of Software. This Agreement will terminate immediately without notice from Sun if you fail to comply with any provision of this Agreement. Upon Termination, you must destroy all copies of Software.

7. Export Regulations. All Software and technical data delivered under this Agreement are subject to US export control laws and may be subject to export or import regulations in other countries. You agree to comply strictly with all such laws and regulations and acknowledge that you have the responsibility to obtain such licenses to export, re-export, or import as may be required after delivery to you.

8. U.S. Government Restricted Rights. If Software is being acquired by or on behalf of the U.S. Government or by a U.S. Government prime contractor or subcontractor (at any tier), then the Government's rights in Software and accompanying documentation will be only as set forth in this Agreement; this is in accordance with 48 CFR 227.7201 through 227.7202-4 (for Department of Defense (DOD) acquisitions) and with 48 CFR 2.101 and 12.212 (for non-DOD acquisitions).

9. Governing Law. Any action related to this Agreement will be governed by California law and controlling U.S. federal law. No choice of law rules of any jurisdiction will apply.

10. Severability. If any provision of this Agreement is held to be unenforceable, this Agreement will remain in effect with the provision omitted, unless omission would frustrate the intent of the parties, in which case this Agreement will immediately terminate.

11. Integration. This Agreement is the entire agreement between you and Sun relating to its subject matter. It supersedes all prior or contemporaneous oral or written communications, proposals, representations and warranties and prevails over any conflicting or additional terms of any quote, order, acknowledgment, or other communication between the parties relating to its subject matter during the term of this Agreement. No modification of this Agreement will be binding, unless in writing and signed by an authorized representative of each party.

JAVA™ 2 SOFTWARE DEVELOPMENT KIT (J2SDK), STANDARD EDITION, VERSION 1.4.X
SUPPLEMENTAL LICENSE TERMS

These supplemental license terms ("Supplemental Terms") add to or modify the terms of the Binary Code License Agreement (collectively, the "Agreement"). Capitalized terms not defined in these Supplemental Terms shall have the same meanings ascribed to them in the Agreement. These Supplemental Terms shall supersede any inconsistent or conflicting terms in the Agreement, or in any license contained within the Software.

1. Software Internal Use and Development License Grant. Subject to the terms and conditions of this Agreement, including, but not limited to Section 4 (Java Technology Restrictions) of these Supplemental Terms, Sun grants you a non-exclusive, non-transferable, limited license to reproduce internally and use internally the binary form of the Software complete and unmodified for the sole purpose of designing, developing and testing your Java applets and applications intended to run on the Java platform ("Programs").

2. License to Distribute Software. Subject to the terms and conditions of this Agreement, including, but not limited to Section 4 (Java Technology Restrictions) of these Supplemental Terms, Sun grants you a non-exclusive, non-transferable, limited license to reproduce and distribute the Software, provided that (i) you distribute the Software complete and unmodified (unless otherwise specified in the applicable README file) and only bundled as part of, and for the sole purpose of running, your Programs, (ii) the Programs add significant and primary functionality to the Software, (iii) you do not distribute additional software intended to replace any component(s) of the Software (unless otherwise specified in the applicable README file), (iv) you do not remove or alter any proprietary legends or notices contained in the Software, (v) you only distribute the Software subject to a license agreement that protects Sun's interests consistent with the terms contained in this Agreement, and (vi) you agree to defend and indemnify Sun and its licensors from and against any damages, costs, liabilities, settlement amounts and/or expenses (including attorneys' fees) incurred in connection with any claim, lawsuit or action by any third party that arises or results from the use or distribution of any and all Programs and/or Software. (vi) include the following statement as part of product documentation (whether hard copy or electronic), as a part of a copyright page or proprietary rights notice page, in an "About" box or in any other form reasonably designed to make the statement visible to users of the Software: "This product includes code licensed from RSA Security, Inc.", and (vii) include the statement, "Some portions licensed from IBM are available at *http://oss.software.ibm.com/icu4j/*".

3. License to Distribute Redistributables. Subject to the terms and conditions of this Agreement, including but not limited to Section 4 (Java Technology Restrictions) of these Supplemental Terms, Sun grants you a non-exclusive, non-transferable, limited license to reproduce and distribute those files specifically identified as redistributable in the Software "README" file ("Redistributables") provided that: (i) you distribute the Redistributables complete and unmodified (unless otherwise specified in the applicable README file), and only bundled as part of Programs, (ii) you do not distribute additional software intended to supersede any component(s) of the Redistributables (unless otherwise specified in the applicable README file), (iii) you do not remove or alter any proprietary legends or notices contained in or on the Redistributables, (iv) you only distribute the Redistributables pursuant to a license agreement that protects Sun's interests consistent with the terms contained in the Agreement, (v) you agree to defend and indemnify Sun and its licensors from and against any damages, costs, liabilities, settlement amounts and/or expenses (including attorneys' fees) incurred in connection with any claim, lawsuit or action by any third party that arises or results from the use or distribution of any and all Programs and/or Software, (vi) include the following statement as part of product documentation (whether hard copy or electronic), as a part of a copyright page or proprietary rights notice page, in an "About" box or in any other form reasonably designed to make the statement visible to users of the Software: "This product includes code licensed from RSA Security, Inc.", and (vii) include the statement, "Some portions licensed from IBM are available at *http://oss.software.ibm.com/icu4j/*".

4. Java Technology Restrictions. You may not modify the Java Platform Interface ("JPI", identified as classes contained within the "java" package or any subpackages of the "java" package), by creating additional classes within the JPI or otherwise causing the addition to or modification of the classes in the JPI. In the event that you create an additional class and associated API(s) which (i) extends the functionality of the Java platform, and (ii) is exposed to third party software developers for the purpose of developing additional software which invokes such additional API, you must promptly publish broadly an accurate specification for such API for free use by all developers. You may not create, or authorize your licensees to create, additional classes, interfaces, or subpackages that are in any way identified as "java", "javax", "sun" or similar convention as specified by Sun in any naming convention designation.

5. Notice of Automatic Software Updates from Sun. You acknowledge that the Software may automatically download, install, and execute applets, applications, software extensions, and updated versions of the Software from Sun ("Software Updates"), which may require you to accept updated terms and conditions for installation. If additional terms and conditions are not presented on installation, the Software Updates will be considered part of the Software and subject to the terms and conditions of the Agreement.

6. Notice of Automatic Downloads. You acknowledge that, by your use of the Software and/or by requesting services that require use of the Software, the Software may automatically download, install, and execute software applications from sources other than Sun ("Other Software"). Sun makes no representations of a relationship of any kind to licensors of Other Software. TO THE EXTENT NOT PROHIBITED BY LAW, IN NO EVENT WILL SUN OR ITS LICENSORS BE LIABLE FOR ANY LOST REVENUE, PROFIT OR DATA, OR FOR SPECIAL, INDIRECT, CONSEQUENTIAL, INCIDENTAL OR PUNITIVE DAMAGES, HOWEVER CAUSED REGARDLESS OF THE THEORY OF LIABILITY, ARISING OUT OF OR RELATED TO THE USE OF OR INABILITY TO USE OTHER SOFTWARE, EVEN IF SUN HAS BEEN ADVISED OF THE POSSIBILITY OF SUCH DAMAGES.

7. Trademarks and Logos. You acknowledge and agree as between you and Sun that Sun owns the SUN, SOLARIS, JAVA, JINI, FORTE, and iPLANET trademarks and all SUN, SOLARIS, JAVA, JINI, FORTE, and iPLANET-related trademarks, service marks, logos and other brand designations ("Sun Marks"), and you agree to comply with the Sun Trademark and Logo Usage Requirements currently located at http://www.sun.com/policies/trademarks. Any use you make of the Sun Marks inures to Sun's benefit.

8. Source Code. Software may contain source code that is provided solely for reference purposes pursuant to the terms of this Agreement. Source code may not be redistributed unless expressly provided for in this Agreement.

9. Termination for Infringement. Either party may terminate this Agreement immediately should any Software become, or in either party's opinion be likely to become, the subject of a claim of infringement of any intellectual property right. For inquiries please contact: Sun Microsystems, Inc. 901 San Antonio Road, Palo Alto, California 94303 *(LFI#109998/Form ID#011801)*
